THE EDUCATION OF MINORITY GROUPS

The Organisation for Economic Co-operation and Development (OECD) was set up under a Convention signed in Paris on 14 December 1960, which provides that the OECD shall promote policies designed:

- to achieve the highest sustainable economic growth and employment and a rising standard of living in Member countries, while maintaining financial stability, and thus to contribute to the development of the world economy;
- to contribute to sound economic expansion in Member as well as non-member countries in the process of economic development;
- to contribute to the expansion of world trade on a multilateral, non-discriminatory basis in accordance with international obligations.

The Members of OECD are Australia, Austria, Belgium, Canada, Denmark, Finland, France, the Federal Republic of Germany, Greece, Iceland, Ireland, Italy, Japan, Luxembourg, the Netherlands, New Zealand, Norway, Portugal, Spain, Sweden, Switzerland, Turkey, the United Kingdom and the United States.

The Centre for Educational Research and Innovation was created in June 1968 by the Council of the Organisation for Economic Co-operation and Development for an initial period of three years, with the help of grants from the Ford Foundation and the Royal Dutch Shell Group of Companies. In May 1971, the Council decided that the Centre should continue its work for a period of five years as from 1st January 1972. In July 1976 it extended this mandate for the following five years; and in July 1981 it granted a further extension to 1986.
The main objectives of the Centre are as follows:

- *to promote and support the development of research activities in education and undertake such research activities where appropriate;*
- *to promote and support pilot experiments with a view to introducing and testing innovations in the educational system;*
- *to promote the development of co-operation between Member countries in the field of educational research and innovation.*

The Centre functions within the Organisation for Economic Co-operation and Development in accordance with the decisions of the Council of the Organisation, under the authority of the Secretary-General. It is supervised by a Governing Board composed of one national expert in its field of competence from each of the countries participating in its programme of work.

Centre for Educational Research and Innovation

Organisation for Economic Co-operation and Development

The Education of Minority Groups

An Enquiry into Problems and Practices of Fifteen Countries

Ministry of Education, Ontario
Information Centre, 13th Floor,
Mowat Block, Queen's Park,
Toronto, Ont.　　　M7A 1L2

Gower

© OECD, 1983
Application for permission to reproduce or translate all or part of this publication should be made to:

Director of Information, OECD,
2 rue André-Pascal,
75775 PARIS CEDEX 16, France.

Published by

Gower Publishing Company Limited,
Gower House, Croft Road, Aldershot,
Hampshire, GU11 3HR, England

British Library Cataloguing in Publication Data

The Education of minority groups.
   1. Minorities — Education — Economic aspects
   I. Organisation for Economic Co-operation and
Development, *Centre for Educational Research and Innovation*
371.97   LC3719

ISBN 0-566-00639-1

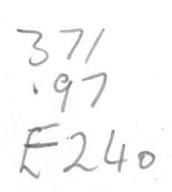

Contents

List of tables ix

List of figures xi

Preface xiii

PART I

An overview of experience in fifteen countries 1
W. Donovan, A. Fordham, G. Hancock
ACT Schools Authority, Canberra, Australia

1 The political, social and educational context 5

2 National policies and performance 9

3 Synthesis and conclusions 43

PART II

Principles and issues 61

4 Recognising students in need of extra resources: the Swedish experience 63
Esse Lovgren
Swedish National Board of Education

5 Screening categories relevant to special education 83
Pierre Dague
Centre National d'Etudes et de Formation pour l'Enfance Inadaptée, Université R. Descartes, Paris V

6 Rationales for providing additional resources 101
Erik Jorgen Hansen
Danish National Institute of Social Research

7 Unequal resource distribution 119
Jean Blackburn
Australian Schools Commission

8 Educational autonomy for special populations: Canadian experience 139
Edward N. McKeown
Toronto Board of Education, Ontario, Canada

9 A researcher's assessment of the autonomy problem 155
Kjell Eide
Royal Ministry of Church and Education, Norway

10 Service delivery: an analysis of systems of administration 165
Jane Hannaway
Columbia University, USA

11 The delivery of special education services for minorities 177
K. McDonagh
Carysford College, Ireland

12	Costing for special populations *Maurice Peston* *Queen Mary College, University of London*	191
13	How the cost of the provision may be determined *R.A. Rossmiller* *University of Wisconsin, Madison, USA*	211

PART III
Linguistic and cultural minorities — 231

14	Problems and policy instruments in the provision of special education *Stacy Churchill* *Ontario Institute for Studies in Education, Toronto, Canada*	233
15	Language and literacy: programmes for linguistic minorities in five countries *Ray C. Rist* *Cornell University, Ithaca, New York*	267
16	Indigenous cultural minorities — concepts pertaining to their education *Frank Darnell* *Centre for Cross-Cultural Studies, University of Alaska*	293
17	Reactions to these concepts from Aboriginal Australia *Colin J. Bourke* *Centre for Research into Aboriginal Affairs, Melbourne, Australia*	317
18	The situation of the Sami people in Norway *Anton Hoem* *Institute of Educational Research, University of Oslo, Norway*	325

19	An American Indian view on education for indigenous minorities *William G. Demmert* *University of Washington, Seattle, USA*	337
20	A response for the Maori population of New Zealand *Allan F. Smith* *Department of Education, Wellington, New Zealand*	349

Appendix	363
Index	365

Figures

2.1	The special populations in each country to whom special educational resources were allocated	14
2.2	The styles of provision of educational resources in terms of type of special population	25
2.3	Major sources of funding of special education in the countries participating in the inquiry	35
6.1	Current expenditure per student and per successful student for selected educations, 1977–78	103
6.2	Expenditure per pupil in Ishøj and Søllerød, 1974–77 (Kroner)	104
6.3	Some social characteristics of the adult Danish population (20–69 years) who have children of pre-school age, 1976	110
6.4	Percentage distribution of young people in the age group 16–19 years who were not receiving any education/training after leaving primary school. Percentages for 1965 and 1973, by social class of parents and sex of the young people	112

ix

13.1	An example of a complex programme structure: educational programmes for handicapped individuals	215
13.2	An example of a simple programme structure: educational programmes for linguistic minority populations	216
13.3	A typology of systems for delivering educational programmes to special populations	217
13.4	An illustration of Full Time Equivalent student computation and use	222
13.5	An illustrative format for reporting data on programme costs	226
14.1	Linguistic and cultural minorities here considered in the light of information provided in country reports to the CERI inquiry	234
14.2	Multilingual situations for a selection of minority groups according to the level of development of their aspirations	242
14.3	Major models of problem definition and policy responses	246/7
14.4	The role of the home language of minority pupils (L1) in selected jurisdictions	253
15.1	The form and source of funding for language and literacy programmes	279

Tables

2.1	Provisions for education of the intellectually and physically disabled, slow learners and the specifically learning disabled	22
2.2	The styles of provision and the types of services for the education of special populations	26
2.3	Type of provision, source of funding and locus of control for the education of special populations	36
6.1	Special groups in the education system	113
10.1	Control agents and the levels on which they can operate	167
13.1	A continuum of objectives in programmes for special populations	213
13.2	A matrix illustrating programme structure and programme delivery modes for a special population	219

Preface

The essays in this volume all speak with the authority of special experience on some aspect, or aspects, of a problem still highly topical in many industrialised countries — the education of young people designated (for one of several widely different reasons) as being in need of special attention. Minorities, indeed; but minorities with a growing significance.

By origin, these papers were an essential part of the documentation for an extensive programme of inquiry carried out by the Centre for Educational Research and Innovation for the Member countries of the Organisation for Economic Co-operation and Development. Many of these countries have been active in recent years in reducing disparities in educational access and performance across social groups; alongside this has gone widespread demand for public policy to reflect more fully what may be termed 'equity' or 'justice' in respect of the differing needs of individuals as well as groups.

The progressive recognition of these concerns in the actual allocation and distribution of educational resources has, however, given rise to important questions about the linkages among, and the effects of, different kinds of financing, organisation and governance for what are generally regarded as 'special populations'. This has been the area of the CERI inquiry: simply put, the aim of the project was to elucidate the policies and processes by which some groups are designated as special and by which differential treatment is legitimated, organised and financed.

Basic to the inquiry were surveys of current practice carried out in fifteen countries and detailed accounts of how a few — Canada, England and Wales, France and Germany — were addressing some of the less tractable policy problems related to the making of provisions for special population groups. These original and authoritative studies were made widely available as they appeared in the countries participating in the programme, and copies will continue to be held in the OECD for perusal by anyone professionally interested in the statistics of the time.

It is this body of material that provides the substance for the three chapters in this book that give an overview of countries' policies, practices and (sometimes) thoughts for the future — globally by Greg Hancock and his co-authors, for linguistic and cultural minorities by Stacy Churchill and, for five European countries with particular linguistic minority problems, by Ray Rist.

These national accounts and their authors are listed in the Appendix. When any of the three assessors refers to a country by name it will, more often than not, be that country as represented in one of these papers.

In a limited sense, the three chapters just mentioned epitomise the results of the CERI inquiry. But no less important, in terms of long-term results, are the specialised contributions that make up the rest of the book. These, as already said, gave continuing sustenance to the programme as it developed; but in our view they continue to have a high potential usefulness even after its termination. We are glad, therefore, to have readership among those who are concerned at the national level with the development of social and educational policies.

I take this occasion also to thank the United States Department of Education for their generous grant that made it possible to reach the conclusions here recorded.

PART I

An overview of experience in fifteen countries

W. Donovan, A. Fordham, G. Hancock

*ACT Schools Authority,
Canberra, Australia*

Our report aims to provide a descriptive and analytical overview of the total project as reflected in its documentation. In chapter 1 we briefly describe the context in which the inquiry was set. In chapter 2 a two-stage analysis of the papers is made. First, the country surveys of current practices, principles and issues are explored to present an analytical structure for the provision of services to special populations; secondly, an overview is provided of the case studies of provisions for the two special groups — linguistic and indigenous cultural minorities.

Chapter 3 synthesises the principal points developed hitherto, outlines major conclusions and policy directions, and makes some suggestions for future work.

The origin and aim of the CERI inquiry into the financing, organisation and governance of education for special populations have already been made clear by the Centre's Director in his Preface. The fifteen countries to which he referred as participants are: Australia, Canada, Denmark, England and Wales, France, the Federal Republic of Germany, Ireland, the Netherlands, New Zealand, Norway, Portugal, Sweden, Switzerland, Turkey and the United States of America.

The specific elements of the project that provided the basic documentation for the overview on which we here embark (and, indeed, for the rest of the book) were these:

— a 'mapping' of current practices and policies in the field of special provisions in education for schoolchildren in the fifteen countries (these 'country surveys' are listed in the Appendix);

— a more detailed examination of how some countries address persistent and intractable policy problems in making provision for two special populations — linguistic and indigenous cultural minorities (see the chapters in Part III);

— an analysis of five crucial issues pertaining to any special provision, namely identification, rationales, autonomy, service delivery and costing (the content of Part II).

1 The political, social and educational context

Changes in society undoubtedly affect education and those who provide it. Social structure changes in response to political and economic forces that mould the pattern of national life. Thus, the social structure in the developing countries has changed in response to fundamental processes that have influenced it. Some of these are cyclic, such as economic booms, migration flows, periods of protest and turbulence, employment patterns and so on. Many of the changes, however, are permanent and alter power structures. These consequently set the pattern for change in education. Some of the permanent changes that are affecting the provision of education are those dealing with technological advances, leading to demands for a more highly skilled workforce and making it more difficult for people from the lower end of the educational spectrum to obtain jobs. The spread of institutionised education, evidenced in higher retention rates in formal education establishments and the growth of continuing education activities, provides an example of how an irreversible shift towards a better educated society can lead it to view political power and influence in an increasingly sophisticated way.

Women's place in the societies we here survey has also radically changed in recent times: more women are better educated; more are entering the workforce; and in particular attitudes to family life are changing. The emerging structure of the family is also making demands on education different from those of the past. In many OECD countries a static or declining birth rate and the consequent aging of the population are changing the characteristics of our community and of educational provisions.

Another new feature is the pervasive role of the media. Most people in the industrialised countries can now gain instant access to information that they can use in politically influential ways.

The past twenty years have seen a growth of major educational programmes in advanced countries providing a range of services in special areas such as provision for ethnic minorities, for the mentally and physically handicapped, for the gifted, for the socially disadvantaged and the economically or emotionally deprived. Whether these provisions are motivated by cost-benefit reasoning, by some welfare concept of need or by straight social demand is relevant to the discussion which follows.

In the fifteen countries under review, the financing, organisation and governance of educational services are remarkably varied. Since we are specifically concerned with education, it is worthwhile to consider at this stage some major issues that cut across the education systems in these countries. The first of these is *decision-making*. This can be seen as dealing with educational programmes, finance, and school organisation. A rough generalisation is that, depending on the constitution and law of different countries, there are up to four levels of decision-making: national, state, community and school. There is little evidence however of a major emphasis on the last of these. On the other hand, apart from Turkey, there is little evidence of decision-making vested at the national level. There is, in most countries, a balance spread over the four levels with degrees of integration, overlap and commonality. In the United States for example (despite cyclical fluctuations brought about by changes of government) local boards of education, the States and the Federal Government are integrally involved in nearly all facets of decision-making about education.

Countries like Australia, Canada and the Federal Republic of Germany, while having some national responsibilities for education, in the main base their decision-making at the State or Provincial level. There is in these countries much less involvement at the local community level, especially with funding and curriculum decisions. Other countries such as New Zealand, Norway, Sweden and Denmark have a strong involvement at the national level in decision-making yet with local communities having a large say in this process.

A second major area is the *nature of the special programmes*. We take a narrow definition and divorce it from the organisational and administrative aspects of school life. Here generalisations are difficult because there can be major differences in curriculum offerings between not only different parts of the school system, but also different States and school communities. There appear, however, to be some aspects that help to set the context for special provisions: in most countries primary or elementary education operates in a more clearly defined age-range than secondary education; and the more diffuse the decision-making processes, the more diverse the curriculum. Again, countries such as Turkey and Portugal with centralised decision-making have fairly specific education programmes for their schools. In the United States, States vary widely on curriculum offerings, some determined by State legislatures, others by school districts and still others by individual schools. Specific national initiatives such as testing programmes have, however, led to uniformity across the nation in some teaching areas, less by legislation than by accountability measures (that is test results).

In the area of school *organisation and administration*, it seems that in many countries, schools have considerable freedom, within the general constraints of funding and curriculum, to set their own priorities for the target groups and special services. Whether they actually provide these services is, of course, a different matter. From many of the reports from participating countries it can be assumed that schools and their communities have been reluctant, until recently, to move into the politically sensitive and financially very expensive area of special provisions, and have concentrated their efforts on the mainstream school populations.

2 National policies and performance

Identification of special students

Within any country there are several distinct groups of people who cannot be adequately catered for by the education programmes provided for the general population. These groups, referred to here as 'special populations', require particular learning environments if they are to reach a level of development typical of the general population or congruent with their potential. Before we identify these populations, four points should be made.

The composition of special populations is not fixed but changes over time. Just as curriculum changes, so too will the populations which are unable to cope adequately or be stimulated fully by the curriculum. In fact, there are many educators who argue that all children should be treated as special and that the notion of the typical or normal student is anathema to the educational process. It must be said, however, that while there can be some fairly easy movement from the 'normal' to the 'special' curriculum, the movement in the opposite direction is difficult and often requires special integrative measures, which may be beyond the capacity of the school.

Not only will curriculum evaluation result in changes to the nature of special populations but so too will alterations to economic and social circumstances. Recognition of those people in need of further assistance will be at least partly dependent upon prevailing political and social conditions. At some times rather than others it may be more politically viable to recognise the existence of special populations and to develop policies in their interests. Recognition and action are usually separate political acts. The claim for recognition (that is legitimation as an individual or group in special need) is followed by claims for special attention (usually within existing structures) which in turn leads to the claim for particular programmes and finally the claim for control of these programmes (often by means of a separate administrative structure). Sometimes the general population may become more socially aware and feel it their obligation to recognise special groups who deserve or need special assistance. At other times it may well be their inclination to treat all such people in a manner that is more typical of the general population.

The identification of special populations, particularly the labelling of people as belonging to a special population, may lead to preconceived judgements concerning their potential for development both on the part of the person and of the general population. Notions of limited growth potential in turn affect the type of learning strategies and richness of learning environments afforded special populations. Such preconceptions are readily transmitted and become part of the attitudes and values held by the general population.

Such differences in the understanding of special populations do not only occur over time. They also exist among geographic localities within the same country or even city, and among groups in the general population.

Hence, while being aware of the problems associated with the identification and labelling of people as belonging to special populations, such categorisation is usually considered necessary for the development of policies directed towards the generation of resources over and beyond those given to the general population. Although it is possible to differentiate a very large proportion of the population into groups of people who would benefit by specialist teaching, it is usual to consider the following groups as representing the range of special populations within the total population of a country. These are:

(a) *Intellectually disabled*   Students with degrees of intellectual disability: mildly, moderately, severely and profoundly. For each of these categories of intellectual disability there are fairly well accepted definitions.

(b) *Sensorially disabled*   Those who are blind and visually disabled, deaf and with impaired hearing or a combination of both. This group will also consist of people with reduced speech development.

(c) *Physically disabled* Those who are physically disabled but have fully developed sight and hearing and are not intellectually disabled.

(d) *Gifted and talented* Students of very superior, all-round intellectual ability or those who exhibit consistently exceptional levels of performance in particular scholastic areas or in music, art, sport or dance.

(e) *Slow learners* People who consistently perform poorly in general academic work but who are not found to be intellectually disabled.

(f) *Specific learning difficulties* Students who generally perform adequately in most areas of their academic work but have a depressed performance in a specific area.

(g) *Emotionally and socially disturbed* Those whose behaviour is unpredictable and incompatible with the behaviour of the general population.

(h) *Economically disadvantaged* Families in depressed socio-economic circumstances and therefore living in communities where public and private resources are generally low. Children of such families are at severe risk in a situation of decreased employment opportunity. Students in this group generally attend schools where achievement is traditionally low and thereby possess expectations of poor performance and probable failure (expectations often reinforced both by parents and teachers). Teachers of these students typically possess a different set of values and behaviour from their students and are often unable or unwilling to accommodate to or even recognise students' values.

(i) *Ethnic minorities and indigenous populations* These consist of both immigrants to and natives of a country. The concerns of these groups tend to be three-fold: assimilation into the general population; preservation of ethnic characteristics (linguistic and cultural); and the accommodation of the general population to the sub-culture.

(j) *Geographically disadvantaged* There are at least three types of geographically disadvantaged populations. The first is the geographically isolated and is defined by the distance of students' homes from a permanently established school: this may also include students who are isolated from cultural and social opportunities. The second covers the children of itinerant families who do not attend a particular school but rather are reliant upon a variety of schools (and inherent educational practices) for their formal education. A third group comprises students temporarily absent from their home school, including those in hospital.

(k) *Students about to enter the workforce*   With growing unemployment in many OECD countries, there is concern being expressed that many students about to leave school are 'at risk' of not obtaining satisfactory employment. These students constitute a special population characterised by reduced job opportunity.

(l) *Sex*   There is less opportunity for girls to participate in the educational process, especially tertiary education, or to be employed in particular occupations. That population which has the generally restricted access — the female half — can be considered a special population.

These categories are, in many cases, artificial if not arbitrary because a child may fall into more than one of them. However, for the purposes of this analysis it is necessary to identify their range.

The first set of categories represents the traditional view of special populations — the intellectually and physically disabled. Educational systems have for a long time been concerned with special provisions for the education, albeit a limited one, of these groups. There is only now widespread concern expressed for providing special assistance to the education of the socio-economically disadvantaged, ethnic minorities, the geographically isolated and the gifted.

It is evident that identification with the classifications described above may reside 'within' the individual, and again this has been reflected in the traditional understanding of special populations. Alternatively, the basis may reside 'outside' the individual and be a part of his or her general social or specific school environment. Lovgren, in his chapter on Sweden, argues that the identification of students requiring special provisions is based upon interpretations and decisions which reflect different views as to how difficulties arise and how they are to be dealt with. These underlying models of student development can be classified as: medical, psychometric, administrative, sociological, pedagogic and behavioural therapy. Three examples will illustrate the point being made. In the case of the medical model, deviations are considered somatic defects or diseased states in the individual. By contrast the sociological model emphasises the importance of identifying the problems experienced by the individual within the social environment. The administrative model places students into special groups traditionally created by educational systems for deviant students, rather than creating specific programmes for individual students.

Some countries, for example Norway, while accepting groupings based on location, ethnicity, language and sex, reject on philosophical grounds the notion of classification into special groups. Officially the Norwegians only make differential provisions in order to provide more equitable chances for educational success.

Having established the set of special populations which might exist, policy can be directed towards special assistance for them. This effort can be directed towards the elimination of the characteristic, compensation for the characteristic by the development of other skills or the distribution of particular facilities for maintaining or nurturing the characteristic.

In summary, special populations are defined as those groups of people not adequately catered for by the educational programme developed for the mainstream. We consider the identification and recognition of special populations at the national level to be dependent upon political and social factors operative at a particular point in time, and therefore any classification of special populations is likely to change over time. Special populations can be described in terms of factors intrinsic to the individual or inherent in the social environment. For these reasons what constitutes a special population in one country may not constitute a special population in another; and what may be a well-recognised special population in one country may be either emergent in another or even not recognised. Furthermore, a country's social structure may limit the types of special populations which could emerge.

From the reports of each of the countries participating in this study, we have summarised in table 2.1 the special populations to which supplementary educational resources are allocated. Several points should be noted when interpreting the table. First, we have amalgamated the categories 'remedial', 'specific learning disabilities' and 'slow learners' because it was often not clear how or by what means countries had differentiated these groups of students. Secondly, we stress that this listing is not exhaustive and that some countries may provide special resources for groups which were not indicated in the survey reports on which this table is compiled.

Table 2.1
The special populations in each country to whom special educational resources were allocated

Special population	Aust-ralia[1]	Canada[2]	Den-mark	England & Wales	FRG[3]	France	Ire-land	Nether-lands	New Zealand	Nor-way[4]	Portugal	Sweden	Switzer-land	Turkey	USA
Intellectually disabled	X	X	X	X	X	X	X	X	X	–	X	X	X	X	X
Physically and sensorily disabled	X	X	X	X	X	X	X	X	X	–	X	X	X	X	X
Slow learners and specific learning disabilities	X	X	X	X	X	X	X	X	X	–	–	X	X	–	–
Emotionally and socially disturbed	X	X	X	X	X	X	X	X	X	–	X	X	X	X	X
Ethnic minorities	X	X	X	X	X	–	–	X	–	–	–	X	–	X	X
Indigenous groups[5]	X	X	–	X	X	–	–	–	X	–	X	X	–	–	X
Gifted and talented	X	X	–	X	–	–	X	X	–	–	–	–	–	X	X
Socio-economically disadvantaged	X	X	–	X	–	X	X	X	–	–	X	–	–	X	X
Geographically disadvantaged	X	X	–	–	X	X	X	–	X	–	X	–	X	X	–
Students about to enter employment	–	–	–	–	–	–	–	–	–	–	–	X	–	–	–
Girls	X	–	–	–	–	–	–	–	–	–	–	–	–	–	–

1 Since the collection of information for this project, a Commonwealth School-to-Work Transition Program has been introduced.
2 Ontario.
3 The FRG provided a restricted listing of special populations to whom resources were provided.
4 Norway did not provide a listing of special populations to whom resources were provided.
5 Includes resettlers of national origin.

The equitable distribution of resources

There is a common pattern discernible in the types of special provision being made by the fifteen countries even though there are widespread differences in financing, organisation and governance. All the countries provide special assistance to the physically and intellectually handicapped and for the emotionally disturbed. Many make provision for the socially disadvantaged. Some give additional help to the gifted and talented, to children of itinerant workers, and to indigenous populations. The rationale for the unequal distribution of resources derives from a desire for equality of opportunity for all, regardless of innate ability, ethnicity and social circumstance. Just how much progress towards equality of opportunity might be achieved or even what the ideal of equality of opportunity means in policy terms is not so readily agreed upon. Blackburn, in her chapter that follows, notes that there has been a shift across time in the understanding of equality of opportunity. Initially, equality of opportunity was taken to mean that all individuals would receive the same amount of resources no matter what their social circumstance. As a result, differences of educational attainment would only reflect the ability of individuals. This was followed by a belief that, by altering the structural characteristics of schools to suit individual differences, individuals would be provided with an optimal learning environment. A more recent understanding of equality of opportunity is one where extra resources are allocated to disadvantaged groups so that they may aspire to similar sets of educational objectives as does the general population. There appears to be a trend currently towards applying the equality of opportunity principle to justify extra resources for the education of the gifted and talented, with the express aim of allowing this group to reach a level of achievement above that of the general population because of differences in potential.

Inequality of resource allocation is a general feature of the educational process across all countries. In some cases, such inequality is not readily recognised. In others it is a deliberate feature of the political and educational scene in that disparities are readily recognised by both the special population concerned and by the general population. Whether such inequality of resource allocation remains hidden or is made visible will depend upon governmental intentions for creating or permitting it. In either case the inequality will only occur to the extent to which it can be tolerated. This depends in the long run upon the general population's belief as to whether the inequality is fair and represents an equitable distribution of funds. There are various concepts of educational equality used, deliberately or unconsciously, by education systems to distribute funds according to different notions of justice. Darnell, in his discussion of educational equality in a later chapter includes:

(a) the foundation system concept which guarantees a minimum allocation to all students regardless of available local resources;

(b) the equal dollars per pupil concept which provides each individual with the same allocation of resources;

(c) the competition concept which distributes educational resources to students according to their ability without reference to other characteristics;

(d) the fiscal neutrality or negative concept which ensures that the nature of a student's education should not be dependent upon parental circumstances;

(e) the levelling concept which requires that resources be allocated in inverse proportion to the ability of each student;

(f) the minimum attainment concept which requires that each student shall receive educational resources until a specified level of achievement is reached;

(g) the full opportunity concept which provides each student the opportunity to develop his or her abilities to the maximum.

The interpretation of equality differs markedly across each of these approaches to the distribution of resources. Equality is associated with the equal distribution of resources in the first two approaches which treat all students as equals. In the others there is an unequal distribution of resources on the basis of individual differences, some deriving from the social environment. In the case of the competition model, the interpretation of equality results in greater resource allocation going to students of higher ability or aptitude. By contrast, in the case of the levelling concept, more resources have to be allocated to students of lesser ability in order to ensure basic competence.

It is clear, then, that when we examine the notion of equality we must focus upon both the allocation of resources and the pursuit of educational outcomes. Even though it is possible to define the approaches to the concept of educational equality, the specification of what actually constitutes equitable distribution of resources is far more difficult. For example, if cost-per-student is used as a basis of establishing need for subsidies, then the capacity to contribute to education by the family and the neighbourhood is ignored. Many would argue that such contributions ought to be taken into account.

A further difficulty in determining equitable resource allocation is that the functioning of educational institutions is multi-faceted, that is, there is rarely one source of funds, rather resources are often received from national, state and local governments. Therefore, justice in one particular source of funding can only be determined with reference to the other sources. Similar problems arise if one wishes to define the benefits of schooling which should accrue to a special population following an equitable distribution of resources. Here the problem is one of identifying legitimate ways to measure outcomes. The attainment of minimal levels of competency for the basic skill areas is often cited as one such measure. However, it may well be that longer term outcomes are the significant indicators of wise educational policy. These would include job status and satisfaction, earning capacity, and general quality of adult life. Therefore, the whole notion of equality of opportunity revolves around the question of 'opportunity for what?'.

Thus, the concept of educational equity is closely associated with the distribution of resources in terms of what is considered just and fair, politically and educationally, by both the general and special populations. Often the rationale is couched in terms of the overall goal of equality of opportunity. Yet, as has been pointed out, meanings vary. It may mean the provision of equal resources to all students who are alike so that each will have the opportunity to develop to the limits of their ability. Alternatively, it may refer to the unequal provision of resources in an attempt to give students of differing ability and social background the opportunity to achieve similar educational outcomes by either increasing the resources and enriching the programmes they are already involved with or enhancing their opportunity to participate in existing programmes. The extent to which this is considered legitimate and tolerated will be dependent upon the type of special populations receiving the unequal treatment and the extent of differential treatment.

Styles of provision

In order to achieve an equitable distribution of resources to special populations, four distinctive *styles* of provision exist:

(a) provision to achieve territorial justice by equalising the capacity of areas to have educational services of an appropriate standard;

(b) provision to supplement the regular curriculum for 'target' groups;

(c) provision of alternative educational experience for groups in special need;

(d) provision to encourage greater participation in educational offerings by under-represented groups.

Each of these four approaches may be applied to the treatment of all special populations. This is shown by the array of programmes described in the various countries' reports and the manner in which the programmes (or resources) are distributed. It should be pointed out that the concern here is with the more general style of the provision, rather than resources themselves. Within any approach to the provision of resources, the type of resources as well as the financing, organisation and governance of it, may differ. For example, in the case of the provision 'to encourage greater participation in educational offerings', the resources distributed may refer to direct student grants, transport facilities and boarding facilities.

Each of the four styles of provision can be related to practices existing in member countries. In some instances we have 'force fitted' some of the provisions for purposes of the analysis.

Equalisation across areas: territorial justice

Attempts to equalise the capacity of areas to have educational services of an appropriate standard is evident in the general approach taken by several countries. This principle is fundamental to the financing of all aspects of education in Norway. There the administrative responsibility for compulsory schools rests with about 450 communities with an average size of 10,000 students, although communities vary considerably in size and economic strength. The fiscal capacity (in terms of taxable income per capita) in the poorest communities is only one fifth of that of the richest. To some extent this is compensated by general equalisation grants from the central government. In addition, the refunding by government of educational expenditures is graded according to the economic strength of communes. The effects of this are felt by all students. The Norwegian educational orientation is one where legislation does not recognise special education and categories of handicapped children as a basis for funding. Rather the central government places major responsibility for needs assessment on institutions and individuals at the local level while the resulting extra expenditures incurred at the local level are charged to the government account.

Some form of area equalisation funding policy is also found elsewhere although it is not as highly developed and as extensive as Norway's. These countries have, at least in part, directed resources to particular areas for the education of students on the basis of characteristics of target groups within the areas. This reflects an attempt to equalise educational standards across identified areas or communities, but in contrast to Norway, the principle of 'equalisation of areas' is not fundamental to the provision of education as a whole.

In England, direct grants to local authorities take into account the socio-economic characteristics of local authorities and compensate those authorities whose taxable income is below average. This forms part of the general funding procedure used for the education of both general and special populations. As well as the general funding procedures, England also provides resources to inner-city areas characterised by social disadvantage: poverty, high levels of unemployment, overcrowding, lack of basic household amenities, inadequate community services, inferior educational performance and so on. Again, the provision is made on the basis of area characteristics rather than the identification of particular groups of students. Attempts to equalise education opportunities for socially disadvantaged and geographically isolated areas by general funding procedures rather than the identification of target individuals were also found in several other countries' reports.

The Canadian report describes the provision of compensatory educational programmes in Ontario. This occurs on the grounds of socio-economic attributes of the community in which schools are located rather than upon the identification of particular disadvantaged pupils within the school. This bears certain similarities to Australia's Disadvantaged Schools Program in which schools are selected for participation on criteria that, at the national level, are based on a complex of socio-economic descriptions of neighbourhood populations. However, eligible schools do not automatically receive funds from this programme. Rather, staff and parents develop programmes which they believe will lead to more effective learning, more meaningful and enjoyable schooling and improved school—community interaction. Funding is then dependent upon the quality of the proposals made. This contrasts markedly with the Ontario scene where schools are granted funds automatically and provide compensatory programmes accordingly.

This important difference between Ontario and Australia highlights a defining characteristic of this style of provision, namely that once the socio-economic and geographical characteristics of an area (or community) are established, these become the sole criteria for the allocation of resources within the programme. Both Australia and New Zealand provide extra resources in the form of staffing to selected rural schools. As well, there are zone allowances and promotion incentives for teachers working in remote areas.

The approach to the equitable provision of resources to remote areas in Ontario is also worth noting: they are funded on a straight per capita basis with additional financial resources provided to compensate for the higher cost of goods and services and the higher administrative and instructional costs of operating small schools and school boards with a low enrolment base.

In these various ways the authorities hoped to maintain a standard of education in rural areas commensurate with that in more densely populated areas. But care must be taken that funding of areas rather than schools does not lead to an inequitable distribution of resources to schools within areas which have received an equitable allocation from central sources.

So far we have been describing the provision of resources first to areas and then to schools based upon characteristics of the general areas and local communities. Such provision is not based upon identified characteristics of students within the schools although, of course, there is a high correlation between community and school population characteristics. The principal aim of these provisions has been to equalise the capacity of areas to provide educational services of an appropriate standard across-the-board. By contrast, provision of resources to areas or schools might also be made on the basis of identifiable special population characteristics.

To sum up, there are two bases on which an equitable distribution of resources to special populations might be made. The first is that of the area in which schools are located, and reflects an underlying philosophy favouring territorial justice. The second is that of the incidence of a special population in attendance at particular schools. In either case the schools to which resources are allocated may be regular schools or specialist. In regular schools, resources are provided for the supplementation of the regular curriculum or for the provision of separate education experiences such as special classes or sometimes the restructuring of regular school curricula to reflect better the abilities and aspirations of those attending the schools.

Curriculum supplementation and alternative experiences

A tension running through the country survey reports is that of whether good practice lies in supplementing the regular curriculum or in providing alternative educational experiences for target groups. This also comes to the fore in the integration—segregation debate. On the one hand, countries like Norway and Denmark have adhered fairly strictly to supplementing regular curricula rather than providing alternative educational experiences such as special classes or schools. On the other hand, Turkey and Ireland are among the countries which have a greater tendency to make alternative provision for their special populations.

Whichever approach to resource provision is adopted is dependent upon the particular special population being focused on and the attitude of the school and educational system to it. In some cases it may be necessary to provide alternative educational experiences. In respect of other groups, there can be a choice. There is an emerging interest in retaining special populations within the ordinary school curriculum and supplementing the regular curriculum where necessary. For example, in providing education for the intellectually or physically disabled, Denmark, Canada and the United States have clear policy statements on the desirability of integrating provisions for these groups into the ordinary school curriculum. The limiting effect of the severity of the disability upon the nature of the provisions is illustrated in figure 2.1 which is taken from the Canadian (Ontario) country survey.

The needs, interests and capabilities of each student will determine where the placement of students should be made. A similar approach to the education of the physically and intellectually handicapped was found in many of the countries reviewed. Yet there are difficulties faced by educational systems in their attempts to integrate partially intellectually and physically disabled students into ordinary classes. Ireland has restricted full integration to some physically disabled and hearing-impaired students. Factors that militate against integration include the relatively high pupil—teacher ratios of most urban schools in Ireland, the bilingual curriculum and the absence of any local or regional controlling bodies.

Generally, provision has been made for the less severely disabled within the regular school for some degree of supplementation to the regular school curriculum. Such provisions might be in the form of specialist staffing and materials for the education of these students either within the normal classroom or on a withdrawal basis for particular times of the school week. Such an approach is more common in the education of the slow learner and those with specific learning disabilities. Hence we find countries such as Australia, Canada, Denmark, England, Ireland, New Zealand, Norway, Sweden and the United States supplementing the regular school provision of permanent specialist teachers in a school by others who visit schools on a regular basis for remedial work in the areas of numeracy, literacy and oracy.

Not all provisions are within the regular school. Supplementation of the regular curriculum might well be in the form of remedial centres for educating slow learners or students with specific learning difficulties, both during school hours and after school. Ireland has augmented its remedial teaching programme in the regular school in this manner. Several other countries also indicated that as well as providing for the slow learner or student with a specific learning difficulty by means of supplementing the regular curriculum, they also have developed separate learning facilities for these students.

Students may be enrolled in special classes or specialist schools for differing periods of time for remedial purposes. Ireland reports a period of from one to two years for students with specific learning disabilities in their specialist schools. New Zealand also provides clinics for students

```
←——————Proportionate number of children——————→
```

Most learning and behavioural problems accommodated by modification of regular programme

Regular programme with consultation for class room teacher (special education consultant, psychologist, etc.)

Regular programme plus supplementary instructional services

Itinerant teachers

Resources room

Withdrawal for scheduled special work

Part-time special class

Full-time special class or school

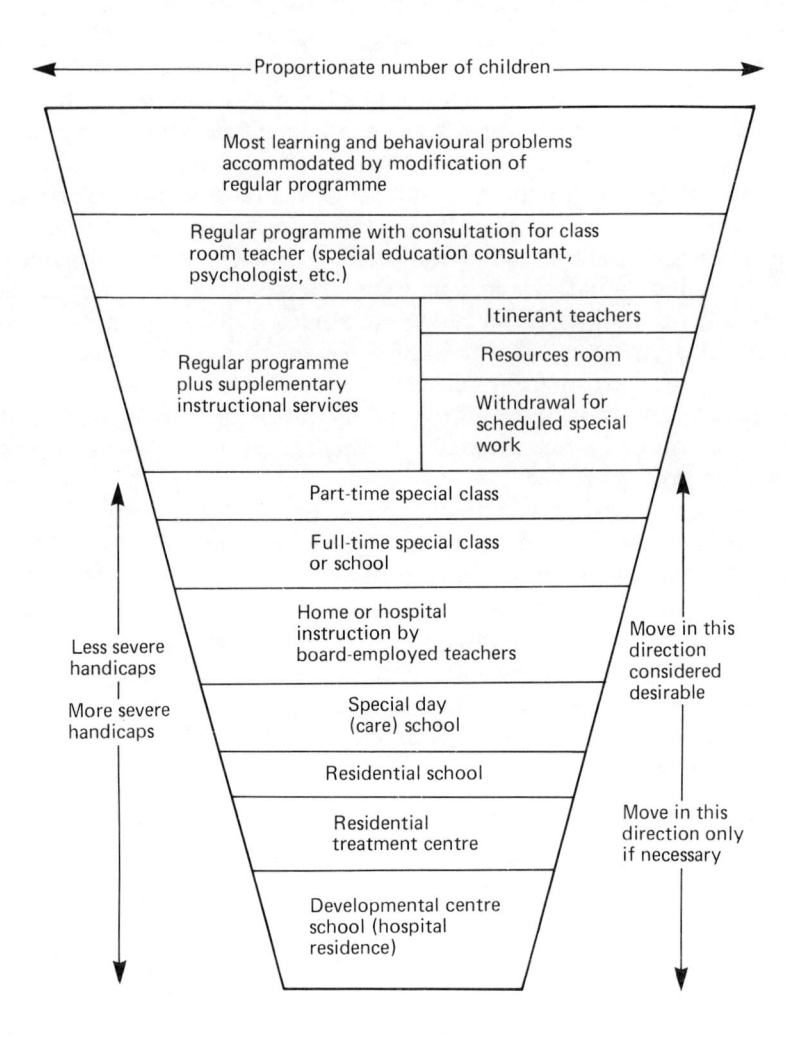

Home or hospital instruction by board-employed teachers

Special day (care) school

Residential school

Residential treatment centre

Developmental centre school (hospital residence)

Less severe handicaps
|
More severe handicaps

Move in this direction considered desirable

Move in this direction only if necessary

Source: Benson and Burtnyk, Survey of Current Practice: Canada.

Figure 2.1 Provisions for education of the intellectually and physically disabled, slow learners and the specifically learning disabled.

of average ability with severe reading retardation and who are considered unable to learn in a conventional classroom situation. The reports of Denmark and Sweden also made reference to special classes and schools for these types of students but again the intention is for them to return to the regular school curriculum as soon as possible.

Another approach to the provision of alternative educational experiences outside the classroom is undertaken by New Zealand. In this instance assistance is provided to parents to tutor their children at home. Similarly, in Ireland, home tuition is provided for a small group of physically handicapped children unable to attend school regularly.

Such divergent styles of provisions are not limited to the education of the physically and intellectually handicapped or the slow learner or student with a specific learning disability. Policies for supplementation of the regular curriculum and the development of alternative educational experiences are characteristic of the education of almost all the special populations identified in this study. The only groups for which both provisions are not made are the socially disadvantaged, although in one sense homogeneous socially disadvantaged communities might constitute an environment for an alternative educational experience if curricula were adapted to meet local needs. Even the largest special population of all — girls — is treated separately in some countries through the provision of sex-segregated schools.

In the education of children of itinerant workers, ethnic communities, of indigenous populations and children who are gifted or talented, there are examples given by countries of both forms of provision. In the education of children of itinerant workers special provisions within ordinary schools are sometimes made as well as the establishment of special schools for their education. For example, in Stockholm, a small group of adult gypsies undertook a general basic education programme in a school administered by a local school board. In the Netherlands there are schools for bargees' children, schools for caravan-dwellers' children and children of fairground operators which teach a curriculum governed by a special education decree and in which teachers work with smaller classes than is usual within an ordinary school. In both these examples, the central authorities have opted for a segregated approach to educating the special groups rather than integrating them into the regular school curriculum.

This integration/segregation dilemma is examined in the Irish report on the education of itinerant workers. Whilst the central government's policy is for the integration of these children into the curriculum of ordinary schools, this has not been easily implemented, as shown by a low rate of participation — less than 50 per cent of the target population were attending school sufficiently regularly to acquire basic literacy and numeracy skills. The Department of Education in Ireland has no machinery for initiating schemes at local level and the initiative for the provision of facilities must come from local instrumentalities and people. Budgetary constraints have restricted much local initiative including the provision of suitably qualified welfare staff to assist in the integration of this group into ordinary school and community life. The situation has been worsened by active resistance by ordinary communities towards the integration of children of itinerant workers into ordinary schools. As a result several special schools for this group have been established at the primary and secondary level. A further complicating factor for the older students is their generally low level of literacy and numeracy skills. In order to enable the present generation to acquire essential educational and vocational skills, training centres in Ireland have been established for the development of skills in metalwork, woodwork, domestic crafts and industrial machine work.

All the country surveys indicate that, with respect to the education of indigenous peoples, ethnic minorities and minority language groups, provisions in terms of both supplementary regular curricula and alternative educational experiences (often through separate schools) are made. Yet as Eide points out in his paper on autonomy in Part II of this account, each country seems to be facing a dual problem in the education of these groups. The first is educating them in a curriculum which is aimed at developing the necessary skills for a full adult life which often subjugates their minority values in favour of those of the dominant culture. The second is the maintenance of the culture of these minority groups; and to this end, countries have developed multicultural programmes, resource materials for the promotion of minority cultures, special language programmes and bilingual schools.

Increasing the participation of under-represented groups

The distribution of resources by countries to gain greater participation in education is common in the case of the geographically isolated and socially disadvantaged. These resources are generally directed towards the individual student in the form of travel allowances, scholarships and boarding facilities to enable him to attend school regularly. For example, many countries provide school transport for students living a minimum distance from their nearest school. Rather than bring the student to the school, several countries have developed means of bringing schooling to the student by providing visiting teachers, by correspondence courses and by the school of the air (radio and television). In the case of children of workers abroad, France, Italy, Portugal, Sweden and Turkey subsidise schooling in foreign lands. The participation of the socially disadvantaged in education is also facilitated by the provision of scholarships in a substantial number of the countries. For example, in France scholarships to primary and secondary school students of low income families are available. Free boarding and scholarships in secondary schools are also available for Turkish students of low income families who have demonstrated high achievement in their previous schooling.

Summary of styles of provision

In summary, four styles of providing resources for the education of special populations have been identified. From table 2.2 it is evident that in the education of most of the groups identified in the reports the styles of provision are diverse.

Table 2.2
The styles of provision of educational resources
in terms of type of special population

Special population	Distribution of resources to identified areas to maintain educational standards	Distribution of resources to gain greater participation by under-represented groups	Distribution of resources for the supplementation of regular curricula	Distribution of resources for the provision of alternative educational experiences
Intellectually disabled	X		X	X
Physically and sensorily disabled	X		X	X
Slow learners and specific learning disabilities	X		X	X
Emotionally and socially disturbed	X		X	X
Ethnic minorities			X	X
Indigenous groups		X	X	X
Gifted and talented	X	X	X	X
Socio-economically disadvantaged	X	X	X	X
Geographically disadvantaged	X	X	X	X
Students about to enter employment			X	X
Girls				

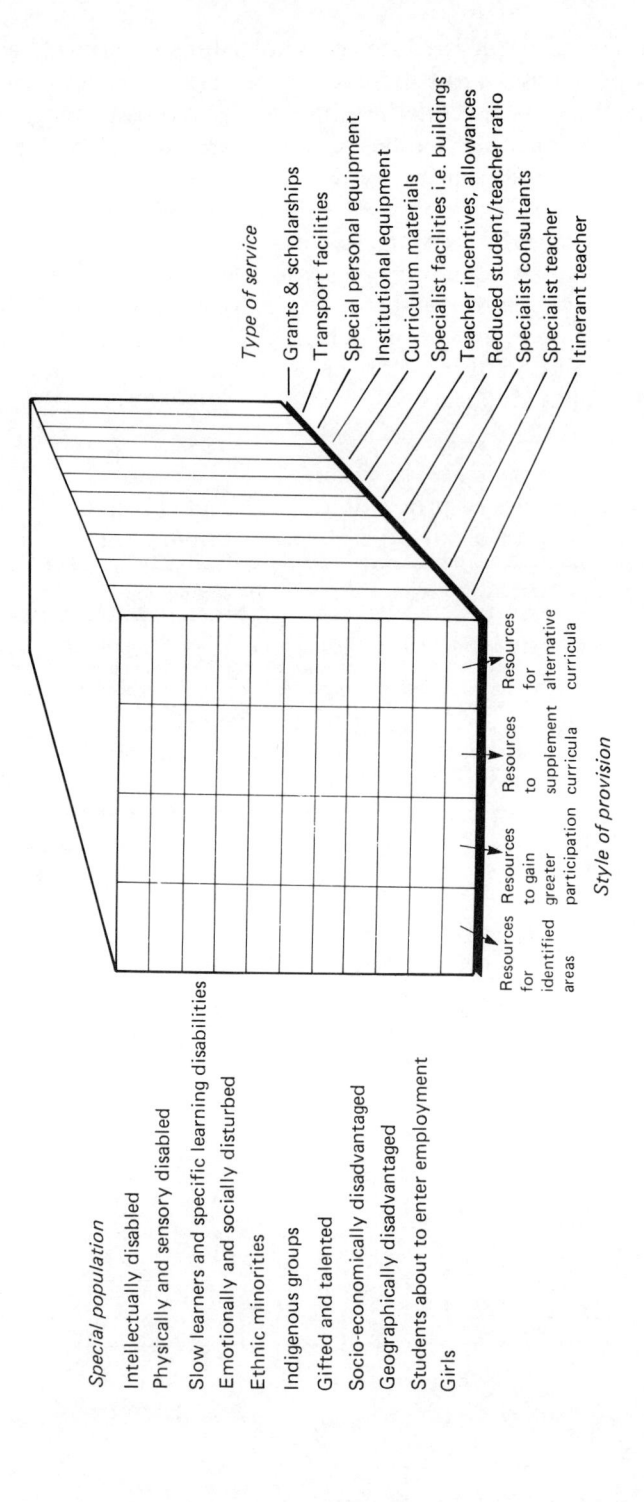

Figure 2.2 The styles of provision and the types of services for the education of special populations.

Within each style of provision there is a range of services which may be established for the education of particular populations. From this we can consider the allocation of resources in accordance with figure 2.2. While many of the cells of this three dimensional diagram remain empty, it does however, provide a representation of the choice of alternative provisions available for the education of special populations.

The final choice of which provision to make available depends upon many factors. McDonagh, in his discussion of service delivery in Part II, lists the following factors as influencing the choice and affective implementation of the provision:

- the structure of the regular school system
- the existing structure of special education
- the role of voluntary organisations
- finance and fundings procedures
- attitudes and values of teachers
- community attitudes to special populations
- parents' attitudes to special services
- inter-institutional and inter-government co-operation.

To this list we must add the political condition of the country. For while the effects of particular political persuasions will be felt in educational as in other government instrumentalities, the political climate of any country varies. When instability exists, pressure groups representing special populations or strategies for the education of special populations may exert sufficient influence to overrule the influence of many of the factors listed above. For governments rarely make such decisions on purely educational grounds, even if such grounds do really exist. Rather, decisions concerning the allocation of educational resources are largely affected by politics, economies and culture.

Funding strategies

Provision for the education of special groups may be made to local areas, particular schools or individual students. We have seen how many factors, often contradictory, determine the most appropriate type of provision and the extent to which it is implemented. These relate to the means of financial support available, the organisation of agencies associated with the education of special populations and the types of control exercised.

There are two aspects of finance for special education which require close scrutiny: the *allocation and distribution* of funds and the *generation or source* of funds. In examining the first, we are concerned with the special groups to whom the resources are being allocated and the form that the resources take, that is, the programme, the personnel and the facilities. Of particular interest are the criteria upon which authorities allocate resources and the means by which they establish costs. Also of interest is the allocation of resources to the same programmes from different agencies and the interdependence of such provisions.

As for the generation of funds, the concern is with the proportion of revenues to be provided from the whole range of educational fund sources, the types of receipts which are to be raised, and the relation of educational revenue with that of other areas of government. Darnell, in providing an analytic framework for the study of provisions for indigenous populations, stresses the need to keep each of these two aspects of finance separate since individuals or groups, depending on their basic orientation, are often more interested in one than the other.

Funding at the level of central government

The specification, generation and distribution of funds can be examined at several levels of government. First, the financing of education for special groups can be examined at the central level. In this case, the relationships between the department of finance, department of education and other relevant central government departments can be explored. Of major importance at this level is the relationship between the political arm of government and the administration department. Secondly, raising, allocating and distributing of resources can be the responsibility of local government or even the school itself. This represents a second level at which the finance of education for special populations can be examined. Finally, the finance of special education can be examined at the level in which resources flow from central government to some more local form of government (including state, provincial, local, education board or school). We will consider first the funding arrangements at the central level of government.

The method of financing special provisions at this level has marked effects upon the establishment and maintenance of educational programmes for special populations. There are a number of such approaches to funding. McDonagh in his paper on service delivery comments on three strategies:

(a) *Funding for the department of education through a general finance vote for the education system as a whole.* The major advantage of such a funding strategy is that it facilitates the provision of educational programmes for the handicapped and disadvantaged within the regular school system. It may also enable educational systems to establish their own educational priorities and even to transfer surplus funds from one programme to another. While this may be seen as a plus when the education department places a high priority on the education of special populations, of course it is not so when the department is not so sympathetic to the needs of these groups. Educational administrations may view it as being more educationally sound or more politically expedient to place higher priority upon other educational programmes and so distribute funds accordingly.

(b) *Funding for the department of education through a finance vote for special provisions.* This funding procedure restricts the capacity of the education department to alter the intended priorities of the central government for the funding of special provisions, but at the same time retains special services within the regular school system. A separate budget for special education ensures a continuity of programme and increases the likelihood of a more sophisticated (and often numerous) management structure.

(c) *Funding of a special education authority independent of the department of education.* The clear limitation of such a funding strategy is the separation of the education of special populations, at least at the financing and organisational levels, from the regular school system. At a time when the blending of education for special populations with the mainstream is a high priority among the countries participating in this study, great difficulties could be faced in trying to establish a separate 'special provisions' authority with administrative and organisational links at all levels to that of the general education system.

A fundamental question that needs to be explored is on what basis are funds allocated from central government revenue for the purpose of special education and to which central agency are these funds directed? The link between the central government, the central education authority and other government departments which assume some responsibility for the education of special groups is at the heart of this.

It is difficult to make an unequivocal statement on the extent to which government revenue is tagged to the education of special populations before it is received by education authorities (hence reflecting the second funding strategy described by McDonagh) because the capacity or willingness of central education departments or other central government agencies to allocate their general revenue to particular educational programmes is not dealt with in depth in the background papers.

The Disadvantaged Schools Program in Australia is, however, one example where there is some mention made of the link between central government and a central education authority. This programme is funded from consolidated revenue available to the central government from income and other taxes. The amount allocated to the programme derives from advice to the government from an advisory Commission, but such advice is not binding on the government.

The financial relationship between the central government and the central education authority in regard to the provision of resources for the education of special populations reflects the interaction and interdependence of both political and economic forces within government policy-making. The frail grasp on continued existence by many programmes for special populations, and their utter dependence upon central government is illustrated by the educational development policy for disadvantaged children described in the Country Survey of the Netherlands. There is no legislation governing the finance for educational development policy, unlike provisions made for normal funds to schools. The Dutch paper points out that because there is no legislative yardstick to determine the scale of educational development funds, in theory drastic cuts in expenditure can be made when a new budget is drawn up. However, such a situation is improbable, due to the likely political consequences of such action.

Funding arrangements between central and local government, and schools

There are several funding strategies evident from the Country Surveys that can be dealt with under this rubric:

(a) earmarked allocations from central education to local authorities;

(b) earmarked allocations from the central authority directly to schools;

(c) general allocations to local authorities who are responsible for its disbursement;

(d) fiscal autonomy of local authorities;

(e) fiscal autonomy of schools;

(f) joint allocations of earmarked funds from several central government agencies to local authorities and/or schools.

Central government funding of specific services to local authorities. The Title 1 programmes for compensatory education in the United States are illustrative of this form of funding, with general revenue funds of the central government being directed to State governments and local educational agencies. The Urban Programme (inner-city) in England and Wales covers industrial, environmental, and recreational as well as educational provision and funds flow directly from the central government to local authorities for the overall improvement of community life. In both these examples the central government allocates funds for specific purposes. This strategy is reflected in the reports of other countries. There are variations, but the common element is that the central government provides resources for a particular purpose to be used at the regional or local level for the particular purpose of educating special groups.

In Norway and Ontario, the notion of expenditure in excess of that used in the education of regular students is adopted and the central government reimburses local areas for the extra cost incurred in the provision of special education. The Norwegian government provides resources to communes, based upon their size and economic strength, for the provision of compulsory education to all students. Expenditure by communes in educating pupils with learning difficulties which is beyond that used on average for educating normal pupils is made good by the central government.

Ontario employs the concept of population grant ceilings to allocate resources to school boards in the province. This ceiling includes adequate financial resources for the education of all students in a typical area, including a small (representative) proportion of students belonging to special populations and high cost categories. Above this figure there are special provisions made from the ministry of education to school boards – for example, to strengthen minority language programmes and the development of language curriculum materials. In the case of the minority language programme the allocation of funds to school boards for the education of special populations is based on the number of students in the category. The number of teachers used is the funding base in the case of the English as a second language – ESL – programme: this, rather than the number of students, avoids the labelling of students but instead specifies the type of programme and service.

Central government funding of specific services directly to schools. The funding strategy which has been outlined above refers to the distribution of funds from central government to local educational authorities. Another strategy is for direct funding from central government to schools with special populations. For example, in some countries the central government is financially responsible for the establishment and maintenance of schools for the severely intellectually and physically handicapped. This may be the case even if local authorities are generally responsible for provisions for the education of special populations. Hence, in Denmark we find that provisions for special education in ordinary schools are funded by the local municipality; observation schools and centres for the severely handicapped are funded by the counties; and 'special care' services (generally special schools) are funded by the central government.

The distribution of funds to schools by central government may be by means of a local authority (the county in the case of Danish special care provisions). Alternatively, resources may be distributed directly to schools. In the Netherlands both practices apply: the central government reimburses either directly or by means of the local authority the special schools established for the education of children of itinerant parents; in the education of disadvantaged students the government pays the extra subsidies directly to the schools themselves. Similarly, the French Minister of Education is financially and administratively responsible for the establishment of special primary schools with boarding facilities to accommodate the children of bargees and other itinerant workers.

Overall, there are large differences across countries in the extent to which federal or central government funds are designated for particular educational programmes for special populations. All federal aid for public education in the United States is identified for use for specific purposes or for special populations, with the major responsibility for financing general education held at the state and local levels. In fact, the level of federal funding, as in the case of compensatory education programmes, may be dependent upon local effort. By contrast, Turkey and Portugal are examples of central funding being specifically directed to the total provision of all services for special populations as well as the provision of general education.

Allocation of general revenue to local authorities. It would appear that for the greater part of resource allocation for special populations, central governments in most countries do not 'tag' funds to special educational programmes. The government may allocate resources to districts or regions for the provision of education and from these resources the local or state education authorities distribute funds. For example, in England the central government provides a Rate Support Grant to local authorities. Not only is the education share of the total grant indeterminate but it also falls within the legal and professional responsibility of each local authority to distribute funds to the various sectors of education within and to strike a balance of the allocation of these resources between mainstream and special education. Similarly, local education boards in New Zealand fund most of their special educational programmes from general grant money received from the national Department of Education.

While this model of resource allocation is similar to the first of the strategies described by McDonagh, neither the central government nor its education ministry allocates resources to various education programmes. This is seen to be the role of local government.

Fiscal autonomy of local authorities. The local authority may have the capacity to raise its own revenue and allocate part of this for the purpose of educating special groups. In the case of the local education authorities in England and Wales, they must provide additional revenue from property and trading tax for the provision of educational services. This may be in the form of a matched grant system — for example, the Urban Programme requires local authorities to provide 25 per cent of resources and the central government the other 75 per cent for disadvantaged programmes in the inner-city areas.

In brief, the contributions made by local authorities in many countries to the education of special populations form another funding strategy. In the United States, the local contribution at the school district level to the financing of special education varies from no contribution to about 70 per cent. In general, districts spending large amounts of money on special education programmes are characterised by a high property wealth and traditional commitment to special education. Norway is another country in which there is a potential contribution by local authorities to the education of special populations. Only relatively rich communes go beyond what is being partially refunded by central government and thus the amount of discriminatory spending at the commune level is limited, a situation which contrasts with that of the United States.

School based financing. Another resource allocation strategy is that initiated within the school itself or from charitable and voluntary organisations. While this approach is not dealt with in detail in any country's report, several countries (particularly Ireland) stressed the important contribution made by voluntary organisations, both financially and administratively, in the educational provisions for target groups.

Joint earmarked allocations. So far, the funding of education for special populations has been viewed as the concern solely of education authorities, whether they be national, state or local. However, several government departments may be responsible for the provision of education to special populations. The care and education of disabled children in Ireland is the joint responsibility of the Departments of Education and Health. Education pays teachers' salaries and allowances and the cost of school transport, together with grants for building, equipping and operating schools. Health makes grants in respect of boarding, day-care, psychological, medical and para-medical services provided at special schools.

Funds from departments other than education may be indirectly allocated to the provision of education for special populations. In the education of children with learning and behavioural problems in the Netherlands, monies spent on special schools are reimbursed by central and by local authorities. The Ministry of Education and Science pays the cost of teachers' salaries and local authorities pay the remainder, the money for which comes from the Ministry of Finance and the Ministry of Home Affairs.

While such dual funding sources may operate to the benefit of target groups, the Portuguese report notes the difficulties experiences from the involvement of several government departments in special education. This has led the Ministry of Education and Scientific Research in Portugal to accept responsibility for providing for all children, both general and special.

Summary of funding strategies

Table 2.3 presents a summary of the main sources of funding in each of the countries under review. As to establishing a level of funding for the provision of services there appear to be several quite distinct approaches and these often reflect philosophical differences in the countries' consideration of special groups. One equitable basis takes into account the economic strength of the areas or community, using indices such as the proportion of the community receiving social welfare benefits, the per capita income of the community, and the number and type of housing units. A second approach is based upon the relative costs of servicing different types of student. Student weighting systems take into account factors such as student numbers, grade level and the type of educational need as a means of adjusting for cost differences in the education of special groups. An alternative approach which does not focus directly upon student characteristics is a weighting formula based upon the number of specialist teachers employed. In this case, the number of teachers is used (rather than the number of students within the special group) in a deliberate attempt to avoid stigmatising students.

Several difficulties were encountered in attempting to identify the

Table 2.3
Major sources of funding of special education in the
countries participating in the inquiry

Country	Source of funding		
	National/Federal	State/Province/ Country	Municipalities/School Districts/Local Educational Authorities
Australia	X	X	
Canada (Ontario)		X	X
Denmark	X	X	X
England and Wales	X		X
Federal Republic of Germany		X	X
France	X	X	X
Ireland	X		
Netherlands	X		
New Zealand	X		
Norway	X		
Portugal	X		
Sweden	X	X	
Switzerland	X	X	X
Turkey	X		
United States of America	X	X	X

Note: A significant source of funding in many countries is charitable organisations. These have not been included in the table.

strategies by which special education programmes are funded across the participating countries. The English study makes the point that it is often extremely difficult to identify clearly costs associated with the provision of services since costs may be both direct and indirect and may be financed from different sources: central, county, local, voluntary, and so on. Direct costs are generally clearly identified: curriculum materials and development, additional and support personnel, and pre-service and inservice training. Indirect costs, by contrast, may be associated with the higher cost of plant operation and maintenance, administration and additional ancillary staff. The difficulty of isolating the sources of funding is well illustrated in the provision for the schooling of behaviourally disturbed children at the Hanover Children's Centre in the Federal Republic of Germany. The Centre is financed by a variety of public and private agencies: the German Federal Government, the rural district of Hanover, the City of Hanover, the Hanover

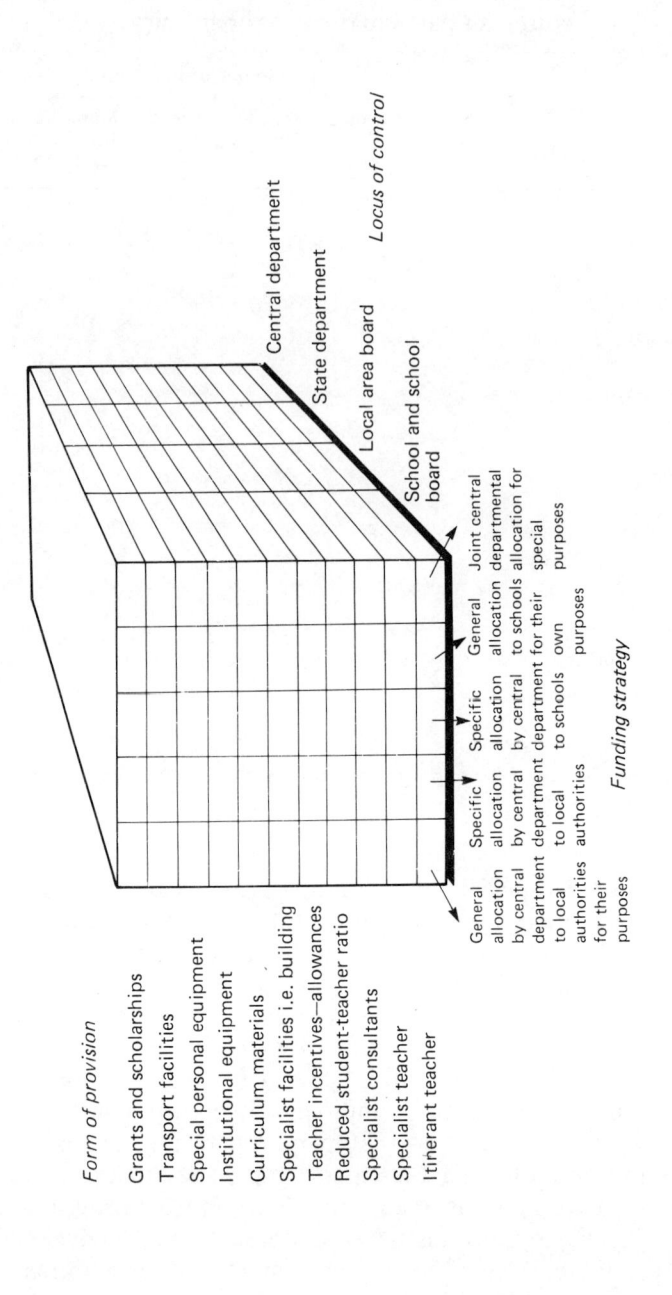

Figure 2.3 Type of provision, source of funding and locus of control for the education of special populations

Children's Hospital Foundation, the Contergen Foundation as well as a handicapped children's association.

No one funding strategy characterises the provision of education for special populations in a particular country. Rather, many of the forms outlined above will be found in any one country, although one could expect that certain approaches would dominate, depending upon the political orientation of the country.

We have listed both the types of provision and the types of funding strategy to be found in the participant countries. To this must be added the governance of the provisions and, more particularly, the locus of control for the definition and implementation of the provision. 'Definition' means the specification of the educational content and processes which characterise the provisional, rather than the labelling of the special population. Clearly, in some instances, the definition of the provisions rests with the central government. For example, in the case of student allowances and transport subsidies, it is generally the body to define the eligibility criteria. In other cases the central government also plays a major role in the definition of the educational programme for particular groups. An alternative is for the central government to act as the funding source for a provision but for a provincial authority to specify the form the provision should take. Several of the provisions for the severely intellectually and physically disabled are characterised by this form of control. Finally, the locus of control may be held by the local school board or the school itself. This is the case when schools or school boards are provided with earmarked funds and are able to develop their own curricula to best suit their particular needs. This is common in those countries where there is a high level of devolution of curriculum responsibility.

In the analysis of the provisions for the education of special populations the central concerns have been:

(a) type of provision;
(b) the type of funding strategy adopted;
(c) the locus of control for the definition and implementation of the provision.

The linkage between type of provision for a particular population, source of funding and locus of control is represented in figure 2.3.

Case studies of provisions for indigenous and linguistic minorities

Many countries have had a 'multicultural society' for centuries. Others have seen the recent emergence of such societies through mass migration. Two educational issues arising from such multicultural societies are the provisions for linguistic minorities and indigenous cultural minorities. This matter was considered distinct enough, and important enough, to merit special treatment in the CERI inquiry and two sets of comparative studies were initiated, one for each kind of minority. Their main purposes were to:

(a) examine in detail how countries address these two persistent and intractable policy problems in making provision for special population groups;

(b) throw comparative light on the different ways that different countries approach similar policy issues;

(c) illuminate the effects that different modes of financing, organisation and governance have on the attainment of similar objectives.

Indigenous minority populations

The methodology employed in dealing with this issue was to invite Professor Frank Darnell (University of Alaska) to write an 'issues' paper on this topic and for spokesmen for the indigenous populations in Australia, New Zealand, Norway and North America to respond with 'reaction papers'. All of these are reproduced in Part III of this volume.

As will be seen, Darnell did not undertake a detailed account of provisions for indigenous minority education found in the participating countries, nor does he compare provisions. What he attempted was to introduce certain governance and financing notions that may pertain universally to education among indigenous minorities. The major issues canvassed relate to the education of indigenous peoples from an international perspective and provide us with an informed state of the art in this field. Thus, Darnell has attempted, by drawing generalisations from dissimilar stances, a synthesis of an extremely complex cultural process.

The main message is that indigenous populations in modern industrialised nations are experiencing profound dislocations in their traditional lifestyles. Education increases this tension; while providing a means to cope with change, it also usually forms a basis for assimilation of the minority population into the dominant culture rather than being a support for the language and culture of the minority groups and help for them to cope better with change.

The necessary criterion for success of educational programmes among indigenous minorities is the provision of an education which relates to their interests, norms and values. This 'legitimates' the schooling offered. The reactors to Darnell's paper take up this theme but tend to turn it into a needs analysis of the indigenous population in their area. There are, however, some common threads to their arguments that correspond to Darnell's position.

Efforts to cater effectively for indigenous groups in societies which have come to acknowledge their pluralism are not coming from the establishment in a form satisfactory to these minorities. All the authors assert that effective provisions are dependent on a grassroots movement from within the special groups rather than from an outside analysis of needs. This is, of course, a circular argument. For a basically uneducated (in western ideological and political terms) population to reach a stage where at least some of its members are sufficiently politically and educationally sophisticated to help their fellows determine the fundamental needs to bring them to the attention of the power élites and to initiate educational action at the local level, it is necessary to have a suitable education provision provided from outside the group.

One 'reactor' suggests that Darnell tends to equate formal education with institutionalised schooling although education for indigenous groups might well be more appropriately conducted in and by local communities rather than through schools provided, staffed and run by the mainstream.

Each of the responding authors, themselves members of indigenous minority groups or closely involved with them in educational planning, argue for a needs based analysis of the communities in terms of their survival as an identifiable cultural group within the wider societies in which they live.

Bourke, writing about Australian Aboriginal communities, submits that educational programmes should be designed, staffed (if appropriate) and run within the Aboriginal communities as a basis, not only for maintenance and development of their cultural identity, but also to enable them to operate effectively in multicultural mainstream Australia. This will require Aboriginals to take initiatives and for funding agencies to support these moves. Bourke argues that all Australians will benefit from this because successful education programmes will develop a deeper appreciation of cross-cultural situations.

It is apparent from Smith's reaction that the Maori people of New Zealand have moved along a line of self-reliance and self-determination. While favouring integration of their people with the country's majority group, they are nevertheless maintaining the line of bicultural development.

Hoem, discussing the situation of the Sami people in Norway, argues that the degree of integration of the minority into the larger society will determine the function of education for the Sami minority. However, he sees the establishment of individual Sami schools leading to the development of other Sami institutions. The teaching of the Sami at school presupposes some form of Sami language institutes. The teaching of Sami literature presupposes specialised publishing and printing houses. Living Sami literature presupposes Sami theatres, radio and television. All this presupposes Sami organisations and bureaucracy to take care of the various cultural activities, and this in its turn presupposes Sami people with various educational backgrounds. The education of Norwegians in Sami language and culture to help such cultural revival and development is, in principle and in practice, a nonstarter. If there is to be revitalisation of Sami culture, this must be brought about by the Sami people themselves. Otherwise it will end up as an advanced form of museum activity.

Demmert, in dealing with Indian communities in the United States, clearly sees indigenous peoples as having developed societies as complicated and demanding as any. Thus he sees the need for the Indian people to determine clearly their own goals for education and for them to be given financial and political support to carry out a plan directed towards these goals. He concludes that we should concentrate on an educational system for indigenous minorities that is flexible, allows a sense of community ownership, is well supported financially and politically, has a good mix of competent, sensitive and dedicated professional and community people, and represents a joint venture between the people served and the responsible government.

There is, then, some consensus on the directions necessary for the education of indigenous minority groups. However, the process of carrying this out presents a complex, political problem for the countries concerned.

Linguistic minorities: language and literacy

This part of the inquiry deals with the manner in which language diversity is addressed within the educational systems of four developed countries. In his overview of the reports from these countries (Canada, France, FRG, United Kingdom), Ray Rist has been able to generalise in order to obtain a better understanding of the rationale and implementation of educational programmes within multicultural societies. His paper, too, can be read in Part III.

Several key points emerge from Rist's overview. First, it is apparent that some countries create a climate in which the dominant language is paramount and is used in business, government and schools. This situation retards language diversity and its integrated provision in schools. Secondly, there are marked differences between countries related to the length of time that linguistic minorities have been present. These differences have led to a different treatment of long-term as distinct from short-term populations. Two countries — France and Germany — have policies concerning recently arrived linguistic minorities. Canada and the United Kingdom (in Wales) have, to varying degrees, legislated for provision to provide for historically-rooted linguistic minorities. Thirdly, the four countries offer language and literacy programmes in the mother tongue for quite different political and social reasons. It is therefore important to analyse policies of provision in different contexts. Fourthly, it is evident that the provisions vary from country to country about the continuum from centralised to locally administered. In this regard most governments appear willing to establish policies concerning language and literacy programmes against a background of how the different linguistic minorities want to, or are prepared to, define their own presence in particular countries.

Within this context, four main conclusions can be drawn from the case studies. The main conclusion is that, viewed historically, the policies of all four countries have evolved in the last few decades towards the increasing recognition of the special needs of minority language populations. This tendency is manifest in the gradual elaboration of a multitude of policy instruments showing progressively more sensitive adaptations to take into account both the educational needs of the populations served and the specific organisational/political context faced by the responsible educational authorities and administrations. The following conclusions can be derived from viewing the policies as they have evolved.

(a) *Organisation* While there is diversity of organisation in the four countries, it is evident that preservation of, and education in, the mother tongue has only been guaranteed on a significant scale if the countries concerned have adopted specific policies creating or accepting multicultural/multilingual national identities, that is, a long-term commitment to the maintenance of more than one culture within the country.

(b) *Finance* Finance follows policy. In all four countries the recognition of multicultural needs and priorities has been followed by the adoption of financial measures to provide adequate resources for the implementation of language and literacy programmes for affected minorities. In those countries lacking long-term commitments to a bilingual national identity, financial support is provided generally on a temporary basis, that is with no sense of long-term commitment; the size of the affected populations and their growing permanence is now calling into question the assumption that solutions can be of such a short-term nature.

(c) *Governance*   Political and ideological stances govern the provisions towards linguistic minorities in quite observable ways. For instance, newly arrived immigrants of whatever nationality will, in some countries, be put into educational programmes to enable their ready assimilation into the dominant language and culture. In other countries, the same immigrants could find themselves forced to learn a third language because of those countries' bilingual policies. A mark of the importance of political and ideological stances in provisions made for linguistic minorities is that the five countries involved in the study have little or no knowledge of whether their language programmes achieve teaching/educational outcomes based on the real needs of pupils. The policies in the five countries have also a marked effect on the various linguistic minorities. Most such groups would probably prefer to determine whether they would like to preserve their language and culture or to assimilate into the dominant linguistic group. However, policies and practice in the various countries virtually dictate which choice they must make if they are to live and work in that country.

It is apparent from the four country papers that changes are in train. Most countries are in the process of transition as far as language and literacy policy is concerned. Taken together the four countries embrace a wide variety and complexity of cultural and linguistic populations. It is also evident that this complexity has had very little influence on the language and literacy policies of these countries. There seems however to be little information available on the results flowing from educational programmes for minorities in those countries. Whether the language programmes provided produce educational benefits matching the aspirations of the children concerned has implications for further work which is taken up at the end of this overview.

3 Synthesis and conclusions

In this chapter we bring together the observations we have already made in order to point out some interesting practices that OECD countries could seriously consider in their future planning for the education of their special populations. In so doing we offer some general conclusions and implications for action, comment on the research design for the inquiry and point to some possible future directions for further co-operative work.

The analytic framework developed in the previous chapter provided a means of ordering the large body of information contained within the diverse set of reports produced for the inquiry. In so doing the financing, organisation and governance of the education of special populations across the participant countries might appear clear-cut, rational and perhaps even deterministic. This is certainly not the case and exemplifies the first limitation which we see in the study. The framework does not, and cannot, incorporate the many factors influencing decisions about each of its major dimensions, namely, the identification of special populations, the rationale for equity, the style of provision and the funding strategy employed. Furthermore, the framework does not take into account the relationships between identification, equity, style of provision and funding strategy. Yet the interrelationships among the four aspects of the financing, organisation and governance of education of special groups in fact dictate the nature of provisions for special groups within any country. Decisions made by governments about each of these aspects are not independent of each

43

other. Nor are they independent of the political, economic, social and technological context in which these decisions are made. It is the interaction between contextual factors which determines the course of action taken by a government at a particular point in time which provides a dynamic dimension to the seemingly static analytic framework which has been proposed.

This limitation of the analytic framework comes about because the country survey reports did not, and could not be expected to provide the necessary insight into the context in which decisions regarding the education of special populations were taken. For example, there is little sophisticated analysis of the political or economic background to many of the policies examined in the reports. Yet such analysis is necessary in order to develop a full understanding of the processes and procedures underlying the education of special groups.

A case in point is the Australian country survey. To understand fully the identification, labelling and legitimisation of girls as a special group in Australian education, one must be aware of party policies and politics that operated during the early 1970s. This period saw a change at the national level after twenty-four years from a somewhat conservative government to a more left-wing government and at the international level resulting from Women's Year. Another example is the provision of special services for unemployed youth which has occurred in several countries. The type and extent of services provided will be determined by the prevailing economic situation and the political orientation of the governments of the day as well as by educational factors. Governments which, in the current economic climate, opt for a policy of reducing monetary inflation in order to try to reduce unemployment, may treat quite differently the educational needs of unemployed youth than will a political party whose primary intent, if in power, would be the initial reduction of unemployment. Both examples illustrate the importance of a detailed understanding of the contextual background to the finance, organisation and governance of education for special populations. Yet such information is generally lacking from the reports provided by the participant countries. It is within this context that Eide's paper in Part II calls for a greater contribution to research on education and equality by political scientists, anthropologists and historians.

A second limitation of the inquiry was that detailed comparative analysis of the educational provisions for target groups had to be so restricted. Granting countries the opportunity to select examples for detailed examination limited the extent to which we could explore the influence of background factors such as the nature of the education system and the political orientation of the central and local governments upon particular programmes.

It remains to take note of the place of the five sets of 'theme' or 'issues' papers which are reproduced in full in Part II of this volume. These played an integral role in understanding both the processes underlying the education of special populations and the variety of factors influencing the nature of those processes. They were thus germane to those parts of our analysis dealing with the identification of special populations, equitable distribution of resources, styles of provision and funding strategies. Often they were relevant to more than one of these factors. This again reflects the interrelatedness of each of the aspects of the financing, organisation and governance of education for special populations. For example, Rossmiller's paper on costing describes procedures for deriving cost estimates of educational programmes which include identifying the special population to be served, the programme structure and the programme delivery system.

Eide's paper on autonomy brings together with respect to ethnic and indigenous minorities the nature of the special population, the rationale underlying the equitable distribution of resources and the style of provision and examines the resultant interaction. McDonagh's treatment of service delivery focuses upon the identification of target groups and the assessment of educational needs, the provision of services and funding strategies. Lovgren's analysis of identification is likewise broad-ranging and considers both the identification process, the nature of special populations and the provision of services. As a further example, Blackburn's paper on the rationale for distributing resources unequally deals with the different bases for the equitable distribution of resources in relation to different styles of provision and funding strategies. The various theme papers acknowledged the interrelationships which exist within the financing, organisation and governance of any educational programme.

Finance

In the preceding chapter the financing of education for special populations was considered from the perspective of the rationales for the equitable distribution of resources and the funding strategies employed by each of the participant countries. Concepts of equality of opportunity employed by educational systems to justify the distribution of funds were described as a basis for understanding the notion of equity. This was later followed by an examination of three features of funding strategies: the generation or source of funds; the distribution of funds; and the locus of control concerning expenditure. From this analysis three issues emerged: equity and funding; costing; and factors affecting changes in the fund availability.

Equity and funding policies

The most appropriate basis for an equitable distribution of funds for atypical educational provisions differs according to the type of special population being considered. One group receiving resources for ostensibly the same purpose as a similar group in a different jurisdiction or system may accrue different benefits because of different rationales for equitable distribution which underlie the funding strategies employed. It is important, therefore, to examine funding policies for particular programmes in terms of their notion of the concepts of equity. This could be done in several ways. For example, the funding policies for particular programmes could be analysed in terms of their attention to the seven concepts of educational equity described in chapter 2. This is particularly important in the case of those educational programmes designed to benefit a wide range of students or special groups: while one concept of equality might benefit one group, it may have a detrimental effect upon another.

Regarding the outcomes of the funding policy, three principles have been commonly used to assess whether a service is operating equitably. The first is that students who are alike should receive equal resources, as reflected in such indices as uniform expenditure per student and uniform student–teacher ratios. The second principle which emerges is that since students differ in cognitive, physical and socio-economic characteristics, differences amongst students should result in differential resource allocations. The outcome of this is to try to break the correlation between student achievement and the particular characteristics such as ethnicity or geographical location. The third principle concerns the concept of equal opportunity for participation in education amongst students of similar background. In the short term this means that participation in education should not be influenced by such characteristics as wealth, race or sex: in the longer term, employment opportunity should not be influenced by such characteristics.

An analysis of the concepts of equality underlying funding policies and an assessment of the outcomes of the policies in terms of the principles of equity provide a useful basis for evaluating funding policies.

Estimating costs

A major difficulty in determining the extent to which there has been an equitable distribution of resources lies in estimating the costs associated with the services provided. There are difficulties in defining precisely the target groups being serviced, the programme being provided, the sources of financial and other resources, the total resources allocated to the programme and the calculation of a price index.

Even if such difficulties can be overcome, a standard must be established against which the cost of a programme for a special population can be compared. Often the criterion has been the cost of a similar programme for the general population. The interpretation of programme costs for special populations based upon such a standard is quite limited, however, unless an evaluation of the outcomes (short-term and long-term) of forms of provision is undertaken. Few countries have undertaken large scale evaluations of their programmes for special populations. It is not until accurate estimates of costs are established and programme outcomes rigorously evaluated that decision-makers at all levels will be in a position to formulate and implement rational policy for the provision of education for special populations.

Student weighted funding systems

Several countries have approached the funding of special need by establishing funding formulas based upon the relative costs of educating different types of students. Weighting factors can compensate for increased educational costs necessarily involved in the special nature of the curriculum designed to meet particular needs. These costs can be direct (for example, specialist equipment and salaries) or indirect (for example, administrative infrastructure charges and non-financial staff incentives). Therefore, before establishing weighting factors for funding the atypical educational provision, policy-makers must identify what the weights are meant to cover. Hence the comparative costing of educational programmes is a difficult and highly technical exercise.

A further obstacle encountered in establishing a student weighted funding system is in determining the total number of students on which the level of funding is calculated. Besides the definitional problems encountered in categorising students, one must decide whether the aggregate or full-time equivalent number of students in the programme provides the basis for funding. The latter index is generally calculated from the number of contact hours of students in the specialist programme. Also, the census interval for counting the number of students in a special programme is a decision which will affect the nature of the programme established. Short census intervals may bring about continual changes in the amount of funds made available (reflecting small changes in student population) and thereby reduce the opportunity for developing a stable educational programme. Long intervals may result in the provision of funds that are not congruent with what is required to meet the needs of the current special population of students.

The size of weights can be established in a variety of ways which can produce quite different funding outcomes. The first approach is to accurately cost current educational programmes which are serving the particular group in question. Per student costs are calculated and funding continued on this basis unless changes are brought about by political intervention and the subsequent implementation of new policies. An alternative method is to establish the theoretical costs of an educational programme designed to cater for the needs of a special group, without reference to existing programmes. This approach requires clear specification of the intended operation and outcomes of the programme. Whichever approach is adopted, the politico-social context is likely to modify the final basis on which weightings are established.

Changes in costing

An issue not generally raised by participant countries but one of importance is consideration of the factors which cause programme costs to change over time. Changes in the respective roles of the private and public sectors in the provision of services to special groups are a major influence. This may be quite subtle, particularly if the services have been initially provided by the private sector, such as voluntary agencies. As the demand on these services increases, there may be pressure for financial support, or even control, to be accepted by the public sector. Furthermore, the voluntary agencies may exert pressure upon the public sector to accept fundings and administrative responsibility for the provisions. In so doing the community's expectations of the nature of the provisions may change, and the community may become less willing to accept from the public sector services of a standard which might be tolerated for voluntary agencies.

A second factor concerns the identification of emerging areas of need. It would appear that there is an increasing number of groups which are being labelled as requiring special resource allocations. Groups which have been most recently recognised in many countries are the gifted and talented and students at risk of unemployment. Currently, a re-emerging special group, viewed within the umbrella of recurrent education, appears to be adults. Although each of these special groups may continue to be educated in regular schools, their recognition brings increased costs. The public sector thrust is towards the differentiation and professionalisation of emergent specialists. Hence, while regular schools might provide the organisational infrastructure for the education of these groups (at little if any extra cost), the regular teaching service is augmented by specialist teachers with resultant resource demands. It is likely that there will be increasing pressure upon resources for providing educational services to special populations, in the minds of some to the detriment of the mainstream. This emphasises the need to monitor costs accurately, in both monetary and broad educational terms, of programmes now provided for the education of special populations.

Organisation

The organisational structures and processes involved in the education of special populations were shown by the national studies to differ widely between countries and between particular groups within countries. However, there are several major organisational issues that are relevant to all countries: identification, integration, delivery services and the role of the private sector.

Identification

The identification and labelling of individuals for the purpose of providing appropriate educational services for them is of growing concern. There have been attempts to move away from practices which determine special educational provision for particular categories of individuals. But such attempts need to be paralleled by a system of financing which is not dependent upon the specification of the individual student or even categorisation of particular forms of handicap, and by a system of accountability that is not concerned with tying specific provisions with specific individuals. One approach that has been adopted is the allocation of resources according to the number of teachers servicing a group of students: thus the teachers are being labelled rather than the students. An alternative is to identify the school or the programme. In this way resources can be allocated to the school and are not tied to the education of specific students.

An important characteristic of any special population is that it is a changing entity. Not all countries participating in this study view their student populations in the same way. While there are several categories of special populations common to all countries, there are other groups which are designated special in one country but belong to the general student population in another. Over time, the categorisation changes. The talented and gifted are one such group: an increasing number of countries are now concerned with the special provision of resources for these students.

It would appear that with the downturn in the western economies and the accompanying reduction in employment opportunities, an emerging special population comprises students who have just completed their formal compulsory education and are expecting to enter the workforce. Changing family life-style has also brought with it the creation of another new special population: children and students requiring pre-school and after school care.

The ability of governments to provide for such special populations necessitates a closer look at the relationship between general and special education. One can envisage tension developing between these alternative delivery mechanisms.

Integration

Together with the growing concern for the identification and subsequent labelling of students is the general move towards the educational integration of disabled students with the regular student population. In some instances legislation has been introduced to effect integration and 'normalisation'. Yet it is not an easy matter in practice, even if legislation is designed towards this end.

General community attitudes, as well as structural and staffing characteristics of school, may prevent the integration of atypical students into the mainstream. Furthermore, integration cannot be considered to be a feature solely of the student's life in school. Integration in the public arena, entailing not only the same access to resources as others but the same opportunities to influence his or her situation and to develop a significant role in society (which may entail an entitlement to above-average resources) must also be a feature of the student's life outside of the confined school environment.

The current emphasis on integration (normalising and mainstreaming) raises a central problem for the design of appropriate educational experiences for special populations. Should students in special need have curricula which are characterised by the values in lifestyles of educators and the regular population of students? This issue is explored in this study in relationship to indigenous populations and ethnic minorities. Clearly, in these cases, curricula are being developed which are aimed both to integrate the group and yet to accommodate the general population to the idea of a continuing separate entity for the group. Could and should a similar approach be taken to the education of those students who are, say, socio-economically disadvantaged and whose families possess a different set of norms from the general population?

Delivery: co-ordination, co-operation and yield

The delivery of services often requires a high degree of inter-institutional and inter-sectoral co-operation, often beyond the scope and control of the school system. This is a recognition that difficulties experienced by the disadvantaged and the disabled, are not restricted to any one area of public policy. Rather, they touch upon many areas of living in a society. For example, we noted that one approach to aiding the disadvantaged was the distribution of resources that could be used by the local authorities for educational, recreational, industrial and social purposes. Merging the boundaries of such traditionally distinct provisions implies a high degree of co-operation and co-ordination.

The tendency towards the placement of atypical students into ordinary schools has also led to a greater demand upon co-operation and co-ordination by various instrumentalities. In the case of severely disabled students this requires the presence of physiotherapists and occupational therapists as well as medical staff working in conjunction with ordinary and specialist teachers within the same institution. Shared responsibility for the growth of the child is not an easy matter when it involves such an array of personnel. It requires a broadening of skills and attitudes that is uncharacteristic of the more traditional provisions. At the same time such shared responsibility at the grass-roots level must be paralleled by a flexibility of governance characterising the wide range of agencies servicing the provision.

Of vital concern to service delivery is the expected yield from allocating extra resources. There is little evidence of attempts to measure the educational and social benefits accruing from provisions for special populations. Assessment of programme impact tends to stop with conventional financial and administrative audits. This is not surprising. With the devolution of authority and responsibility for curriculum development and implementation in a number of countries to the school and classroom teachers, evaluation procedures also become the responsibility of the practitioners. This applies also to the education of special populations.

More important would seem to be a lack of explicit definition of the intentions and objectives of many of the provisions for the education of special populations, at least as they are perceived at both the local area and national levels. While this may be in part due to the trend towards devolution, it is more likely due to the nature of special provisions and the role played by national and local authorities. It is increasingly difficult to specify provisions aimed at integration and normalisation: in the past, programmes were primarily aimed at teaching students a set of survival skills only.

We are now dealing with attitudes and values held by both special and general populations and the extent to which the members of special populations can effectively operate in society at large while retaining their identity. Evaluative indicators in this are difficult to come by. It is even more difficult to put together a general statement about the overall effectiveness of a programme at either the local, regional or national level. Where one of the intentions of the provision is the improved employment prospects of certain groups of individuals (for example migrants or adolescents) then appropriate indicators are more easily defined. Hence, in several countries we see the collection of information relating to the employment rates of these people and their enrolment in further vocational training.

A further factor restricting the development of clear guidelines for the evaluation of provisions in terms of intentions and objectives concerns the establishment of services. Generally, a need is detected and political pressure is brought to bear upon the central government to provide resources to alleviate that need. Pressure groups may force certain educational provisions as a matter of political expediency, even before a convincing educational rationale for such provisions has been developed and its relationship with other educational provisions established.

The role of the private sector

The role of private initiatives (particularly voluntary and charitable organisations) in the education of special groups does not appear to be of great significance in the countries surveyed. Historically, it is often the private sector which takes the first step in some of the now generally accepted areas of public provision for special needs. Moves towards policies of reintegrating special populations into the mainstream open up great potential for the private sector to contribute to the attainment of this objective. Yet few countries mentioned co-operation between both the public and private sectors in the provision of special educational services. Within provisions attempting to develop a range of 'whole life' skills, work and recreational experience must be available. The private sector has the capacity to provide necessary work experience but this resource does not appear to be used greatly.

Governance

The role of legislation in the education of special groups and the locus of control of such provisions have wide ranging implications for the nature of the educational programmes developed for special groups. Issues of governance are therefore of basic importance to the present study.

The role of legislation in the education of special populations

The appropriateness of legislation for the provision of education for special populations remains a vexed issue. One country reported that, as a deliberate means of overcoming labelling and stigmatisation, no legislation identifying provision for particular groups had been introduced. (Yet, in this case, funding and organisational practices had been established which were not congruent with the intentions of such legislation.) Alternatively, countries may be quite explicit in legislation. Such legislation may refer to the specification of particular populations, the allocation of funding and the overall approach to be taken. For example, legislation might direct that disabled children be provided education in such a way that they are taught as far as possible in a regular learning environment.

The situation becomes more complex as one moves from legislation at the national level to state and even local levels. The compounding effects of multiple sources of legislation may lead to different (and unintended) provisions for special populations within a country, and services of varying quality.

Locus of control

The locus of control for the provision of special education may be held by the central government, a local authority or a school board. To the extent that control is closely linked to the source of funding ('he who pays the piper calls the tune') several patterns were evident. It would be unwise, though, to focus solely upon the source of funding as determining the locus of control. Rather it is important to examine the purposes to which funds may be directed and the extent to which such purposes are defined at each level of governance. For example, the funding body may be the central government and allocate funds for the provision of education for special populations in such a manner that schools remain quite free to use those funds as they see fit. Provided that accountability pressures from the central government do not enforce a particular direction of provision, an important aspect of control is vested with the school.

Another important aspect of control is the amount of control exerted by individual students, parents and the local community. This aspect is particularly important in view of the point made earlier concerning the development of curricula for special populations. Few countries reported on the capacity of special populations to influence either the flow of funds in their direction or the types of provision made for their education.

Pluralism: legislated and grassroots movements

Cultural pluralism is a familiar concept in most countries surveyed in this study. Some have longstanding histories of the presence of indigenous populations, others have experience of recent mass immigration, and others still have had periodic mixings of different ethnic groups. Treating cultural or linguistic minorities as target populations is therefore not new. Two aspects of making such provision stand out.

It is apparent that unless policies relating to provisions for bilingualism or the maintenance of ethnic cultures are legislated for, it is highly unlikely that finance will be allocated to produce effective programmes in these areas. Thus, if countries are serious about the maintenance and development of culturally pluralist societies, they will need to consider strongly the necessity to legislate for it.

This legislative process, however, can place countries with indigenous minorities in a dilemma. For no amount of legislation or finance will help such minorities retain their language or culture unless there is a grassroots movement among the people affected. Thus the initial effort of funding needs to be directed towards self-determination by minorities. Subsequently there needs to be legislation based on the views of these groups to ensure resources being made available to provide the necessary educational and community services.

While there is an increasing tendency to acknowledge 'sub-cultures' and the rights of individuals and groups belonging to them to an equitable share of educational resources, what is not widely accepted is the right and propriety of special populations to exercise control over how those resources are used. This is a question of governance.

Implications for Member countries of the OECD

The governance of special provisions as described in the various papers is generally beyond the grasp of the special populations concerned. The contribution that special populations can and ought to make to the control of their education, and the effect such control might have upon the broader education system, is a policy issue still to be fully addressed.

A basic question set for this study is 'how are public policies for special groups shaped?'. Despite the common brief for the country surveys, the individual authors tended to describe the political situations in their countries in a straight factual way that gave little indication to us of the reality of the policy processes behind them. For example, while the Australian report provided an excellent analysis of actual provisions for special populations and an accurate description of the governance mechanisms in Australia, one would have to have lived and worked in Australia to detect the subliminal factors which influence policy-making. For, while educational policy-making at the national level is indeed based on a federation-of-states model, as the report suggests, it is also a fact that the two major political parties in Australia have different conceptions on what federalism means. Thus, some local knowledge will allow the reader of the Australian survey document to interpret it in the context of the political realities of policy determination as well as that of the formal educational structures and processes provided in the document.

General observation about governance is that policy decisions are more frequently influenced by historical and political quirks than by the formal structure of government. Therefore in analysing the provisions of individual countries one should not necessarily look for consistency with other countries but more for divergences and examples of 'good' principle or practice. Judgements about particular provisions should be made as much in terms of historical and political antecedents as, for example, of how the provisions fit against the concepts of equality outlined earlier.

There is a distinction, at least in political terms, between recognition of a special need and action to satisfy that need, that is, recognition and action are not a single event. It has been easier to analyse actions of various countries in providing for special populations than to identify, or analyse, the political processes leading to this recognition. Thus, the onus is on readers to review provisions in their own countries against our framework in the light of intimate knowledge of local idiosyncrasies.

The research design

In the introduction to the general report of a previous CERI study of 'Educational Financing and Policy Goals for Primary Schools', the OECD secretariat analysed the methodology used and made some suggestions for conducting the present project. As in the primary schools' study, the research design had to provide data to describe different countries' provisions to enable analysis of these provisions — this time to draw out principles concerning financing, organisation and governance of education for special populations.

From experience with the previous study, the research design was broadened to include specialist papers on specific issues and in-depth case studies of educational provisions for selected minority groups. How well did this expanded methodology satisfy the three purposes required of the research design?

Country studies

The major strength of the country studies was the emphasis in seeking a comprehensive listing of all provisions and populations with a detailed examination of a small number of provisions. The papers provided a wide range of data to satisfy adequately the mapping requirement, presented well-documented cases for these provisions (which proved extremely useful in our analysis of general principles) and provided 'live' examples that enabled us to relate general principles to practical reality. The papers were sufficiently concise and followed the specifications provided well enough to enable an analysis of major trends without becoming lost in tedious detail.

There were, however, some omissions and weaknesses. First, while there was adequate treatment of legislation governing general education at each echelon of governance in most countries, there was virtually no discussion of such legislation in respect of special populations. It was, therefore, difficult to derive from the illustrations the overview so necessary for our analysis. Secondly, it was difficult from the data provided to calculate the expenditure as a percentage of educational expenditure or as part of the gross national product. This made it hard to compare expenditure across countries. Thirdly, while authors were given the option of concentrating on interesting and important programmes in their country, it would have been more convenient from the analyst's point of view to have also asked them to describe at least one common programme.

In summary, the diversity of approaches to the format of reports, while providing excellent and diverse material contained too wide a range of different material for ease of analysis and synthesis. This was particularly so where the formally correct details of governance provided only a superficial framework of decision-making and left unsaid the sophisticated dynamism of the political process.

Case studies of some minority groups

This second element of the study was conceived of as an extension of the mapping exercise into topical (and indeed controversial) areas; and, in the research design, to overcome limitations of the broad treatment in the country studies. It was also meant to illustrate the five themes that were to be elaborated at a conceptual level. The case studies selected, however, were so atypical of special populations that the issues raised were in fact quite different and accordingly treated separately in our analysis. We were able to find sufficient material in the country studies and issues papers to provide adequate data for critical analyses of general principles governing special provision for 'target' populations.

In future comparative studies, for analytical purposes, case studies should be selected which represent the general as well as the unusual. Case studies are a powerful means of illuminating particular examples of the provision being examined in such a way as to provide participating countries with a model or scheme against which to compare their own provisions. Such studies could perhaps be used as the first stage in a research design so that, for example, the framework for a wider range of country studies could be informed by the analyses of data on issues from samples of cases.

Principles and issues

The main role of the issues papers reproduced in Part II was to conceptualise contentious issues in the field of special provisions and to form themes for the analytic overview. They supplied good ideas for the analysis and helped in the conceptualisation of the issues behind special provisions. Since they were written at the same time as country surveys they could not, of course, focus the direction of these surveys, nor could they draw from examples in the country studies: if the elements of the study could have been staged consecutively rather than concurrently, the potential of the study overall would have been enhanced.

Like all research designs which deal with major projects conducted over an extended period, the final products differ from the original intentions. This has led to the analytic framework used in this paper differing somewhat from that originally envisaged in the research design. The abundance of available data made it possible to take into account the methodology actually adopted by the contributors to the project.

Future directions

We have suggested earlier that it is important for participating countries to pursue this study with a review of their own practices against the financial and organisational framework discussed in chapter 2. In their analyses members would need to take into account the realities that govern decision-making in their countries. Apart from such individual reviews, suggestions for future work at a cross-national level are taken up in this the last section of our report.

Our analysis of the various papers that make up the overall framework of this project and our comments on methodology point to several areas which could profitably be the focus of future research and investigation.

Governance of education

One limitation to the interpretation of the data was the difficulty of classifying the educational structures and processes influencing decision-making about provisions for special populations. In particular, it was difficult to determine who controlled or made decisions in an informal and latent as well as a formal and manifest sense. A comparative analysis of the governance of education in member countries would be most valuable in providing basic data against which to carry out future analyses target provisioning. Also, in this context, studies of control mechanisms in specific educational programmes could be undertaken.

Special populations

Several areas in the identification of target populations could profitably be examined. The first of these is the method used to label and characterise students in special populations. As Lovgren and Dague posit in their 'issues analysis' pieces on this topic in Part II, it might well be that there are good arguments against thinking of these students in terms of being in special groups. Several countries are opposed to labelling. It would be interesting to compare the outcomes of educational programmes in such countries with those which consciously label special groups, in order to determine whether the fundamental direction of education should be the treatment of special populations in a group or individualistic way.

Another area that might be investigated is that of provisions for students who fit simultaneously into different special groups. What are the difficulties in catering for students who have multiple special needs and multi-dimensional groups? There is also the specific question of what constitutes atypicality. From many of the papers in the project, it is obvious that in some countries the majority of students fit into a special population of some sort or another. This situation reinforces the previous suggestion that a future study could focus on whether students or provisions should be the policy and resource allocation focus. Studies could be undertaken in determining the emergent special populations. From this project it is apparent that for political as well as pedagogical reasons, the talented and gifted are presently a popular target of identification and provision. Other populations that seem to have moved into the limelight over recent years are those students in transition from school to post-school life who are 'at risk'; women and girls; and very young children for whom early childhood services are needed before the provision on compulsory education. The problems of identification of emergent special groups could focus on how to identify these populations and how they fit into a general framework of priority programmes.

Provision

Several areas could usefully be investigated under the heading of provision. The first concerns the question of whether education should continue to be equated roughly with schooling or whether education should not be looked at in broader terms. This question arose time and time again in connection with the education of minority groups and could be looked at in terms of how provisions should be made within a community service rather than in a school system framework. For example, an analysis could profitably be made of children's services provided for target populations in the community as distinct from educational services in schools.

Another question that arose from many papers was the political activity required to provide satisfactory education for students from minority groups. The point was made that unless there were grassroots movements leading to political pressure on national governments to provide an appropriate resource provision to such populations it was unlikely that an adequate and effective education would be provided for these populations. Further studies could be carried out on how such grassroots movements could be encouraged, whether any of them now operate and what lessons could be learned.

Another area in the provision of educational service for special groups that could usefully be followed up, is the difference between the types of programmes that operate in member countries. Is it the norm to have special classes or schools for students who benefit from special provisions or is it a question of enrichment of regular curricula? Finally, studies could be carried out to describe specific programmes as models of the type of provisions made for particular target populations.

Outcomes

An important area of future study could be to consider the outcomes that are expected of programmes in various countries and to see how far these outcomes are achieved. In particular, research could focus on specific issues such as interpretations of equity; individuals versus groups as the unit of treatment; how far outcomes meet the social as well as educational needs of different communities and populations. An additional focus of such studies could be on the forecasting and monitoring of long-term trends and outcomes of provisions.

Resources

There are three areas that might be investigated under this rubric. First, descriptions of the type of resources employed in special programmes to see whether there are any common trends in the curriculum provisions for special populations. Secondly, there is a need to monitor trends, in both distribution and receipt in the resource provision for special populations. Finally, a project could be mounted to obtain more information about the contributions of human and physical resources to special programmes. Such a project might look at the quality of these rather than merely at the quantity or monetary costs.

Linguistic and cultural minorities

In most countries it is apparent that linguistic infrastructures to service multicultural societies are very complex. Full descriptions of these infrastructures are necessary to understand more fully the context of providing education for cultural minorities. Particularly in the area of providing education for cultural minorities there is a need for considering the issues concerned in the case studies, beyond the general area. A number of OECD countries are increasingly recognising the educational needs of multicultural groups within their societies and are making educational provisions for them accordingly. CERI is already taking steps in considering further studies in this area and is proposing to focus on education and cultural minorities. Whatever methodology is adopted we see a need to include some measure or measures of learning outcomes for students in typical programmes. This would involve the collection of quantifiable data, at least for a sample of programmes, in selected countries or a sample of similar programmes in a range of member countries. Such data, coupled with illuminating case studies and mapping exercises, could provide a rich source of data for international analysis and ultimately assist in providing member countries with useful yardsticks with which to evaluate their own provisions.

PART II

Principles and issues

4 Recognising students in need of extra resources: the Swedish experience

Esse Lovgren
Swedish National Board of Education

Possible strategies

The resources at the disposal of the school are both personal and material. The former can be taken to include not just the work of the teachers but staff inputs of many different kinds, including those by the staff involved with administration, student welfare, school health, counselling, extra-curricula activities and so on. Material resources include not only the regular premises and equipment, and libraries, but also the special equipment and adaptation of premises needed for special students.

Whether or not any given students will have access to resources over and beyond those available to students in general is determined, essentially, in three ways:

(a) the school can place students in a special group (examples of which are given below) or otherwise make a selection of students to be allocated extra resources;

(b) the students and their parents can choose freely, without any decision being made by the school;

(c) the school seeks out students and recruits them to draw upon certain extra resources.

Trends in educational policy have not always, therefore, been applied in a consistent way.

Strategy (a) has been applied in respect of starting school (the school decides whether or not children are mature enough to start school), and the special treatment of mentally retarded students and those with various kinds of physical handicap. Previously, this strategy was also applied to slow learners. Pierre Dague, in the paper that follows, draws attention to the rapid increase in special instruction and auxiliary teaching. This also applies to the Swedish 9-year comprehensive in the late 1960s and early 1970s.

Strategy (b) can be exemplified by the instruction given in Sweden to immigrant children in their 'household language'. The parents and students themselves decide whether they would like such teaching — the school cannot force students to accept it.

Strategy (c) can be illustrated by the procedure used to recruit unemployed young people who have only the 9-year compulsory school, or less, behind them.

In Sweden we speak of 'difficulties' at school — a term that is somewhat ambiguous. It sometimes means the inability of a student to achieve certain results in relation to the demands and expectations of the school; but 'difficulties' can be general, or limited to a given function. The expression can also relate more to the students' experiences, their sense of inadequacy when faced by the demands and expectations of the school environment. Such difficulties can arise in connection with teaching, relationships with peers and teachers and so on. Obviously, there is a correlation between poor performance in the objective sense and a sense of inadequacy.

The concept of 'school difficulties' is ambiguous also in another sense. The term can relate to a discrepancy between demands and ability in the school situation as such, or to the individual's internal conflicts and disturbed relationships in general. One can also, naturally, speak of the difficulties produced by the educational system itself, its organisation, selection procedures, working methods, and environment.

A Government Committee on working conditions in the Swedish schools[1] has ranged the causes of difficulties in three groups:

(a) factors within the individual;
(b) factors in the individual's social environment;
(c) factors in the teaching situation.

The Committee further considered that a system of measures to deal with these difficulties should be aimed at three levels:

(a) the public level (the allocation of public sector resources outside the educational system for children and young people);

(b) the school level (inputs within the educational system: organisation, methods, content and so on);

(c) the individual level (measures specific to the individual, for example, in respect of physical handicaps, or measures via the school health, psychology and welfare systems).

The identification process

Different approaches

The identification of students who are experiencing various kinds of difficulties at school and need extra resources is based on interpretations and decisions made from different basic views as to how such difficulties arise and how they are to be dealt with. We can speak of different approaches to the identification of such students. The Committee referred to above has discussed six such models: medical, psychometric, administrative, sociological, pedagogic and behavioural therapy.

With the *medical* model, deviations are described as somatic defects or diseased states in the individual. An attempt is made to arrive at clearly delimited groups on the basis of medical properties: the deaf, the mentally retarded, spastic students and so on. The medical model must always be supplemented with behavioural data for identification.

The *psychometric* model is based on the assumption that the personality of the individual consists of a number of measurable properties such as intelligence, motivation, interests, attitudes and so on. Owing to the unreliability of personality measurement, the emphasis has been on intelligence tests. The psychometric model has been of great importance in defining and delimiting the difficulties experienced at school. Work has been based, for example, on concepts relating to correlations between intelligence and difficulties at school, the ability of intelligence tests to measure intellectual capacity, and the possibilities of forecasting difficulties and success at school with the help of intelligence tests. Pierre Dague notes their limitations when it comes to designing programmes of pedagogic measures.

The *administrative* model is based on the placing of students in the special groups traditionally created by educational systems for deviant students. One example is the expansion of special instruction for students with learning difficulties. When difficulties are observed, resort is made to an administrative cliché rather than an analysis of the problems, and suggestions for educational action.

The *sociological* model takes as its premise the necessity of identifying the problems experienced by the individual in his social environment. The variation observed in the behaviour and adjustment of individuals can be ascribed to different demands, expectations and standards in their social environment. School difficulties are regarded as relative to the individual's social environment.

Central to the *pedagogic* model is an analysis of the student's properties with regard to such processes as comprehension, learning, problem solution, memory, attention and so on, and the individual's profile with regard to the learning of skills, content-matter and concepts in the school.

With the *behavioural therapy* model, difficulties at school are the result of a faulty learning process. Satisfactory social behaviour patterns must be reinforced and unsatisfactory patterns extinguished.

The various models (or rather combinations between them) can be illustrated by some examples. We have chosen students with impaired hearing, an illustration of the concept of 'school readiness', and measures for immigrant students.

The placing strategy: deaf and partially deaf students as an example

The criteria for identifying students in special need of extra support can be illustrated by the measures taken for children who are deaf, or whose hearing is seriously impaired. The medical and psychometric measures provide a starting-point when placing is to be considered. These, however, have to be interpreted with care, and supplemented by a more all-round investigation. A common criterion of the degree of deafness is the audiogram, for example. However, an audiometric average provides little guidance for measures to be taken *within* a group with impaired hearing. Consideration of the hearing curve affords a more reliable basis, but can still be unreliable when it comes to judging the child's ability to discriminate language sounds.

The distinction between the 'deaf' and 'partially deaf' is often made on the basis of the degree of linguistic handicap among people with normal hearing. Norden and Ang[2] observe that it is not uncommon among children and adults with impaired hearing for an individual to attach himself voluntarily to a group that communicates in sign language. By this choice of group allegiance, these people indicate that they feel themselves to belong to the 'deaf' group. It is reasonable to give children too the opportunity to choose their group allegiance in this way.

School readiness

According to an earlier basic approach, which was genetic in nature, the maturing process could not be influenced to any great extent by environmental factors. The age at which schooling should start was regarded as essentially dependent on the degree of biological maturity, which should be established and in doubtful cases tested with special 'school readiness tests'. Early developers could start a year earlier, while late developers were recommended to postpone their schooling for a year.

In recent decades, research has emphasised the importance of stimulation and learning for children's readiness to avail themselves of teaching when they start the Lower Level. A Swedish researcher, Bror Johansson, has shown that the home background of children greatly affects their ability to meet the demands made by the school on new pupils. According to his investigations, the attitude of the parents to the school, and their own formal education, had the greatest influence on the readiness of children to attend school, while their economic status was of lesser importance. The social handicap is a significant one:

> The effect of the social factors on the assignment of children to school readiness classes implies a certain discrimination which is incompatible with the goal of the school, which is to promote the self-realisation of each pupil.
>
> The aim of the school is not to sift out a gifted élite successively, at least not at the primary level. Nor is it to *classify* beginners into school 'ready' and school 'unready' before they have been studied carefully. The respect for the child as an individual which is the fundamental idea behind the new comprehensive school gives rise to the demand that each child has the right to begin his school life without first being classified in a way that may lead to permanent categorization.[3]

For children whose development is retarded by reason of a social handicap, the postponement of schooling would delay it still further. Instead, the school should provide supplementary support and training for these pupils at as early a stage as possible. For this reason, Swedish local authorities are now required to offer all 6-year-olds and certain 5-year-olds pre-school places (ordinary schooling starts in Sweden at the age of 7).

School readiness is not a static concept, a boundary line between the pre-school and Lower Level. It is an extremely relative concept which is difficult to define. It contains various components, and is naturally dictated largely by the demands made on the child's capacity by the school and its teachers. From the standpoint of developmental psychology, there is a considerable overlap between children in the pre-school and the Lower Level. Therefore, there must also be a considerable overlap between the activities and pedagogic methods of these two stages.

For the above reasons, school readiness tests have now been abolished in Sweden. To achieve a smooth transition, teachers in the pre-school and Lower Level co-operate, and establish joint contact with the parents. An extensive and mutual exchange of information takes place between the pre-school, the Lower Level and the parents as the child starts its schooling. This is particularly important in order to be able to plan in time for children with special needs.

A number of special pedagogic screening methods are used to identify students with different kinds of school difficulty. Above all, the extensive body of ATI research already performed has stimulated new efforts to arrive at more specific diagnoses, so that more individually geared measures can be deployed. As an example, let us consider briefly a joint Nordic development project.

Around the mid-1970s, a joint Nordic research project was started on the learning problems of children. Commonly known as the 'Bergen project', it was originally initiated by Professor Hans Jörgen Gjessing in Bergen, Norway. Its background was partly the considerable resources being devoted in the mid-1970s to special teaching in the Nordic compulsory comprehensives. Special teaching claimed between 15 and 20 per cent of total resources. At the same time, both Nordic and international research shows that with many students the effects were unsatisfactory.

The philosophy underlying the Bergen project is that special pedagogic measures must be considerably more specific to the individual. This presupposes more careful diagnosis. Its main purpose is to point the way to a research method that follows the individual weak performer more analytically, that analyses the various measures employed in special teaching, and tries to show which weak performers benefit from specific forms of pedagogic and human support. This is being done by a qualitative, long-term process — and function-orientated study of individuals and their environment. The emphasis in analyses will be on difficulties with reading and writing (different forms of dyslexia). The dyslectic group is heterogeneous, and includes individuals with widely disparate patterns of disturbances. One factor of major importance is termed linguistic awareness, that is, the ability to reflect upon the formal aspects of language.

The individual investigations of weak performers, together with introductory counselling, cover ten hours per student. The diagnoses incorporate various tests and observations in respect of general maturity, and the diagnoses of learning difficulties and areas of function in which weaknesses are evident. In connection with reading difficulties, a study is made of, for example, linguistic development, laterality, visual processes, and socio-economic factors. This will provide a basis for diagnosis and the planning of measures in which neurological, cognitive, emotional, social and pedagogic components will be incorporated in a functional context. Certain special follow-up studies are being made, which cover the audiological, ophthalmological, neuro-psychological and clinical psychological fields.

The strategy of choice: immigrant students as an example

A special problem of identification is afforded by the teaching of immigrants in Sweden. The aim is that the school, by various measures, should be able to give immigrant children such an education and such a knowledge of Swedish and the household language that they will be able to develop a positive cultural identity and enjoy equal opportunities with Swedish children in their future studies and working life. Immigrant students receive teaching in their household language (as a subject) and study guidance (in respect of various school subjects) given in their household language. They also receive teaching in Swedish (as a foreign language), and can obtain study guidance (in respect of various school subjects) in the Swedish language.

The scale of teaching in the household language as a subject, and given in that language, can vary according to the needs of students, and the opportunities of the local authority to organise such teaching. In 1978, the number of students whose household language was other than Swedish broke down as follows:

received teaching in the household language as a subject	42,000
received study guidance, given in the household language	14,000
wanted household language teaching but were unable to obtain it	4,000
did not use their right to receive household language teaching	21,000
Total	81,000

It is statutory for the municipal authorities to arrange household language teaching. They are also required to inform students of their right to such teaching, and the possibilities of obtaining it. The students with a right to such teaching are those who use a language other than Swedish in their household environment. This normally means that at least one of the parents should have a language other than Swedish as his or her mother tongue, and speak that language with the child. The children themselves need not possess any given skill in order to obtain household language teaching.

One motive of immigrant teaching is that students should become bilingual. This objective makes great demands on teaching in both Swedish and the household language. Both researchers and the immigrant organisations have stressed that the status of the household language is important for teaching in it to succeed, that is, give a bilingual result.

Teaching in the household language is at present organised on the basis of voluntary choice by the students. It has been maintained in various quarters that it should be made compulsory. Among the reasons quoted why the school rather than the students and parents should identify the students to be accorded extra resources for household language teaching are the following:

— it would give the household language higher status;
— parents are not aware of the importance of the household language;
— it would make it easier to plan the supply of teachers.

The arguments quoted for a continued voluntary basis include the following:

— compulsory teaching in the household language is contrary to the freedom of choice aimed at in Swedish immigrant policy;
— immigrants should not be forced to adopt publicly a position on what is a sensitive question;
— if the household language is compulsory, it will either replace other subjects or lie outside the regular timetable, leading to conflicts of ambition between the household language and other subjects.

The central educational authority is now discussing a compromise proposal which involves a distinction between teaching given in the household language (either in the form of study guidance/auxiliary teaching in the household language parallel with regular teaching, or in the form of teaching given entirely in the household language) and teaching in the household language as a subject (teaching that for immigrant students corresponds to the teaching given to Swedish-speaking students in the subject of Swedish). Auxiliary teaching (study guidance) in the household language, and to some extent teaching given entirely in the household language, would by this view be compulsory for students during a period when the school judged this to be necessary for the imparting of knowledge. Under the present rules, parents and students can refuse the offer of household language teaching. The result is sometimes that the school is unable to impart to students knowledge at a level corresponding to their general development. This means that the students themselves cannot fully utilise their capacity in communications with the school. However, the compromise proposal involves that it should not be possible to place a student in a permanent household language class against the wish of the parents.

As regards teaching in the household language as a subject, it includes, as does teaching in Swedish for native Swedish speakers, elements relating to the culture, history, social order and so on of the country or cultural region in which the language is spoken. This may be one of the reasons why some parents choose to refrain from household language teaching on behalf of their children. This applies particularly to political refugees and linguistic minorities from countries where only one language is officially approved. In the latter case, the children often have several household languages. Sometimes they have a better command of the official language in their country of origin than they do of their parents' native language. The parents thus have strong emotional reasons to oppose teaching for their children in a particular language.

A large group of immigrant children has grown up during a period when Swedish policy led to the assimilation of immigrants. Some of the parent generation may not wish to be reminded of their background. Other parent groups may now be regretting that they did not teach their children their mother tongue. For the former group of parents, it can be a violation of their integrity to insist that their children should participate in household language teaching. To the latter group it can be taken as an equal affront that, when they want household language teaching for their children, they should be questioned as to the extent to which that language is used in the home.

The advantages of reasoning along these lines are that it can cater for the needs of both the school and the parents or minority group, and also help raise the status of immigrant languages: on the one hand the school recognises that the immigrant languages are necessary as teaching languages, on the other it confirms the right of the linguistic minorities to obtain teaching in their languages in accordance with their own wishes.

The procedures for identifying groups in need of special resources then differ. In the case of teaching given in the household language, the school can resort to the methods of pedagogic diagnosis used to establish the students' communicative ability (strategy (a)). When it comes to teaching in the household language as a subject, the school is required to inform and advise without adopting any position on behalf of the students and parents, who instead make their own decision (strategy (b)).

The case-finding strategy: the training of unemployed youth as an example

As an example of strategy (c) — in which the school performs case-finding or outreach activities in respect of the special populations to which it wishes to assign extra resources — we will take activities for young people who are unemployed. The schools and the Employment Service are jointly responsible for giving all young people the best possible opportunities for education or work. In most municipal authorities, much work is devoted to following up the young people who leave the compulsory comprehensive without a job or further studies being arranged. At the beginning of the autumn term, as well as catering for normal enrolment at the *gymnasium*-level (upper secondary) comprehensive, we call in young people who have left the compulsory school without having obtained either a place in upper secondary education or a regular job. This facilitates the task of finding suitable training or work for these young people. For a period of five weeks they receive more detailed collective and individual educational and vocational guidance. 'Guidance groups' are set up from the school and Employment Service staff. The aim is to help each student to find suitable training or work. Students are prepared so that they can enter regular education when places become available. They also receive practical vocational orientation and take part in study visits.

Compared with the students in regular education, these young people require major inputs in the form of individual instruction after absence, student welfare counselling, and contacts with the parents. Personal case-finding and individual information demand large inputs of both personnel and time.

Summary of trends

Alongside the changes in the identification of special populations that have occurred during the past two decades, the following shift in emphasis may be observed:

from	*to*
Diagnosis	Treatment
Work directly with problem students	Work via others
Concentration on individuals	Concentration on groups
Inputs when problems have already arisen	Preventive inputs in the school environment

At the same time change has also occurred in the staffing policy for the provisions, narrow specialists being replaced by teams of differently qualified people. This can be seen, for example, in the following outline programme for dealing with the problems and difficulties of individual students.[4]

		Performed by
1	Pedagogic analysis level of knowledge level of skills working method motivation	Educationist
2	Psychological and socio-psychological analysis social functions emotional functions intellectual resources	Psychologist (Educationist)
3	(Social-) medical analysis somatic psychological-psychiatric	School nurse and school doctor
4	Social and socio-psychological analysis home environment community environment	Social worker
5	Studies and career analysis background interests study opportunities labour market	Ed. and voc. guidance personnel

6	Socio-psychological analysis of the school environment
	Functions:
	  social
	  emotional
	  creative
	  aesthetic
	  cognitive
		All those active in school

Working method: Analysis; synthesis + hypotheses; programme of treatment; new analysis; new synthesis, possibly new hypotheses; new programme of treatment.

Integration and normalisation

The measures taken in schools to deal with the students' difficulties have been dominated by different kinds of special teaching. Such teaching has expanded rapidly. In 1945 only just over 1 per cent of students were involved; in 1960 just under 3 per cent, and in 1974 between 35 and 40 per cent. At the same time, the shortage of trained 'special teachers' has erased the special character of such teaching. It has become the subject of lively discussion, partly because pedagogic research has failed to demonstrate any clear and positive effects of teaching special classes.

The present aim in Sweden is therefore, that the bulk of pedagogic activity should take place in regular classes, not in clinics or special classes. Supportive and auxiliary teaching will then be part of teaching at large. The working team that functions in a unit consisting of two or three classes can then be assigned joint responsibility for finding solutions to the problems of individual students by, for example, flexible groupings of students, increased time for learning, the redistribution of resources, an efficient use of personal and material resources, and cooperation with parents, recreation leaders and the staff specifically concerned with student welfare (welfare workers, school psychologists, school nurses).

Only in special cases and in the final resort should students be separated in permanent groups outside the work units. This is necessary when special pedagogic inputs are required that lie outside the competency of the working team (for example, speech and hearing difficulties), or when special medical and psycho-therapeutic treatment is needed. Students with severe physical, learning or behavioural difficulties must be taught outside the working team. Even for students with severe handicaps, the possibilities of 'integration' and 'normalisation' are being discussed. According to the terms of reference given to a committee set up to study the integration of handicapped students in the regular school system, the purpose of integration is to create 'a normal environment for the handicapped students, and to provide favourable conditions for social affinity and understanding between different groups of student'.

The mentally retarded

The concepts of 'integration' and 'normalisation' can be illustrated by the application of the special provisions made for the mentally retarded, including the special schools for such students. The principles of integration and normalisation were formulated as ideological lodestars in the late 1960s. The mentally retarded were to be offered an existence as close to the normal as possible. They were to live and attend school among other children, and not be isolated in special institutions. This approach was essentially a reaction to the view previously dominating, which had led to separative measures such as placing in institutions and segregated schools.

The background to this change in the approach to the mentally retarded was an altered view of humanity. By the view previously dominant, a mentally retarded person was considered to suffer from an absolute property which could not be altered and about which nothing could be done. It was impossible to influence mental retardation, since it reflected, essentially, the disposition of nature.

In the approach prescribing integration and normalisation, the emphasis is instead on the relative nature of the handicap. No property is a handicap in itself. Properties become handicaps only when demands and expectations on the individual cause certain properties or weaknesses to appear as such. The static pessimism that had prevailed was called into question by a succession of studies which show that even the severely mentally retarded react, sometimes in a surprisingly positive manner, to conscious influence. The previous separative measures appear as actually aggravating a handicap. Special social and pedagogic measures of this kind confer a label and a stamp. The deviating individual is given a designation that reduces his chances of being accepted as 'normal'. Both the designation that stamps him and the physical separation cut the mentally retarded person off from 'normal' human life and normal human contacts. The placing and treatment over which the authorities and the school have control are experienced as contributing to the handicap.

During the late 1970s, researchers, theoreticians in the field of care, and the relatives of the mentally retarded and other handicapped have all become aware that an integration of the handicapped into the regular school system does not automatically lead to social integration. Obstacles exist in the 'normal' environment in which the handicapped are placed. The mechanisms of segregation are to be found in the reality outside the school, in the students' free time and above all after schooling has finished, particularly in working life. There are labelling and segregating mechanisms outside the school which have strong effects on activities within the school. Integration in the school does not automatically lead to integration in society.

The pendulum towards integration may swing slightly back. In a 'normal' school environment, the mentally retarded can see for himself that rewards are given precisely for the sort of intellectual performance that he is unable to produce by reason of his handicap. In this way the 'normal' school environment can actually hamper efforts to build up the security and self-confidence of the handicapped student. The 'normal' school environment cannot remain unaffected if the social aims of integration are to be achieved.

Different forms of integration

A Swedish sociological researcher[5] who has analysed the provisions made for the mentally retarded has identified four separate forms of integration: physical, functional, social and public.

By *physical integration* (integration of premises) is meant, in the context of the school, that the teaching premises of the special school for the mentally retarded are in or adjoining those of the regular school.

By *functional integration* is meant the joint use of common arrangements and resources. In its ultimate form, such integration implies a simultaneous use of these resources.

By *social integration* is meant that the mentally retarded are included in a group affinity with the non-retarded and have regular and spontaneous contact with the latter, and experience themselves as a natural part of the group.

Public integration entails that the mentally retarded, as adults, should have the same access to resources as others, the same opportunities to influence their own situation, and that they should have a working role which resembles that of others.

We sometimes speak of 'individual integration'. By this is meant that individual handicapped students during parts of the school day, or sometimes for the entire school day, work together with other students, but with special supportive and auxiliary measures, such as technical aids and personal assistance.

In Sweden during the 1970s, the classes of the separate compulsory comprehensive for the mentally retarded and the training school catering for the most severe cases have rapidly been integrated, so far as their premises are concerned, with the regular schools. Classrooms have been assigned to the same buildings, or immediately adjoining premises. Common resources are used to some extent. Co-operation in actual teaching, however, has been fairly unusual, relating perhaps to PE lessons and joint end-of-term arrangements and other festivities. Social integration has been negligible. Part of the reason why there has been so little co-operation in activities, or social integration, may be that neither the special nor the regular schools have arrived at suitable forms because they have not yet acquired experience of how to co-operate. Another difficulty is that the staff of the 'ordinary' school do not have the training or experience to work with special school students. As, however, they acquire greater experience of working in teaching teams, the conditions for co-operation between the special schools and 'ordinary' schools should become more favourable.

As regards social integration in the schools whose premises have been integrated, it is difficult to pass any general judgements: 'The mentally retarded are generally accepted by their peers in the ordinary classes. There is practically no systematic bullying or mobbing, but any more positive relationships are also unusual'.[6] Among the difficulties involved in social integration is the fact that the students of special schools are recruited from a wider geographical area than those in the ordinary schools, which is an obstacle to the retarded and their peers in the class or school getting together in their free time.

Integration and normalisation:
the deaf and partially deaf

In Sweden the term 'normalisation' means in the school context a normalisation of the environment of the handicapped.[7] The concept can be taken in a more narrow or a broader sense. In the narrow sense it implies the creation of optimal environmental conditions by means, for example, of special equipment. In the broader sense it implies a change in the overall public environment in order, as far as possible, to make all functions of the community available also to those with handicaps.

In the case of certain handicaps, the debate on integration is affected by discussion as to the most suitable methods. In the majority of countries one finds, for example, in the case of deaf and partially deaf students a conflict between the adherents of oral methods (spoken language) and manual methods (hand alphabet, sign language and so on). Adherents of the manual methods have no wish to exclude the spoken language but are concerned to use all possible means of communication to stimulate the development of language. No parallel need be drawn between the oral method and integration, or the manual method and segregation. Doubt is also felt about attempts to integrate the deaf and partially deaf to such an extent that the aim is assimilation, that is, to recreate the deaf so that they resemble those with normal hearing. These students can never acquire normal hearing, but are forced to live 'as if' they could hear, which may threaten their self-confidence. They are constantly made to feel that they are inadequate, that there is something wrong with them.[8]

A respect for deaf and partially deaf students as individuals implies that we must respect their choice of communicative channel, and give them an opportunity to choose. The parallel with the aim of freedom of choice in immigrant teaching is clear. Immigrant students must be given a real chance to preserve their cultural and linguistic identity. Just as immigrants and their children come together where they find a group affinity, so too do the deaf, finding in this way a security they have lacked in the normally hearing environment.

Deaf and partially deaf children are probably the group most difficult of all to integrate in ordinary classes. A single student with impaired hearing who is placed in an ordinary class finds himself in a situation that can create 'social deafness'. It is extremely difficult in an ordinary class to follow teaching via a hearing aid, owing to the natural noise occurring in the classroom. The sound impressions communicated by the hearing aid differ from those experienced by normal hearers in the same sound environment. The deaf even so accept their situation, since their upbringing and teaching has schooled them to behave as if they could hear. They have nothing to compare with, and therefore accept their situation. They have become masters in pretending to understand even when they do not.[9]

In the case of deaf students, we must ask ourselves whether integration in ordinary classes is not the more limiting environment for their development, compared with special classes. Difficulties in communicating lead to a social isolation that impedes their personality development. The ideal solution, if it is possible, would be to create opportunities for social contacts with both deaf and normally hearing groups. In particular, deaf children must be given the opportunity to meet deaf adults.

The effects of identification and special treatment

The effects of treating specially those students who have learning difficulties (special teaching) have been the subject of lively interest in an extensive international research and debate. It has not been possible to demonstrate any major and positive effects of teaching in special classes.[10 & 11] This applies both during schooling and in the longer term.[12]

Emanuelsson[13] has presented a model of how educational handicaps can be studied before, during and after education. His model integrates both general experience and theories in the fields of learning and personality psychology, and educational psychology. Among other things, he has followed a group of educationally handicapped over a period of thirty-five years, from the time they were ten. As 'educationally handicapped' Emanuelsson reckons groups encountering greater difficulties than is normal in school, above all students of low aptitude or with more specific difficulties, such as reading, writing and calculating difficulties, or emotional disturbances. The object of different kinds of special teaching is to reduce the difficulties of the educationally handicapped, usually by trying to achieve the best possible adjustment to the school and its demands. We must assume that the measures taken in special teaching in some cases have positive effects on the students, but it has been asked whether we should not even so be justified in speaking of educational handicaps that are caused by or expressed through the activities of the compulsory school system.

One may sum up this line of thinking as follows:

Educational handicaps prior to schooling	Examples of school experience	Expected 'effects' of educational handicaps after schooling
	No influence	Low status occupations dominate
	Reinforcing	Few individuals in managerial and supervisory positions
	New handicapping experiences	Low-wage domination
	Repeated failures	Difficulties common in making a livelihood
	Negative experiences of educational situations	High risk of layoffs and unemployment
	Experiences of being specially treated and non-normal	High frequency of retraining
	Poor results (marks)	Poor internal and external adjustments in society
	Shorter schooling (studies discontinued)	Little participation in adult education
	Leaving certificates not conferring competency, abbreviated courses etc.	Weak interest in studies
	Little opportunity for supplementary studies	Low educational aspirations for own children
		Little variety in leisure activities

Emanuelsson's empirical studies largely confirm the expectations of this model. Experiences at school that could function as educational handicaps later in life are common. The placing in a special class has become definitive, in the sense that a person so placed at the beginning of his schooling often spends a very large part of his schooling in a special class. Another general feature is that school difficulties start very early on. A negative school career with repeated failures is common.

Stangvik[14] has studied the connection between groupings of slow learners and their self-concept development. Research into the effects of educational grouping on the motivation and personality of low-aptitude students has produced divergent results. Certain trends, however, can be observed. The students in ordinary classes tend to comprehend success and failure more quickly than those in special classes. Students in ordinary classes show greater aspirational shifts following evaluation of performance than special class pupils. Placing in a special class means that the social significance of school failure is emphasised also outside the classroom.

The grouping of low-aptitude students has been attacked from various angles by research workers. It has been analysed in terms of status, role, interpersonal communication and expectancy, and teaching processes. The negative results of placing in special classes can be meaningfully interpreted in terms of a 'segregation syndrome'. Particularly important in this context are the dimensions pointing to teaching at a low cognitive level, the dependence of the students on the teacher, non-academic values and low motivational orientation.

Placing in a special class affects the students' self-concept development in various ways:

— Such a placing can be regarded as a sanction of the failure definition.

— The characteristics of the special class, above all from the socio-economic standpoint, shape the specific comparative relationships which exist between the group and each of its members. These differ radically from the corresponding relationships between low-aptitude students and an ordinary class.

— Teaching in a special class is characterised by adjustments to the failure definition with a more personally 'clinical' orientation than in an ordinary class, a less accentuated academic value orientation, lower teaching objectives, and modified time frameworks.

From the premise of the 'segregation syndrome', the connection between self-concept and placing in a special class can be assumed to be as follows. As long as the self-concept is related to internal aspects of the school environment, a positive evaluation can be expected in the special class. When, however, the self-concept is related to the external aspects of the school environment, then the positive self-evaluation of special class students disappears owing to the secondary effects of the placing. This is due to the symbolic relationship between the placing in a special class and the failure definition. This symbolic connection also affects social interplay outside the school. In a survey of the literature on self-concept, Stangvik finds this explanation to fit. The picture is further confirmed by his own empirical studies.[15]

According to Stangvik, previous effect research with regard to special teaching can be interpreted with the help of social system theories. Special class students feel more comfortable with their low level of performance than weak students in an ordinary class. They judge their school capacity more positively and express a lower motivation to improve their performances. This may partly explain why weak students in special classes produce worse performances than corresponding students in ordinary classes. Their self-concept and the teaching reinforce each other. The two different environments (special class and ordinary class) create a different internal readiness and self-concept. The special class conveys social and cultural values. An adjustment is made to the definition of failure. This is a successive process over time. At the same time, this view must be balanced by the results of studies showing that students with learning difficulties can experience severe mental pressure in an ordinary classroom, and that this can lead to high ambitions and self-devaluation.

Emanuelsson[16] asks whether it is the students who fail to cope with the school or the school that has failed with the students. Our answer to this question will decide what special measures we can contemplate in order to solve the problems we refer to as 'school difficulties'. If we seek faults in the properties of the students, then it becomes natural to try to 'cure' the student and alter his behaviour so that he adjusts to and succeeds in the school. If we see educational handicaps rather as signs that the school has failed with its students, then it would seem more reasonable to try to analyse and alter conditions in the school so that failures can be prevented. How this can be achieved lies beyond the scope of this paper.

Notes and references

1   Utredningen om skolans inre arbete — SIA, *Skolans arbetsmiljö*. (The working conditions in school) Stockholm; Allmänna förlaget, 1974 — (Statens offentliga utredningar; 1974:53).

2   Norden, K. and Ang, T., *Skolplacering av döva och hörselskadade barn. Vad vet vi om integrering?* (School placement of deaf and hearing impaired children. What do we know of integration?) Stockholm, National Board of Education, 1979 (MS).
3   Johansson, Bror A., *Criteria of school readiness. Factor structure, predictive value and environmental influences*, Stockholm, Almqvist and Wiksell, 1965 (Acta Universitatis Stockholmiensis. Stockholm Studies in Educational Psychology: 9). Diss.
4   Wiking, B., *När nu skolan ändå finns* (Yet the school is there), Stockholm, Prisma, 1973, p.64.
5   Marten Södar, University of Uppsala (MS).
6   Ibid.
7   Ibid.
8   Norden, K. and Ang, T., *School placement*.
9   Ibid.
10 Osterling, Olle, *The efficacy of special education. A comparative study of classes for slow learners*, Uppsala, Almqvist and Wiksell, 1967.
11 Stangvik, Gunnar, *Self-concept and school segregation*, Göteborg, Acta Universitatis Gothoburgensis, 1979 (Göteborg Studies in Educational Sciences, 28), Diss.
12 Emanuelsson, Ingemar, *Ubildningshandikapp i langtidsperspektiv* (Educational handicap in long-range perspective), Stockholm, Pedagogiska institutionen, Lärarhögskolan i Stockholm, 1974, Diss.
13 Emanuelsson, Ingemar, *Ubildning för anpassade. Skolan i langtidsperspektiv. Analys och debatt* (Education for adjustment. The school in long-range perspective. Analysis and Debate), Stockholm, Rabén and Sjögren, 1977 (Tema nova).
14 Stangvik, Gunnar, *Self-concept*.
15 Ibid.
16 Emanuelsson, *Education for adjustment*.

5 Screening categories relevant to special education

Pierre Dague
Centre National d'Etudes et de Formation pour l'Enfance Inadaptée, Université R. Descartes, Paris V

If it is agreed that children or adolescents suffer from such serious handicaps or difficulties that they must have a special education, the first problem is to identify or screen these young people. We mean by this, first, definition of these categories according to their special characteristics; secondly, technical ways of detecting these characteristics; and, thirdly, the process of screening, and particularly the point in the life of the subject when screening is most necessary or most feasible, the conditions under which it is made, the persons or institutions which have to make it and its reliability. We cannot therefore speak of 'screening' in an abstract and general way: we must state who we wish to screen, how and why.

Screening criteria. Extension of the concept of maladjustment

Determining the screening criteria proves less simple than it seems: in fact, according to the various categories considered, these criteria are far from being of the same kind and possessing the same sort of objectivity. We shall therefore begin by enumerating them and analysing them critically before turning to their implications. In a fairly traditional way, the difficulties which justify a special education are divided into three major groups: physical, mental and social.
Physical handicaps include sensory disabilities, diseases affecting the

main vital functions and motor handicaps. It should at once be noted that two very different situations are encountered here. There is first the case of children whose substantial loss of visual or hearing acuity — especially if this is congenital or precocious — makes it impossible for them to do their basic schooling under normal conditions and calls for the use of original pedagogical techniques: Braille learning for the blind, auditory training, speech training for the mute, lip-reading and sign-language teaching for the hard-of-hearing. It is thus possible, in this case, to speak of a special education.[1]

Such is also the case for children afflicted with serious diseases or motor handicaps who must undergo special treatment or rehabilitation, medical attention or operations and are obliged for this purpose to spend a more or less lengthy period in a hospital type of institution.[2] They cannot attend ordinary schools during such periods and must be taught at their place of treatment. Can such teaching nevertheless be called special? In point of fact, these children often have the same learning capacity as healthy children: it is rather the teaching which is 'under special conditions' and must be adapted to the constraints of rehabilitation or medical treatment. Only in the case of certain children who have motor handicaps and suffer from serious impediments in their upper limbs and/or speech must the teaching allow for these handicaps and use original methods.[3] It is thus apparent that the screening criteria and especially their pedagogical implications differ in these two cases.

Handicaps of mental origin are a very mixed category. They include, first and foremost, the more or less profound intellectual disabilities. Historically, most attention has been paid to the more serious of these: feeble-minded or imbecile children who are very disturbed as a result of their mental handicap and for whom an education is provided which is mainly based on sensory-motor exercises.[4] Subsequently and with the general spread of education, this category has extended to milder handicaps compatible with a school education whose pace and methods were made to allow for these impairments.[5] It was in order to screen such children that the first intelligence measurement scales were drawn up since they only attracted attention through their learning difficulties and not through any physical deformation or excessive development retardation.[6] For these 'mildly feeble-minded' children, the screening criteria are therefore both learning problems and mental retardation, the latter explaining the former. But neither is so objectively clear-cut as for children with physical handicaps since their setbacks may be due to other causes than mental deficiency[7] and since any psychological examination may be subjected to the criticisms which we shall mention later.

In any case, it is not only the existence of an intellectual disability which may be the source of maladjustment, since a marked and very precocious superiority may also be the cause. In certain countries, special education has been introduced for the highly gifted, while in others such a measure has been demanded in order to pay due respect to differences and especially to the need to make best possible use of this intellectual potential, particularly in developing countries.[8] But, here too, certain questions must be asked: concerning the criteria for screening these children and marking them out, since certain subjects suffer from psychotic disorders; concerning the relationship between this superiority and membership of the more privileged classes; and, finally, concerning the necessity for a special education on their behalf or concerning the conditions for keeping and integrating them in ordinary schools.

Another category consists of children who have behavioural disorders (called psychoneurotic or 'problem' children). There are of course serious neurotic or psychotic disorders which call for specific treatment in special institutions. But certain less dramatic behaviour (for example, instability) may appear increasingly 'normal' (in the statistical sense of the word) insofar as it is caused in a great number of children by the conditions of modern city life. It may also develop as a reaction to a temporarily or permanently disturbed situation — usually family — requiring psychotherapeutic aid which does not rule out education in ordinary schools, either full- or part-time.[9] It should be noted, finally, that the concept of 'behavioural disorder' depends to a certain extent on the degree of tolerance of the social and especially school environment towards any phenomenon of 'deviance' and therefore on more or less subjective 'norms', even when these are defined by reference to the popularised accepted facts of psychiatry or psychoanalysis.

Lastly, the existence of certain types of learning problem has led some countries to establish a category which requires special education: children with serious learning difficulties, which include what are also called dysgraphia, dyslexia-dysorthography and dyscalculia. The problem is then to define criteria for screening such subjects. But doctors, psychologists and educationists are far from agreeing concerning the specific nature of these disorders and their origin: a genetic often hereditary disposition, hidden brain damage, visually handicapped orientation or backwardness, too precocious and misdirected learning, or serious emotional disturbances inhibiting the learning process by a rejection of the symbolic meaning of verbal communication. The screening criteria — where they are not simply confined to observing problems — as well as the remedies proposed differ considerably according to whether one explanation is accepted or given preference over another.[10]

The third group of difficulties, for its part, is based on social criteria.

Screening depends here on membership of a minority social group in a given society and the assumption is made that such membership creates difficulties for the pupil which make school learning under normal conditions impossible or difficult. But, here too, this criterion covers a variety of different situations.

In certain cases, the main obstacle lies in the language spoken by the child in his family environment: the case of recent migrants of foreign origin or of pupils who speak a different language or dialect from that spoken in school and for whom the national language seems in part to be foreign.[11] It is then considered that basic education can only be acquired with the help of special methods (original or derived from adult education or based on the language spoken by the child) and with homogeneous groups separated, at least for a certain time, from other children (language induction classes, for example, for foreigners). But we are justified in asking whether social integration should begin with such segregation.[12]

The concept of 'linguistic handicap' covers the case of children from backgrounds which are socio-culturally disadvantaged for mainly economic reasons: poor vocabulary and ungrammatical language spoken by the parents, few verbal exchanges, insufficient cultural support to help with learning, and so on. While special education is not regarded as a necessity for these children (although they are subjected to a certain segregation if it is thought that they should progress at their own pace in groups corresponding to their level), it should be noted that intelligence tests often show them as slightly mentally retarded and that they may then be put into special education classes: we shall return to this point.

Finally, the concept of cultural handicap sometimes covers much more debatable cases: those of children who for various reasons have no family (orphans in social service care) or whose family has no fixed residence (gipsies and other travellers, boat or barge people), or whose parents are temporarily out of action (because they are sick or in prison) or have been deprived of their rights as a result of their misconduct. But there is nothing, in any case, to prevent these children from going to school under the same conditions as their comrades. In what way can the teaching they are given be regarded as 'special'? And yet it is in certain countries.[13]

This rapid survey reveals that in many countries the concept of maladjustment — which justifies the existence of a special education — has been gradually extended to increasingly wide and numerous categories of children. From being first reserved for retarded and sensory handicapped children, it has been extended to the physically handicapped (open-air or hospital classes), then to children who have fallen behind at school and finally to disadvantaged social groups. The criteria on which the screening of these categories is based have become less and less objective and more dependent on assumptions or opinions, if not on a certain educational policy. Above all, some confusion has set in between the kind of special education which has had to invent its techniques and methods in order to adjust to sensory or mental handicaps or to serious emotional disturbances, thus making learning and education possible which would not have been the case under ordinary conditions, and an education, on the other hand, which does not differ greatly from normal practice but is given under special conditions (limited possibility of movement, hospitalisation, absence or indifference of the family). It is regrettable that the title 'special education' should have been indiscriminately made to cover all these situations: it has not facilitated discussion. This had to be pointed out at once.

The consequences of this extension

Be that as it may, this extension (not to say this tendency to expand) of special education has entailed a certain number of consequences, of which we shall analyse the most important for categories themselves, for institutions and for their staffs.

For categories

More specific sub-groups have been established within each major category of handicap or disability. A distinction has thus been made between the blind and the partially sighted, the deaf and the hard-of-hearing, and the mildly, moderately or profoundly mentally retarded, who come under different institutions (and sometimes different Ministries). In France, the word *surhandicapés* is even used for cases in which the handicap is of maximum severity (for example, motor-handicapped children suffering from severe athetosis or quadriplegia). It was then necessary to refine the diagnostic criteria, to perfect the measuring or evaluation instruments and to train more specialised staff. This refinement has had several consequences.

First of all, the borderline between these categories is often theoretical and debatable when based on quantitative data. For example, the classification of hearing handicaps (mild, moderate, severe, profound) is based on losses in decibels for certain frequencies; but account should also be taken of the conditions under which these losses have been calculated (subjective or objective audiometry), the methods used and other factors such as examination of the child's voice, speech and way of expressing himself: calculating the hearing loss alone is therefore insufficient.

If we take the case of the mentally handicapped, we also find a classification (mild, moderate, profound disorders, profound retardation) based on intelligence quotient intervals. But, here again, we have to know what test has been used to obtain this level. Above all, this apparent numerical accuracy should deceive no one: when we put the dividing line between mild mental retardation and moderate mental retardation at the IQ of 60, what real difference is there between subjects with 59 and those with 61? None, no doubt. In any case, these two figures merely have a probability value in a confidence interval which at this level is about five points, which means that there is no statistical difference between an IQ of 60 and one of 65 or 55. In actual fact, when a guidance decision has to be made, more account is taken of certain factors (such as the proximity of a special institution, the number of vacant places in it, the wishes of families) than of numerical criteria, even though these officially define the conditions for acceptance. Quantitative accuracy is therefore purely formal.

Secondly, as the definitions are increasingly narrow and cover fewer and fewer subjects, there is a growing chance that children will drop into a sort of 'no man's land' between two categories. We will have an example of this with those who are shown by psychometric examination to be mentally retarded and by psychiatric examination to be perhaps psychotic (and we know how difficult it is sometimes to differentiate the diagnosis between these two possibilities). We have resorted to creating intermediate categories such as 'psychosis with expression impairment' (*psychose à expression déficitaire*) or 'evolutive irregular disturbances' (*débilités dysharmoniques évolutives*).

Lastly and above all, it should be noted that a handicap rarely occurs in an isolated form: it is often accompanied by impairments due to the same pathogenic cause — usually an associated mental retardation, but sometimes also sensory losses or functional disorders[14] — all of which are a secondary consequence of the primary handicap, particularly retarded psychomotor and verbal development and especially emotional disturbances. We then have to define a new category (which becomes something of a 'hold-all') of 'multiple' or 'poly' or 'pluri-handicapped' combining all sorts of disorders. Children who suffer from multiple handicaps experience great difficulty in finding a place in the existing structures.

For institutions

There has also been increasing specialisation on the part of institutions on the basis of medical or psychological criteria. Their structure, staff and equipment correspond to a particular type of handicap or disease, to a certain intelligence zone and to certain types of behavioural disorders. When they were still too few to meet all demands, a selection could be made at the time of admission and only those cases accepted which raised least problems and were closest to the 'typical case'.

But, with the extension of the policy of taking complete care of the handicapped and the rising number of institutions, but also with the reduction if not the disappearance of certain diseases, these institutions have in some cases begun to compete (especially when they come under different organisations, associations or Ministries and when their location has not been the subject of concerted agreement) and in others to accept more handicapped children whom they would have refused only a few years earlier. This inevitably raises problems of internal organisation, finance, staff training and integrating the new arrivals in the old structure.

Some of them even have to convert completely because they were designed in accordance with predictions of a state of affairs which has evolved in an unexpected direction. Such is the case for the institutions intended for children suffering from rickets, tuberculosis of the bones or pulmonary phthisis and poliomyelitis. For want of staff, they have been obliged to convert in order to meet new demands: for children with poliomyelitis who come from countries which are underequipped for vaccination and treatment, and the increasing number of handicaps (such as brain or spinal damage caused by road or traffic accidents) or those for which better therapeutic possibilities are available (mucovisicidosis, spina bifida, progressive muscular dystrophy, chronic renal deficiency, leukaemia, and so on). But such conversion raises financial, material and human problems. This may be seen in particular when these institutions wish to keep their numbers up and have to accept children who combine certain impairments with a major handicap (retarded or deaf motor-handicapped, for example): staff, children and also their parents have to be persuaded to accept the presence of these newcomers, who seem to be 'deviants' compared with the original inmates.[15]

For staff

Medical assistants, teachers and educators have had to specialise in order to work with these children.[16] But, here again, this specialisation has been obtained in order to face a fleeting situation. With the changing intake, some staff feel unable to face the new situations or are unsatisfied with their new working conditions. The forms of basic training must therefore be redesigned and in particular continuing training introduced in order to inform staff about the current state of medical and psychological research, new techniques for use in the classroom, the possible forms of action with the children and the outlets for the different types of training. In certain cases — such as, for example, regarding the sequels of post-traumatic coma in children — almost everything remains to be discovered and invented. Not to speak of finding the necessary resources for doing so.

Still more important is the problem of diagnostic teams. In view of the growing number of such children, the multiplication of categories and the difficulties of differential diagnosis, the bodies responsible for recruitment are faced with a dilemma. Either, in order to cope as best they can, they form themselves into multidisciplinary teams consisting of qualified staff (doctors, psychologists, welfare workers, teachers and re-educators) with the necessary time and money, working near the place of treatment and education, but at the risk of eating into the financial resources available for special education, or else they are inadequately equipped, for lack of the necessary means, and their screening is quick and summary and based on one or two criteria (the prevailing handicap or the family situation, or usually the IQ), which may lead to errors of guidance that are difficult to correct subsequently, to overcrowded institutions and to parents' dissatisfaction.

In any case, who is to be responsible for this screening and guidance? If it is to be the services or people who depend directly on special institutions, selection or rejection might be made on the sole justification of these institutions' needs or possibilities (a feedback process) without always allowing for the child's interests. If it is done by services independent of these institutions (which should be more objective), they will depend, at national, regional or county level, on responsible Ministries, and there is then the danger that decisions will be taken in the light of budgetary or policy imperatives by people who will not always be familiar with the institutions (nor even with the children when decisions are based on records alone) and that parents will be partly deprived of the possibility of choice.[17]

Main characteristics of special education

Turning now to special education itself, we wish to concentrate on two of its main aspects: its increasingly early introduction into the child's life and its relations with ordinary schools.

A policy of early screening and intervention

What is striking, to begin with, is that in the last few years the policy of dealing with disorders or failure when they were observed has tended to stand down in favour of preventive action based on the early screening of handicaps or impairments.[18]

The justification and effectiveness of this early screening for certain cases cannot be denied. In particular, when in the absence of definite signs at birth, there is some reason for suspecting the existence of a disease or handicap which will only appear later. Techniques have therefore been prepared for revealing in young and sometimes newborn children any hearing impairment or genetic aberration which might cause mental retardation (phenylketonuria) or motor disorders (progressive muscular dystrophy), or neonatal brain damage which might be responsible for subsequent severe motor disorders (spastic or athetosic children). Such early screening justifies the use of special equipment or treatment, as well as education in the family environment. In some countries, nursery schools have special classes for such children.

It will be noted, however, that these are mainly physical handicaps. But when it comes to mild mental retardation or behavioural disorders, does this early screening prove as easy, desirable and justified? As far as the latter are concerned, it has already been observed that they could develop as a reaction to disturbed family situations or to social factors (habitat, living conditions), which themselves generate family indifference or tensions[19] although they cannot be regarded as 'emotional' or be classified with the psychotic structures. It would be a grave mistake to interpret as 'constitutional' and an early sign of serious disorders behaviour which may only be transitory and curable by simple means where it does not disappear of its own accord. This is not to deny the existence of psychotic or pre-psychotic disturbances in children. But, under the pretext that they were for long disregarded and even rejected, is there not at present a tendency to refer to them systematically whenever the teacher or parents are faced with behaviour which baffles them? There is thus a constant danger of 'psychiatrising' disorders because it satisfies the need to classify, the desire for a medical explanation and, finally, the uneasiness felt when faced with anything different.

Turning to mild intellectual disturbances — by far the greatest number who benefit from special education — we feel obliged to criticise the process of screening them. Our criticisms mainly concern intelligence tests and the interpretation of their results.[20] It must be remembered, first, that these tests were prepared on the basis of a certain definition of intelligence, regarded essentially as the capacity for learning, particularly school learning.[21] But it has been objected that these 'traditional' tests measure intelligence mainly by verbal tests which penalise certain categories of pupils such as those of foreign origin or who have bilingual or culturally disadvantaged backgrounds. Attempts have therefore been made to work out tests requiring no verbal replies ('performance' tests) or which are least sensitive to cultural factors ('culture-free' or 'culture-fair' tests). But no test is completely independent of these factors, as has been demonstrated by comparative studies carried out on very different populations (in Africa, for example) or by the failure of Bells' attempts in the United States to eliminate these factors from tests.[22]

At the same time, the form of measurement most frequently used to express the level of intellectual development, the IQ, is not as accurate as might be desired. As already pointed out, it is subject to a systematic error which gives it a probability value only. But, above all, there is no reason for claiming that this measurement, made at a particular moment in the child's development, will remain constant throughout that development. Many researches, especially in the United States, have shown that the correlation between the IQs measured at two points in a child's life is all the smaller the earlier the first is taken and the later the second, and that it is practically non-existent between the ages of 3 and 16.[23] In other words, apart from the case of serious retardation, early measurement of a level of intelligence has very little prognostic value.

Finally, it remains to be proved that an IQ lower than a certain norm (80 for example) can only be explained by global congenital and irreversible retardation — in short, mental deficiency — justifying recourse to special education. Indeed, such retardation may be due to various causes: peri- or post-natal brain damage, chromosomal or genetic aberrations causing brain dysfunctioning, of course, but also congenital or early sensory or motor deprivation delaying sensory, motor and verbal development, emotional blockages ranging from a simple inhibition to psychotic breakdown, as well as insufficient cultural support in a socially underprivileged background. Can all these cases be bundled together under the pretext that the IQ of these children is in the same zone? In point of fact, they call for different attitudes and action: suitable education for specific handicaps, or remedial education for deficiencies, or psychotherapy, or a policy of very early education (in day nurseries for example). Putting these different children in the same 'class for the mentally deficient' is an indefensible solution; yet it is the one currently adopted.

What we have just said about early screening and its dangers can be extended to any diagnosis in general. It is tantamount to labelling the child with his predominating handicap without trying to consider how his total personality is built up around this handicap (displacement or compensatory process, for example) and reacts to the family and social background. The child is assimilated and reduced to his handicap, to the figure which measures it and the word which designates it. He becomes a 'case' defined by all the characteristics common to all other subjects in this category. He is now only thought of via these clinical pictures: he is a 'case of cerebral palsy', a 'mongol', a 'psychotic' or 'hyperactive', as though a whole range of differences did not exist within these categories. And once this label is attached, it tends to stick and remain unchanged. No further question is asked about the possibilities and conditions of change for the subject; very little scope is provided for checking and correcting the diagnosis and measurements. The handicap becomes a permanent social characteristic.

Existing and possible relationship between special and ordinary education

The fact is that this special education tends to become a parallel stream in which children and adolescents will remain until they attain their majority. This state of affairs has been responsible for many criticisms which have led to support of the principle of educational integration. But it is no doubt possible, after having examined the arguments in favour of both policies, to suggest a series of possibilities between these two extremes.

Special education as a parallel stream

From being first confined to the primary cycle, from 6 to 12–14 years of age, this education has been extended both 'upstream' — with early screening and the opening of special nursery-school classes — and 'downstream' with the creation of vocational training institutions for adolescents up to the end of compulsory schooling and even until they reach adult age. Beyond that limit, other structures take over such as work help centres and protected workshops with or without an associated hostel. A relatively independent school and educational stream has thus been built up, with its own special staff, recruitment and guidance bodies and its own forms of finance.

This system risks operating in 'closed circuit' since it provides permanent care and assistance.[24] For various reasons — not excluding financial concerns — institutions tend to keep children as long as possible, even when the medical symptoms no longer justify such maintenance.[25] It then becomes increasingly difficult for them to go into the ordinary cycle of study; in any case, they are not always prepared for such integration. Furthermore, when institutions are specialised in treating a single handicap which calls for highly qualified medical teams, they can often only recruit on a nationwide basis, which then necessitates a boarding system and all its consequences such as the loosening of family ties and conditioning for a constantly protected life often cut off from social reality.

At the same time, teachers in the ordinary cycle tend increasingly to send children who give them problems into special education because they seem to 'deviate' from the 'norms', which are in fact often relative and subjective. Thus, Terman put the upper limit of mental deficiency at the IQ of 70 and special-class enrolment was for long based on this figure. But, in many countries, this limit has gone up gradually to 75 and then to 80, and it is not even rare nowadays to find children in these classes whose IQ is above 80 (especially where this has been found with non-verbal tests) and who are not therefore really retarded. This change of recruitment does not in any way correspond to any raising of the level of the basic education curricula and therefore to greater demands on intellectual capacity. It is more a reflection of teachers' growing intolerance of slow learners or culturally disadvantaged children who only 30 years ago would have had all their education in ordinary schools.

The same intolerance — or at least the same reluctance — is encountered when sensory or motor handicapped children have to be integrated in ordinary classes. The objections mentioned include the risks of accident, these children's slow performance and the teachers' lack of preparation. But, at bottom, the argument — whether stated explicitly or not — is as follows: 'Since special institutions exist for these children, they would be much better off there than in our own classrooms where there is no real reason for taking them'. We thus come to a sort of 'consumer society' for special education, whose very existence becomes its justification. In the extreme case, ordinary education becomes the recruiter or supplier of special education but, at the same time, it neither considers its own possibilities for retaining these children, nor the reforms it should make to this end, nor above all its own responsibility for causing certain learning difficulties or certain behavioural disorders.[26] All in all, it can be said that the two systems operate to their mutual satisfaction.

Special education and segregation

But is this self-satisfaction general? Is this momentum irreversible? It must not be forgotten that, for many decades, retarded or handicapped children could find no place in ordinary education or elsewhere. The introduction and extension of special education have helped to repair this injustice: that cannot be denied. But has it not, at the same time, been responsible for a segregation institutionalised in a certain kind of exclusion which might be called a 'guilded exclusion'?[27] As a reaction to this state of affairs, a policy has developed for some years in many countries with the aim of integrating the maximum number of children who traditionally depended on special institutions into ordinary classes. The opposition between these two policies is sometimes expressed in a downright and exclusive fashion; but, in the light of the facts and not of the doctrines, the problem is not a simple one.

The opponents of special education level several criticisms at it. *From the educational standpoint*, it encourages the tendency to reject deviants, salves the conscience of teachers by justifying their intolerance and dissuades them from any effort of thought or invention to adapt themselves and their teaching to the difficulties encountered. They are even accused of being the involuntary accomplices of a policy which exacerbates inequalities of social origin.[28] At the same time, special education is developing, becoming diversified and extending without ever querying the validity of the guidance and maintenance decisions, the soundness of its pedagogical plans, the occupational and social outlets to which it leads or, in a word, its own justification.

From the social standpoint, this special education sometimes involves family separation which is prejudicial to emotional development and, even if this is not the case, it does in any event prevent the child from living with his equals and from establishing the sort of relationship in which all children get to know each other and to adapt mutually. Yet it is mainly during childhood that differences are accepted best. Early segregation is no preparation for future integration. In handicapped children, it develops the attitude of being always assisted, the difficulty of coping with frustrations, emotional immaturity and fear of outside reality. In adults, it encourages indifference and sometimes rejection, as well as the tendency to think that this is a problem which is the sole responsibility of the medical or social services. Lastly, this system avoids any criticism of the causes of certain kinds of failure: economic and social causes, as well as political causes in the end. For when we speak of prevention, it is mainly with regard to physical handicaps and the learning of basic skills, but practically never with regard to the social causes of retardation and failure. It is therefore no matter for surprise to find that the defenders of special education include certain partisans of social conservatism and of the genetic proofs of differences between individuals and races.[29]

From the economic and financial standpoint, lastly, it is suggested that the public and private resources devoted to handicapped children or children in difficulties could be used more effectively than by financing special institutions alone, whose investment and operating costs are very high. Maintenance in ordinary schools — with the help of technical and financial aid for teachers, children and their parents — would release resources which could be used to develop small treatment and education units to which children would go for short periods commensurate with their real needs; this would not rule out the existence of centres equipped for research and medical treatment. This is a problem which should be given serious consideration, but it is not within the scope of the present study.

Limits and conditions of integration

These arguments plead in favour of the integration of handicapped children in ordinary schools. However, such integration raises problems in its turn and assumes that a number of conditions have been fulfilled.

It must first be agreed that integration is impossible for children who are too seriously affected mentally (severe and profound mentally retarded), who are obliged permanently or temporarily to undergo strictly controlled vital medical treatment or who have multiple serious handicaps (blind-deaf, motor- or sensory-handicapped mentally-retarded children). Integration cannot therefore apply to all children. Furthermore, even in the case of less serious disorders than those mentioned above, it may be illusory if it is just purely formal: such is the case, for example, for certain special classes or sections annexed to ordinary schools but in which the children have no opportunity to meet other pupils and to join them in common activities; theirs is a case of virtual 'internal segregation'.

Moreover, true integration is not accomplished once and for all by waving a magic wand. It is a process which assumes that a number of conditions are satisfied. The teachers must be prepared for it through information and personal contact to overcome their reluctance and prejudices. They should be given this preparation during their basic training itself. The parents of healthy children must be persuaded of the possibility and necessity of this integration; yet they are often against it for fear that the level of education provided will be aligned to the less gifted. The parents of the handicapped must fully realise that their children will experience difficulty in getting themselves recognised and accepted. Material facilities must be provided for ease of access and movement. Handicapped children will almost always have to be given help by special staff such as speech therapists, Braille teachers, physical or occupational therapists, special education teachers and psycho-therapists, for the ordinary teacher cannot cope with all the difficulties he will come up against.[30]

Finally, a pedagogical and educational plan will have to be worked out for all categories of children, as well as the pace and methods of learning. The champions of integration often quote the example of the successes with sensory or motor handicapped children possessed of normal intelligence.[31] But in the case of the moderately mentally retarded, for example, we have the problem of teaching curricula, the maximum level of learning we are entitled to expect, the pace of this learning and the place which should be given in school to practical and social education so that the child has maximum autonomy when he grows up. If we want integration, we must recognise its limits and, above all, provide the institutional framework and the necessary resources. Otherwise, it will fail and the child will have to go back to a special institution: this is a serious setback for himself and his family, but also for integration policy, which might then be condemned out of hand. In any case, certain parents of handicapped children are not much in favour of this policy since they fear it will remain purely formal and perhaps lead to a disguised form of exclusion.

A range of intermediate possibilities

In point of fact, there are many solutions already existing or which lie between the two alternatives we have just analysed. For instance, special centres operating only for the purposes of diagnosis, special treatment and special education can take children for the time strictly necessary while the latter are at the same time enrolled in a special class or in an ordinary school but with the benefit of the necessary assistance (in school, in the centre or at home). Or else the school can arrange its syllabus to include time for such special assistance (speech training for the mute, ordinary speech training, Braille teaching). In extreme cases, home help and treatment services comprising a special staff can help in the home with children who are too young to go to school or too handicapped to move, or even with children who go to an ordinary school but need help and support. The various forms of assistance may be given by different services according to the gravity of the disorder.[32] These are only some of the existing possibilities; others might be thought of. In any event, we must not get bogged down in the ordinary education/special education dilemma as though only these two alternatives existed or could exist.

Conclusion

Special education, which was made necessary by the existence of certain physical or mental handicaps in some children, has been extended to an increasing number and variety of categories. The screening criteria come up against the problem of their content (physical, mental or social handicaps) and the pertinence of the measurements made (quantitative evaluation) or definitions given (qualitative evaluation).

This extension of special education has educational consequences (establishment of parallel streams and, finally, of two systems of education), social consequences (segregation, exclusion) and economic consequences. The outcome has been the recommendation that the children concerned be integrated in ordinary schools. But that is not always possible and depends on certain conditions being satisfied.

There are many intermediate possibilites between these two extremes. They should be considered in the light of the different categories of children and their age levels (since nothing will be gained by combining all cases under the heading 'handicapped' or 'maladjusted'), as well as from the standpoint of the use to be made of the financial and human resources. Co-ordination and a common policy should be worked out through discussion between the Ministries concerned (Education, Health, Social Affairs), associations and parents. The respective roles and responsibilities of the public services, private bodies and parents should be defined.

Notes and references

1   It was for these children that the first special institutions were opened in France: in 1760, by the Abbé de l'Epée, for the deaf; in 1784, by Valentin Haüy, for the blind.
2   Such is the case, for example, for children afflicted with serious cardiac, renal or respiratory deficiencies, mucoviscidosis, diabetes or epilepsy (at least during the period of treatment). It is also the case for the motor handicapped such as children with cerebral palsy, spina bifida, myopathy and those with scoliosis in need of operations, rehabilitation or treatment which cannot be carried out at home.
3   The case of children with cerebral palsy who cannot write by hand or speak.
4   By Itard in 1802, Seguin (1845) and Guggenbuhl (1841), and also by Halle (1863), Perray-Vaucluse (1876) and Corre (1881), speaking of Europe alone.
5   Classes for 'the retarded' (*classes pour arriérés*) were opened in France in 1905 which later became 'improvement' classes (*classes de perfectionnement*).
6   The metric intelligence scale of Binet and Simon in 1905–1911; Terman's Standord-Binet in 1917.
7   In *Les idées modernes sur les enfants* (1908), Binet quoted some dozen causes, including mental deficiency.
8   Rémy Chauvin, *Les Surdoués*, Stock, 1970.
9   As in the case of the *'Centres médico-psycho-pédagogiques'*, (rehabilitation centres) or the part-time day hospitals.
10 The reader is referred for an overall view of the problem to *La dyslexie en question* (a collective study), A. Colin, 1972.

11   Such is the case in France for Alsatians, Basques and Bretons, but also for West Indian children who speak creole.
12   This may be only partial: in induction or adaptation classes, certain times in the school day may be set aside for such language learning, the child spending the rest of the time with the other pupils for certain activities.
13   In France, for example, for most of the 'social handicapped'.
14   For example, in children with cerebral palsy: motor and speech disorders may be accompanied by visual and/or auditory handicaps, mental retardation and epilepsy.
15   In some institutions for the motor handicapped, overt hostility may be found among children and their parents towards pupils who are also moderately retarded. The rate of tolerance towards these multiple handicapped children is very low.
16   In France, for example, the teachers must have the *Certificat d'Aptitude à l'Education des Enfants Déficients ou Inadaptés* (CAEI) (Certificate to teach retarded or maladjusted children), which comprises a choice of nine specialities corresponding to specific handicaps or difficulties.
17   In France, the *Loi d'orientation en faveur des handicapés* (30 June 1975) has set up various bodies which are responsible for advice on special education. They include representatives of Ministries, institutions and parents. But provision had to be made on parents' behalf for the possibility of appeal against the authors of or administrations responsible for these decisions.
18   In the case of France, see the Circulars of 15 February 1970, on the prevention of maladjustment and on special classes, and that of 25 May 1976 on the operation of the *Groupes d'aide psychopédagogique* (GAPP).
19   M.J. Chombart de Lauwwe: *Psychopathologie sociale de l'enfant inadapté*, CNRS, 1959.
20   These criticisms have been the subject of many books, some of which (such as: Michel Tort, *Le Quotient Intellectuel*, Maspéro, Paris 1974) are more polemic than scientific.
21   Binet could claim that his was a good test of intelligence because its results were strongly correlated with educational success. The same opinion will be found in Terman and Zazzo.
22   The reader is referred for a review of this research to: P. Dague, *Psychologie de l'enfant en Afrique noire francophone et à Madagascar*, Ivory Coast Ministry of Education, School Television Programme, vol. V, and the articles by M. Reuchlin and A. Zampleni in *Milieu et développement*, PUF.
23   Particularly the research by Nancy Bayley and Marjorie Honzick.

24 See the Preamble to the 1975 *Loi d'orientation en faveur des handicapés*.
25 In the report by M. Bloch-Lainé, which unfortunately has not been published, there was talk of 'misappropriation of public funds'.
26 For example, fatigue and educational setbacks as a result of the pace of school work, long school hours and the arrangement of holidays. In spite of the many researches published by doctors on this school fatigue, nothing has been done to remedy it.
27 The reader will find R. Lenoir's *Les Exclus*, published by Le Seuil, Paris, 1974, very useful.
28 For example: P. Bourdieu and J.C. Passeron, *Les Héritiers*, Editions de Minuit, 1964, and *La Reproduction*, ibid., 1970; and C. Baudelot and R. Establet, *L'Ecole capitaliste en France*, Maspéro, 1971.
29 For example, the articles by A. Jansen in the United States, the publications in France by Editions Copernic (*Les inégalités de l'homme*, *Race et intelligence*) and Debray-Ritzen: *Lettre aux parents*....
30 We have examples of this in France with deaf children in ordinary classes: the teacher is assisted on a part-time basis by one or two specialists.
31 We may remember with Mme Mottier (*L'enfant sourd*, Cahiers Baillière, Paris 1978) that in 1848 Dr Blanchet had practised this integration of deaf children in the ordinary environment of State schools in Paris. The demand for, and practice of, integration are not new, therefore.
32 For example, in France, the degree of assistance depends on the pedagogical support and assistance given by the GAPP in the school itself, the rehabilitation centres outside school hours and the part-time day hospital, according to the degree of severity of the child's disorders.

6 Rationales for providing additional resources

Erik Jorgen Hansen
Danish National Institute of Social Research

This paper examines reasons that can be discerned for allocating additional resources to certain categories of pupil in the educational system. Initially we can note all of the categories in which the average investment per pupil is below the average for the whole educational system. This means that these groups are to be found among those receiving the shortest possible education.

It is, and has always been, the rule that differences will exist in the per capita investment in the main categories of pupils. It will therefore be reasonable to take as the starting point the general motives behind distribution of any educational resources unequally among individuals.

The general view in this consideration will be that by investing in education we aim — consciously or unconsciously — at achieving certain central social objectives. We also hold that the education system can to a certain extent be compared to a complicated productive apparatus in which the nature as well as the quantity of production factors (in this case, teachers, buildings, school psychologists, text-book material and so on) and their relative composition at a given time are of the greatest importance to the production result — here the educational result. In an assessment of the reasonableness of allocating additional educational resources to certain pupil categories, considerations as to the nature of these resources must, therefore, also be included.

Not only is the education system a complicated apparatus but its framework also shows great variation from society to society. However, there are so many common features of the education systems in western industrial societies that it is possible to let the following considerations be applicable to the whole of this field. At the same time the considerations will, however, gain in clarity if they are related to a specific education system at a certain moment. Thus, in what follows the frame of reference will be the Danish education system which perhaps, very roughly categorised, can be characterised as something in between the Scandinavian and the Central European education 'model'. Incidentally, some of the central problems in this education system have recently been described in an introduction to long-term planning in Denmark. This is available in English.[1]

Rationales for disbursing educational resources unequally

Introduction

In all established education systems educational resources are distributed unequally among different categories of young people. For example, it will appear from statements for 1977–78,[2] see table 6.1, that in Denmark the total public expenditure on young people who take university entrance examination after completing upper secondary school, is Kr.56,000 per pupil, while the expenditure on those who take the primary school teacher examination is Kr.109,000, and that it runs into Kr.1,050,000 per graduate for those who obtain a degree in natural science. Owing to differences in the social recruitment for various types of education within higher education where young people from the working class are under-represented, these figures are at the same time rough indicators of the redistribution via public finance of funds from the less well-off to the better-off population groups which takes place through the educational sector.

However, it is not only differences from one individual to another in the duration of their educational career which result in these disparities. The annual public expenditure per pupil also shows very great differences between various types of education at the same level. To give an example, the annual expenditure per pupil in the upper secondary school and on higher preparatory courses was Kr.18,000, on apprentices within trade and commerce Kr.3,000, and on students receiving basic vocational education aimed at the iron and metal trade Kr.13,000.

It goes without saying that all these figures are average figures, and considerable variation in the expenditure per pupil can also be shown within education which is both at the same level and of the same type. A more recent Danish study[3] of the conditions of primary school pupils in two municipalities, both situated in the Greater Copenhagen

Table 6.1
Current expenditure per student and per successful student
for selected educations, 1977—78
(Kr.1,000)

	Annual current expenditure per student	Total current expenditure per successful student*
Nursery school class — 10th class	10	108
Upper secondary school	18	56
Apprentices in trade and commerce	3	9
Apprentices in metal trades	6	24
Basic vocational educations (efg) in metal trades	13	60
Kindergarten and youth centre teachers	16	55
School teachers	22	109
Engineers (at technical schools)	50	220
Engineers (at academic schools)	40	190
Engineers (at technical university)	72	530
Dentists	79	460
Pharmacists	42	300
Veterinarians, etc.	74	560
Theologians	17	290
Social Sciences	10	105
Arts, Copenhagen University	11	380
Arts, Arhus University	11	210
Medicine, including clinical training	48	481
Natural science	46	1050

*Annual current expenditure per student, multiplied by the average number of years spent on the particular education, divided by the success rate (the share accounted for by those who complete the education).

Source: *Enhedsomkostninger i uddannelsessystemet 1976—77 og 1977—78, Uddanelsesanalyser 1979, no.2, Undervisningsministeriets økonomisk-statistiske konsulent.*

area, thus shows that in 1977 the expenditure per primary school pupil was Kr.13,429 in one municipality (Ishøj) and in the other (Søllerød) Kr.22,813 (table 6.2).

The most interesting feature of these figures is probably that Søllerød is a municipality with a population composition of mainly salaried employees and large-scale self-employed persons who, besides, have a high average income, while Ishøj has a much higher proportion of workers, a relatively low average income per inhabitant and also a

Table 6.2
Expenditure per pupil in Ishøj and Søllerød 1974—77
(kroner)

Amount per pupil	1974—75[1]	1975—76[1]	1976—77[1]	1977[2]
Ishøj				
Primary school	4,271	8,490	9,505	12,735
Leisure-time education	316	584	619	694
Total amount per pupil	4,587	9,074	10,124	13,429
Søllerød				
Primary school	8,426	15,316	16,105	20,319
Leisure-time education	686	987	1,029	2,494
Total amount per pupil	9,112	16,303	17,134	22,813

1 Net figures
2 Gross figures

Source: Liselotte Taarup and Else Hammerich: *Graenser for faellesskab* (Limits to community). *Unge Paedagoger*, Copenhagen 1979.

large element of foreign workers. These are selected examples of the existing inequality in the distribution of educational resources. In the following paragraphs we shall look at reasons normally underlying this unequal distribution.

Different kinds of rationales.
A suggestion for systematisation

The above examples should immediately give us a clue about some of the reasons. That society all in all invests many times more in, for example, a natural scientist than a primary school teacher is first and foremost connected with the division of labour in society, which means that different people perform different work functions. Thus the same people do not circulate among the different functions. However utopian this may be, it makes it clear in any case that, other things being equal, a circulating division of labour would presuppose equally great investments per individual, while the existing division of labour must necessarily result in inequality in the distribution of resources.

However, the example also illustrates two other reasons, reason number one being that, at a given time, society will work at a certain technological level — chosen more or less voluntarily. The maintenance and further development of this technology presuppose a rather cost-consuming instruction of youth in the prerequisites and mode of operation of this technology. Secondly, the example illustrates that the particular political system has chosen a specific distribution of activities between the public and private sector, so that central and local educational authorities will undertake the financing of a large proportion of the advanced — and as is well-known also the basic — theoretical qualification of labour.

As concerns the example showing differences in the expenditure on primary school education per pupil in two different municipalities, this indicates that the reasons for an unequal distribution of resources can be that the particular society puts a high value on the local (decentral) right of decision. It should, however, be added in this connection that the central authorities have at the same time ensured that the expenditure per pupil cannot be less than an amount which secures a certain minimum standard. The principal reason for this is the desire to restrict the differences between pupils from different geographical areas of the country in regard to basic educational skills and possibilities of climbing up the social ladder. This reason can be termed social equalisation.

The last-mentioned reason can also be said to apply when pupils who have educational difficulties are referred to special education. Thereby the annual expenditure on the schooling of these pupils will exceed the cost of the instruction provided for the other pupils, but as a rule the total expenditure on such pupils will not become greater as this will, in particular, depend on the total length of the individual pupil's education. However, one should be aware that the reason for such measures can equally well be that, by segregating those who adjust less well, the educational opportunities of the other pupils are supposed to be improved — in other words a reason assuming more the character of achieving an educational elite.

The above discussion points to some, at any rate, of the rationales for the unequal distribution of resources which make themselves felt at the central societal level. They may possibly be systematised in rationales applying to the maintenance of the economic system securing economic growth (division of labour and technology), maintenance of the political system (decentralisation and specific division of activities between the public and the private sector) and the securing of a certain social equalisation (centrally fixed minimum standards and possibly special education).

These central main objectives of an economic, political and social character, however, do not pinpoint all the rationales which are of importance to the actual cost differentiation. In practice, educational policy is controlled by agents at a societal intermediary level, that is, the institutions which are to implement the central objectives.[4] In the case of Denmark, primary school education, for example, is controlled partly by municipalities and partly by the Ministry of Education, and upper secondary education by the Ministry of Education, while vocational education at the same age level is in practice controlled by labour market organisations, and higher education by the Ministry of Education.

Thereby at least two further conditions will be co-determinants of the cost differentiation. In the first place, the internal 'power fights' between various parts of the state apparatus for a share of public resources which manifest themselves in expert valuations of what is a necessary minimum standard — for example in regard to average class size, number and nature of necessary subjects, number of lessons per week in each subject and so on. Secondly, we are presented here with conceptions of what is the necessary training for teachers and thus their relative wage level. For example, the wage level is higher for upper secondary school teachers than for primary school teachers because, among other things, it has been decided to educate them at different institutions. Yet these conditions cannot only be related to the mode of operation of the state apparatus as, obviously, they are also connected with the policies pursued by the trade organisations.

But also at the micro-level of the educational sector (that is, decisions made by teachers and administrators at the individual schools) supplementary rationales with important bearing on the resource distribution among the pupils make themselves felt. Decisions made at this level will, for example, be which and how many pupils are to be referred to special education, and which and how many pupils shall be encouraged to stay on in the education system after the statutory leaving age. Within the framework and possibilities of the system, the nature of these decisions can to a certain extent be related to the teachers' conception of what is to be understood by 'clever' and what is to be understood by 'adjustable pupils', and perhaps the individual teacher's more or less conscious conception of how large a proportion of a given age group — irrespective of absolute size — is considered qualified for transfer to the upper secondary school.[5] Thus we deal here with more traditional rationales concerning the conception of a bright and a dull pupil.[6] As a main rule, these rationales will not have any impact on the differences in the fixed average expenditure norms for different categories of pupils. But they will influence the actual average expenditure level and the total distribution pattern of the expenditure, because these rationales will have an effect on the decision of the number of pupils to be referred to each category.

To the central societal rationales of an economic, political and social nature we must thus add rationales from the state apparatus and trade organisations concerning standard norms in the educational process. Moreover, we must add rationales concerning the reasonable earnings of different teaching staff and, from the individual teachers, the conception of which and how many pupils are at a certain qualification level.

These considerations lead to a picture of the nucleus of an anatomy of rationales for the current distribution of educational resources as outlined in Statement 1 (where some explanatory phrases have been added to indicate the multivarious processes underlying the individual rationales).

Statement 1

Societal level		Rationales
Central societal level	Economic	(preservation of the existing economic system, economic growth)
	Political	(decentralisation, distribution of activities between the public and the private sector)
	Social equalisation	(or care for the élite)
'Implementing' intermediary level	Vocational norm requirements etc.	(caused by, among other things, efforts of autonomy in the state apparatus, traditional conceptions of necessary teaching requirements and, obviously, more 'objective' basic requirements)
	Particular interests of trade organisations	(wage differentiation)
Micro-level	Selection decisions, assessment (awarding of marks)	(stereotypes concerning pupil performance and, obviously, more 'objective' evaluations)

This, as already said, is only a nucleus; nor are all the processes instanced equally relevant to all education systems or at any one time. On the other hand, I maintain that here we have pinpointed some of the more central rationales.

It should be added, at the same time, that the anatomy must be supplemented with a further two dimensions which are only indirectly indicated in the Statement. First, that some of the rationales are open and others hidden. In reality this will often be a distinction between formal and real rationales. For example, vocational norm requirements at the societal intermediary level can be characterised as both open and formal rationales, whereas efforts of autonomy in various parts of the state apparatus correspond to rationales which are at the same time hidden and real.

The second supplementary dimension concerns current and historical rationales. Some reasons for the allocation of resources can be regarded as functional in the light of the current conditions of the given society. Others are dysfunctional and simply an expression of a timelag in the conception of society's mode of function and in the conception of value as a result, among other things, of the fact that teachers, for example, have received their training in a different historical period.

Most of the economic rationales are supposedly an example of functional rationales, and teachers' stereotypes concerning pupil performance must be an example of dysfunctional rationales.

Rationales for providing additional resources for special populations

Introduction

The above anatomy should assist us in pinpointing rationales that will be valid if the problem is to obtain additional resources for specific pupil categories. The starting point here is that these categories must be the ones that manage less well in the education system. Moreover, it is assumed — at any rate for the time being — that these pupils' school performance can be changed in a positive direction through the allocation of additional resources for their education.

The central social rationales for such a financial disposition in education policy can be localised to rationales of a social and economic character. The social rationales in this context can be specified as the desire to equalise differences in educational opportunity between pupil categories while, supposedly, the economic rationales are first and foremost based on the classical approach to the problem of utilisation of the 'intelligence reserve'.

Concerning the rationales at the societal intermediary level and at the micro-level, as outlined in the Statement, they will hardly, as a main rule, support measures in the nature of increased resources for categories doing less well at school. On the contrary, they must be considered rationales which in this respect will counteract the aforementioned central rationales.

From a realistic point of view, measures in the nature of increased resources for the categories we have in mind will not be a question of removing all — in regard to additional resources — counteracting rationales from the educational sector, but a question of a shift in the relative weight of the individual rationales.

However, such an educational policy presupposes that the above observations about the conditions of the special groups become much more specific. In particular it seems evident that it is not satisfactory to answer the question of why some categories should have additional resources without first answering the question of 'what categories' they are, and next how they are going to receive these resources. The reasons adduced for the last question are simply that the specific use of the additional resources must depend entirely on what category one has in mind. To this should be added that the question of 'why' can be further diversified when we have looked more closely at the composition of the special groups.

In the following discussion I will therefore try to answer these three questions: what categories; why should they receive additional resources and how should the resources be allocated?

What categories?

All our experience shows that society in interaction with the education system will create special groups in the sense that they benefit only to a small extent from schooling. If we are going to pinpoint these groups, it seems fruitful to consider the pupils at the time when they appear as input in the education system, the period during which they are in the educational process and the time at which they appear as output from the system.

Already by the time children enter the education system, there are categories among them who find themselves in a special social and cultural situation. The socialisation process in early childhood will in particular create differences between children from different social classes and geographical regions and from regions of different degrees of urbanisation, just as it will result in social differences between boys and girls.

The result of this early socialisation process first and foremost manifests itself in the fact that working-class children, and in some countries also children from industrially less developed areas of the particular society, already have a number of educational handicaps when they enter school. The degree of these handicaps will, however, to a large extent depend on how middle class-oriented and how metropolitan-oriented the particular education system is.

If one were to identify special groups at the time they enter school, this could result in a segregation into a special group of all working-class children and children from families in a corresponding material and cultural situation. It will, however, be possible to arrive at a more realistic delineation by combining several indicators of a situation threatening living conditions, for example low social class, poor housing, low income and single parent.

Let us for the sake of convenience use the term Category I for pupils at the time of entering school — when several combined indicators of living conditions show that they are in a vulnerable and exposed position.

How many children could this concern? We have grounds enough for estimating their number on the basis of the Welfare Survey carried out by the Danish National Institute of Social Research.[7] It is true that this survey covers adults between the ages of 20 and 69, however, one can look at the proportion who have children of pre-school age and select a few social indicators of the living conditions of these adults. This has been done in table 6.3 and, in particular, it should be mentioned that this table — because of the above information about the group of persons included in the survey — does not comprise the proportion of children with the particular characteristics, but the proportion of adults with children. If the starting point had been the children, the percentage rates would probably have been slightly different due to a varying average number of children in different social classes.

Table 6.3
Some social characteristics of the adult Danish population (20—69 years) who have children of pre-school age, 1976

	Per cent
Proportion falling into Social Class V (unskilled workers)	16
Proportion with poor housing standard	34
Proportion with low income	20
Proportion of single parents	4
Proportion falling into Social Class V *and* having poor housing standard	8
Proportion falling into Social Class V *and* having poor housing standard *and* low income	2
Proportion falling into Social Class V *and* having poor housing standard *and* low income *and* being single parents	0

Source: Material from the Welfare Survey by the Danish National Institute of Social Research, see Erik Jørgen Hansen et al., *Fordelingen af levekårene* (Distribution of Living Conditions), Publication no.82, Danish National Institute of Social Research, 1978.

The figures show, however, that Category I can become fairly big if one considers a single social indicator, for example housing standard, and disappear completely if one considers an accumulation of poor conditions arrived at by means of a combination of many social indicators. According to a rough estimate the just under 10 per cent who have at the same time unskilled work and a poor housing standard must have children who, with the structure of the education system, will have social and cultural handicaps when entering school.

For some of these children in Category I the succeeding educational process will compensate for the original handicaps, for others experiences in their school career will mean an accumulation of the original handicaps and, finally, the educational process will create new categories of special groups — for instance children from social environments which should not be specially predisposed to having children with educational handicaps. However, the meeting with the educational situation will nevertheless create low motivation, a feeling of not being at ease and unsatisfactory school performance for some of these children. Let us call this group whom the very educational process places in a poor — or even poorer — educational position Category II. This will consist of part of the population from Category I plus a number of new groups, while the rest of the children in Category I cope satisfactorily with the educational process.

No investigations have been carried out which directly approach the Category II problems if we keep to the Danish frame of reference used here. Yet there was a Danish investigation[8] carried out in the 1960s with the object of locating children from about 9 to 12 years of age who showed disturbances in 'personality development or social adjustment'.

The assessment of the mental state of these children was made on the basis of an assessment of their school adjustment — an assessment made by psychologists and teachers in common. The proportion of these 'problem children' out of all school children varied from just over four per cent in rural districts to just over ten per cent in Copenhagen. There were twice as many boys as girls among them. Moreover, the investigation — in which the 'problem children' were compared with a control group — showed that 'problem children' were found rather more frequently in families living under the socially and economically least favourable conditions, and not so frequently in families with the best conditions.

A follow-up investigation of the same children was made 6 years later, and it was found then that three times as many of the 'problem children' as of those in the control group had left school as early as possible.

It holds true of both categories dealt with so far that they have been segregated according to the criterion of ability to cope satisfactorily with basic education. However, it is quite decisive, both for the opportunities of the individual pupil in adult life and for economic growth in society that he/she should receive satisfactory vocational education/training. Quite a few do not, among whom first of all are those who get no vocational education/training at all. Let us call this group Category III. This category consists to a large extent of the same people as are included in Categories I and II, but it is special because it caters for the many children who cope well with basic education, but nevertheless receive no vocational education/training. This is again bound up with the fact that the objective of schooling is not identical with that of vocational education, a fact which is explained by these two lines of the educational system being controlled from different power centres in society. In the case of Denmark, the basic vocational education/

training is first and foremost controlled by the parties of the labour market, as previously mentioned.

How big is Category III and who falls into it? As far as Denmark is concerned, we know a good deal in this respect. Category III, which in Danish educational policy is called the residual group, has been described in some depth in surveys by the Danish National Institute of Social Research.[9] Briefly, the results of these surveys can be summed up as follows. The group comprises about 30 per cent of all young people born within the same year. This proportion has remained constant over a number of years, that is, from the mid-1960s to the mid-1970s. There is a larger proportion of girls than of boys — just under 40 per cent as against just over 20 per cent — and there is great social imbalance in the recruitment to this category, which is particularly pronounced in the case of girls. In 1973, 6 per cent of the girls from social class I thus fell into the residual group, as opposed to 40 per cent of the girls from social class V (table 6.4).

Table 6.4
Percentage distribution of young people in the age group 16—19 years
who were not receiving any education/training
after leaving primary school
Percentages for 1965 and 1973, by social class of parents
and sex of the young people

	I	II	III	IV	V	All social classes
Boys						
1965	5	12	25	17	35	24
1973	10	10	18	19	31	21
Girls						
1965	13	24	31	40	55	38
1973	6	18	31	41	50	37

Source: Bente Ørum, *Fra skole til erhverv*, Paper no.7, table 2.13, Danish National Institute of Social Research, Copenhagen, 1974.

We can thus conclude that the three categories dealt with here contain different groups of educationally under-privileged young people, but that at the same time they greatly overlap, as shown in figure 6.1. We can term Category I the 'socially under-privileged', Category II those 'not adjusting to school' and Category III the 'residual group not receiving any vocational education'. The group most threatened and with the poorest future possibilities is indicated by the

Socially under-privileged

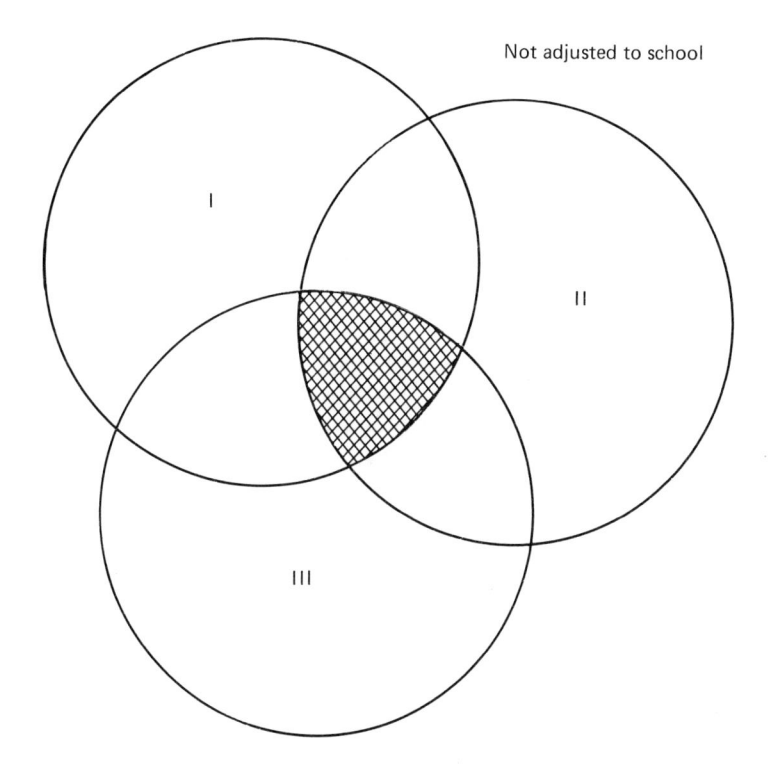

Not adjusted to school

I

II

III

Residual group not receiving
any vocational education

Figure 6.1   Special groups in the education system

shaded field — those who started as socially under-privileged, could not adjust to school and ended up in the residual group not receiving any vocational education.

Why additional resources?

By taking our anatomy of rationales as the starting point, we have already indicated the social and economic reasons for channelling additional resources to special groups, here specified as Categories I, II and III. The review of who falls into these categories points to a further specification of these rationales. For example, social rationales are a question of compensating for poor conditions of upbringing — that is to say for example, poor housing, poor hygiene, low income, an environment not stimulating the acquisition of knowledge — compensations which the education system, depending on the level of development, has certain possibilities of providing. It is evident that the reasons for these rationales are the desire to create a society fit for all human beings, but they are also justifiable solely on the grounds that a reduction of these handicaps can increase the effectiveness of the education process. The reasons for this improvement of effectiveness can in turn be the general socio-economic rationale. Here one should bear in mind, however, that only in the long term may they lead to an increase, combined with an equalisation, of the pupils' educational qualification. For example, it is not unlikely that — with the existing situation in trade and industry, and the prevalent forms of production — Danish economy has been directly interested in maintaining, over a number of years, a residual group of constant size as a recruitment basis for unskilled workers. Thus we have also at the central societal level counteracting rationales of an economic-political character.

Finally, this review of the special groups points to the fact that slightly more diffuse but fundamental humanistic rationales also exist, for example the securing of personality development. Rationales of this nature have always played a central part in Danish educational thinking. Traditionally, one has tried to live up to them by securing freedom — with public grants of considerable size — to run so-called free, private schools.

How should additional resources be allocated?

In considering what kinds of resource should be allocated to particularly exposed groups in the education system, it is important to distinguish between the three categories segregated above. It is true that all three will be in need of an increased pedagogical effort, but Category I, 'the socially under-privileged' seem, in addition, to be in need of a development of a number of social measures related to their schooling, for example medical and dental inspection, school meals, arrangements for the children to be looked after at the school, stays at school camps and so on. Category II, 'those not adjusting to school', will probably be in particular need of help from the school psychologist and extra teacher efforts. For Category III, 'the residual group not receiving any vocational education', we can point to an extension of the vocational guidance system.

It is characteristic of most of the above examples that they are extremely traditional and may not have much effect other than creating extra employment for teachers and other professional categories in the educational sector. This must, at any rate, be the case if the explanation for the creation of special groups in the education system is first and foremost to be looked for in the selective structure of the education system, in the school's value content and in the prevalent educational methods. To this should be added that the examples mentioned in most cases presuppose — or at any rate in practice will result in — a real segregation of pupils in need of special help. In this way the processes of segregation and stigmatising in the education system will be reinforced.

From this follows the primary importance of discussing thoroughly whether the rationales pointing to the necessity of providing additional resources to specially exposed groups are to result in the allocation of resources directly to particular pupils or indirectly in the form of changes in the educational structure, content and method. In this respect the present situation (greatly simplified) could be that the direct method is used in relation to the special groups, while the indirect method is used in favour of the educationally privileged pupils. In the basic education system educationally successful pupils will not directly receive more resources per pupil per year, but they will indirectly, as the relatively largest amount of resources is allocated to activities, arrangements and methods which are more in conformity with just their needs than the needs of the special groups.

A somewhat more effective effort for the special groups, in particular Categories I and II, would therefore be a change of school curriculum and methods aimed at greater weight on ways of thinking and forms of work which are close to working-class culture. This can probably be done by producing other forms of educational material, by giving greater attention to 'the hidden curriculum' — that which is *not* learnt as a result of the official guidance given to class teachers and writers of textbooks, but as a result of the daily routine and the behavioural forms which are encouraged and rewarded — by abandoning detached training situations, the division of the timetable into subjects and the division into lessons, and by abandoning the traditional examination and assessment (awarding of marks). However, it must be admitted at the same time that a good deal of development work is required before we know exactly how all this is to be done.

For Category III, the residual group not receiving any vocational education, there are, however, further problems which will not be solved by means of the above suggestions. The existence of a residual group is primarily connected with the fact that after the primary school stage there are simply not places of education corresponding to the number of young people born within the same year. This in turn is bound up with the fact that the control of basic vocational education in practice lies with the labour market organisations — as previously mentioned. Thereby the fixing of the number of vocational education places will be influenced by the conception of these organisations of how big an intake at different qualification levels the labour market will need with the existing technology and organisation of the work. However, experience shows that the time perspective in these conceptions is very short. Economic considerations in the longer term could very well point to more places in vocational education, but such a policy can hardly be secured unless central and local authorities in actual fact take over the control of all basic vocational education in its entire course.

Even if this does not happen, the composition of the residual group can nevertheless be changed. This could be done most effectively by systems of quota arrangements for the recruitment to vocational education, discriminating in favour of working-class pupils, girls and pupils from special regions.

These remarks quite clearly point to a preference for indirect methods when additional resources to special groups are concerned, especially because the direct methods have a built-in risk of escalating the processes of segregation and stigmatising. This does not mean that the direct methods should be consistently rejected provided that the term direct is not defined as direct to individual pupils, but direct to other units, for example individual schools or school districts. Here I think especially of town districts or parts of the country where the social composition of the population indicates that expenditure on education should simply be higher than usual if the objective of equal educational opportunity is to be promoted.

Notes and references

1   *U-90. Danish Educational Planning and Policy in a Social Context at the End of the 20th Century*, Central Council of Education, Ministry of Education, Copenhagen, 1978.

2   *Enhedsomkostninger i uddannelsessystemet 1976–77 og 1977–78* (Finance in the education system, 1976–77, 1977–78), Uddannelsesanalyser, 1979, nr.2. Undervisningsministeriets økonomisk-statistiske konsulent.
3   Liselotte Taarup and Else Hammerich, *Graenser for faellesskab* (Limits to community), Unge Paedagoger, Copenhagen, 1979.
4   The distinction between agents at three levels used here, and the importance of this distinction to the analysis of the development in education have been reviewed by Erik Jørgen Hansen in 'Some Aspects of the Total Qualification Process in Denmark since 1960', *Acta Sociologica*, Supplement, 1978.
5   This hypothesis has been developed in Erik Jørgen Hansen, 'The Problem of Equality in the Danish Educational Structure', *Acta Sociologica*, vol.16, no.4, 1973.
6   Such stereotypes seem to have been demonstrated at any rate in the case of pupils, see Torben Fridberg and Carl Nørregaard, *Uddannelsernes formidling af den sociale arv* (The social heritage handed down through education), Study no.35, Danish National Institute of Social Research, Copenhagen, 1978.
7   Erik Jørgen Hansen et al., *Fordelingen af levekårene* (Distribution of Living Conditions), no.82, vols I, II, Danish National Institute of Social Research, Copenhagen 1978.
8   Jacob Vedel-Petersen et al., *Børns opvaekstvilkår* (Children's Conditions of Upbringing), no.34, Danish National Institute of Social Research, Copenhagen, 1968; Mogens Nord-Larsen and Jacob Vedel-Petersen, *Tabere i skolen* (Losers at School), no.69, Danish National Institute of Social Research, Copenhagen 1976; Mogens Nord-Larsen, *Tabere i skolen – 7 år efter* (Losers at School – 7 years later), no.80, Danish National Institute of Social Research, Copenhagen 1977.
9   Bente Ørum, *Fra skole til erhvery* (From School to Job), paper no.7, Danish National Institute of Social Research, Copenhagen, 1974; Bente Ørum, *Uddannelsernes restgruppe* (Residual Group in Education), paper no.13, Danish National Institute of Social Research, Copenhagen, 1975.

7 Unequal resource distribution

Jean Blackburn
Australian Schools Commission

In all public education systems, students benefit unequally from resources provided. Many of the decisions which bring about this result are either so traditional that they are unexamined, or are made by professional educators within flexible budgets without being publicly visible or justified.

Over recent years, these unexamined or hidden resource allocations have been supplemented by specific public and often politically initiated direction of funds by legislatures for particular purposes or for the benefit of identified sub-populations of students. While these differentiations naturally draw greater public attention, they are indistinguishable in principle from those which have often been protected in the past from public scrutiny. Without full knowledge of both types of differentiation, it is difficult to obtain a full picture of the extent to which students differentially draw on publicly provided resources in their formal education.

One effect of specifically directed funding is increasingly to bring into the public arena the grounds on which differences in treatment of students are considered appropriate, and by whom. This interest may be expected to rise further as the rate of increase in educational spending slows and new priorities can only be followed at the expense of diverting resources from existing uses. Specifically directed funding, especially where it has to be accounted for separately to a funding authority which does not have responsibility for running school systems and is not a major funder of schools, raises operational issues which are comparatively new and which require a somewhat different analysis from that examining the justification for distributing resources unequally.

Equal and unequal resource distribution

The notion of unequal resource distribution assumes some idea of equal resource distribution from which it is a deviation. It is not entirely clear, however, what an equal distribution of resources would look like. There are three types of difficulty. The first arises from the necessary assumption that costs per student is an appropriate basis for comparison. The second refers to the time span over which resource provision will be compared, the third to what units are being compared to establish the basic equality. Restricting the count to those resources for which cash payments are made and which are made available in educational institutions ignores the differing resources of families and neighbourhoods with which institutional resources must be combined to get a total of resources applied to the education of individuals. The resources of the peer group are likewise ruled out; these may be particularly significant where students of similar background are concentrated in particular schools. The cash measurement of resources can take no account of the differing knowledge skills and dedication of teachers of comparable cost; nor can it register whether the beliefs of teachers are equally sustaining to students of differing backgrounds and attributes. Unequal costs may be a necessary condition of making roughly equal provision for students in different locations, and student allowances designed to equalise access to publicly provided educational services will affect costs per student without necessarily making provision unequal. Equal costs per student in school are imperfect indicators of equal provision, but for all practical purposes are generally used as a substitute measure.

The period over which equal provision is being considered is highly significant, since the greatest differences in public expenditure on the education of individuals are those related to length of participation in the education system. Those who stay longest have most resources made available to them, not just because of the longer period of time over which they are consuming the resources, but because of the traditional pattern of educational expenditure, according to which each successive educational stage is more expensive than the preceding one.

The units being compared to establish a base equality against which unequal provision may be identified also present problems. Equal expenditures per student across a district or region may co-exist with very great inequalities among districts or regions, as in the United

States. The greater the dependence of schools on local sources of finance, the more likely is this to be the case. The inputs of a single level of government cannot be considered in isolation in defining equality or inequality of resources. National governments often distribute their inputs into school finance unequally per head among regions in an attempt to make per pupil expenditure in schools more equal across the nation. State governments similarly may make unequal payments across districts. These differing payments are not cases of unequal resource provision, except where, having established a base of equal total per pupil expenditure from all sources, payments above it are made according to particular justifications.

When schools are the unit of comparison, and population density is not at issue in comparing them, the notion of equal resource allocation is more complex than is often assumed. Equal provision interpreted as equal expenditure per pupil, or equal provision of staff and other resources to schools of comparable size, must assume that all students will have identical treatment or that those requiring special treatment of some kind are randomly distributed among schools. But if such students are not randomly distributed in the sense of being the same proportion of students in all schools, unequal resources among schools will be needed if students classified as requiring special treatment of some kind are to have equal access to it in all locations. This approach throws new light on much so called 'positive discrimination' in favour of schools having a concentration of students of particular kinds.

Several school systems now in fact distribute resources among schools on a basis which responds to the attributes of students in them. The staff schedules operating in Winnipeg, in Lodi (California) and in Denver (Colorado) are examples which weight students according to a range of characteristics presumed to affect the intensity of teacher attention they require or demand. Several Australian school systems also now marginally vary resources to schools according to socio-economic characteristics of neighbourhood populations, and some American school districts according to the proportion of students scoring below certain levels in standardised tests. The test of equal provision has, in these cases, been transformed into one which requires unequal expenditure per pupil in order to provide appropriate treatment which is not identical for all students of comparable age. Whether this approach is any more destructive of the notion of equal resource allocation than that of the past where the main differentiations were those associated with length of schooling is a moot point.

With all these qualifications, we may assume that it is some deliberate deviation from an equal expenditure per student of comparable age and educational stage which requires justification in the present study of resource distribution.

Orientation of the education system

Differences in age specific expenditure are perhaps the most revealing indicators of the orientation of school systems, within which the claims of individual and social differences are considered. The annual cost differences per student between primary and secondary levels, between compulsory and post compulsory school years, and between tertiary education and each of the preceding years of education, perhaps say more about the values and expectations on which the education system is based than do any other types of cost differences. The wider the differences between primary and tertiary costs, the more strongly is the system geared towards the academically talented with strong home support, the less towards developing latent academic talent among socially disadvantaged groups and towards supporting all youth towards independent participation in the society, where such participation requires some threshold level of certification and of formal academic and social negotiating skills.

The per student cost differences between primary and higher education vary among countries, yet in all cases the same considerations justifying progressively higher costs as the student goes up the system presumably apply. These are the increasing weight and complexity of the material to be taught and learned and the higher salaries needed to attract teachers whose knowledge gives them access to alternative well paid employment. Other, less overt, justifications are also involved. These are historically derived, going back to the early days of public education when it was presumed that only a relatively small minority, selected by their higher social status or outstanding ability, would progress beyond elementary level. Mass education was in those days elementary education, to be provided in the cheapest possible way, and often paralleled by private education for those who could afford to pay for it. Systems which preserve wide differences between lower and higher levels of education would seem to have this presumption still written into them, even although mass secondary education is now the rule and the scale of higher education has expanded greatly. Both the higher costs at higher levels and the public funds attracted by staying for several years beyond compulsory levels result in great differences in the total amount spent on the survivors in the system as compared with early leavers. In some countries this difference is of the order of 10:1.

The scale of such differences is now being questioned. This questioning has three grounds. The first is that while the whole society benefits from the application of advanced knowledge in production, services and government, there are also social and individual costs associated with failure of a significant proportion of the population to gain certain threshold levels of academic and social competence. The second is that equality of opportunity to participate in higher levels of education is now generally accepted as requiring greater support in the early stages of learning for those whose social position is least conducive to school success. The third is that it is difficult for the school to provide viable secondary education for those whose access skills are below certain levels. High and persistent youth unemployment has given a new emphasis to the compulsory years and to the claims of early school leavers to more intensive attention during their years of schooling and to the achievement levels which it is important for them to reach.

When we turn to the narrower, but still significant, differences in expenditure between primary and secondary and between compulsory and non-compulsory secondary years, the persistence of the same historically derived justifications is also revealed. The differences vary among countries. The Swedish system stipulates smaller maximum class sizes at primary than at secondary level, but this is not the case in all systems. In all systems, moreover, the range of curriculum is narrower at primary than at secondary level, teachers have less non-contact time, fewer specialists in such areas as art and physical education are employed. Where the margin between primary and secondary student costs is wide, it can only be presumed that old beliefs that schooling for the masses should be as cheap as possible persist, along with the assumption that most students will move out of school early, with minimal levels of accomplishment, allowing proper concentration on selected survivors. Yet such assumptions have long been rejected by the provision of secondary schooling for all, and by providing it increasingly in a common comprehensive school, with delayed selection.

The tendency towards prolonged schooling is unlikely to diminish unless new institutional forms arise, because advanced societies have increasingly restricted places for the young, inexperienced and poorly qualified in productive activities. The alternative to high school retention is high levels of youth employment, with its associated financial and social costs. The school therefore has to live with early learning failure in a way which did not concern it in the past. In countries like Australia, where half the age group is out of school by age 16, the dimensions of this problem are only beginning to be recognised as attention is drawn through unemployment to the fact that the equipment which early leavers take into the adult world has received scant attention in a school system still oriented towards the minority who enter tertiary studies. If students are to stay longer in school, and the school is ill equipped for learning which does not rest heavily on the printed word, early elimination from the possibility of engaging in such learning through poorly developed access skills can create problems hard to rectify at later stages.

From a societal point of view this is important in another way. As technological advance brings increasingly capital intensive methods to a whole range of tasks in service industries as well as in manufacture and primary industry, alternative futures seem possible. Assuming that full employment on the old terms is less likely in the future than in the period recently ended, one possibility is a permanent division between paid workers and unemployed ones sustained by public payments. Another is to develop more flexible options for all in the balance of paid and unpaid activities over their working lives. This possibility, which appears to have positive merits as well as being less individually and socially destructive, is largely ruled out if the gap between low and average school achievement cannot be narrowed by improved formal achievement among the lowest fifth of school achievers, since capacity to learn on the job or to engage in job training is constrained by poor reading and number skills and by low confidence in capacity to learn. Moreover, since it is the least skilled jobs (including those involving what used to be regarded as middle level skills) which are largely replaced by machinery and electronic devices, school systems predicated on some sharp distinction between the skilled and the rest may no longer be appropriate.

It is possible to discern some common pattern in the types of special provision being made in the countries participating in this study, even accepting that the special provision is injected into school systems having different orientations, structures of governance and financial support. All countries provide extra resources for special services to the handicapped and for remedial assistance to those in regular schools and classes. All make special provision for ethnic minority groups and some for the children of migratory workers and for early school leavers. Some select relatively poor neighbourhoods for special action and resource supplements. All these provisions could be said to affect those disadvantaged in some way, either by personal attributes, low performance, family circumstances or discriminatory schooling. However, some countries also make special provision for the gifted. In the allocation of resources to selected populations, the United States is distinctive in the number of special programmes supported — national programmes alone number 120. Most countries in the study, however, have few special provisions directed at selected populations of students within the regular school, and generally operate those they do have on a basis which avoids dividing up school populations into predetermined and inflexible categories.

Justifications for special treatment on the basis of individual differences have long been rehearsed. In the case of those variously described as 'handicapped' or 'unable to benefit fully from the programme and teaching of the regular classroom', the justification is generally non-controversial, even if there is dispute about how to operate special provision and about where it should be located. Within the range of difference normally accommodated in regular schools, it is very difficult to generalise across countries and school systems regarding the nature, cost and extent of special provision. Not merely educational philosophies are in question, but the degree of public information about provision made. Concentration on specifically funded provision gives only part of the picture.

If we compare Scandinavian, American and Australian school systems, it becomes clear that the types of special provision arise out of differences in the orientation of systems. Scandinavian systems operate a uniform curriculum of a traditionally academic kind, taught in socially and functionally diverse groups to the end of compulsory schooling. Since staff schedules are also public we know that, in the Swedish case, 20 per cent of the age group are seen as requiring remedial assistance. We know little about what the range of outcomes at the end of compulsory schooling relating to these common and academic goals is, but we do know that the rationale, or intention derives from an interpretation of equality of opportunity which seeks to eliminate organisational structures discouraging to some students and to ensure that as high a proportion of the age group as possible is qualified to enter vocationally differentiated post-compulsory education.

American systems maintain high retention by enabling students of very different levels of academic achievement to continue to participate through diverse curriculum offerings and wide student choice. It is not surprising, therefore, that specific funding of various kinds aimed at asserting a common core of learning, at ensuring minimum standards of competency in basic skills at various levels, and providing supplementary instruction for the slow learning and gifted should have emerged more strongly there than in systems having less diverse goals and defining opportunity in more confined terms. Australian systems, as previously indicated, are slowly moving from being strongly academically selective, with high early drop-out rates, to more comprehensive goals and greater remedial support. As in the United States and the United Kingdom, this emphasis is bringing forth special programmes for the gifted within flexible education budgets or through specifically allocated funds.

New issues are arising in the accommodation to individual difference. Characteristics of students and organisational considerations are only two elements in the school situation. Curriculum content, the limited means explored for the development of talent, beliefs about student capacities and rigidities in instructional methods are being acknowledged as variables affecting outcomes which should also be examined. A case is being advanced for greater experimentation to establish what levels of resource supplementation might make a difference for students facing difficulties in the mastery of access skills. Some see literacy and numeracy difficulties as symptoms of wider problems of an emotional, social and motivational kind. Such a case would support experimentation with a one to one relationship with a concerned and skilled adult, who may not necessarily be a teacher, in a situation which removes competitive pressures and provides emotional support. Experimentation along these lines has been very successful in some places, as has tutoring by older students. Attention is also being drawn to the greater motivation, confidence and achievement which develops among students in situations where access skills are a by-product of engagement with an activity which produces tangible results of importance to them.

We may need to know more about what produces engagement with learning before we settle for intensive instruction of traditional kinds as the approach most likely to improve the participation of discouraged students. When we know more about the range of possibilities, their costs and effectiveness, we shall be in a better position to make rational choices about ways of approaching individual differences. This could justify, at least in the short term, the extra expense of non-traditional and high resource intensity approaches. In the long term, of course, it raises difficulties, because once we begin to define essential learning itself in ways beyond traditional academic disciplines, relating claims to each other becomes even more complex. But increased concern about those students who gain least from traditional schooling, and are even incapacitated by it, inevitably leads sooner or later to a questioning of 'outcomes' as traditionally defined. This is especially so if the interplay between individual attributes and outcomes on the one hand, and social background on the other, becomes a focus of interest.

Social difference

When we compare social groups constituted by slicing the population by income, occupational level, ethnicity, location and sex, very different patterns of educational achievement and participation are revealed. There are many different explanations of why this should be so, some concentrating on qualities of the people concerned, others on societal arrangements and aspects of educational institutions.

Traditional equality of opportunity analysis has focused primarily on social groups defined by socio-economic level; extension of the analysis to ethnic groups and to females is more recent. This extension has provided insights which advance understanding about how the school itself may discriminate against particular groups of students in positive ways, as well as by omission.

Husén[1] has distinguished three historical phases in the interpretation of equality of opportunity.[2] The first assumes that if school provision is equal, treatment uniform and financial barriers removed, the outcomes in achievement will reflect innate differences in ability, freed from constraints of social background. The second attacks structural impediments in the school system itself which early channel children into different futures, and maintains that ability is not fixed, but subject to continuing change. It favours comprehensive schooling in mixed ability groups and delayed selection. The third sees structural changes in the school as insufficient to give equal chances of success to students of all backgrounds. It calls for unequal inputs into schools in a partial attempt to compensate there for home and social environments unequally conducive to success in the school's terms, and for a broader definition of the terms of success itself. It emphasises equal outcomes across social groups and changes in school orientation and inputs in order to promote them. It also requires action beyond the school within the education system as a whole, expanding the opportunities for participation at pre- and post-school levels; and broader social changes improving the conditions of life of least advantaged groups.

The justification for action, in terms of this analysis, is an equity one. In an unequal society, and as a result of social arrangements which they have not participated in making, some children get a better home back-up for success in school than do others. Therefore the school should attempt, at least marginally, to iron out these differences by action which makes starting points more equal and through organisational structures which keep all children in the mainstream of opportunity as long as possible. Once broader definition of the terms of success comes into the picture, however, issues arise which are different in kind from those involving the removal of financial and structural barriers and providing greater school support for children of particular backgrounds.

These issues are addressed in a somewhat different type of analysis which has more recently gained currency.[3] This focuses less on home 'culture', on school resources and intensity of instruction and more directly on aspects of the school itself. It sees particular social groups as being disadvantaged by the attitudes, expectations and social understandings of teachers and by the selection and organisation into subject categories of the knowledge considered valuable by the school. It suggests that the school plays an active part in socialising students into an acceptance of social hierarchy and in its perpetuation across generations. The institutional definition of 'brightness' is seen to be narrowly related to occupations requiring academic preparation of an academic kind divorced from practice, so devaluing a wider range of competencies, characteristics and knowledge actually valued in diverse positions in the society. The expectation of a normal curve of performance as a preamble to eventual selection for higher academic pursuits leads to the acceptance of failure at all levels of the system; it is, moreover, accepted that children of some low status backgrounds will be more strongly represented among this group than children of high status backgrounds. (A recent Swedish study[4] gives support to this hypothesis, showing that among students below a given level of performance, those of high social status backgrounds were seen by teachers as being in need of remedial assistance twice as often as those of low status background.)

The failure of the school to interact with social reality as experienced and perceived by students in different social positions is also pointed to. The school may be seen as having little directly to say to the relatively poor and to economically depressed ethnic minorities if their reality is excluded from reflective examination and the connection between view of self as an individual and as a group member is not appreciated in ways which make a positive self-definition possible. Failure to bring expectations based on sex stereotypes under conscious scrutiny particularly disadvantages girls, and both sexes confronting a world very different from that of their parents.

There are thus two different approaches to equality of opportunity now running. The first stresses action in schools to equalise chances of students to enter high status occupations, irrespective of background. Its implications for resource allocation are clear, although at the operational level the resulting action may be indistinguishable from that directed at low achievers or the gifted. The second calls for school change which would both make the content of schooling more socially comprehensive and attempt to alter the attitudes of teachers and the expectations embodied in the institutional ideology. This second position has implications for the means by which more equal opportunities in the first sense may be brought about, but it is also concerned with more general propositions about the democratisation of schooling which would place academic pursuits in perspective as one avenue through which intellectual activity is related to action.

The resource implications of this position are unclear. While general school change may be the objective, extra funds to support action research in schools where low achieving, low status students are congregated, could, in the short term, be justified by it, although the objectives sought cannot be confined to those relevant to the academic competition as it is presently operated. This raises difficulties because, if different goals are being pursued through alternative action, there is no simple way of comparing needs, which must be related to the gap between some existing state and a desired end. This difficulty emerges sharply in resource allocations justified by ethnic difference, as we shall see, but it also has its relevance to special action directed towards groups identified on general socio-economic grounds. This difficulty is avoided by justifications for extra resources for schools having a high concentration of low status students which draw on both equality of opportunity perspectives. Extra resources are then justified by the need to improve the competitive position of students in standard accreditation terms, using curriculum and institutional change as a means of doing this as well as of advancing broader aims related to the democratisation of schooling.

Groups identified on a socio-economic basis

It is recognised that a complex of social indicators, rather than any single one, best identifies, on social grounds, those students likely to be least well sustained in home and school in ways which positively assist educational success. But since such statistical associations have no predictive power for individuals, and because it is in any case offensive to identify students for special treatment on such grounds as parental education and occupation, family income or structure, special funding or provision is usually directed to schools or regions having a concentration of students from similar low social status backgrounds. Some general justifications for doing this may be enumerated. The first is a simple social justice one, which has nothing to do with school performance. It is that where social arrangements give children less access to resources in home and neighbourhood than are available to the mass of children in their upbringing and education in the broadest sense, the society should ensure that the provision it makes through the school is better than average. Where parents are least able to afford musical instruction, to take one example, then there is a good argument for giving priority to its introduction in schools where children of such parents are concentrated. The same would apply to such things as excursions, bush holidays or visits to the city, as the case may be.

Following this argument is the need which exists to make up for the social discrimination of the past where schools in poorer neighbourhoods have often been less well provided for, calling for positive discrimination in the present. Where families subject to greatest economic pressures are concentrated, there will often be a need for the school either to extend its normal provisions or to be closely associated with a welfare or referral network which can be available to families. Schools in poorer areas are often cut off from parents and they wrongly assume that the parents are indifferent to their child's school progress. There may be a need for extra resources to bring families and school into closer interaction for the benefit of the child and, perhaps more particularly, so that teachers may learn about social realities of which they have little direct experience and knowledge of which is essential for effective teaching.

The most common arguments, however, relate to the association between home background and success in school-related tasks. Preference in funding for schools in poorer communities is normally some response to this. The argument is particularly strong if it can be demonstrated that concentrations of children of like background have an effect on learning over and above that of the family considered in isolation. The Swedish study already referred to, covering a sample of children who entered the schools in 1972, reaffirms this proposition, once held to be true, but more recently contested. It shows children of low social status backgrounds perform on average less well in schools or classes where they are concentrated than is the case where the composition of the student body is more heterogeneous. It also points to other effects of concentration in schools of children of similar background. It sees the spatial segregation of social groups as reinforcing experiences of belonging to a subordinate or superior group, as leaving the segregated groups ignorant or uncertain of the conditions of other groups, and so having inadequate knowledge of the society and differing in their perceptions of their own power to influence it.

Unless there is pronounced spatial segregation of the population by social level, arguments favouring extra resources to some schools on the basis of their social composition are considerably weakened and special provision which might be said to be attending to the effects of social condition on school learning are more likely to be based on arguments relating to low performance or social maladjustment of some kind at the individual level. There is some ambiguity about whether social indicators are merely proxies for low average school performance, or whether they relate to broader social grounds favouring positive discrimination and drawing attention to possible social bias in the presumptions and processes of schools.

To illustrate the variety of rationales which may be associated with ostensibly similar action, we may look briefly at funding directed at low income populations. Canada, for example, makes stimulation grants to school boards on the basis of the percentage of population in them on public welfare payments, having an income below a certain level, having a first language other than French or English and on the number of public housing units per 1,000 persons. The United Kingdom, using similar measures, pays a special supplement to teachers in defined areas and, through the Inner Urban Programme, supports integrated social action (of which educational action, especially at pre-school level, is a part) in an effort to improve the quality of life and the life chances of children there. The Australian Disadvantaged Schools Program makes extra funds available, on certain conditions, to schools identified on socio-economic criteria. The United States, through a number of programmes, of which Title I of the Elementary and Secondary Education Act is by far the largest, makes extra funds available to schools and school districts serving poorer populations. Concern that the school system has not succeeded in serving poorer populations as well as more affluent ones, and social justice considerations generally underlie all these provisions. But in order to illustrate the different rationales which may support such apparently similar provisions, Title I and the Australian Disadvantaged Schools Program will be looked at in more detail.

Title I began in 1965 as part of the Johnson era War on Poverty. It has been alternatively described as the poor conscience of white America responding to the very limited social mobility prospects of American blacks, and as a means of breaking the cycle of poverty through education. Although the federal government provides only some eight per cent of all expenditure on public schools, the greater part of this contribution comes to schools through Title I, and all of it through categorical grants. Federal policies thus discriminate in favour of poorer communities. But although the funds are in total considerable, they fall far short of bridging the wide disparities in expenditure per pupil which continue to exist among districts and regions unequal in wealth. The funds in the Australian Disadvantaged Schools Program average only some $50 per student in eligible schools as against $300–$400 which comes through Title I to eligible students in eligible schools. But the Australian funds add to an expenditure per student by tradition roughly equal with State public systems, minor differences among which have themselves been equalised through federal payments. The Australian programme thus represents positive discrimination in a sense which the American does not, if total expenditure per student is compared across the nation.

After Title I funds have been distributed among districts on the basis of percentages of low income families in them, they are directed towards services to students identified within schools on the basis of achievement scores in standardised tests which fall below the median of a wider group. The Australian programme is a whole school one which does not distinguish externally among students in the school. In practice, and largely because of the perceived need for close federal supervision to ensure that Title I funds benefit only those students whom Congress had intended to benefit, the overwhelming proportion of Title I funds is spent on remedial assistance during the early years of schooling to low achieving students in poorer districts, given in most States in groups pulled out of the regular class. The rationale for this approach (as distinct from operational imperatives) is that if the school performance of students in poorer neighbourhoods could be improved early in their school lives, the cycle of poverty, repeated across generations, could be broken through improved school success.

The Australian programme, on the other hand, is low-keyed in justifications affecting income distribution and has broad, somewhat vaguely defined objectives which eligible school communities interpret in their own situations. Schools are selected for participation on criteria which at federal level are based on a complex of socio-economic measures applied to neighbourhood populations, but which systems may vary within the general philosophy of the programme. (The selection of schools has proved contentious in some systems, indicating that spatial segregation of social groups may not be as pronounced as federal policies assume.) Eligible schools do not automatically receive additional funds. Staff, involving parents as far as possible, are required to analyse what the school is presently doing and to devise plans for improving it, bearing the needs of the community served in mind. The resulting action funded is diverse, but must be justified in terms of the programme's three objectives — more effective learning, more meaningful and enjoyable schooling and improved school community interaction. Funding varies according to the judgement of representative systems or regional committees according to their estimate of the quality of proposals made. The programme is thus one of general school improvement, based on the belief that the commitment of people who have to operate changes will be greater if they themselves devise them on the basis of their own analysis of the situation, and on the contention that there are no known generalisable ways of improving the effectiveness and relevance of schooling in poorer communities, since the correlation between social background and school achievement leaves explanations for it open. The programme thus has echoes of the second approach to equality of opportunity, calling on school personnel to examine operating assumptions and to focus change on the school rather than continuing to 'blame' families for the poorer outcomes of some schools.

Different social and pedagogical assumptions underlie the two programmes, both of which are directed at improved schooling for poorer populations and are supported by national funds. The Australian programme leaves open a number of crucial issues about which the American one seems to assume that closure has been reached. The financial and structural situation in which the two programmes operate is very different. Significant features of their operation may be attributed to this, without regard to theoretical structures at all. The American programme is moving through more levels of school governance and financial support than is the Australian, which can in turn afford to be more open and less prescriptive in dealing with six public systems as against the 14,000-odd districts which draw funds under Title I. The constitutional position also affects what is possible from the national level, the situation here being more circumscribed in the United States than in Australia. Comparison of the two programmes is instructive, providing a heavy caution against trying to generalise too far at the theoretical level about rationales for what is ostensibly the same action even in two countries.

Ethnic minority groups

While socio-economic differences are the most pervasive social ones affecting school success, and are in many ways the most difficult from the point of view of designing action, ethnic minority groups are generally accepted as being a social classification requiring special provision.

Among ethnic minority groups some distinction needs to be made between the claims of indigenous groups whose way of life has been largely destroyed by conquest and whose economic position is now severely depressed (Australian Aborigines and American Indians) and involuntary immigrants imported as cheap labour (American Blacks) on the one hand, and recent and voluntary immigrants on the other. The claims of the two first groups may be seen as involving reparation for historical injustice, justifying special action of a distinctive kind and supporting a revival of pride in group affiliation.

Special provision for teaching the dominant language to students raised primarily in another language is clearly desirable to give most such students a fair chance of success in schools and other social institutions conducted in what is, for them, a second language. If it can be shown that initial bilingual instruction assists the mastery of the dominant language or that cognitive development in the second language is constrained by its level of development in the first, the equity case may extend to provision going well beyond special assistance in learning the second language. The minimisation of conflict between school and home through special provision to improve home/school contact, and action in the school to make the minority culture officially visible there in various ways, may all also be justified on equity grounds.

Establishing the limits of this equity claim presents problems. Does it extend to special provision throughout the student's whole school life, or is its duration limited either in time or by the demonstration that certain levels of proficiency in the second language have been reached? The population may be sliced in many different ways to produce groups whose levels of school success may be compared. Socio-economic categorisation may, for example, show that students raised in languages other than the dominant one perform no worse than their dominant language counterparts when matched on socio-economic grounds. Which categorisation then takes precedence on equity grounds? It is clear that the claims of native speakers and second language learners requiring special assistance must at some stage be reconciled.

There are justifications for special provision for ethnic minority groups in school which go beyond overcoming handicaps in relation to the dominant language. Although both in Sweden and the United States school instruction is given in over fifty languages, the justification in each case is different. The American justification is overwhelmingly an equity one — to give access to the cultural mainstream, with all its implications for social mobility. Swedish provision also has this justification, but it also speaks of advancing 'equality, freedom of choice and partnership' in an attempt to build an international society.

Special provision, confined to ethnic minority group members, which has as its aim the preservation of home culture and the capacity to operate in two cultures, raises special issues. Ethnicity is only one aspect of cultural difference, albeit one in which language plays a significant role. Other aspects of cultural variety which might be seen as having significance for school provision are non-standard forms of the dominant language, belief and value systems, different ways of life facilitated and constrained by income differences and varying views parents hold about how they want their children educated. When the preservation of ethnic variety is placed in this broader context, difficult issues about the definition of culture and about the forms of pluralism which should be reinforced by the school arise. Some decision then has to be made about whether the schools should build on common aspects of varying cultures, and extend knowledge and tolerance of their differences, or regard sub-cultures as distinctive entities, with little interpenetration and overlap.

Girls

Girls participate less in post school education than do boys and in some countries leave school earlier. They participate hardly at all in technical education which is an important avenue of further development for boys who leave school relatively early. Girls from families of low socio-economic level are a more serious concern than those raised at higher levels in the social scale. The latter are more aware of options because they see females with whom they are able to identify taking higher education and, increasingly, moving into responsible professional and managerial jobs.

Education is often only valued as a means of access to paid employment. Girls who are equivocal about the importance of paid work in their lives and who observe that females with whom they identify are largely confined to low paid work requiring little education, may see no point in extended schooling. This is likely to be especially so if there has been little reflection in schools of the greatly changed pattern of women's lives, or consideration of the alternation of paid and unpaid work over a lifetime. Action taken in schools to make them more congruent with changes in the social roles of the sexes has as its objective the widening of options and the promotion of conscious choices, rather than the unconscious assimilation of sex stereotypes.

The removal of distinctive curricular offerings for the sexes and of curricular content portraying women in reactive rather than in proactive roles, is typical of some action supported by special grants. More positively, attempts are made to make women visible in societies both past and present, in order to assist both sexes to appreciate the significance of sex based divisions of labour in home and workforce. Some action is directed at encouraging girls to be more confident, both as people and as students of maths and science and to consider employment which females do not commonly enter. Special funding is not typically directed towards girls as such, but to school changes promoting sex equality.

All special provision justified on a social group basis raises issues about whether the long-term objective is to change all schools in ways which expose all students to the variety of realities which make up the society, or to promote special benefits for the group in question. Where inequalities are particularly glaring, or social concern about them particularly strong, initial action is likely to be directed towards the group, because general change in schools is slow and school generations short lived.

Specifically directed funding

Where the policies of education systems, and resource allocations within them, are highly centralised and regulated in a detailed way by legislatures, funding for specific purposes is easier to co-ordinate with general policies. Where both political and educational structures are highly complex, a situation of which the United States is an extreme example, specific funding is likely to be directed into school systems from a number of sources, further complicated in this case by legal decisions making particular actions mandatory for school systems, whether accompanied by special funds or not.[5] In the Australian case, the Commonwealth Government is the sole source of specific funding directed into six public systems operated and predominantly financed by the States. While these differences significantly affect the conditions governing grants to schools, the justifications for specific funding may be considered independently of them.

Beyond payments to students, which do not affect the service itself, most specific funding is designed to effect changes for students in schools. Whether the target group is girls, poorer students, ethnically different students, low achieving or gifted ones, specific funding may be seen as a means of bringing about changes which will have benefits for the group concerned, both in their formal schooling and in their life options. It may, however, also be looked at in another way, as being directed at the relationship between the school system, other social institutions and wider social purposes. The school system, for example, may be so mono-culturally oriented as to inhibit the development of a multi-ethnic society, even though the ethnic composition of the population is diverse, and political policies are opposed to the destruction of ethnic bonds. In providing programmes it considers appropriate to individual students, the school system may be insufficiently sensitive to the individual and social effects of wide achievement gaps among students moving out into the world, and of the penalties attached to particularly low performance. It may be operating on outdated assumptions regarding sex roles, or its priorities may be so strongly academically oriented as to contribute indirectly to a shortage of skilled people in industry.

From either of these perspectives, specific funding may usefully be looked at as a mechanism for bringing about school change. Like any other complex organisation, school systems operate according to their own internal dynamics. It is therefore very difficult to alter the operational assumptions on which they have been built. Even minor changes of direction require effort sustained over relatively long periods of time; people have different beliefs and capacities which cannot be changed by fiat, and which inevitably influence what happens in classrooms, whatever official policy may be. If changes are desired, people must be persuaded or induced by incentives of some kind to make them. These incentives may be of several kinds, including professional acclaim, greater job satisfaction, promotion, or other ways of conferring approval. Money may provide a fast moving incentive, especially if it encourages people to face a situation they may previously have overlooked and engages their commitment to seeking out means of effective action by encouraging experimentation and leaving decisions substantially to people at school level who have to operate them.

Very specific conditions attached to special funding are irksome to people in education systems and may have negative unintended consequences. Such funding also, however, often increases the degree of freedom of people at the local level to respond to challenges and to take action which they also accept as desirable. Where the conditions are seen as unduly restrictive of local judgement and initiative, pressures usually mount for giving the schools concerned greater flexibility in the means they use to promote the desired result. This now appears to be happening in the case of Title I grants in the United States. Very little is known about the most effective delivery mechanisms which link intention and outcome. This is the case, not just for special funds, but for educational provision as a whole. Specific funding may provide opportunities for seeking out more effective mechanisms because its patterns of delivery are more easily varied.

Without special funds, the particular needs of groups such as ethnic minority students are frequently overlooked among the competing claims on funds within systems. There is considerable evidence that response of school systems to these and other needs has followed political initiative in the provision of funds, rather than being initiated by school systems themselves.[6]

Specific funding more easily allows experimentation to establish the level of resources which will make a difference in desired directions. It may also trigger off changes in an experimental way which come to be seen as having significance for all schools. This has been the case in The Disadvantaged Schools Program in Australia which has proved an effective way of engaging the commitment of school communities to school improvement and has enabled experimentation with many new approaches in ways which would have been difficult without it. The result is that there are now pressures to extend to all schools the same possibilities for taking action designed by the school community itself. The Californian School Improvement Program, by making funds above a base level to all schools dependent on the kinds of processes which the Disadvantaged Schools Program requires, applies the same method over a wider canvas.

From the point of view of schools and school systems, the bringing together of many different parcels of money into a coherent programme benefiting students undoubtedly presents problems, especially if each is subject to separate accountability and evaluation requirements. Specific funding carries dangers if it is directed towards results which fragment school objectives, singling out limited ones for special attention. It may also encourage the view that there is some necessary and direct relationship between money and easily measurable outcomes. If it requires that students within the school be classified in some predetermined way and stipulates what treatment should be applied to them, there may also be legitimate objections to it. These possible negative effects are strongly related to the conditions attached to funds, rather than to their existence. While from the point of view of the school it may be preferable to have total resources loaded in some ways related to student characteristics, leaving it free to design integrated action within publicly directed priorities, this possibility must depend on the degree of trust existing between funders and operators. It also depends, of course, on the degree to which politicians desire to have distinctive action identified as resulting from funding which they have legislated.

Notes and references

1   Torsten Husén, *Social Influences on Educational Attainment*, CERI/OECD, Paris, 1975.
2   For a somewhat satirical translation of Husén's classification into theological terms, see Guy Neave, *Trends in Research on Equality of Opportunity*, Mimeograph, Institute of Education, European Cultural Foundation, Paris, September 1978.
3   For a survey of this change in emphasis, see the editors' Introduction to Jerome Karabel and A.H. Halsey (eds), *Power and Ideology in Education*, New York, Oxford University Press, 1977.
4   *Social Segregation in Comprehensive Schools in Sweden*, Gören Arnman et al., School Research Newsletter, February 1979.
5   For an analysis of the complexities of sources of funding and decision affecting schools, see David K. Cohen, 'Reforming School Policies', *Harvard Educational Review*, vol.48, no.4, November 1978, pp. 429–47.
6   Jean I. Martin, 'The Education of Migrant Children in Australia 1945–1975' in Charles A. Price and Jean I. Martin (eds), *Australian Immigration*, a bibliography and digest, pt 2, no.3, 1975, Australian National University Press, 1976. This documents the proposition in relation to Australia.

8 Educational autonomy for special populations: Canadian experience

Edward N. McKeown
Toronto Board of Education, Ontario, Canada

The provision of specific or supplementary educational resources for special populations in the City of Toronto and throughout the Province of Ontario is usually determined by groups or institutions other than the special populations directly concerned. In spite of some strongly held positions that these provisions are the result of morality, equity or natural justice, the underlying basis for these provisions is really power. Who has it? What are the priorities of the powerful? What influence do special populations have on these decision-makers who wield this power? As the then Ontario Minister of Education stated to the Legislature, the provision of special education services to exceptional students in school systems through the province is related to, 'the particular attitudes and philosophy (of the school board) toward special education; the amount of money that has to be raised locally to put with the money we provide, and where it (the school board) places special education as a priority against other priorities' (Legislature of Ontario Debates, 10 May 1978). Given this kind of statement, the key questions are how much the provision of services for special populations can be and should be influenced by the special populations themselves?

In trying to answer these questions, specific reference will be made to programmes for four special populations which are currently accorded high priority by the Toronto Board of Education:

1	Special education	— programmes for exceptional students, particularly for the deaf
2	Inner-city	— programmes for students who are economically and/or culturally disadvantaged
3	English as a second language	— programmes for students whose first language is other than English
4	Heritage languages	— programmes in which elementary school students learn a language other than English or French — usually their native tongue

Special education

Special education involves a wide variety of teaching programmes designed for exceptional students attending Toronto elementary (junior kindergarten — grade 8) and secondary (grades 9—13) schools. These programmes consist of self-contained classes, resource and learning centres and individual or group instruction on a withdrawal or itinerant basis. All programmes are open-ended and the progress of every student is evaluated at regular intervals.

All such programmes are operated by school boards under the authority of The Education Act, 1974, Section 147(1) — 38, which says, 'A board may establish, subject to the regulations, special education programmes to provide special education services for children who require such services'. The provincial government is currently considering the introduction of an amendment which would change this to read, 'A board shall, in accordance with the Regulations . . . provide for its exceptional pupils adequate special education programmes and services'. The Regulations mentioned in both versions deal with such things as class size, placement and review committees and requirements for admission to specific programmes.

There is considerable controversy about the exact intent of the proposed change but the Ministry of Education insists it is not 'mandatory special education' as the term is used in the United States. Rather it is intended to require school boards to provide *some* special education as opposed to *no* special education and is primarily designed to deal with school boards which have chosen not to provide special services for their exceptional pupils. The major difference is that the proposal does not incorporate any enforcement provision either fiscal or legal.

From the foregoing, it is clear that the responsibility for the provision of special education services is a legislated responsibility for school boards, or in some specific cases, for the province itself. This legislated responsibility carries with it the necessary power to hire teachers and support staff, provide accommodation, furniture, equipment, supplies, transportation and so on, and the related ability to raise the necessary funds. (In Ontario a school board sets its own budget and the municipal governor concerned *shall* levy the necessary taxes: Education Act, Section 217.)

School boards throughout the Province make their decision about the level of special education service they will provide in various ways. At the one extreme will be boards where the decision is made solely on the basis of staff advice and discussion at committee or board meetings, while at the other extreme will be boards which will go to great lengths to get as much input as possible from as many sources as possible, including the special population concerned or more likely the parents of that special population. Boards operating in the former style essentially are being paternalistic and may pay little attention to the wishes of the parents. As one moves across the spectrum, parental involvement increases but even the board that provides the greatest opportunities for involvement is not really sharing power nor providing true autonomy for the special population. After all the involvement, discussions and consultation are over, the final decision-making power still rests with the school board and the only recourse for any special population which disagrees with the decisions of the board is to lobby trustees to change their minds or to lobby at the provincial level for a legislative change of mind.

Although it is a long way from 'autonomy', the activities of the Toronto Board's Work Group on Special Education provides a good example of an open process which provided ample opportunities for representatives of various special populations to be heard and, through being heard, have an opportunity to influence the decisions that were to be made. This work group was established by the Board in January 1977 on the following basis:

Terms of Reference:

1 Historical background of Special Education in Toronto
2 A review of the current literature concerning special education
3 Current aspects of special education to be reviewed:
   (a) staffing and administration, including decentralisation thereof
   (b) student selection, delivery of service and evaluation
   (c) supervision
   (d) professional development
   (e) interrelationships
   (f) current legislation

4 The work group should receive written and oral submissions from school and non-school personnel, Ontario Secondary School Teachers' Federation, Toronto Teachers' Federation, Elementary and Secondary School Principals' Associations, and other employee groups, trustees, Toronto Home and School Council, Association for Children with Learning Disabilities, Voice, and other interested groups, parent groups and individuals.

Composition:

That the work group consist of Trustees Frasca, Holmes, Maher, McDowell (Chairman), Meagher, Menzies and Spencer; a liaison person to assist the work group, to be appointed by the Director of Education; two persons to be appointed by the Director of Education as interim appointees to act as advisors to the work group from time to time as required (one each from the Departments of Special Education and Student Services), and one Research Assistant to be appointed later. In addition, it is proposed that the work group have the power to co-opt additional members as required.

After two years of activity, the work group published a draft report which contained the following description in its introduction:

The work group has been meeting for twenty-three months. The members of the work group visited special education programmes in many elementary and secondary schools during this period to acquire a first-hand knowledge of the various programmes. Most of the meetings of the work group were public meetings and members of the work group invited those attending our meetings to participate. We are grateful to many people who attended our meetings and shared their knowledge with us.

During May and June, 1978, twelve public hearings were held throughout the City. Twenty-five formal briefs were presented at the hearings. Private hearings were arranged for those who requested their submissions for private session.

Many of the briefs were in response to the Issue Papers distributed in March 1978. The topics of the Issue Papers were:

(a) Aims and goals of special education
(b) Assessment
(c) Curriculum
(d) Race, class and cultural bias
(e) Special Education programmes – Elementary
(f) Special Education programmes – Secondary

The work group received one hundred fifty-four (154) written responses to the Issue Papers. We are indebted to all who spent the considerable time and effort responding to the Issue Papers in an attempt to enlighten the members of the work group.

Copies of the Draft Report were widely circulated, responses were invited and further public meetings were held. The work group, whose membership has been considerably altered by the election of November 1978, is currently considering all of the responses in preparation for reworking the draft into a Final Report.

During this whole process, every individual group who wished to express a particular point of view was able to do so. The opinions ranged far and wide and frequently contradicted one another. Strong demands were made for increased or different kinds of service with a number of groups from the inner-city asking for less special education and more services within the regular programmes. When all has been said and done, however, the ultimate responsibility and the power to make decisions rests in the hands of the elected trustees. The only key piece of autonomy in the hands of the parents of this special population is the right to refuse placement in a special education programme and the right to refuse a change in placement once the pupil is in such a programme. (See: Ontario Regulation 704/78, section 30 (2d) and section 32 (5).)

While a number of school systems have been providing this 'right' to parents voluntarily for some years, it is now mandated and parents in effect will have autonomy as far as refusing or changing programme placement is concerned.

Provisions for some special education populations are made more difficult by significant differences of opinion within a given special population about just what these provisions should be. Perhaps the group where these differences are the most evident is the deaf where the oralists are on one side, the manualists on the other and the Total Communications proponents somewhere in between. For many years, education of the deaf in Toronto was strictly an oral programme based on the premise that a major goal of the programme was to prepare deaf students to cope as well as possible in a hearing world. Manual communication was forbidden in the classroom since it was viewed as hindering the attainment of that goal. The obvious problem with this stand was that it did not prepare the deaf to communicate with one another. In most instances, this ability was picked up informally although formal programmes in manual communication were developed outside the school system in places such as churches and recreation centres.

The adult deaf placed increasing pressure on the education system to provide this kind of programme but no changes occurred until the educators concerned were prepared to support changes. The dogmatism of the manualists was met by the dogmatism of the oralists and the oralists were the more influenced. The constant lobbying gradually started to have an effect as educators grew more concerned about deaf students who did not achieve up to their apparent potential. The first departure from an absolutist approach came in September 1974 when a pilot programme in Total Communication was opened for children whose parents wanted this type of programme. In subsequent years, five more classes were opened but the programme was still considered as an offshoot or adjunct to the auditory/oral approach. In March 1978, a brief was received from the Parents for Total Communication requesting that the programme be recognised as a full-fledged alternative to the oral programme. The contents of the brief were discussed with representatives of Total Communication parents, Auditory/Oral parents, parents of children attending the Metro Toronto School for the Deaf and specialist teachers of the deaf. Out of these discussions grew a series of staff recommendations which supported much of the thrust of the brief. These recommendations were approved by the school board which now offers 'a dual stream programme (Total Communication and Auditory/Oral) in deaf education'.

This is a classic example of a special population using its power to influence when it lacked the power of autonomy. The pattern is typical:

(a) organise;

(b) speak out — formally and informally;

(c) make a written presentation to the decision-makers asking for certain specific matters to be considered;

(d) be ready to provide information and opinions throughout the process;

(e) be reasonable;

(f) be persistent.

When this works, as it did in this case, it is almost as good as autonomy. When it does not work, as happens much more frequently, it may leave the special population angry and frustrated and lead to polarisation and confrontation.

Inner-city

What Toronto calls 'Inner-city programs' are known by a variety of names around the world, with the most common being 'compensatory education'. These programmes are designed to help meet the needs of children who, because of poverty, have special needs which cannot be met by the regular programme. In Toronto, there is a large concentration in the downtown area of children of poor parents and of children of parents who have recently arrived in Canada from many other countries, primarily non-English speaking countries. These parents and their children were handicapped in their dealing with the school system by their very poverty and their inability to communicate fluently their feelings and their needs.

In the late 1960s a few administrators started to have some success in persuading their colleagues that students in a small area of downtown Toronto should have extra resources to help meet their extraordinary educational needs. Small experiments were begun in several schools but the communities being served by these well-meaning efforts felt the attempts were ineffective and too limited. The administrative approach needed more support.

In 1968–69 a small group of residents, tenants and parents organised and began to make their presence felt in the schools and the media. Their demands were simply stated — 'Inner-city kids were not learning as well as other kids and it was the fault of the schools'. They said something had to be done and the 'something' they had in mind involved extra money and resources.

While discussions were going on about what resources and what money, the 1969 election produced several new school board members who had had 'support the inner-city' planks in their campaign platforms. By the following July, a staff-recommended Task Force had been created to investigate inner-city needs. While this task force was at work, these 'inner-city trustees' initiated exploratory programmes which eventually would be used to convince others that there truly were special inner-city needs.

In the 1972 election, the number of trustees committed to championing the inner-city cause was tripled. With a broad community base which coalesced during the election campaign and with a solid minority block on the school board, these trustees helped to initiate programmes that produced a significant redistribution of educational resources based on criteria which weighted poverty heavily.

Elections since that time have maintained the proportion of trustees who give high priority to meeting inner-city needs and there is an ongoing focus on and continuing refinement of the criteria of inner-citiness and of the redistribution of resources.

Economic, immigration and municipal aid policies have produced a true growth of inner-citiness in Toronto to the point that 70 per cent of the schools in the system today are in one of three categories of inner-city schools.

Here we have an example of a special population which, lacking autonomy and the power that goes with autonomy, achieved many of its goals through influencing the decision-making process by way of the ballot box. Although sincerely committed to championing the cause of the inner-city, there is no question that this cause was a useful vote getter in the densely populated inner-city wards. Many of these trustees came as committed delegates to the electorate rather than as representatives and their uncompromising zeal sometimes caused clashes with trustees from non-inner-city wards who saw resources being taken away from their schools in order to bolster programmes in the inner-city. When the needs of special populations can be met through add-on resources, one need only be convinced of the validity of these needs. But, when there is a finite supply of resources and special needs can be met only by taking away resources from an 'ordinary' as opposed to a 'special' population, then confrontations develop and raw power may become the deciding factor.

English as a second language/dialect

'The Every Student Survey' for 1975[1] reported that 46 per cent of the students attending Toronto schools had a first language other than English, while an additional 6 per cent speak Canadian English as a second dialect. In all, there were 21 language groups with more than 200 students, with the largest groups being Italian (9,520), Portuguese (7,227), Greek (6,218), and Chinese (5,794). Although total enrolment in the school system is continuing to decline steadily, approximately 50 per cent of the city's student population are still from homes where English is a second language/dialect. The major shift in the past five years has been among groups with the Italian population moving north-west out of the city and being replaced to a significant extent by a more than tenfold increase in immigration from the Caribbean countries, particularly Jamaica.

The rapid change in the ethnic mix of the city is almost totally a post World War II phenomenon. In fact, prior to the 1950s the city was usually characterised as a WASP (White, Anglo-Saxon Protestant) bastion. As immigration gradually increased during the 1950s, individual schools developed a patchwork of resources and programmes to try to help these students 'fit in'. Assimilation was the order of the day and the overwhelming emphasis was on the acquisition of everyday

English. By the mid-1960s, however, the 'gradual increase' had become a 'flood' (number of immigrants to Metro Toronto: 1963 — 34,500; 1966 — 72,127) and the school system reacted by developing a more organised approach to meeting the needs of this special population.

In 1965, a special school was established as a reception and teaching centre for New Canadian students in the eastern half of the city, while programmes were established at local schools in the western half. In subsequent years, consultants were appointed to assist teachers, and a New Canadian Department was established to co-ordinate programme activities throughout the system. At the same time, the federal government moved to support the concept of a Multicultural Mosaic model for the country[2] rather than the Melting Pot concept espoused in the United States.

In 1974, the Board decided that the Advisory Committee on Philosophy and Programs for the New Canadian Population should be replaced by a Work Group on Multicultural Programs with the following terms of reference:

1. To investigate and explore the philosophy and programmes related to the city's multicultural population. This must include consultation and involvement with staff, students, parents, and the community at large.

2. To examine current practices related to the operation of the Board's multicultural programmes.

3. (a) To recommend to the Board long-range policy related to philosophy and programmes.
   (b) To recommend to the Board implementation procedures for the above.
   (c) To consider the financing and structural needs determined by the proposed policy.

The work group met steadily for nearly two years, received 133 written briefs (43 from ethnic community groups), organised innumerable public meetings and school visits and produced a Draft Report for system and community reaction (114 submissions) which was followed ten months later by a Final Report. As a result of the activities of the work group, three significant shifts took place in programmes for New Canadians. The first, a move from strict language teaching to the more organic and developmental approach of language learning was already well under way although it was being provided outside of the context of multiculturalism. The other two thrusts into Educational Opportunity Deficiencies (EOD) and English as a Second Language/Dialect (ESL/D) were essentially new and significant. EOD refers to the uneven educational background of some students which leaves them deficient in such areas as mathematics, reading and writing for reasons other than the students being intellectually deficient or inherently incompetent to engage in academic work. The addition of 'D' to ESL was intended to help meet the needs of students who came from English-speaking countries in which the spoken form of English was significantly different from Canadian English.

The revised programmes have spread from day school, to night school, to summer school, from programmes for school-age children, to day-night-summer programmes for adults, and from the school classroom, to locations in the work place — factories, offices and so on. All classes are free of charge and open to all who can benefit by them.

Again here, as in the previously mentioned special education and inner-city programmes, the special population(s) concerned have had a significant influence on the shape and nature of the programmes offered to them. This influence is frequently a major factor in the decision-making process and the Board rarely goes against the recommendations of a community group if it is able to accede to these recommendations but, when the final decision has to be reached, the Board and the Board alone must make and be responsible for that decision. The more influence a group has the closer it can get to autonomy, but there is always that final barrier of legislative and fiscal responsibility which stands between any group and absolute autonomy.

Heritage languages

The Heritage Languages Program provides an opportunity for elementary school students to learn a language other than English or French — usually their native tongue. A need to recognise languages and cultures other than English and French was expressed in the Report of the Royal Commission on Bilingualism and Biculturalism.[3] Since that time, a variety of organisations have been aiding the establishment of mother-tongue retention, recovery and development as legitimate goals of all Canadians, whether they were recent immigrants, the children of recent immigrants, or even four or five generations removed from immigrant forebears. The Heritage Languages Program grew, in part, out of the interaction of such groups with the provincial and local education authorities.

Third or non-official languages (English and French are the *official* languages of Canada) have long been taught as academic subjects in secondary schools. At present, there are 18 credit courses and three interest courses in third languages being taught in secondary schools in Toronto. In elementary schools, however, prior to June 1977, it was illegal to use as a language of instruction a language other than English or French. A third language could be used as a component of a cultural programme but the medium of instruction had to be English or French. Toronto had two examples of this type of approach in the period 1973–77.

The first example developed in midtown Toronto based on two elementary schools where 90 per cent of the children were of Chinese origin. The parents of many of these children were seriously concerned about the language and culture gaps that were developing between them and their children. There were after-school Chinese classes in the community but these made much extra work for the children and were too expensive for most families. With the help of community workers, the parents began organising and agitating for a programme, within the context of the school, that would help their children accept and appreciate the Chinese language and culture.

The Board was sympathetic, worked hard to devise a programme that would not contravene the regulations of the Ministry of Education by using Chinese as the language of instruction, that would not displace teachers and that would not commit the Board to extra costs. What evolved was a Chinese–Canadian bicultural programme designed to help the children understand the culture and language of Canada while helping them develop a feeling for the culture and language of their Chinese origin.

What happened is described in some detail in the following excerpt from 'We Are All Immigrants to This Place'.[4]

> The program was finally approved by both the Toronto Board and the Ministry of Education, and it began in September 1974. It was run by the Chinese Parents' Association of the two schools and its direct costs (teachers, supplies, etc.) were paid by the Association from funds they got from government grants and other grants and donations. In its first year about 3,000 students, including a few not of Chinese background (one of the stipulations of this kind of program is that it be open to all students who want it), enrolled in the program. That number represents about two-thirds of the children in the two schools.
>
> The program has two co-ordinators, one community worker, and three teachers, and the students are withdrawn from regular classes for half an hour a day. Courses of study were prepared after some consultation with the permanent staff of the two schools and were approved by both the Board and the Ministry of Education.
>
> The program was first established on a one-year experimental basis and was evaluated at the end of that time. For the evalua-

tion, the Board's Research Department prepared three sets of questionnaires — for students, teachers, and parents. All parents with children in the program received questionnaires and over 85 per cent returned them to the schools — 108 responding in Chinese and 59 in English.

In summarising the results of the evaluation, the research report says:

> 'Most students, parents, and teachers agreed that the Chinese programme was successful in making students more aware of Chinese culture. In general, parents (especially Chinese-responding parents) were the most positive. Students were generally satisfied, but . . . a number of students, especially the older ones, were bored with much of what went on in the program. Teachers also seemed to be relatively satisfied with the program, although many were critical about the content and structure of the program as well as the teaching methodology used.'

One frequent comment by teachers was that the program gave children an unrealistic picture of Chinese life. One teacher compared it to 'teaching people that Canadians live in tents made of animal skins and that they hunt, fish, and trade furs'.

(A similar bicultural program is run by the Greek—Canadian community in two schools in the eastern part of Toronto. Children of Greek heritage are the largest group in both schools but their percentages are less than half the total school population. These programs involved more community opposition and confrontation before they were agreed upon.)

These programmes continued to the end of the 1976—77 school year and ceased operation with the development of the Heritage Languages Program. This programme was announced in the Throne Speech of 9 March 1976 in which the Ontario government refers to Third Language and Culture Programs as follows:

> At the same time, while recognising that French and English are the languages of instruction in Ontario's schools, a Heritage Language Program will be supported, as a continuing education offering, to help Ontario's many ethnic groups retain a knowledge of their mother tongues and continuing appreciation of their cultural backgrounds. The government accepts and values the multicultural character of our province, and believes that encouraging children to understand the language and culture of their parents contributes to the quality of both education and family life.

The rhetoric of the Throne Speech was translated into action by a Ministry of Education Memorandum (1976–77: 46) in June 1977 and, by the end of the 1977–78 school year, the Board was providing programmes for 6,000 children in 15 languages. This has now expanded to 6,400 children in 23 classes ranging from 14 children in Slovenian to 1,491 in Greek.

These programmes received strong impetus from parent and community groups who frequently were exasperated at the apparent inability of the system to meet what they felt were relatively simple requests/demands. Some of the discussions were stormy both before and after the official sanctioning of the programme. Before the sanctioning, the storm usually centred around the Board's position that it could not divert money from existing programmes to fund bicultural programmes while, after the sanctioning, the fight was clearly over autonomy.

The Board's present policy provides for a great deal of parent and community involvement. Liaison committees composed of parents, school and heritage languages staff are formed at the school level, where matters such as the scheduling of classes, staffing and the evaluation of the programme are discussed. At the Board level, a sixteen-member elected Heritage Languages Advisory Committee, assisted by staff, has the responsibility of making recommendations concerning the overall programme. Meetings of these groups are frequent and well attended and are characterised by vigorous debate. Most groups seem satisfied with this process and the programmes themselves but there are exceptions.

In many cases, community or parent-funded third language programmes existed long before 1977. Most of these groups welcomed the Heritage Languages Program and the resulting official involvement of school boards. Some did not. This latter group took strong exception to the following paragraph in the Ministry Memorandum:

> Boards wishing to set up Heritage Language Classes must accept full responsibility for the staff, curriculum, and supervision of the classes, and subscribe to the usual conditions of evening and summer school programming. Classes may be held in a facility other than a school provided the instructors are hired by the board and responsible to them, and provided the boards accept full responsibility for the classes, as mentioned above.

Groups running 'successful' programmes asked why they should give up their longstanding autonomy in matters of staff and curriculum. In effect they said, 'just send the money and we'll continue to run the programmes'. The Ministry was equally adamant that if public money was funding the programme then there would be public control of the quality and content of that programme. Some groups that stayed out the programme the first year have come in under the umbrella this year but there are still several North European language groups who have decided to continue 'to do their own thing'.

Summary

The above four examples are representative of the ways in which the Toronto Board of Education deals with the provision of services for the special populations which are its responsibility. While the amount of influence that can be and is exerted varies from population to population, it is quite clear that in no instance does any one of these populations have what could be described as 'absolute autonomy'. In fact, autonomy is not an absolute but a continuum. How far an individual or a group can move along that continuum is governed by many constraints, for example, legal, fiscal, practical, negotiated, and so on. If the institution responsible for declining supplementary educational services does not have control over these variables, as is frequently the case with school boards, then the drive towards autonomy will be much more difficult. While they may not have control they do have responsibilities and it is simply not possible for a public body which has legislative and fiscal responsibilities for the delivery of services to varying groups to hand off that responsibility to any one or all of these groups. School boards in the Province of Ontario not only have a responsibility for the delivery of services, but also have a responsibility to the local taxpayers who, in Metropolitan Toronto, provide 80 per cent of the funds spent by the school boards.

Even if it were legally possible for the Toronto Board to give control to a special population, the practical problem is that the resources to meet the needs of that special population cannot be add-ons to the total budget. In Metro Toronto at the present time, there is a defined amount of money available for the provision of public education and any increase in resources for one population can be met only by a matched reduction in the provision of resources for part of all of the balance of the population. This is true in regard to the provision of both people and things. Right now, in some of the Board's smaller schools, staffing committees are agreeing to larger regular classes in order to free up a teaching position for such things as ESL or Library. It is obvious that such a move provides additional help for the special populations concerned, but this additional help is at the expense of the general population.

The fundamental question underlying this whole issue is how far can a school system move along the continuum of autonomy for a special population while neither reducing service to the balance of its population nor failing to meet its legislative and fiscal responsibilities. The practical and political answer to this question will vary greatly among school boards but it is not an issue which can be ignored. The approach adopted by the Toronto Board of Education which provides for full and open discussion, which affords opportunities for special populations to state their case orally and in writing, which provides a climate that is viewed as both receptive and supportive and that assigns particular staff members the responsibility for working with special populations, represents the maximum distance which school boards are able and can be expected to go. As long as there is adherence to the democratic process which provides full access to publicly elected school board members, and as long as these elected trustees can be held accountable at the ballot box on a regular basis, then special populations should be well served.

Notes and references

1   Deosaran, R., *Program placement related to selected countries of birth and selected languages (The Every Student Survey)*, Toronto, The Board of Education for the City of Toronto Research Department, 1976 (no.140); Deosaran, R., Wright, E.N. and Kane, T., *Student's background and its relationships to class and program (The 1975 Every Student Survey)*, Toronto, The Board of Education for the City of Toronto, Research Department, 1976 (no.138).
2   Statement by the Prime Minister, House of Commons, 8 October 1971.
3   Canada, Royal Commission on Bilingualism and Biculturalism Report, Ottawa 1967, vol.4, 'The Cultural Contribution of the other Ethnic Groups', Ottawa, 23 October 1969 (Recommendations 4 and 5).
4   'We Are All Immigrants to This Place' (A look at the Toronto school system in terms of governance and multi culturalism), Toronto, Canada, October 1976, p.61.

9 A researcher's assessment of the autonomy problem

Kjell Eide
Royal Ministry of Church and Education, Norway

Most research on educational matters tends to fall into two distinct categories: either education is studied as a passive system, adapting itself to a variety of external forces, or education is studied as a closed system, developing according to pressures generating within the system. Studies focusing on the interplay between external and internal variables are rarely found.

Research on education and equality mostly falls within the first category. Slightly over-simplifying, one might say that, largely, research in this field is based on the assumption that education is a given entity. One may get more or less of it, and it may be differently allocated between individuals and groups. Slightly more sophisticated approaches accept that education has a quality component, mainly related to the amount of resources fed into it, and to its ability to utilise the existing stock of knowledge on how education should be performed.

This happens in spite of the fact that we all know that education can be all sorts of things. In purely cognitive terms, education presents youngsters with a tiny fraction of potentially available knowledge. There is an endless number of alternative selections of knowledge elements which might as well have been transferred. Recognising also that the structuring of knowledge in academic disciplines is a rather arbitrary one, except in historical terms, and that the sequential structure of knowledge elements within each discipline is also mostly artificial, the question of the cognitive content of education is, at least in principle, a very open one indeed. Furthermore, the same content

155

may be presented in a wide variety of ways. Problems may be structured quite differently, the social climate of the school may vary enormously, as may the affective components of the school situation.

We recognise to some extent that individual children may need differential treatment in educational situations because of differences in ability and background experience. We rarely recognise, however, that children and their parents may have a wide variety of interests, values and expectations, with corresponding differences in what they want from education.

Studies on education and equality are concerned with the allocation of education between social classes, geographical areas, religious groups, ethnic groups, the two sexes, age groups, groups with different performance levels and so on. They examine differences between such groups in terms of access to education, the distribution of educational resources, educational attainment, and various measures of 'success' in society at large, presumably related to educational experiences. Usually, an underlying assumption is that the education offered serves all groups equally well, if they can only have it. However, if we want to come to grips with more basic issues relating to education and equality, such an assumption needs to be challenged.

It is generally recognised that many of the problems of the groups studied in the context of equality problems have interests and values, norms and behaviour patterns that deviate from those of other groups. Using the terms somewhat loosely, it might be said that they represent separate cultures, or subcultures, within our societies. It is often assumed that such subcultures will gradually disappear, due to the intensive communication within modern societies, and especially the development of modern mass media. In recent years, however, there is some evidence that the assumed melting-pot principle does not function as effectively as often thought. The cultural characteristics of many special groups within society have proved rather resistant, and we sometimes even experience a revival of such distinct characteristics.

In the case of specific ethnic groups, such as Lapps in Norway, Indians in North America, Maoris in New Zealand, Bretons in France, it has always been recognised that they represent specific cultures. Many more groups are on the point of being recognised as having their own cultural identities, and this is also the case with the increasing numbers of migrants in a great number of countries. Such a recognition, however, is often controversial, and even more so are the political implications of such recognition.

Without the same element of ethnic specificity, many geographical areas show peculiarities that might well be regarded as components of specific subcultures. Traditions of history, dialect, economic conditions, social structures and other traditional behaviour patterns may justify the recognition of a geographically determined cultural identity.

More controversial, perhaps, is the recognition of distinct subcultures linked to the various classes of society. Yet, in many countries most of the elements that constitute the pattern of a specific culture, vary greatly between such broad social groups as workers, farmers, fishers, or the middle-class. Quite often, political groupings reflect such differences in ways which influence profoundly the political structure of a country.

Religious differences influence behaviour in many ways, often related to attitudes towards education. Perhaps more debatable is the existence of a separate female subculture in our societies. Yet, even in this case it can clearly be demonstrated that at least at present, males and females do represent different attitudes in many important relations. Finally, groups defined by deviant performance, primarily in school or at work, and thus defined as 'handicapped', are widely accepted as needing differential treatment. It is less generally recognised that the full integration of such groups in society may require significant changes in general values and attitudes in society as a whole. It might thus be said that even such groups represent different values and norms, which could be seen as elements of a set of subcultures.

In the groups mentioned, it is clear that the separateness of their cultural identity varies considerably, and could often be questioned in some cases. Deviating features might, for instance, be explained as general reflections of a historical under-dog position. Such features, for example among workers or women, might be assumed to disappear the moment such groups have gained access to resources and power to the same extent as the groups now dominating. In educational terms, this would mean that such groups would be satisfied with a just share of the education offered, without necessarily requiring any change in the cultural aspects built into that education. Such a hypothesis cannot just be rejected, it belongs to the general field of uncertainty surrounding the old issue of cultural separateness and identity.

Assuming, however, that in some sense of the word, our societies contain a considerable number of subcultures, this phenomenon adds a fundamental dimension to the problem of equality. Any group claiming equality in educational terms must also be concerned that the education received corresponds to the interests, norms and values of their particular subculture.

There are Indian tribes, literate at the time of Columbus, refusing today to send their children to school. Some migrants in Western Europe also refuse to send particularly their girls to the kind of schools offered by their countries of residence. These are extreme cases, in which no education is regarded as better than the kind of education offered. More usually, special groups tend to concentrate on influencing the kind of education offered to them. Often this takes the form of segregated schools.

Religious groups have in many countries established extensive, separate systems of education for their children. To some extent, ethnic groups have managed to do the same, especially when their language is distinctively different. Decentralisation of decision-making has given a certain freedom to local areas to deviate somewhat from the general pattern of education. Separate schools for girls still have a role to play, and handicapped children are to a great extent put into special schools.

In many cases, such educational segregation may help to maintain the cultural identity of the groups concerned. Yet, quite often such segregated schooling may reduce the chances of those attending them in society at large, at least in terms of some usual measures of 'success'. Whether this is true for separate educational institutions for the handicapped or for women, is a controversial issue. It is more obvious for small ethnic minority groups and for graduates from schools more or less designed for the 'lower' social classes.

The simple solution to the culture dimension of the equality problem, to provide each group with their own forms of education, is thus not easily reconcilable with other equality dimensions related to the social position and general living conditions of the different groups. Educational segregation may further aggravate inequality on more general dimensions.

It should also be mentioned that national policies in education, as well as in other fields, quite naturally have national coherence as a major aim. It may even be argued that such coherence in terms of more egalitarian living conditions for the social classes, more integration between ethnic groups and so on, in the long run will serve egalitarian goals for society as a whole. Strong arguments can be put forward for integration of deviant social groups in all institutional settings, including those of education.

'Integration' of minority groups into some sort of 'mainstream' institutions can take a variety of forms. The 'assimilation' variety assumes that integration primarily requires changes in the deviant individuals, in order to adapt them as much as possible to mainstream behaviours. This has been the typical attitude to the integration of handicapped children into ordinary schools, the increased access of women to all forms of education, the 'catching up' of 'backward' areas in educational terms, and often also the integration of ethnic minority groups.

A different concept of integration accepts the deviant features of minority groups, requiring primarily changes in the 'regular' environment in order to accommodate fully deviant behaviour patterns. Returning to our concept of subcultures, this would imply a change in the 'mainstream' culture to include the norms and values of deviant subcultures. We often seem to take for granted that if this could be achieved, it would be the ideal form of integration. Only in this way can the negative effects of segregation be avoided, while the cultural integrity of the individuals and groups concerned is maintained.

Assessing the degree of inequality between individuals and groups, and the potential of specific measures to promote equality between them, and at the same time accepting that the value structures held by such individuals and groups may differ, raises problems of a fundamental nature. The notion of equality presupposes some form of interaction between the individuals or groups in question. They may interact in productive activities, in sharing elements of a common structure of governance, take part in educational activities with at least certain common features, communicate and exchange ideas and impulses. A policy for equality must be based on the assumption that such interactions can be made to improve the relative position of individuals or groups who are not so 'well-off' as others.

But assessing who are 'well-off' or less 'well-off', and the potential effects of changes in the interaction pattern on the relative position of groups, presupposes the existence of a common scale of measurement. Most attempts to make such assessments have taken for granted that there exist such measures which are commonly agreed as significant, for example income or resources in some wider sense. In doing so, one overlooks the possibility that such measures may have very different meaning for groups with different value structures. Implicitly, there has clearly been a tendency to use measures that reflect the value structures of the strongest groups. Assessment of inequality between groups may thus not reflect the actual inequality as conceived by the weaker groups, and measures to remedy inequality may be seen by them as irrelevant in terms of their values.

One way of defining the equality objective, is to state that no individual or group should be in a position to exploit others. Non-exploitive forms of interactions will thus be interactions which at least do not change the relative positions between two groups so as to widen the gap. But even in purely economic terms, assessing the degree of exploitation is a difficult task. It presupposes some basic assumptions about what a 'just' allocation of resources in society should be. If we accept, as I think we must, that equality has many more dimensions than the purely economic ones, we have even less 'objective' guidance in judging the extent to which exploitation occurs.

Interactions between groups with different value structures may easily make both groups feel that it is being exploited by the other (it is relevant that a recent Norwegian Royal Commission Report on equalising living conditions between industrial workers and farmers came out with exactly this conclusion). In any case, there may be widely differing and equally justifiable views on the equality effect of any specific interaction, as well as on policy measures aiming at changing the nature of interactions.

Essential in this context is the ability of stronger groups to impose their own value structures upon the weaker ones, thus making possible exploitation seem 'just' to the latter. It can hardly be denied that mass media to a great extent serves this function in our societies. Education may be of particular significance in this context. To a considerable extent, education is concerned with the transfer of values. We 'socialise' groups into what is assumed to be a common cultural heritage. This implies, however, that certain groups may have the value structures of other, stronger groups imposed upon themselves and their children. Actually, this may be one of the most predominant forms of 'exploitation' in our modern societies — as well as in the relationship between industrialised and developing countries.

We may, of course, suggest that minority groups should have their fair share in decisions concerning what value structure should be predominant in schools. But we are not, in this case, dealing with a given amount of resources which through some compromise can be allocated, in a manner conceived by all parties as reasonably just. Cultures are different because in a number of points, they reject each other's values.

There are certainly historical examples of the merging of cultures. Usually, it means that a predominant culture has adopted elements of a suppressed one, largely as a matter of convenience. History is rarely written by the losers in such cultural conflicts. There are indications, however, of gross alienation, loss of norms and breakdown of cultural patterns and social structures.

In the short run, it is quite clear that cultures cannot merge simply through some sort of bargaining process. Cultures are whole structures, the elements of which cannot simply be traded off for some elements of another culture. Even minor adjustments in a predominant group culture, in order to facilitate the social and cultural accommodation of weaker groups, often meet fierce resistance. The forced accommodation to a predominant culture by weaker groups may have disastrous and long-lasting effects on many individuals and on the groups as a whole.

Policies for equality facing cultural differences are thus far more complicated than the simple search for more equal distribution of commonly valued resources. To a large extent, the latter may be divided up differently without any major harm to the cultural and social fabric of society. Cultural interactions between unequal partners are much more likely to lead to a feeling of mutual loss. Cultures can be more or less tolerant, but no culture can accept indiscriminately all values as equally valid, and all behaviours as equally acceptable — by definition, it would then cease to be a culture.

In educational terms, this means that the school cannot become everything to everybody. The school must discriminate, it must hold certain values as more valid than others, and certain behaviours as more desirable than others. The ideal of genuine integration is thus no full answer to the claim for equality. Cultures will conflict, even if temporarily they may find ways of peaceful coexistence. Cultures will try to dominate in order to survive. The outcome is a question of the relative strength in political, economic, social and cultural terms. There is no objective ideal of 'justice' to guide such a process.

This does not mean that the quest for equality is futile as a political objective. But it does mean that much more emphasis will have to be put on the dimensions of equality most cherished by the weaker groups. In terms of practical policy, it would mean that such groups must acquire the strength and power necessary to influence its own position, and to make its own definitions of what equality means come through. In the last instance, equality is rarely given to any group; it is achieved through the strivings of the group itself. And in doing so, it is essential that a group is capable of defining what equality means in its own terms. Its ability to do this is, in fact, probably the best measure of the degree of equality it has achieved.

Nor do the problems mentioned above mean that research on education and equality is useless. But it means that such research cannot pretend that it exists in a normative vacuum. It must take off from the assumption that certain groups are discriminated against, in a positive or negative sense. It can examine the forms such discrimination takes, and it can study the ways in which the discrimination may be reduced.

In doing so, researchers cannot overlook the multi-dimensional nature of the equality problem, otherwise their findings could well be fundamentally misleading. If a group is discriminated against in a negative sense, the basic requirement is to build up the strength of that group. It becomes a tactical problem whether this can best be done through maximising the access of the particular group to the educational system as it is, through increasing its bargaining power in relation to that system on matters relating to its content, or through the establishment of separate and sheltered parts of the educational system governed by the group's own values. Probably, the choice of tactic is not only specific for each group; it may change at various stages in the development of any group's fight for equality.

Just as an example, one might suggest that large groups, having gained a fair amount of power in society, such as for instance the workers, could probably achieve most at this stage by using their political influence to change the content of education, and the values predominant in education institutions. Probably, the same applies to women. Ethnic minority groups may in many cases gain most at this stage by achieving more control over a number of schools serving their children, leaving the system at large alone. Based on more moderate ambitions, certain geographical areas may follow similar aims by pushing for more decentralised decisions within the educational system. However, such wide generalisations may not have much validity.

The question of the handicapped is of special interest in this case, as the legitimacy of discriminatory treatment of individuals according to school performance has just recently come under doubt. It may be said that it is the predominant value structure of the school system as such that defines a number of individuals as handicapped although, to a great extent, the school simply reflects the predominant value structure in the economy. Asking for equality in this case, in segregated or integrated terms, thus implies a fundamental shift in the value structure of any educational system. No system primarily aiming at 'performance' can at the same time accept low performance as equally valuable. Whether integration is an appropriate equality measure in this case is thus primarily determined by the willingness of the system to accept a fundamental change in its basic value structure. Segregation may facilitate the maintenance of present value structures, although in that case equality is hardly a realistic objective.

In terms of research approaches, the usual measurement of social mobility through education, as a proxy for the measurement of equality, is based on the assumption that all populations have one common value structure, at least as reflected within the educational enterprise. In addition, it presupposes that access for a few to the highest level of education improves the general situation of the group concerned. Both assumptions are obviously of doubtful validity. The fact is that most studies of this kind tell us very little about the situation of any country in terms of equality, and even less in terms of developments in this respect. An obvious starting point for any discussion of equality must be the dimensions of equality important to the specific groups concerned. Most of the groups in question are primarily concerned with their status as a group, as compared to that of other groups. Access for a few of their members to higher education levels, which often means that they become alienated from their own group, is rarely conceived of as an adequate strategy for equality. On the contrary, it is clearly an expression of the 'mainstream' concept of equality, based on the premises of the predominant groups in society.

Probably, research on education and equality would gain much from stronger input by political scientists, anthropologists and historians, in order to counteract the currently dominating school of sociology in this field, and the even more narrow traditions of economic theory. Equality is not a concept that can be fully accommodated within any single academic discipline, and the contributions research can make to political processes aiming at more equality, would gain from a clear recognition of this fact.

It is also essential in our research efforts to get beyond the simple notions of segregation and integration in purely institutional terms. We need to know to what extent such organisational arrangements influence the general value structure governing institutional activities and their social milieux, the 'cultures' predominant within the institutions. In other words, we need to know more than just the *amount* of interaction between individuals and groups, we want to know the *nature* of such interactions. To what extent are they exploitive, and in whose terms?

Finally, as researchers we have to accept the normative, political nature of the equality concept, or any equality concept we may want to define. This would make us less definite in our judgements, but perhaps more constructive in our contributions to the basically political debate on such issues.

10 Service delivery: an analysis of systems of administration

Jane Hannaway
Columbia University, USA

The basic problem addressed in this paper is how to administer (that is, co-ordinate, control) education programmes for special populations. While the question sounds simple, the answer is not obvious. What I attempt to show is that there is no optimal solution to the problem of how to administer special programmes, rather there are alternative solutions each of which involves trade-offs. The particular alternative chosen depends on the tastes of the actors involved, the nature of the historical situation, and the political and governance structure in the country under consideration.

It is hoped that policy-makers and administrators find the schema developed here useful. Features of administrative systems are likely to have direct effects on the way services are delivered to clients. The discussion that follows attempts to identify some of the dominant characteristics of administrative systems and the ways in which one might expect them to affect service delivery. In order to be applicable to a variety of social and cultural settings, this paper is written in general terms and therefore analyses and prescriptions for particular settings are not included. However, since the author is most familiar with the United States, examples of various points are often drawn from the American experience. I proceed in this paper to identify different agents, different levels, and different types of control; to discuss the implications and consequences of each of these; and to suggest criteria by which administrative systems may be evaluated.

Agents and levels of control

Agents of control are those individuals or groups of individuals who have primary responsibility for determining how special populations are to be treated or how beneficiaries are to be served. Three major categories of control agents are discussed here: consumers, experts, and political figures. Consumers refer to the parents of students in special programmes. Experts refer to the professionals involved such as educational administrators, teachers, doctors, therapists, and so forth. And political figures refer to agents who are responsible to the general public, such as a mayor or legislator.

The role and the extent of the role that different agents play has been the subject of considerable debate, bordering on the philosophical, in a number of different areas. One can cite, for example, recent debates about the role of legislatures in abortion matters; or the roles of parents, doctors, and the courts in disputes about medical treatments that are 'in the best interest of the child'. In regular education programmes, disputes about control usually are not problematic. Generally, community norms and tradition guide practice. In education programmes for special populations, however, the issue becomes more significant. The simple fact that these populations are 'special' or 'different' generates a set of concerns not present in the regular education programmes. Parents with different cultural backgrounds want at least some control in order to ensure that their values and culture are represented in the schools. And parents of handicapped children want control to protect their children from 'labelling' or faulty diagnoses and to guarantee proper treatment.

At times, the preferences of parents clash with the best judgement of the professionals and/or with the interests of political figures. Given the lack of a science of education, questions of how much control different agents *should* have are difficult to answer. Individuals with different value orientations would respond to such a question differently. Undoubtedly, issues of control are of critical importance to both parents and education officials; but their normative nature, that is, what the role of these different agents 'should be', puts it beyond the scope of this paper and the understanding of the author. What follows is a more mundane discussion of what practical effects different agents and different levels of control might have on service delivery to clients.

The accompanying chart shows each of the three categories of control agents and three levels on which they each can operate. Each of these is discussed in the sections that follow.

	Agents of control		
	Consumers	Experts	Political figures
	Individual consumer	Local district teachers/administrators	Local unit
	Local interest group	State/regional agency	State unit
	National interest group	National agency	National unit

Levels
of
control

Figure 10.1   Control agents and the levels on which they operate

Parent control

The polar case of agent control, that is the most decentralised alternative, is control by individual consumers, parents. An example of this type of control is the voucher system, which has been tried experimentally in the United States. Parents are given vouchers by a public authority with which they can purchase needed services from competing vendors. The experiment in the United States was conducted as part of the regular school programme, but the same ideas can describe how a model of parent control would theoretically operate for special service programmes. The system is regulated by parents through choice, that is through purchase power. It is expected that schools that do not provide what parents want, or programmes that are inefficient, would not survive because parents would not patronise these schools.

A number of advantages for control by consumers have been argued and the arguments are familiar. First, consumer control requires little or no monitoring or regulation from public agencies and therefore it is the least costly system of administration. Informed parents perform the regulating function. A second advantage commonly argued is that this system is by its nature adaptable: as consumer needs and tastes change and as technologies and states of knowledge improve, competitive service providers would respond and change accordingly. Otherwise, they would lose their clients.

A major assumption of this model is that 'the consumer knows best'. In the case of special education programmes, this means that the parent understands the specific needs of his/her child and how well a particular service provider would meet that need relative to what other providers could do. Given this assumption, one would expect that parental choice would result in a fairly good match between the needs of the child and the services that child receives. Furthermore, one would expect that only effective and efficient schools would survive parental scrutiny.

Problems are also associated with consumer control over special services, and the main problems stem from the difficulty of consumers gaining a good understanding of the value of different services and the effectiveness of different schools/programmes. While parents undoubtedly have the best interests of their children at heart, they may not be able to make very good decisions about the best education programme for them. Assessing the quality of educational services and predicting its effect on a particular child, even without the complications of emotional interests, and with years of professional training, are subtle judgements at best. Not only do results sometimes take years to be realised but the different outputs of education are also difficult to define and measure.

The above informational problems of the consumer control model also lead to equity and social welfare concerns. Because some parents are more educated, or have more time, or exert more effort, they are able to make better decisions about educational programmes for their child than other parents. Findings from the voucher demonstration and from a private school study[1] suggest that higher SES parents are better informed consumers of education than lower SES parents. This same pattern would probably hold for special educational programmes as well. As a consequence, children would benefit unequally from publicly funded programmes because of parental characteristics.

Another problem associated with the consumer control model is the possible generation of a fragmented education delivery system. Individuals with very particular concerns may band together, leaving little hope for an integrated service delivery system. Special interest groups would compete with each other for the scarce resources available for special programmes and probably also for clients. Children needing multiple or co-ordinated services would be at a considerable disadvantage. In addition, the extremes in the population may not be well served. That is, individuals or small groups with exceptional needs may not be able to compete effectively with larger groups that have more common needs.

As one moves from individual consumer control to control by national interest group, that is, when the level at which control is exercised is higher, the advantages and disadvantages of the consumer model are modified. For example, the match between individual parent preferences and services may weaken so that individual needs would not be as well served. The interest group would generally run the programme based on the average *vocalised* needs of its constituents (probably different from social welfare interests) and again special cases may not be accommodated well. Since centralised programme specification would also lead to standard programmes, less variety and innovation would result.

There are also expected advantages to higher levels of control. One such advantage is that conflict at the local level of programme implementation would be decreased because guidelines, regulations, and programmes would be specified and not open to bargaining and negotiation by individual interests at the programme level. Such a reduction in local conflict might allow programme managers to concentrate their efforts on more or better service delivery. A third expected advantage of higher levels of control is an increased rate of diffusion of any successful programmes or techniques that might develop and this increased rate of diffusion might more than offset the decreased rate of innovation. That is, while the total number of innovations developed might be fewer, the number of innovations that were adopted might be greater. (Of course, it may result in greater diffusion of bad ideas as well as good ones.)

Expert control

A second agent of control is the expert. By expert control, I mean control by educational professionals, either teachers or administrators. This locus of control also has certain advantages. First, it can be argued that professionals know better which services best serve children with special needs; and secondly, there is the equity argument: professionals can see that all children receive adequate and appropriate services regardless of parental characteristics. In this sense, experts can be viewed as agents for social objectives, while parents are agents for private objectives.

In general the expected consequences of different levels of control in the expert model are the same as the effects predicted for the consumer model. That is, the higher the level of control, the less likely that programme services will match special individual needs; that conflict will disrupt programme level implementation; that innovation will occur; and the more likely that new ideas will be diffused through the system.

The issue of equity is also not independent of the level of control. If control is vested in individual teachers, they can control the distribution of resources within their classroom, for example the amount of attention given to each child, but not resources that are distributed across classrooms or schools, for example specialised aides or materials. Therefore children in classrooms with dedicated teachers would receive qualitatively different services from children in other classrooms. If control is vested in higher authorities, then attempts can be made to equalise treatment across districts, schools and perhaps classrooms.

In the case of expert control, we might expect another level effect: the higher the level of control, the greater the administrative costs. In the consumer model, economies of scale might offset increased co-ordination costs of higher levels of control, but this might very well not be the case in the expert model where the levels usually represent public bureaucracies.

In the United States, at least, the regular education programme is decentralised with primary responsibility in the hands of local school districts. However, most of the special education programmes are funded centrally and, although they are administered locally, they are ultimately the responsibility of the federal government. The federal funding of special programmes is designed to allow local districts to provide services they normally would not be able to provide. That is, the federal money is intended to 'supplement' and not 'supplant' local funding; and the aid is 'categorical', that is, for a specific purpose.

Such an arrangement requires, in effect, a dual system of administration at the local and state levels.[2] Local and state agencies must attend to their own administrative needs as well as to the administrative and accountability demands of the special programmes, and these are not insignificant demands. Special education programmes are funded with 'strings', that is, stipulations and restrictions, and compliance with the requirements must be demonstrated to higher administrative bodies, all the way to Congress.[3] In a decentralised system, compliance with central directives is usually demonstrated by audits, reports and evaluations. All of these are administratively costly.

The very fact that these levels represent public bureaucracies also leads to the expectation that higher levels of control would lead to greater administrative costs. In a public bureaucracy, especially one in which the output is unclear, the function of administration is necessarily one of legitimation as well as control and co-ordination.[4] Each administrative level must keep those taxpayers and governmental bodies on which it is dependent satisfied in order to maintain a steady flow of resources. The higher the level of control and the greater the number of levels involved, then the greater the number and diversity of these external groups to which a programme's administration must be responsive. In the consumer control model, however, a national interest group is legitimated by its constituency, those to whom it provides services. This legitimacy is evidenced simply by the existence of the national group since the group is accountable to and provides services to the same set of individuals.

One of the main criticisms of the expert control model is that the interests and the preferences of the educational professionals may not be the same as those of the clients, or for that matter may not be in the public interest in general. Consequently, funds and staff energies may be diverted in ways in which neither funding bodies nor clients would choose. For example, it has been argued that public managers, among them education managers, prefer to allocate a greater share of the budget to administration than either teachers or clients would like.[5]

In the United States this has resulted in some regulations that limit administrative expenditures. Also, the behaviour of educational professionals may not always be directed in ways that maximise educational goals. Since there is no reason to expect education professionals to be more altruistic than the average person, they are likely to behave in ways that promote their own self interests, at least some significant part of the time. This might mean, for example, behaving in ways that increase the chances of career mobility.

In education it is difficult to reward (or in any way sanction) professionals for educational output, that is, student achievement. This is, in large part, due to our general lack of understanding of the complexities of the schooling–teaching–learning process. Consequently, it would not be in the interest of career mobility for professionals to direct their energies exclusively in this direction. They would be better off (in terms of career mobility) to direct their attention to other administrators and outside agencies that provide routes for career advancement. The expectation then is for upwardly mobile education professionals to be more concerned with the administrative aspects of programmes rather than with the service and educational aspects. It is doubtful that parents would share this view.

Another objective of experts that may have a direct effect on the way programmes are managed and services are delivered is the avoidance of conflict.[6] While high levels of conflict are obviously disruptive of services, the active suppression of conflict may conceal real issues which should be addressed. Any level of conflict is to the disadvantage of administrators, which explains why they avoid it. Conflict in public agencies is usually accompanied by increased scrutiny by the outside, making the job of the administrator considerably more difficult.

Political agents

Political agents are those actors who create programmes and appropriate monies through legislation. They respond with solutions (legislation) to needs presented by their constituents. The solutions they generate can take different forms. For example, they can be regulatory or programmatic. If they are programmatic, they can be as simple as stating a general objective and appropriating funds to achieve it; or they may be comprehensive, detailing extensive guidelines about participation rights, programmatic requirements, evaluation criteria, and so on. The initial action by political actors determines the delegation and distribution of control across agents and levels. The interesting questions here are how these determinations are made and why.

One way to begin to understand how political actors go about making decisions about the delegation and distribution of control of education programmes is to analyse their information bases and sources. It is reasonable, indeed if not obvious, that actors will act on problems they are aware of and not act on problems about which they are not aware. They will pay attention to groups that are familiar to them, and not be influenced by groups of which they have no knowledge. They will also respond with solutions that are at hand, and not search very hard for unknowns of uncertain value.

At first this might sound trite, but any analyses of decision-making which do not include an analysis of how the problem or issue was initially defined obviously excludes a critical phase of the decision-making process.[7] A problem brought to the attention of legislators by a teachers' union may be very different from the same problem brought to their attention by a group of parents. For example, a teachers' union may define an educational problem in terms of inadequate time allotted for teacher preparation while a parent group may define it in terms of inadequate teacher accountability. Any solution would most likely be developed in response to the problem as it was posed to the political actors. In some geographic locations, be they at the local or the national level, the presence of an active organised lobby group could monopolise the information channels of political actors who unwittingly develop biased solutions to education problems.

At the national level decision makers would be most vulnerable to biased information channels. Leaders at this level are usually ignorant of local realities. They pass legislation in response to needs brought to their attention by organised groups. They may pass an authorisation for a special interest programme, say for bilingual education, and another, say for reading, without any awareness of how these programmes will be managed together at the local level. Each programme has its own rules, guidelines, and local programme manager mandated at the national level, leading to problems of local implementation. A child could spend the greater part of a school day being shunted from one special service to another without any adult being aware of the total programme to which the child was being subjected. Alternatively, restrictions can preclude a child receiving benefits from two programmes even if both are warranted.[8]

Another local implementation problem that results when higher level political actors create special provisions is that it restricts the flexibility of the local educational professionals.[9] The solutions, that is, the programmes defined at the national level, are the 'givens' into which the local professionals must fit the needs of their clients. This can lead to distortions. For example, students can be intentionally misclassified because of greater resource availability in one programme than in another.[10] Also, local officials and clients are left the task of trying to fit together the pieces of disparate programmes in order to develop appropriate treatments for a child.[11]

Type of control

Not only can control systems differ by agent and level, they can also differ by type of control. Three basic types of control can be distinguished: input control, process control and output control.

Input control involves specifying the characteristics of the clients,

173

the resources, and the service providers. This type of control is often exercised by political agents and education professionals. Political agents usually specify 'who benefits', that is, the characteristics of clients and the amount of resources to be allocated for a problem; and experts, the education professionals (through certification regulations) usually specify the characteristics of the service providers. This is most often in the form of training requirements.

Process control refers to control over the actual teaching/learning tasks. Traditionally in education this has been the weakest form of control. The argument is usually given that teachers are professionals and must use their judgement to decide what is to be done. Recently in the United States, political agents have attempted to exercise indirect control over the educational process for handicapped children. They have done this by giving parents explicit rights to participate in making the decision about the educational programme for their child (Public Law 94:142). Educational professionals can no longer decide independently about classification and treatment for a child nor can they make decisions based on the average need. Each child must have an individually tailored education programme which is approved by the child's parents.

Output control means control by outcomes and implies formal evaluation. This form of control is only effective when the output measures are clear and unambiguous and one can be reasonably sure that the outcomes were largely dependent on the treatment provided. In education, these conditions are usually not met. As a result, significant expenditures are made for evaluation, but the extent to which they are used for making decisions about the actual educational tasks is unclear. They seem, at least in the United States, to be used primarily for purposes of system legitimation. One might also expect that in cases in which ambiguous outcome measures were used for control that considerable conflict would develop with many teachers, for example, feeling that they were being unjustly judged.

Evaluation criteria for administrative systems

There are a number of characteristics that a 'good' administrative system should exhibit; among these are adaptability, flexibility, conflict minimisation, cost minimisation, equity and quality production. Different control systems would affect these in different ways.

A consumer model of control, for example, would exhibit a high degree of most of the above conditions except for conflict minimisation and equity. And those conditions that were exhibited would only result if consumers were well informed, and equally well informed, about the value of services provided by different vendors. If parents were not well informed and were unable to make good decisions then ineffective schools and programmes would be allowed to persist. If some parents were able to make better decisions than others, then gross inequities could develop in services to students. Parents would also not be good decision makers in a society where a stigma was attached to certain handicaps. In such a society, parents would be reluctant to search for information about programmes and a child with a special need certainly would not be well served.

The other major disadvantage of the consumer control model is that it results in a highly differentiated service delivery system in which the consumer is left the task of sorting through and establishing co-ordination of various services.

In the expert model of control equity would be more likely to result, and conflict would be less likely to occur, than in the consumer control model. However, we would also expect the system to be more costly to run and to be less flexible and less adaptable. A system based on equity has a harder time making special expectations; it is managed by rules and regulations. It is also more likely that a system controlled by experts would easily become locked into certain ways of viewing educational problems and solutions making change and adaptability less likely. Group members such as those in professional groups, socialise new members and tend to reinforce each other's views, leading to stable, but sometimes stagnant, belief patterns. This contrasts with the consumer control model where adaptability is based on client choice and competition among service providers. As tastes and technologies change, services change.

The political model also has some predictable consequences. It would be similar to the expert control model in that equity would be likely and conflict at the local level unlikely (relative to the consumer model). However, assuming control would most likely be exercised at the national level, and special provisions would be developed in response to organised interest groups, local professional flexibility in matching services to client needs would be restricted by national guidelines and the resources attached to certain provisions.

It is difficult to predict the consequences of different control systems for the quality of programmes. One could argue that the average quality of programme would not be much different under different control systems. It is the interaction between the teacher and the child, along with peer interaction, that determine most of the learning that takes place in school settings. Since we do not understand just what it is about the behaviour of teachers and students that makes a difference, it is difficult to say how a particular control system would affect quality. However, different control systems would have different distributional effects which are important. For example, it is more likely that some special cases would fare better under the consumer model, where the individual has choice, than under the expert model which is governed by rules, or under the political model in which special service offerings are biased by the vociferousness and intensity of interest groups. However, as explained earlier, this model also has equity problems.

Notes and references

1   Garner, W. and Hannaway, J., 'Competition, Choice and Private Schools: An Exploratory Policy Analysis', in S. Abramowitz (ed.), *Private Schools Today*, National Institute of Education, DHEW, 1980.
2   Many special education programmes are funded by the federal government through state agencies, to local districts.
3   Barro, S.M., 'Federal Education Goals and Policy Instruments: An Assessment of the "Strings" Attached to Categorical Grants in Education', in M. Timpane (ed.), *The Federal Interest in Financing Schooling*, Cambridge, Ballinger Publishing Company, 1978.
4   Meyer, J. and Rown, B., 'Formal Structure of Organizations as Myth and Ceremony', *American Journal of Sociology*, 1977, 83:340–63. This discusses the legitimation and the administration of educational institutions.
5   Hannaway, J., 'Administrative Structures: Why Do They Grow?', *Teachers College Record*, 1977, vol.79, no.3.
6   Cyert, R. and March, J.G., *A Behavioral Theory of the Firm*, Englewood Cliffs, Prentice-Hall, 1963.
7   March, J. and Simon, H., *Organizations*, New York, Wiley, 1958.
8   Birman, B.F., *Case Studies of Overlap Between Title I and Pl 94–142 Services for Handicapped Students*, Menlo Park, SRI International, 1979.
9   Wilken, W.H. and Porter, P.O., 'State Aid for Special Education: Who Benefits?', National Institute of Education, DHEW, 1977.
10   Birman, op.cit.
11   US, GAO, 1974.

11 The delivery of special education services for minorities

K. McDonagh
Carysford College, Ireland

The aims of education for general and special populations

It is taken as axiomatic that the general aims of education for a special population are the same as those for the general population and, therefore, that they would approximate to the following: 'to help the child lead a full life as a child and to enable him to go on to lead a full and useful life as an adult'. In a democracy, which Dewey would see as a way of associated living rather than a form of politics, a society exists in and by communication through consciously shared interests. Education in a democracy therefore is concerned with opening up avenues of communication. Consequently an intervention which cuts off or inhibits communication between the general population and the special population is failing to achieve the aims of education, both for the general and for the special population in a democracy. When, however, the limited technical skills in oral communication, reading, numeracy, and so on, of certain members presents a serious obstacle to communication with the general population, and when it appears administratively or organisationally more efficient to treat these difficulties in isolation from the general society, it is important to weigh the advantages of technical mastery against the disadvantages of cutting the individual off from his natural community. This dilemma is at the centre of the integration/segregation controversy. This proposal of Lloyd Dunn seems appropriate:

An exceptional pupil is so labelled only for that segment of his school career (i) When his deviating physical or behavioural characteristics are of such a nature as to manifest a significant learning asset or disability for special education purposes, and therefore (ii) When through trial provision it has been determined that he can make greater all-round adjustment and scholastic progress with direct or indirect special education services than he could with only a typical regular school programme.

Such a proposal founded on a pragmatic rather than an ideological basis has the administrative merit of centring attention on the pupils' welfare and the appropriate strategies for achieving it.

Identification of target groups

The identification of special populations will depend on the criteria used for assessment. For historical reasons, many special populations have been categorised on the basis of medical criteria. Classification on the basis of physical or mental disability may be adequate for administering the delivery of health services but, at best, such a classification is quite irrelevant for the Education Authority charged with delivering an educational service. At worst, such a classification could seriously impede the education of the child. Many of these medical labels imply a circularity which obscures the problem. For example, the label 'brain damaged' may be accorded to a child because he has failed to make adequate progress in reading, yet the teacher then assumes that this child cannot be advanced in reading because it is brain damaged. The label tells the teacher no more than he already knew; however, the label inappropriately borrowed from medicine or elsewhere suggests that the solution to the problem lies outside the competence of the teacher.

Where education is the special intervention, the criteria for selecting the target group must be the special educational needs of the group.

Assessment on the basis of educational needs

Categorisation on the basis of disability emphasises the way in which some children differ from the general population, yet for the educationalist there may be far greater differences between the educational needs of members within the special population itself than between many members of the special population and the general population. Even within the general population of children who progress satisfactorily through the regular school system, a wide variety of educational needs can be identified and the intensity of the need can be greater for some than for others; nevertheless these children are not regarded as special. One child may need a great deal of sensory training at the pre-reading stage while another needs motor training; both can make satisfactory progress. At a later stage another child may have greater need of concrete experience of shapes in the environment in order to acquire certain spatial concepts leading to a study of geometry — again, this child is not regarded as special. Indeed, the regular school now attempts to cater for individual differences and needs, as is evidenced by present-day classroom organisation in groups and team teaching.

The Warnock Committee considered that up to 20 per cent of children needed some form of special help, and this would vary from a minor intervention such as the provision of special equipment, to a major intervention requiring a separate curriculum. Educational needs can be viewed as a continuum, and the problem may be to establish to what extent the present regular school system can be adapted to cater for all or an extended number of needs along the continuum.

The provision of services

The existence of a continuum of educational needs implies a continuum of provision to meet these needs. Intervention at the level of providing equipment might vary from the provision of a hearing aid for a mildly hard of hearing child, to the installation of expensive electronic equipment for the severely hard of hearing. Intervention at the level of providing personnel could vary from a mere reduction of pupil ratio in the ordinary class (thus increasing pupil exposure to teacher), to the provision of a highly trained specialist teacher. The following list is an attempt to rank provisions along a continuum:

- special equipment, such as spectacles, hearing aids;
- special instructional equipment;
- reduced pupil/teacher ratio in regular classes catering for some children with special needs;
- special education adviser for regular teacher;
- peripatetic teacher helping pupils and advising teachers;
- some specialist teachers in the regular school;
- resource centre in the regular school;
- part-time special classes in the regular school;

- permanent special classes in the regular school;
- combination of special day school and regular school;
- special day school;
- residential special school.

A view of educational needs which gives primacy to the value of social competence or of 'communication through consciously shared interests' will dictate that, as far as possible, special intervention should be of the type specified in the least segregational end of the provision continuum. The objective, therefore, of the special programme should be to make special provision for special populations within the regular school system, and to retain children in special classes or schools only as long as there is evidence that these special services are better for the child than the regular school alone. Many factors, however, can impede the achievement of this objective.

Factors affecting the delivery of services

The structure of the regular school system itself

This in itself may present a serious obstacle to the achievement of our aim because it may view the special population as the problem of the specialist, and it may be unaccustomed to adapting to individual needs, or unable to do so because of underfinancing, poor pupil teacher ratios, or inadequate teacher training. Where the State has financial and managerial control over the entire regular school system, the implementation of a national policy need not be impeded. When the State has to operate through Local Authorities, legislation should be required to ensure that national policy is implemented. However, when the State provides substantial financial support for a private education system with little or no control over day-to-day management, special measures are needed to ensure that national policy is not obstructed. Many secondary schools, for historical reasons, are private institutions, and although financed one hundred per cent by the State, day-to-day management rests with private owners. The delivery of State subsidies to such schools should be made dependent on accepting a certain number of special pupils. However, the mere acceptance of pupils without internal adaptation by the school to meet individual needs could be counter-productive. The Department of Education should direct an information service into these schools through special education advisers and inservice training, and ensure that new entrants to the teaching profession in these schools have been exposed to Unit Courses in special education during initial training.

The existing structure of special education

This, too, can impede placement on the basis of educational needs because where existing services are to a great extent structured on special schools and classes, Government may be reluctant to write off a possible ten-year capital expenditure programme on these schools. Furthermore, the technical excellence of many of these schools has won a public respect which in itself creates an obstacle to their adaptation, even if such were desirable. Staff familiarity with the existing system can be a further obstacle to change. Finally, the special education service, like any other service which consistently works towards meeting a recognised public need, establishes itself as a national institution and inevitably has a vested interest — administrative, managerial and professional — in its own continuation.

The delivery of a service which would seriously alter the existing structure must be justified on the basis of strong empiric evidence of worth. A policy which would close all or a very large proportion of existing special schools in favour of making special provision within the regular school system requires to be justified not only to Government, parents, and the public, but also to management and teachers both in existing special schools and also in regular schools. Even if after rigorous evaluation this evidence were available, the segregation of some pupils in special schools for a considerable time would have created a further obstacle to placement in the regular system. It would appear, therefore, that a policy of gradual strengthening of the capacity of the regular system to offer increasing levels of special provision in order to meet higher levels of educational need, would narrow the gap between present practice in special and regular schools. On the other hand, special schools could be required to establish closer links on a day-to-day working basis with the regular school.

Thus the transition from special to regular school could be brought about more easily and effectively if the regular school had the physical facilities and/or teaching expertise to deal with specific learning difficulties, and if at the same time, the special had extended its social training programme through closer contact with the regular school in order to facilitate the eventual placement of some or all pupils within the regular system.

The role of voluntary associations

It is in the nature of voluntary associations that they come into being to solve a problem which the State has either refused or failed to solve. The more successful the association becomes in gaining public support and providing a service to the community, the more likely it is to acquire a large administrative and professional superstructure and consequently, the less likely it is to engage in its own demise even when the reason for its enterprise no longer exists.

A distinction must be made, however, between voluntary associations such as churches with diversified commitments over the whole education arena, and those associations with a specific commitment to one special population or sub-population. Associations for mentally handicapped, autistic children, the physically handicapped and itinerants are examples of the latter type of voluntary association. The integration of pupils from special schools under clerical management into the regular school system need not give rise to any major problem where the regular schools are also church managed.

In the case of voluntary associations committed to one special population, however, the integration of these pupils within the regular system can render the voluntary association superfluous in relation to its school management role. In control structures of this nature, the voluntary association itself can be a major obstacle to achieving the stated objective.

It would appear that the incorporation of the voluntary association within the control structure of the educational system is undesirable. The role of the voluntary association of its nature demands that it remain outside the establishment acting as an external pressure group, to ensure that the sectional interests of the population it represents are adequately and justly considered by Government and by the educational establishment. Such a role implies that voluntary associations should be represented on official policy-making Boards.

Finance

In relation to the general population, it is conceivable that free market forces could deliver the optimum amount of education for society although, in fact, few societies if any would subscribe to this view. The operation of a free market demands that the consumer has sufficient knowledge of the product, and of alternative products, in order to make a free choice. Special populations, however, almost by definition do not have this knowledge of the product (education), and consequently it is taken as axiomatic that the responsibility for providing and financing education for the special populations falls entirely on the State.

The methods of State financing, however, can have serious implications for the delivery of services, namely:

(a) Exchequer funding of the Department of Education through a general finance vote for that Department This method of financing has

the merit that it facilitates making special provision within the regular school system. Furthermore, surplus finance from other programmes can be directed into special interventions, thus enabling the extension of special provision to an increased number of individuals.

The disadvantage of such a structure, however, is that since funds are not specifically designated for a special purpose, an unfavourable administration could trade off the welfare of the special population against that of the general population — of course, the existence of an active voluntary association would act as an effective check against this.

However, the controls applied by the Exchequer might be a more serious obstacle to good delivery. The accounting function of the Department of the Exchequer tends to limit the discretion of the Department of Education in relation to discriminating positively in favour of those in need. This limiting influence can be a serious obstacle to initiating new interventions.

(b) Exchequer funding of the Department of Education through a finance vote for special educational provision This also has the merit of facilitating the making of special provision within the regular school system, but it has the added merit which ensures that finance is available for special provision over and above the provision made for the regular system. It has the further advantage of giving the special education section of the Department control in a trade-off situation. This, in the event of less resources being required for making provision at one end of the continuum, these resources can be reallocated to special programmes at another point on the continuum. This system also provides incentives for management to evaluate services, and through internal transfer of resources to initiate new services.

(c) Exchequer funding of a special populations education authority independent of the Department of Education This system has the advantage that the Authority would have full control over the financing of special interventions. However, it would face very real difficulties in feeding into the complex regular school system, and would have to set up an elaborate organisational structure to ensure that it could collaborate — not only with the Departments of Health, Justice, Environment, and so on, but also with the complex federation of institutions making up the regular education system. The administrative and organisational difficulties are so great that the Authority might feel it was forced to operate a system parallel to the regular system, thus compounding the needs it was designed to meet.

This is not to say, however, that such an Authority would not have a valid overseeing role with an official forum to comment on the effectiveness of special services, and also having the power to ensure that necessary inter-Departmental co-operation was forthcoming.

Of the three methods of financing special interventions, Exchequer funding of the Department of Education through a finance vote for special populations would appear to have greatest merit.

School atmosphere

Even within a centrally controlled regular school system purporting to work to a child-centred curriculum, a wide variety of approaches can be detected as between one school and another and even between teachers in the same school. In a school attempting to offer a child-centred approach, it is not unusual to find one or more teachers whose teaching style is authoritarian, aimed entirely at the average group in the class with scant attention to the aptitudes and needs of individual pupils. A school which expects and insists on conformity of behaviour and achievement is unlikely to provide the best setting in which to deliver special provision for special needs. While lack of concern for the child with special needs is regrettable, it would be counter-productive to place special pupils in such a school or classroom. The inculcation in teachers of attitudes receptive to these pupils is a problem which should be tackled during the initial training period in a college of education. The teachers' registration council could require that trainee teachers take a course in special education for their final degree examination. Such a course would not attempt to provide specialist teaching skills, but would aim to heighten awareness of the individual needs of different populations.

The problem of bringing about attitude change in serving teachers is a more intractable one. It may indeed be necessary to make a realistic decision that certain teachers or schools are not suitable for dealing with special educational needs, although — even in these circumstances — efforts should be made to make the appropriate information available to those teachers through teachers' journals and inservice training courses. Official recognition in monetary terms should be seen to be given to those teachers and schools deemed to be capable of meeting special needs. While teachers in regular schools engaged in special intervention should be paid a special allowance in recognition of their added responsibility, those who acquire specialist training should receive an additional allowance. A post of special responsibility appropriately remunerated should be reserved for the teacher heading special intervention programmes within the school.

The present system of providing specialist training for teachers of the mentally handicapped and a different training for teachers of the deaf, blind, and so on, has undoubted advantages for those children at the extreme end of the continuum of educational needs. It may be, however, that fewer of these specialist teachers may be required than was previously thought necessary. It may be also that a special training aimed at meeting the less extreme type of needs of mentally handicapped, deaf, blind, and so forth, as well as those of special populations such as itinerants and language minority groups — emphasising similarities of achievements rather than differences — might provide a specialist type teacher who could function very effectively as a specialist class teacher in the regular school and, at the same time, act as a consultant on special needs to the regular staff.

Community attitudes to special populations

The delivery of a special service can be impeded in whole or part by the attitude of a hostile host community. Hostility to minority language groups, itinerants, or certain ethnic groups stem from factors outside the school system, and the resolution of these difficulties may rest principally with other agencies. Social acceptance at some level of the special population is essential, and frequently acceptance may depend on the proportionate balance between host community and the special population. Similarly with the school itself; a disproportionate intake of members of the special population into a school can change the nature of the school and establish it in the community's view as a special ghetto school.

In this context, the Education Authority might find the notion of a *pareto* improvement, a notion borrowed from welfare economics, a useful one — a pareto improvement is defined as 'a change in economic organisation that makes everyone better off — or more precisely, that makes one or more members of society better off without making anyone worse off'.

This notion applied to educational intervention on behalf of the special population would attempt to ensure that benefit to the special population did not involve a reduced service to the host population. In the longer term, benefit to the special population would be seen to confer benefit on the general population.

Parents' attitudes to special services

The aspiration of parents to have their child at home and participating in the regular school system must influence the type of provision offered. A special intervention on behalf of the child in the regular school may frequently require that an educational social worker would form a link between the home and school. The provision of an indirect special service such as this to the parents must be seen as an educational support service and consequently should come within the control of the

Educational Authority. In the absence of such an educational/social service, or even if such a service exists, the school itself should have available within the school a teacher charged with the responsibility of opening lines of communication between the parents and the children in receipt of special services.

Working relationships with other agencies

While many government departments and agencies contribute towards the provision of special services for special populations, a distinction is made between — on the one hand — those departments whose contribution cannot in itself limit the effectiveness of the educational programme and — on the other hand — departments whose policies may have the potential, not only to limit the educational service, but in fact contribute towards the creation of a new category of special educational needs. For example, assessment of children on the basis of disability by the Health Department does not prevent the Education Authority from classifying special populations on the basis of special educational needs and making provision accordingly — of course co-operation between both Departments could, no doubt, ensure a type of assessment which would meet the requirements of both Departments at reduced inconvenience to pupils and teachers, and at a reduced cost to the taxpayer.

However, the allocation policy of the Housing Authority could, in itself, result in the creation of a new special population whose special educational needs could be met only to a limited extent by a special educational programme. In this latter case, the special education Department should seek representation as of right on the policy-making committee of the Housing Allocation Authority where the educational implications of housing policies could be examined. Such representation should be regarded as an educational intervention of a preventive nature, and intervention at this stage would undoubtedly be infinitely more effective than any type of subsequent remedial provision aimed at the resultant ghetto population.

The representation of the Department of Education on the Housing Authority's Planning and Allocation Committees, as well as on State and semi-state committees charged with providing physical facilities for itinerants or other special populations, should have statutory support.

In the case of Departments such as Health, Justice and Manpower which can be seen in some of their functions as offering a support service to the Education Department, co-operation may frequently depend on the nature of the working relationship carefully built up by diligent, well disposed officials over a period of years, and such efforts are to be encouraged. Legislation to control such inter-departmental endeavours could well result in a formalism which would inhibit initiative. However, the importance of co-operation demands that present endeavours in this direction be given official support, and that some pressure be exerted on sections of departments which are negligent in this area. A national council for special populations appointed by the Government charged with the responsibility of reporting to the Government on the effectiveness of co-ordination procedures and recommending improved strategies as required, would strengthen the position of co-operative departments and bring pressure to bear on the less co-operative section.

Arrangements for delivery of services

Arrangements for delivery of service, therefore, must allow for these factors already discussed. Certain stages can be identified which guide us towards achieving the goal of making special provision as far as possible within the regular school system.

(a) Departments of Education and Finance should seek Government approval for funding through a separate finance vote for special education services to ensure that special interventions in the regular school system were not dissipated over the general population.

(b) Assessment of the existing school populations in receipt of special services in terms of their educational needs could then proceed.

(c) The Department of Education would compile a register of regular schools considered suitable and capable of offering special services.

(d) A number of these schools might be selected on a trial basis and special provision made within them to accommodate children from special populations. Special services — for example equipment, physical adaptation of the building, more favourable pupil-teacher ratio in certain classes, special teachers, and so on — would be provided. Placement of pupils with special needs within this school would be made by an area placement committee which would include the Department of Education Inspector or Education Officer, the principal teacher of the regular school, the teacher having a post of responsibility for special services within the regular school, and a principal teacher representing special schools in the area.

(e) The Director of Special Services within the school would be responsible to the principal teacher for providing the necessary information both to parents and the community on the one hand, and to the Department of Education on the other.

Structure for evaluating services

Efficient delivery of service demands that adequate information collection and processing procedures be built into the structure of the service so that the effectiveness of the service itself can be evaluated. A striking feature of some present services is the vast amount of detailed information assumed to exist. It is claimed that the special teacher who has this information is making vital day-to-day decisions about the individual child's learning programme, and indeed this detailed understanding of the individual is often cited as one of the major merits of special education. Undoubtedly, most special services amass a considerable amount of information about individual children's needs and progress, and this can be found in school assessment forms and progress record cards. This information, however, tends to be used only within the confines of a triangular interaction between pupil, teacher and parent.

A relatively minor adjustment to the information collection and processing system at school level would provide invaluable management information for the school authority which could evaluate its own effectiveness and alter procedures in the light of its analysis of effectiveness. If the information collection and processing is effectively co-ordinated as between schools, the central management authority could be in a position to evaluate the effectiveness of general programmes, and the formulation of future policy would be based on a clearer knowledge of the potential of sub-programmes rather than on the impressionistic claims made by professionals whose major experience may be of a day-to-day exposure to operating a programme with little responsibility for programme analysing and evaluation.

In the absence of structured information systems, the administrator must be directed by the consensus view of professionals as well as by the results of limited sample surveys. The administrator is then less than effective, not only in making decisions as to which services should be developed and to what extent, but he is also severely limited when arguing the case for increased financial assistance from the State or the public.

The extra cost of comprehensive data collection and processing service need not be great — a large amount of information is at present being provided by schools, but it is of such a nature that it helps the central administrator to discharge his traditional accounting responsibility for the disbursement of public funds rather than his less widely acknowledged responsibility to Government for ensuring that a service is achieving its objectives.

With the minor adjustments suggested, the information system at school level would be the responsibility of the Director of Special Services in the school; processing at area or regional level would be the responsibility of the Schools Inspector or Education Officer, and the final processing of the data supplied from the regions would be done by the central Department of Education. This information would be used on an on-going basis to evaluate the effectiveness of various interventions, and consequently would form the basis for future policy-making. A similar information system would operate in special schools, thus facilitating comparisons between special interventions.

12 Costing for special populations

Maurice Peston
Queen Mary College, University of London

The study of costing is, of course, interesting in its own right, but the purpose of the present essay is to consider the matter in much broader terms. The purpose of the analysis of costs and costing procedures is to assist the process of decision-making, and to help in identifying those areas in which policy changes are possible and, perhaps, desirable. It should also be emphasised that costing is a *part* of the governance of an educational system or subsystem. It is not the *whole*. There is a widespread belief (influenced occasionally by harsh experience) that issues of finance are only raised in education when the intention is to reduce expenditure. When resources are relatively abundant there is less concern with the efficiency of their use. Only when decision-makers feel severely constrained do they look for stringent economies within what they are already undertaking. Against this it must be said that there is no logical reason why financing should be considered seriously only in conditions of contraction. Furthermore, resources are never available in such abundance that policy-makers are free to do anything they like. In particular, while economic growth means greater availability of funds for action, it is noteworthy that desirable projects increase just as rapidly. It is, therefore, not always the case that the governance of education is unequivocally easier in times of rapid economic expansion than in other circumstances.

But all this is, of course, academic at the present time when economic performance is poor and the economic outlook poorer still. At the moment there is no doubt that costing must be taken most seriously, and procedures devised so that resources made available for special populations are used as efficaciously as possible. This should enable the case for providing support for special populations to be considerably strengthened, and should lead to a choice of superior as opposed to inferior means of helping those populations. While it is true that the interests of the special populations must be continually emphasised, it is wrong to believe that these are served by obscuring problems of cost or finance.

The central cost concept used in economics is opportunity or alternative cost. From the point of view of the economist something is a cost if it is avoidable. If it is unavoidable, no matter how burdensome, irksome, or even painful it is, it is nonetheless not a cost. The idea of cost in economics, therefore, is closely related to choice and the taking of decisions. The costs of a decision or the pursuit of a particular activity are what is incurred as a result of that activity compared with what otherwise would be the case. If nothing is incurred, nothing is given up as a result of pursuing the activity, then no cost is involved.

This doctrine of opportunity cost is transparently easy to comprehend, but is frequently misunderstood. It is to be compared and contrasted with two other cost doctrines. One is that of so-called real cost, or pain cost. This regards cost either in physical terms as the amount of resources used up by an activity, or in psychological terms as the painful experience imposed by the activity on a person or group of people. From the economist's point of view these are costs if they are avoidable, but not otherwise. What is important to comprehend is that the economist is not denying the existence of the phenomena of resource depletion or of unhappy mental states. He simply does not identify them with costs. To take an obvious example: the special population may suffer from whatever it is that makes it special, but it is a mistake to refer to a physical disability (say) as a cost. It is not a cost if it is unavoidable. It is a cost if it is avoidable, for example, the cost of saving a given amount of public expenditure, or using the funds for some other purpose will be the extent to which the special population continues to suffer from its various disabilities.

A second concept of cost is that of cost incurred in the past or historical cost. Again it is always interesting and important to explore what was given up in the past in order to allow some activity to take place. It may be that that past cost enables some activity to continue in the present and on into the future. But, if there is no way of avoiding or reversing this cost incurred in the past, it no longer becomes a cost as far as the continuation of the activity in question is concerned. Once certain resources are irreversibly sunk into an activity or certain commitment irrevocably entered into, they cease to be part of the costs of the activity in the sense of varying as the activity varies. This is, perhaps, the most difficult idea for the non-economist to accept. It must, therefore, be emphasised that the economist is not arguing that past commitments are unimportant for the present, and may be ignored. Quite the contrary: commitments are of considerable significance in the analysis of costing and the governance of education. What is being stated here is much simpler, namely that commitment once incurred constrains present and future action, and influences other costs, but is no longer a cost itself.

The concept of opportunity cost relies heavily on the distinction between what is given and what is variable. Its application in practice, therefore, requires a careful specification of the nature and scale of the activity or class of activities under consideration, and the circumstances in which decisions about them are taken. Whether we are discussing the choice between undertaking an activity or not, or varying the scale of an activity, or substituting one activity for another, we are obliged to concentrate on what we have to give up as a result.

Consider, for example, a programme of additional education for some special population. The cost of that additional education may include the extra teachers we have to recruit for it. In normal circumstances we may evaluate that at whatever it is that these extra teachers have to be paid. Suppose, however, that (temporarily at least) teachers are rather scarce, and that the teachers recruited for this programme will have to be moved from some other one. In that case the value of the work they are doing exceeds what they are currently being paid, and it is this which has to be counted as a cost for the new programme. In other words, in a time of teacher scarcity the costs of helping one special population may have to be measured as the value or benefit foregone by not helping or ceasing to help another. Of course, the point also holds in reverse. If teachers are in excess supply and would otherwise be unemployed, their cost, as far as the whole economy is concerned, is less than the salaries they are paid.

This last consideration applies to the treatment of such comparatively fixed resources as school buildings. Obviously, if the economy is fully employed and new buildings must be constructed to cater for the special population, the costs of those buildings (suitably amortised) must be included in the relevant costing exercise. But, if the buildings are already there, and cannot be used for other purposes, the only new cost involved is the additional wear and tear resulting from more intensive use on behalf of the special population. To say that the new activity must meet its 'fair share of the original or already committed cost' of the building is an irrelevance when considering whether or not to undertake it. Such a consideration only becomes important when the new activity squeezes out an existing one, or gives rise to the necessity of new construction even if it is not directly for itself.

The analysis here gives rise to an interesting and significant contrast between the public and private sectors. Suppose there are two empty buildings identical in all respects except that one is in the public sector and the other is privately owned. It would be argued that in pure theory it is a matter of indifference whether education for a special population took place in one rather than the other. The only costs involved are the additional wear and tear of the building if used. But in practice the position is rather different. If the special education programme is a public one, and the building is a government one and cannot (as presently foreseen) be used for any other purpose, the authorities may decide not to include any cost for it in assessing whether or not to proceed. But, if the building is in private hands, the authorities may be asked to pay rent for it. Strictly speaking this rent is a transfer payment from the public to the private sectors, and is not a cost to the economy as a whole. Nonetheless, the authorities will not view it that way, and will actually treat the payment as a cost. This type of complication, arising from the imperfect working of the economic system, can be taken further. Suppose the special education programme is a private one (albeit one undertaken by a voluntary or charitable body). In this case the authorities may regard the transfer of the empty building to their use as a cost to the public sector and may demand a rent. Thus, although the reality of the empty buildings and the special education programme may seem fixed, institutional forces in practice will determine whether the use of a particular resource is regarded as costless or not in the process of taking decisions.

Now, it is important not to take this example too far. There may be other perfectly good reasons why the different cases should be treated differently. There may be legal constraints on the availability of public buildings for private uses. The condition of uselessness for other purposes may not be met and, in particular, because of uncertainty about the future, there must always be some probability that the buildings may be required for other purposes. Nonetheless, the general point holds that, although purely theoretical and abstract considerations may lead to one result, this may be changed, even distorted, once institutional reality has to be taken into account.

A similar problem occurs when the relationship between separate public sector agencies is taken into account. One agency may be in charge of buildings and be empowered to levy a fee for its use. The agency concerned with education for the special population may have a budget, part of which it can use to rent buildings. The first agency may endeavour to take a fee from the second, even for a building that is not in use, in order to meet its financial objective. The second agency may discover it cannot afford this, and overcrowd an existing building in order to save money. Relative to the constraints imposed on both agencies the building in question would impose a cost on an educational programme and may have to be treated as such despite the fact that in a wider context it is an idle resource.

These paradoxes and pitfalls can be multiplied endlessly. The purpose of mentioning them is to stress the central proposition that costs depend on circumstances and are not in some crude sense objectively given. Since circumstances change, costs change. Moreover, since circumstances are not known for certain, there is an additional complication of all decision-making involving costs, namely allowing for uncertainty.

Uncertainty, timing and scale

The costs of an activity are the value of what is given up as a result of the activity, but this may not be known for certain. The question arises, how is this uncertainty to be taken into account? One answer to the question which is widely accepted is to regard the uncertainty itself as a cost (that is, what we incur as a result of the activity is a lack of certainty of what the outcome will be).

Even without uncertainty economic and social change mean that costs vary over time. Thus, the circumstances pertinent to the estimation of the costs of an activity include its timing. There are two aspects of this which are worth mentioning. If the activity is regarded as finite and self-contained (for example, raising the literacy level of a specified group), undertaking it in one time period may be cheaper than undertaking it in another. (It is necessary to add at this point what underlies everything written here, namely that cost is not all. Since benefits also vary, a rule based on cost minimisation need be neither efficient nor optimal.) Secondly, if the activity is regarded as a continuous one, its costs at any one time need not be the same as at another. This is so even if the real resources it uses are constant, since it is the alternative use to which those resources can be put which is important.

A related question on dynamics is that the costs of an activity need not coincide wholly in time with the activity itself. What is actually foregone as a result of doing something now is to do something else in the future. This aspect of the problem is exceedingly important for the education of special populations, for a failure not to deal with certain aspects of this early on in life (that is, a decision not to incur certain costs now) can give rise to much more intractable problems later (that is, a need to incur greater costs in the future). What we are discussing here are not the costs of the activity as such, but the costs of deferment.

One final point on circumstances concerns scale. Just as the cost of an activity may depend on timing, it will also depend on scale in several ways. Firstly, there is the simple point of how many members of the special population are to be assisted. Secondly, there is the level of education and educational performance to be aimed at. Thirdly, there is the speed with which it is intended that all this should happen. Costs will increase with numbers and levels. *A fortiori* they may be expected to increase with the intensity of the educational process, especially after a point. Beyond this it cannot be assumed that the special population, no matter how carefully it is selected, is completely homogeneous. An increase in scale may imply, therefore, an extension of education to more and more difficult individuals. Costs will, therefore, rise with scale simply because of the heterogeneity of the group being educated.

This leads to an important symmetry in the explanation of cost. If the population is heterogeneous, as attempts are made to reach the same set level of educational achievement for increasingly difficult cases, costs will rise disproportionately. Alternatively, costs in that sense are held constant, and average and marginal educational achievement diminishes with scale. What we are foregoing in this latter case is the greater educational achievement of the less easily educable people. In other words, the cost does not disappear because resources are not committed for a particular purpose, they merely emerge in another form, and are borne by one lot of people rather than another.

In point of fact, the opportunity-cost doctrine is dominated by a symmetry principle. If X and Y are mutually exclusive alternatives, the cost of X is Y, and the cost of Y is X. This is extremely important, because in common practice the concept of cost is frequently taken to imply what new commitment is incurred when the *status quo* is changed. The decision to do something involves costs, the decision not to does not. In economics that is an erroneous proposition. The cost of change is the giving up of the *status quo*, and the cost of the *status quo* is the giving up of the change. Thus, a decision to help a special population certainly involves whatever it costs to do that. But a decision not to help that same population equally involves accepting as a cost its poorer educational performance.

Costing as an approach to programmes

We have argued above that, although it is true that many people who are actually engaged in education are fearful of a costing approach, their fears are misplaced. It is, of course, a matter of historical fact that costs, costing, and the like tend to be emphasised in times of economic difficulty and, therefore, are correlated with attempts to reduce educational activities and to put brakes on expansion, especially expansion into new fields. But there is no necessary connection between a concern with costs and the contraction of education. Moreover, there is a necessary connection between a correct examination of costs and a correct specification both of the activity in question and its alternatives. Those who are directly involved in education, especially that directed at groups with special difficulties and disabilities, must want to see resources used for such groups in the most efficacious ways. They are obliged, therefore, to ask exactly the same questions of the activities to be pursued as lead on to an assessment of costs. It is not too much to assert that irrationalism about costs is inevitably accompanied by irrationalism in the process of education itself.

Of course, we must not be too sanguine about all this. Administrators, especially those whose business is finance, do misuse the cost concept themselves, identifying, as they tend to do, costs with expenditure. They are able to do this partly because traditional costs and expenditure are regarded as the same thing and, indeed, for everyday purposes, they are most likely to be so. In addition, expenditure is a seemingly hard phenomenon, while many costs in the extended economic sense are elusive and hard to grasp, let alone measure. It follows that in advocating a costing approach, we must be careful not to play into the hands of the financial controllers, and accept their concept of cost as all there is worth taking notice of. One way of doing this is to put in a certain amount of effort identifying other costs, and also arguing on relevant occasions that financing is not a cost that should influence the decision in question.

But, having said that, it is important not to go to the other extreme. Financing of education is not a trivial matter. Teachers have to be paid, and other bills have to be met. Where fees and other user charges are not levied, taxes have to be raised or other forms of public expenditure limited. Thus, although not all expenditure is a social cost and, therefore, should not be taken directly into account when assessing the desirability or optimality of a project, it still gives rise to serious problems, not least to do with administrative feasibility. In addition, financing involves costs in two indirect ways. One is the administrative burden of raising, dispensing and controlling the money. The other is the possible distortion of resource allocation consequent on some but not all public expenditure and tax structures.

This leads us on to note that there will be costs in assessing costs and benefits of particular projects. Although the nature of certain costs is apparent, how to estimate them can often be obscure. Suppose the problem to be decided is which of two special populations to help. An example might be which of two inner city areas is to be given first priority. (For the sake of argument assume that the educational process is such that sharing the available resources between them is grossly inefficient.) The cost of going ahead with one will be the fact that the other is neglected, possibly temporarily but, perhaps, even permanently. (Since we have assumed that the resources are already committed, the cost of these may be ignored for the problem in hand.) How is the one alternative to be evaluated compared with the other? One of the inner cities may be dominated by literacy problems connected with an influx of immigrants; the other may have educational difficulties simply due to the poverty of the domestic population who live there. Without pursuing these seemingly non-comparable cases further, it may be recognised immediately that there is no obviously objective answer to the question, what is the cost of helping this special population? Without asserting that the answer to the question is entirely arbitrary, it is apparent that it contains a large subjective element.

The motivating force behind this and similar discussions is the special population itself and its education. The natural sorts of question to ask, therefore, seem to be: how much is being spent on this population? What are they costing the community at large? What share of the cost are they bearing themselves? Certainly, these are interesting questions both about costs and expenditure, but they do direct attention solely and probably excessively to distributional issues. While such matters of equity must be given a due place in any approach to economic policy, efficiency and effectiveness must not be neglected. This requires a different formulation of questions with greater attention being paid to the policies themselves and the policy instruments.

Insofar as the educational process itself is a good thing, a quantification of the means gets very close to being a quantification of the ends. Thus, to ask what share of educational resources is being devoted to West Indian teenagers or to the blind or to the inhabitants of the inner cities is important. But it is also the case that education must be judged by results or performance. It is then necessary to try and identify a particular means—ends relationship, and to associate with it an assessment of costs and benefits.

An example would be remedial literacy classes in secondary education. Suppose we define the special population as illiterates of secondary school age. A programme of literacy within the secondary school can then be costed and related to the performance of these literacy classes. The purpose of this is to gain some measure of the resource costs of reducing the fraction of illiterates by x per cent. What is relevant here is not so much that resources are being directed at illiterates, but how effective those resources are, and what it costs to reduce the illiteracy rate. (It is possible to go further and to state that sometimes concentrating solely on the funds themselves, that is, we are spending £Ym. on illiterates, may detract from considerations of effectiveness of the programme. To commit the resources and incur the costs is generally only a beginning, not an end in itself.)

Programme performance and their benefits

Having emphasised costing as an approach to programmes and as providing one basis for a consideration of their effectiveness, it is again possible to state a principle of symmetry which helps in giving a perspective to the discussion. We may start from programmes and their costs and proceed to performance and their benefits. The special population may then be defined as whoever are affected, actually or potentially, by the programme. Alternatively, we may start with the population, see what costs are incurred and benefits received in educating them. The programme or set of programmes may then be defined as those that influence, actually or potentially, this population.

In the latter case, the general and symmetric position would be via a matrix, the rows of which would define various education programmes and the columns various populations (special or otherwise). An entry in the matrix would describe how the programme relates to the population, in terms of resources committed, costs incurred, educational benefits achieved, and a valuation of those benefits. An empty cell simply means that the programme in question has no effect on the population in question. A row with no empty cells means that the programme affects all populations. A column with no empty cells means that the special population is affected by all programmes. Very specific programmes should have many empty cells in their rows and, if programmes are also tailor made to special populations, each population should have many zeros in their columns. If a cost matrix is calculated separately from a benefit matrix, a successful educational programme overall would have the structure of entries and their relative sizes very much the same in both matrices. The sum of the entries in any row are the total costs of (or benefits to) a whole programme. The sum of the entries of any column are the total costs of (or benefits to) a whole special population. Thus, formulating the subject in matrix terms shows the essential unity of an approach via programmes or populations.

The dynamic context

We have attached some weight to the proposition that costs and costing must be placed in a dynamic context. This is the counterpart of the proposition that decision-making and governance must be placed in a similar context. Dynamics here means several things:

(a) there are fixed costs of starting up any operation, to which must be added the variable costs that depend on its scale in various dimensions;

(b) there are the costs of reacting to new circumstances as they arise;

(c) there are the costs of continually testing whether the policy is being effective; both in achieving the desired objectives for the individuals being educated and ensuring that these individuals do comprise the whole of the special population under consideration;

(d) there are the costs of innovation, which include both the direct costs of new approaches to a particular area of education, and the indirect costs of changing over from the existing one;

(e) finally, there are the costs of identifying and rectifying mistakes, both of method in general and of misdiagnosis of individual problems, in particular.

An inevitable consequence of the dynamic approach to the subject is the need to distinguish between costs *ex ante* and costs *ex post facto*. We may consider the following:

(a) the cost as an annual flow incurring in helping the special population;

(b) the cost as a lifetime sum (suitably discounted) spent on an average member of the special population;

(c) the incremental cost of extending the range of educational provision;

(d) the incremental cost of extending the level of provision;

(e) the incremental cost of extending the intensity or speed or provision.

In all these cases planning and decision-making starts with estimating such costs *ex ante*. It is trivially obvious that the feasibility of a programme of education for a special population (let alone its desirability or optimality) cannot be determined without such cost estimates. At the very least a subset of costs, namely expenditures, must be related to the available financial provision. This may also be put in the form that desired or needed financial provision will depend on estimated costs and expenditures.

What is less frequently appreciated is that costs must be monitored at regular intervals. Again one reason for this is the financial control of the programme, that is, the need to maintain proper accounting standards. But all that is far less important than the use of costs as a first step in the assessment of actual effectiveness and value for money. An *ex post* analysis of costs enables the decision-maker to see whether the resources made available to the programme were actually used for the original purpose. The categories and headings under which the original plans were made are also appropriate for *ex post* analysis. In addition, and more important still, concern with cost *ex post facto* leads irresistibly to the question of whether the programme worked in the way intended, and did yield the returns that justified its inception.

All programmes of this kind must be interpreted in terms of learning, or of feedback from experience to new plans and actions. The discovery that costs differ in either direction from what was planned may lead to a modification of the education provision. Some activities which were justified because they seemed inexpensive relative to what they were supposed to achieve may subsequently be reassessed as too dear, while others may turn out to give much greater returns than expected. Subject to the points made below about costs of change, there will be a tendency to shift the programme in the latter direction and away from the former.

Of course, there are clear difficulties in the way of *ex post* analysis. The collection of the relevant data is difficult and can be expensive. Such monitoring can also get in the way of the actual education. In addition, effectiveness can often only be judged in the longer term, so that concentration on costs and expenditures may make the decision-making process rather myopic. Nonetheless, while it will be necessary to be on guard against an undue emphasis on control of actual resource use, to place no weight on it at all would surely be foolhardy.

There is an additional technical point on dynamics that must be made at this stage. Economic systems grow and are subject to inflation. It is customary to argue that inflation, in particular, is the business of finance ministries and not education departments. Thus, it is suggested that the correct procedure for costing of an education programme is at constant average prices, which can then be adjusted for inflation subsequently, especially when it comes to working out financial budgets. The justification of this is that inflation is not supposed to influence relative prices and, in particular, will affect costs and benefits equally, leaving any decisions about net benefits unchanged. In these circumstances it is then asserted that budgets determined on the basis of zero inflation should and will be fully supplemented to an extent equal to the actual rate of inflation.

The objection to this position is twofold. One is that inflation does not actually leave relative prices unchanged. A second is that nowadays finance ministries do not provide full inflation supplementation, but use so-called cash limits as a means to damp down the rate of inflation. The result is that at the present time there are considerable doubts of how decision-makers (notably in the public sector) ought to allow for inflation in their plans. In particular, should they take cognisance of the possibility of non-full supplementation, and set aside financial provision to avoid the contingency of not being able to meet their bills?

The significance of economic development is that it affects relative prices, especially those of labour and capital. Thus, education projects of a long-term nature should not base all their plans on the relativities existing at their start date, but should take account of changes in those relativities. In particular, a long-term project might aim to be more capital intensive (if that is feasible) to take full advantage of the benefits of the fall in the price of equipment compared with that of teachers.

This proposition too is complicated by the reality of unemployment, and stagflation. Although the opportunity cost of bringing the unemployed part of the labour force into work appears low, in inflationary circumstances it may be extremely high. The reason for this is that when people experience a high rate of inflation and expect it to continue, they may respond in an even more inflationary fashion to increases in public expenditure rather than raising output. In other words, if an additional education programme involves an increase in net public expenditure this may add to the rate of inflation even though there are plenty of resources that remain unemployed. This is the paradox of public policy in conditions of stagflation and inflationary expectations which so far governments have not solved.

This is the stage of the argument to emphasise, therefore, that it is likely that most education for special populations will be publicly financed and publicly provided, so that most costing exercises will take place within a public sector context. We have already pointed out that, although from many theoretical points whether an activity occurs in the public or private sectors is an irrelevance, in practice it makes a great deal of difference.

In many countries there will be charitable provision of education for certain special populations or charitable sources of finance. This will occur typically with the physically disabled such as the blind or deaf, and for the mentally disabled. In this area where the medical and the socio-educational merge into one another, governments may actually choose to act via public finance and public subsidy of private sector agencies, so that these do more than cater for a tiny minority of members of a special population.

Beyond that a government may include as part of its own programme an obligation on firms to deal with various aspects of the educational and training needs of special populations. To the extent that it is agreed that young people nearing the end of their formal secondary education or during the course of their further education require a programme which brings the workplace and school or college close together, the requirement will hold *a fortiori* for special populations who face major difficulties with respect to employability. Thus, firms may be required to employ a quota of people with special disabilities and organise a course of training for them in association with their education. This may be funded directly by the State (possibly in association with a tax levy on all firms), or by allowing firms extra tax reliefs to offset revenue.

While using the private sector may complicate the financial arrangements and lead to difficulties of accountability, the education programme may itself become less costly as a result. This would be the case if an education programme designed to prepare the special population for the world of work were confined entirely to schools and colleges. It is highly likely that many more resources would have to be used taking the workplace to the educational institution rather than allowing the two worlds to operate in parallel each complementing the other.

Categories of cost

Most of our discussion of costs can be regarded as divided into the following four themes:

(a) the costs of identifying and monitoring the special population, that is, decision and organisation costs;

(b) the costs of offsetting whatever are regarded as the deficiencies and disabilities of the special population, for example, making transfer payments to them to make up for an inability to earn a high enough income;

(c) the costs of remedial action, for example, the provision of special medical care which might raise their learning capacity, or catering to their educational needs when they differ from those of the population at large;

(d) the costs of preventative action, for example, the diagnosis of particular conditions, and the provision of special services to prevent these arising in the future.

Not all of these are costs in the same sense. In addition, the categories are highly interrelated and merge one into the other. It is also obvious that a decision not to incur costs or commit resources to one category may lead to an increase in costs in another. Thus, no attempt may be made to monitor the state of a special problem or pay attention to the education it is getting or whatever needs are peculiar to itself. Eventually, this may give rise to a state of affairs which is so socially damaging that action is called for by the population at large either on grounds of general principle or because they themselves are beginning to suffer from the neglect of the special group. Monitoring and preventative costs were saved, but remedial costs and transfer payments are increased. Furthermore, the latter may turn out to be much larger than the former, especially if the need for action itself is regarded as a crisis.

It may also happen that a decision to monitor a special population (even if it is stated as involving no greater commitment than that) discovers and makes public problems that would otherwise be ignored. In practice, therefore, it is most likely that pressure will develop to commit resources under the other three categories. Theoretically, this will only happen if it is adjudged that national welfare will rise as a consequence. But the more cynical officials in finance departments would point out that decision-making is never as accurate or as cold blooded as that. In the administrative and political systems characteristic of the OECD the discovery of a problem is tantamount to devoting some resources to solving it or offsetting its bad consequences, no matter what careful analysis might suggest about effectiveness. In other words, in a costing exercise the key issue is the identification of the special population and its needs. A commitment under that heading leads rapidly and virtually unstoppably to a commitment under one or all of the three others.

The four categories, identification, transfer payments, prevention and remedial action, can also be related to a categorisation of who bears the costs. The following classification is worth considering:

(a) the cost the special population bears because of its problems;

(b) the cost the special population imposes directly on the rest of the community because of its problems;

(c) the cost (notably the tax burden) imposed on the general population by measures to help the special population;

(d) the cost (again notably the tax burden) imposed on the general population by measures to help those connected with the special population.

In a sense it could be argued that incurring costs under headings (c) and (d) give rise to benefits in the form of the reduction or disappearance of costs under headings (a) and (b). It is also worth remarking that the successful commitment of resources under heading (c) will simultaneously deal with (a) and (b) and remove the need for expenditure under (d). Thus, raising the educational (and related economic) performance of the special population to the average of the community at large will also remove the need for special help for (say) the families of the special population. Of course, it is necessary not to be too sanguine about this last contingency. Special educational help for the physically disabled will help them more easily to make their way in the world and will cause them to become easily employable. But their physical disability as such will remain, so that additional aid for their parents and dependents will probably continue to be a necessity.

This does lead the discussion on to the point of inter-disciplinarity and the interrelationship of the different social services. The theme of this essay is the costing of educational programmes for special populations. In the first instance the education system will see these populations as special precisely because of their educational deficiencies and requirements. Nonetheless the origin of their problems will often lie elsewhere, and thus the special education programme may itself be a *pis aller* or offset to difficulties which really ought to have been dealt with in other ways.

The obvious examples are educational problems that arise for economic or social reasons. A remedial reading class may contain many young people whose problems arise from the bad housing in which they live, or the size of their families, or sheer shortage of income at home. They may play truant to supplement the family income, and may be able to do so because of lack of parental control. This is not to argue against remedial reading classes. Quite the contrary. But it is to say that a careful costing of such an education programme may lead to the conclusion that resources used to deal with the origins of the problem will ultimately yield a larger return.

Perhaps, more significant than that, a joint programme extending well beyond education could be more effective relative to the costs incurred than a series of separate programmes. Thus, although the main focus of this paper is the financing of education, it is necessary to stress continually that the subject of special populations is inter-disciplinary in character and involves simultaneously all the social services. As we have already stated, therefore, the usual problems arise whether resources available for one set of policy measures could not be better employed by other agencies controlling other instruments. Policy needs to be co-ordinated, especially as success in one area may lead to increases in costs in another. Expenditure on training may lead to a greater improvement in educational performance than expenditure on education itself. Expenditure on health care may enable a group which hitherto were unable to attend school now to do so; thus raising the costs of education.

Analysis of these problems is likely to be most successful if all the social sciences are brought to bear rather than just a single one. To take an obvious example, the employability of a special population may depend on their acceptance by the population at large the conditions for which may be clarified by sociologists or social psychologists even though the consequences of their studies will be economic. In other words, a costing exercise will often need to be much broader than just a study of the resources committed to the education of a special population.

The question of transfers

Reverting to our main theme, the question of transfers is worth exploring a little further. It is about at least three things: (a) Who pays? (b) Who bears the other cost burdens? and (c) Who receives the benefits? It is thus not merely to do with transfer payments or social security and taxes.

It could be argued that the whole subject is essentially distributional in that it arises from a concern in the population at large with the condition of the special population (or special populations). Nowadays in society there is a general concern with issues of equity, and a desire to seek out examples of inequity to see what can be done about them. This might be thought of as part of what we have already described as the cost which spills over from the special population to the general one.

But there is much more to this interrelationship than just a broad psychic spillover. The special population may prove burdensome in much more direct ways. An inability to understand the language may at the very least be a nuisance when it comes to using shops or quite dangerous if it results in a failure to understand traffic signs. A failure to find work, apart from the deadweight loss of output, is now generally recognised to lead to a variety of forms of social disruption which the general population finds itself having to control and offset. Thus, if education for the special population makes its members more employable, there will be a resource saving to people at large as well as a reduction in social security benefits. It follows that a costing exercise which concentrates solely on the taxes paid by one group to finance the education received by another can be misleading.

A correct analysis of transfers would have to take account of payments being made to the special population as a result of broad social policy which might be reduced by a successful programme of education. It would also have to take note of any taxes paid by the special population, especially out of the income they earn from subsequent improved employability.

This is not intended to lead to the conclusion that there is no net transfer from the one group to another. Indeed, it is possible that the total transfer of resources far exceeds that which is committed initially. To start to help the special population on a small scale may increase people's consciousness of the wider issues, both for this group and for others similar to it. The so-called arguments of 'the slippery slope' or 'the thin end of the wedge' are not always invalid. The correct conclusion, therefore, is simply that the analysis of transfers must be undertaken in broad terms, and cannot be confined to the specific education programme itself, who pays for it and who benefits at a particular point in time.

Programme size and intensity

Our opening discussion referred to the importance of costs varying as the scale of the education programme increased. This leads on to the question of the size of the special population. This will vary over time either for reasons exogenous to the education programme (for example, the economy may attract more migrant workers) or because of the education programme itself (for example, the success of the programme may attract new customers or encourage its practitioners to seek them out). Before a programme starts, therefore, one costing exercise will be required relative to the problem as it is then perceived, and another needs to be based on alternative possible expansion rates (including the zero one).

In doing this, attention must be paid to an aspect of the matter which we have already referred to, namely the costs of changing the scale and intensity of the problem. If the latter are likely to be unduly high, it will be sensible to take account of this in the initial planning. The system as set up may be large and rather too expensive relative to the best estimate of population size, but can as a result be more easily and cheaply varied in response to changing demand and need. In other words, planning might be based on several possible costing exercises in which the risks of excess capacity are weighed against the risk of high costs of change if that proves necessary. Of course, in areas in which experience is limited the reverse is also true. A system may be started at too low a scale compared with the size of the population it is envisaged will be dealt with ultimately. Although this may add to the costs of expansion, this is worthwhile if sufficient experience is developed to modify the nature of the education programme and guide it in a more useful direction.

All these considerations about the size of the programme are also relevant to its intensity. A case can be made out in some circumstances for too intense a programme and in others for a comparatively quiet beginning. The relevant facts are again the costs of change and the costs of acquiring experience. A low intensity approach may be expensive to gear up, but it has the merits of enabling special teaching skills to be developed and of gaining an acquaintance with the requirements of the special population and how they are to be met.

One further change that should be taken into account is that of technology and teaching method. Here too there are costs of being flexible and not too specific in method and technique. But to offset against them are the benefits of being able to invest in new approaches as they become available.

There may be great economies by standardising the teaching of the deaf in terms of certain kinds of equipment and how it is employed. This may appear to be cheaper and easier to manage, but it may also turn out not to be the best system technically and may become prematurely obsolete. There is another point to be made about technology in education. The most up-to-date system may be exceedingly durable (and expensive), but also rather transitory. While a programme based on it may look extremely advanced, it may not be long before it becomes out of date, but may have to remain so because funds are lacking for new investment. A superior system might be one that was never perfectly up to date, but was also never tremendously out of date. In other words, there are great costs as well as benefits in being first in the field.

Costing as a continuous process

All of this leads to a conclusion which dominates the present contribution, namely that the emphasis throughout should be on costing and not just on costs. While *ex post facto* it may be possible to state what an education programme has cost relative to what it has done, *ex ante* cost is much more problematic. There is no such thing as *the* cost of an education programme in its broad terms, only a set of possible costs depending on circumstances and the precise nature of the programme as it is planned and as it develops subsequently. Thus, costing should not be regarded as a once for all exercise, but as something that must be undertaken continuously as long as the education programme itself continues.

Before concluding there is one final technical problem to be mentioned. Assume that the special population has been defined satisfactorily so that it is possible with a fair degree of accuracy to identify its members in practice. Let us also assume that it is possible to state what is the education being received by the special population. The problem still remains of assessing how much of that education is being given to it as a result of its special nature and, therefore, of estimating the extra costs of educating it.

Presumably, the special population will be receiving some education as part of the country's usual education system. It is tempting to take the unit cost of that education as the base point from which all other calculations follow. The objection to this is twofold. Firstly, some special populations may be getting less than their fair share of resources. They may be subject to discrimination; indeed, that may be part and parcel of why they are 'special'. Secondly, some schools may already be endeavouring to cope with the problem of the special population which they will view as the difficulties of individuals within the norm. This second consideration partly reverses the first in that it may mean that resources are devoted to the special population as well as away from them.

This leads on to a further difficulty involving the definition of the special population. A group of individuals may (and probably will) have been defined as such independent of the education they are receiving, but the group nonetheless has educational difficulties. This means that an educational programme prescribed for them as a whole may cut across other education programmes. Apart from the question of efficiency this also makes costing very much more difficult.

Consider, for example, the children of immigrants to a country. They may be classified as part of the group which has language difficulties which the ordinary schools have to cope with. A literacy programme may then be mounted, and the relevant costing exercise will be of that programme. Alternatively, emphasis may be placed on immigrants as a group, especially their children, and a literacy programme may be developed for them. This will give rise to a different costing exercise. In practice, both these programmes may exist simultaneously; that is, schools are given extra resources for language tuition of difficult cases, and more resources still to cope with immigrants. The problem in practice is to disentangle these different resources in order to say what the children of immigrants are receiving over and above the norm, the costs of which can be compared with the benefits.

It is not enough, incidentally, to consider what resources are set aside in various plans, because reality may be different, especially if discrimination is taken into account. The resources, teachers, books, buildings, equipment, which are actually used are what is relevant.

(It should be added that, if some special populations are discriminated against in the *quality* of resources assigned to them, this too must be allowed for in a costing exercise. If they are given poorer teachers and inferior buildings and equipment, lower unit costs must accordingly be used to multiply resource quantities by to arrive at total costs.) One final point on all this is that our example is based on members of the special population being affected by two additional educational programmes. In practice some individual people may be affected by many more still.

This takes us back to whether the population is defined *sui generis* or simply as those at whom the educational programme is aimed. Starting from the former leads to all the difficulties we have outlined in determining what education it receives, and estimating how much of that education is peculiar to it. Starting from the latter leads to a different set of difficulties, namely determining who actually (and potentially) is influenced by the special education programme. It may be possible to cost the programme itself, but for decision purposes it is necessary to know which individuals and groups it reaches. Of course, for some purposes it may be possible to accept that a literacy programme helps illiterates, and nothing further need be known. But usually the degree of heterogeneity of the clients of an education programme is such that it is not sufficient to define them as a group in their own right. Indeed, they must be assigned to other groups recognised for social policy purposes, and the costs of the education programme apportioned correspondingly.

The purpose of this essay has been to clarify the concept of cost and indicate its importance for the analysis and design of policy measures for special populations. We have argued that any discussion of costs raises questions of great interest to the policy-maker, especially to do with the definition, and practical identification of the population he is seeking to help. He is immediately confronted with policy issues to do with the scale and intensity of the activity he is undertaking. At the same time the theoretical framework which is suitable for the measurement of costs is also suitable for the estimation of benefits. Indeed, the former can hardly be discussed sensibly without due attention being paid to the latter.

13 How the cost of the provision may be determined

R. A. Rossmiller
University of Wisconsin, Madison, USA

The purpose of this paper is to identify and describe procedures which may be used to estimate with reasonable accuracy the costs involved in providing educational programmes for special populations. The term 'cost' as used in this paper is synonymous with expenditure. That is, we will not deal with opportunity costs (the cost of foregoing alternative courses of action) or other economic costs, but with the actual expenditures associated with the programme under study. The term 'special population' refers to members of groups who, for whatever reason, are outside the educational mainstream. Typically, such groups are comprised of individuals who have needs that cannot be satisfied by the programmes provided for the general population, for example, individuals whose native language is not that of the country in which they currently reside; individuals with physical, mental or emotional problems severe enough to impair their educational progress; or individuals whose level of cultural development makes it difficult or impossible for them to benefit fully from programmes provided for the majority of the population.

It is assumed that information concerning the cost of programmes for special populations is of interest primarily to decision makers at local, regional and national levels. Decision makers need information concerning the cost of programmes to aid them in planning and providing programmes appropriate for the special population of concern. To obtain information on programme costs, several tasks must be accomplished. In the sections which follow we will discuss the tasks of identifying the special population to be served by the programme, defining the programme structure and programme delivery system for which costs are to be obtained, determining the strategy to be used in the collection and analysis of data, and interpreting the results.

Identifying the special population to be served

Although the task of identifying the special population appears at first glance to be simple, in practice it often turns out to be quite complicated. This step is crucial because failure to identify the special population accurately may jeopardise the validity of any information on programme costs which is developed. It is not sufficient to identify the special population merely as linguistic minorities, persons with physical or mental handicaps or groups who are culturally disadvantaged. In addition to identifying the general characteristics of the population which make it 'special', it is also necessary to specify the criteria for participation in a programme. That is, one must identify those individuals who will be the 'targets' of the programme. In special programmes for linguistic minorities, for example, it is necessary to define the conditions under which individuals are eligible to participate in the programme. An individual's surname obviously is not necessarily indicative of one's linguistic ability. If a programme is designed to remedy a deficit such as lack of fluency in a given language, criteria for determining whether or not potential participants have attained fluency in the language will be needed.

The purposes of programmes for special populations may range over a broad continuum, as illustrated in figure 13.1. At one extreme the primary objective of the programme is to eliminate the attribute(s) that make the special population 'special'. At the other extreme the primary objective may be to preserve the attribute(s) of the special population. Between these two extremes would fall such objectives as compensating for or accommodating to the attributes which distinguish the special population. In programmes for linguistic minorities or indigenous populations, for example, a host nation might wish to discourage their assimilation into the general population by programmes designed to maintain and preserve their language and culture. Or a host nation might wish to encourage rapid assimilation of the linguistic minority group into the general population by programmes which aim at rapidly increasing their language fluency. The nature of the programmes that flow from these diverse policy objectives are likely to differ very sharply.

```
─────────────X─────────────X─────────────
Eliminate the    Compensate for    Accommodate to    Preserve the
 attribute(s)     the attribute(s)   the attributes(s)  attribute(s)
```

Figure 13.1 A continuum of objectives in
programmes for special populations

Programmes for handicapped individuals also can be placed on such a continuum. Programmes for persons with speech defects, for example, generally seek to eliminate the defect. Programmes for the blind or partially sighted, however, attempt to help persons compensate for and/or accommodate to the handicap since it cannot be eliminated.

A number of criteria have been used to identify individuals eligible for participation in programmes for special populations. Occasionally the criteria are educational in nature, but more frequently they are based on physical, mental, linguistic, economic, or cultural attributes. If the criteria for participation are not primarily educational in nature, the programmes often will include non-educational components, such as therapy for physically handicapped individuals or counselling for emotionally disturbed individuals. These non-educational services must be considered in determining the cost of the programme. It is also necessary to identify the extent to which those characteristics which qualify individuals to participate in the programme are related to their educational needs. For example, deficits in vision or hearing often are used as criteria to identify persons eligible for special programmes, and sometimes economic or cultural characteristics have been used as criteria. Such criteria, however, are not necessarily related to the educational needs of participants. One blind person, for example, may already be adept in the use of Braille and another may not. The educational needs of these two individuals will differ significantly despite the fact that both are blind.

Regardless of the criteria applied to identify the target population, they must be applied uniformly and consistently. If they are not, it will be impossible to draw generalisations concerning the cost of the special programme. Each programme will be essentially unique and there will be no basis for aggregating or comparing data.

Identifying the programme structure

Identifying the structure of the educational programme to be analysed is the next step in the process and one with many potential pitfalls. The nature of this task can best be portrayed by an example drawn from the field of special education for the handicapped. The literature in the field generally identifies a taxonomy which includes programmes for students who are intellectually handicapped, speech handicapped, visually handicapped, auditorily handicapped, and orthopaedically handicapped; programmes for students with learning disabilities; and programmes for students who are emotionally disturbed and/or socially maladjusted. Some of these categories are further subdivided. Programmes for the intellectually handicapped are often directed to the educable mentally retarded, the trainable mentally retarded, and the severely retarded. Programmes for auditorily handicapped persons are subdivided into those directed to the hard of hearing and the deaf. To complicate matters further, these programmes may be provided at several levels within the educational system.

Table 13.1 illustrates a complex educational programme structure which can yield a high level of detail on the cost of educational programmes for the handicapped. The use of such a programme structure will, if the needed data are available, yield a comprehensive and detailed set of programme cost estimates. It should be noted, however, that the data required by a detailed programme structure such as that illustrated in table 13.1 are very high indeed.

Table 13.2 illustrates a much simpler programme structure which might be appropriate for analysing the costs of programmes for linguistic minorities. Note that programmes are identified at three levels — pre-school age, school age and adult. Two programme types are distinguished in each of the latter two categories.

Considerable care must be exercised in identifying the programme structure most appropriate for the cost analysis. The adoption of a particular programme structure has implications for the size of sample needed, since each cell must be represented and should occur with sufficient frequency to enable meaningful conclusions to be drawn. Secondly, the utility of a particular programme structure must be evaluated in terms of its compatibility with the availability and composition of the data necessary to compute programme costs. A third consideration is the use to be made of the cost information. The level of detail necessary for projecting the cost of a national programme will differ from that needed to evaluate the costs associated with alternative programme structures or delivery systems. The programme structure which is adopted should provide enough detail to identify meaningful distinctions between the programmes being analysed and the attendant costs, but should avoid irrelevant details.

Table 13.1
An example of a complex programme structure: educational programmes for handicapped individuals

1. Programmes for very young children
   - (a) Nursery school
   - (b) Kindergarten

2. Programmes for children
   - (a) Intellectual handicaps
     - (i) Educable retarded
     - (ii) Trainable retarded
     - (iii) Severely retarded
   - (b) Learning disabilities
   - (c) Emotional problems
     - (i) Mildly disturbed
     - (ii) Moderately disturbed
     - (iii) Severely disturbed
   - (d) Speech handicaps
   - (e) Visual handicaps
     - (i) Partially sighted
     - (ii) Blind
   - (f) Auditory handicaps
     - (i) Hard of hearing
     - (ii) Deaf
   - (g) Orthopaedic and other health handicaps
   - (h) Multiple handicaps

3. Programmes for adolescents
   - (a) Intellectual handicaps
     - (i) Educable retarded
     - (ii) Trainable retarded
   - (b) Learning disabilities
   - (c) Emotional problems
     - (i) Mild or moderate
     - (ii) Severe
   - (d) Speech handicaps
   - (e) Visual handicaps
     - (i) Partially sighted
     - (ii) Blind
   - (f) Auditory handicaps
     - (i) Hard of hearing
     - (ii) Deaf
   - (g) Orthopaedic and other health handicaps
   - (h) Multiple handicaps

4. Programmes for adults
   - (a) Intellectual handicaps
   - (b) Visual handicaps
   - (c) Auditory handicaps
   - (d) Health handicaps

Table 13.2
An example of a simple programme structure:
educational programmes for linguistic minority populations

1	Programme for pre-school children		
2	Programme for school-age children		
		(a)	Elementary school
		(b)	Secondary school
3	Programme for adults		
		(a)	Employment based
		(b)	Community based

Defining the programme delivery system

The third step in the process of determining programme costs is to identify the alternative ways in which the programme under consideration might be made available to participants. Although this step is not always given explicit attention, differences in the cost of a programme are closely linked to the system used to provide the programme. Table 13.3 identifies several alternative ways of delivering special programmes to handicapped individuals. The typology includes regular school, classrooms, instruction at home or in a hospital, and instruction provided by community organisations.

Delivery systems that use regular classrooms exemplify the concept of 'mainstreaming', where the special student spends a part of the school day in a regular classroom with members of the general population. Variations of this concept include situations where the regular classroom teacher is provided with consultation from a specialist in the teaching of exceptional students; situations where the regular classroom teacher receives help from itinerant teachers who are specialists in teaching exceptional students; and situations where regular classrooms are used in combination with a resource room in which the exceptional student receives instruction from a special teacher for part of the day. The special classroom organisational pattern can be subdivided into two types. One is the situation in which students spend all of their time in a segregated special education classroom; the other is when the exceptional student spends most of the day in a special classroom but participates in some activities with students from the general population.

Table 13.3
A typology of systems for delivering educational programmes to special populations

1		School-based programme delivery systems	
	(a)	Regular school organisation	
		(i)	Regular classroom, no additional services
		(ii)	Regular classroom, consultative assistance to teachers
		(iii)	Regular classroom, itinerant specialist teacher
		(iv)	Regular classroom, resource room to supplement
	(b)	Special classroom organisation	
		(i)	Part-time, some instruction with general population
		(ii)	Full-time
	(c)	Special day school	
	(d)	Residential school (institutional care)	
	(e)	Instruction by itinerant teacher at home or in hospital	
2		Community-based programme delivery systems	
	(a)	Day-care centre	
	(b)	Religious or charitable organisation	
	(c)	Social or recreational organisation	
	(d)	Place of employment	

The utility of cost data can be substantially enhanced by differentiating among the types of delivery systems used in providing programmes for special populations. Rather than merely obtaining gross information about the cost of programmes, discrete information concerning various methods of providing programmes for a special population can be obtained, thereby greatly enhancing the value of the information for planning purposes. It must be cautioned, however, that the degree of detail involved in a typology of delivery systems has implications for the data collection phase of the study and can impose data requirements that are very high. As with the educational programme structure, a balance must be struck. The programme structure and delivery systems included in the analysis should provide data which meet the needs of decision-makers without being so detailed as to be unmanageable.

Determining a strategy for collecting data

The preceding steps will yield a matrix which identifies the special population of concern, the nature of the programme structure and the systems employed to deliver the programme to the special population. Figure 13.2 illustrates such a matrix. With a programme matrix in hand, the next task is to decide how to obtain the data needed to ascertain the cost for the programme structure(s) and delivery modes of interest. Three possibilities exist: (a) obtain data from existing programmes, (b) extrapolate from the results of studies of similar programmes in other states or nations, or (c) determine the resource requirements of a programme recommended by specialists in the field and estimate the programme's cost.

If one decides to use existing programmes as a basis for determining costs, it is necessary to decide whether to use a random sample or whether to use a set of case studies. The choice will depend upon such factors as the number of programmes available for sampling, the amount of variability that exists among programmes, whether or not the programmes have been proven effective and perhaps most important, the availability of data.

As a general rule, careful case studies are preferable in situations where the number of programme sites is limited, the variability is great, the effectiveness of the programme has not yet been proven and the data needed are not easily obtained. Case studies have the advantage of facilitating investigations in greater depth and thus help investigators identify the reasons for differences in cost in programme structures and/or delivery modes. If the programme is well established, a random sample of programme sites appropriately stratified on factors likely to influence programme costs is preferred. Experience indicates that cost estimates based on data obtained from actual programmes have greater credibility with decision-makers than do cost estimates based on the opinion of experts.

If no programmes currently exist for the special population of interest, the results of studies of similar programmes in other states or nations may be used as a basis for cost estimates. Another alternative is to base cost estimates on expert opinion concerning the resources required to mount effective programmes for the special population. For example, if one wished to estimate the cost of a programme to reduce adult illiteracy, one could obtain recommendations from experts in adult education and literacy with regard to the programme structure, delivery mode(s) and human and material resources needed in such a programme. The factor cost of each resource could then be estimated and aggregated to arrive at the total cost of the programme.

Unfortunately, each of these two methods has drawbacks. If one attempts to extrapolate from cost information obtained in other states or nations, it is necessary to either assume that the programmes themselves and the factor costs are comparable or make arbitrary adjustments in the data. If expert opinion is used to determine the level

Programme delivery modes	Programme structure			
	1	2	• • •	n
a.				
b.				
• • •				
n				

Figure 13.2 A matrix illustrating programme structure and programme delivery modes for a special population

of resources needed, it is often the case that experts do not agree on the 'best' configuration of programme elements. Another problem is the fact that the programme configurations recommended by experts cannot be subjected to external validity checks and cost estimates derived from them may lack credibility in the eyes of policy-makers.

Collecting the data

The next stage in the process of determining programme costs is the collection of data. The first step at this stage is to identify the cells in the matrix for which data are needed. This may be either a simple or a complex task, depending upon the nature of the special population and the programme. If the special population consists of illiterate adults, for example, the special population is immediately obvious and the programme structure and delivery modes may be very simple — perhaps either employment-based or community-based programmes to attain basic literacy. However, if the special population consists of mentally handicapped individuals, the programme structure(s) and delivery mode(s) are likely to be quite complicated.

Obtaining information on expenditures for special programmes is often the most difficult (and certainly the most tedious) aspect of programme cost studies. Accounting systems and formats tend to differ from one agency to another even within the same region or state. Few educational agencies use programme accounting procedures. It is typical, for example, to find that the salaries paid to instructional personnel in all of the programmes operated by an agency are lumped together in a single accounting category. Unless the agency maintains separate accounts for each programme, it is necessary to disaggregate the accounting data in order to identify the expenditures associated with the programme under study. This is a particularly difficult task in the case of personnel, because some individuals may work in two or more programmes. When this situation occurs it is necessary to determine the amount or percentage of time each person spends in each programme and then prorate the individual's salary and fringe benefits accordingly.

Occasionally programme responsibility will be divided among two or more agencies. For example, the educational components of a programme may be the responsibility of a local or state educational agency and the health care aspects of the programme may be the responsibility of a local or state health agency. Where this condition exists, it is necessary to obtain data from each of the agencies involved in order to identify the total cost of the programme under study.

Another potential complicating factor exists where the agencies involved use different accounting periods. In this situation it is best to identify a common accounting period, for example, a week or a month, and work from the accounting data of each agency for such time periods.

The generally accepted procedure for deriving programme costs is to identify and attribute to the special programme all of the costs associated with that programme and then calculate the total programme cost. There are two distinct steps in this process — attributing direct costs to programmes and attributing indirect costs to programmes. Direct programme costs are those costs that can be directly and logically associated with a specific programme. For example, in educational programmes direct costs include the expenditures made for the salaries of teachers or other persons working directly with students in the special programme.

Indirect costs are those which cannot reasonably be attributed only to a special programme or to a group of special programmes. Expenditures for general administration of an agency, salaries paid to personnel such as librarians, counsellors and secretaries, and the cost of operating and maintaining buildings and equipment are examples of indirect costs. Indirect costs are attributed to all programmes (both general and specific) on a pro rata basis. The general rule in attributing programme costs is to attribute to specific programmes those which can be directly associated with individual students and attribute to all programmes on a pro rata basis those costs which cannot be associated directly with a given student or programme.

Some expenditures cannot be attributed to only one special programme, but can be attributed to several special programmes. Examples would include salaries paid to persons who direct or supervise several special programmes or salaries paid to psychologists who divide their time among several special programmes. Expenditures of this type can be attributed to the appropriate special programmes on a pro rata basis.

One essential item of data is the number of individuals participating in the special programme being studied. It is strongly recommended that student data be reported on the basis of full-time equivalent (FTE) students, especially in situations where students do not spend all of their time in the special programme. The FTE basis makes it possible to isolate the portion of time a student spends in the special programme from that time spent in programmes for the general population and allocate costs accordingly. Most conventional methods of counting students (such as daily membership or daily attendance) indicate only that a student is enrolled in or attending school; they do not indicate the division of the student's time among and between various programmes. In order to determine programme costs accurately in situations where students divide their time between two or more programmes it is necessary to allocate costs between and among programmes and this task is best done using FTE students.

The FTE measure is sometimes confusing to those not familiar with its use. It is *not* the same as a student head count. If, for example, five students each spend 20 per cent of their day in a resource room, they would be equivalent to one FTE student, but the *head count* of students in the resource room would be five. If the same five students each spend 80 per cent of their day in the programme provided for the general population, they would be equivalent to four FTE students, but the *head count* of students would again be five. The use of the FTE student measure affords a way to avoid the problem of 'double counting' of students.

Table 13.4 illustrates the computation of FTE student units and shows how they are used in cost calculations. Let us assume that an educational agency reports the data shown in the table on the distribution of the time of seven students between regular and special programmes. Let us further assume that the cost of the regular programme is $1,000 per FTE student and the cost of the special programme is $5,000 per FTE student. The data shown in the table 13.4 indicate that Student A spends a full 30-hour week in the special programme and therefore is counted as 1.0 FTE student in that programme. Student B spends half time (15 hours per week) in the special programme, which is equivalent to 0.5 FTE student.

Table 13.4
An illustration of Full Time Equivalent student computation and use

Student	Special programme Hrs/wk	FTE	Regular programme Hrs/wk	FTE	Programme cost/student Special $	Regular $	Total $
A	30	1.00	0	0	5,000	0	5,000
B	15	0.50	15	0.50	2,500	500	3,000
C	10	0.33	20	0.67	1,650	670	2,320
D	5	0.17	25	0.83	850	830	1,680
E	1	0.03	29	0.97	150	970	1,120
F	0.5	0.017	29.5	0.983	85	983	1,068
G	0	0	30	1.00	0	1,000	1,000
7 students		2.047		4.953	$10,235	$4,953	$15,188

Student E spends only one hour per week in the special programme, or 3 per cent of a standard 30-hour week, the equivalent of 0.03 FTE. When the FTEs in the special programme for these seven students are totalled, the sum is 2.047 FTE, with the balance of their time (4.953 FTE) spent in the regular programme. Note that the sum of the FTEs in the regular and special programmes is 7.0, the total number of students involved.

With regard to the cost of each student's total programme (both special and regular), the FTE basis clearly shows that the cost varies for each student depending upon the proportion of time the student spends in the regular and special programmes. Student F, for example, spends only one-half hour per week in the special programme and the additional (or excess) cost of the special programme for this student is only $68 ($1,068 minus $1,000). Student B's total programme, on the other hand, carries an excess cost of $2,000 ($3,000 minus $1,000), because Student B spends a higher percentage of time in the more costly special programme.

It is particularly important to use the FTE student measure in programmes for special populations in which students spend a portion of their time in a special programme and the remainder of their time in the programme provided for the general population. Failure to identify and allocate costs on the basis of full-time equivalent students will seriously distort the data. As illustrated in table 13.4, it is easy to convert FTE data to student head counts, but it is not possible to convert student head counts to full-time equivalent students.

Analysing the data

Expenditures for personnel merit very close attention because they typically constitute the largest single component of the total programme cost. Personnel expenditures are very sensitive to teacher/student and staff/student ratios. Special programmes which require low teacher/student and staff/student ratios generally are very expensive on an FTE basis. Where geographic or demographic conditions (for example, mountains, rivers or widely scattered settlements) make it impossible to gather together the optimum number of students, it is unfair to compare the cost of such a programme with the cost of a programme in areas where optimal class sizes can be maintained. One must differentiate between necessarily expensive programmes (that is, where the choice is to either maintain an expensive programme or no programme) and inefficient programmes where a high cost per student served can be reduced without impairing the programme's effectiveness. Caution also must be exercised in cross-regional or cross-national studies where the conditions under which special programmes are offered are likely to differ widely.

Most compensation schedules are weighted to reward the professional preparation and experience of individual teachers. It is important to have data of these two variables for each of the individuals employed in the programme under study. Unless these data are available, the analyst will be unable to identify the reason why a programme in which the staff is highly trained and experienced is considerably more costly on an FTE basis than a similar programme in which most members of the staff are at the entry level in terms of their training and experience.

One question which sometimes arises is whether actual expenditures or standard costs should be used in the analysis. The possibilities range on a continuum from standard costs at one extreme to actual expenditures at the other extreme. If standard costs alone are used, all actual expenditures for salary are disregarded and a standard compensation schedule is constructed for each category of personnel. This schedule is then applied to the personnel involved in the programme to arrive at the total cost. The primary advantage of this approach is its simplicity. The calculations are simple and straightforward once the standard compensation schedule has been determined. The burden of making appropriate adjustments to reflect local conditions is placed upon the users. The major disadvantages of this approach is its lack of credibility and the likelihood that prospective users will have limited knowledge of the adjustments which would be needed to fit local wage market conditions. There is also greater potential for misuse of the cost data developed using this procedure. The disadvantages of this approach appear to outweigh the advantages, particularly where reasonably accurate data on actual expenditures are available. This approach would be most useful where no programme currently exists and experts are asked to define the staffing and other characteristics of a programme which would meet the specified objectives.

A second approach is to adjust the actual expenditures for personnel to standardise salaries in a manner that will 'correct' for regional or state variations in the salary paid persons with comparable training, experience and responsibility. For example, cost of living indices might be applied to adjust for variations in this factor. Another possibility is to use the average salaries received by persons filling comparable positions in the region or state on the assumption that they are likely to reflect variances in cost of living or labour market conditions. The advantage of this approach is that data on salaries paid to various types of personnel generally are available on a regional or state basis. However, state or regional averages can mask a great deal of variance in labour market conditions within a state or region. And it may be difficult to obtain data for all personnel categories. Although this approach is usually preferable to basing estimates entirely on standard costs, it does have disadvantages. The utility of this procedure depends primarily upon the availability of accurate data for each major category of personnel and for each region or state.

A third approach is to use actual expenditures. This approach has the advantage of utilising fully all of the available data. It is reasonable to assume that the wage rates paid by agencies take into account all factors that influence the labour market — cost of living, amenities or disamenities, labour supply, and so on. Although this assumption may not be entirely accurate, it is likely that the labour market adjusts for all of the relevant factors more adequately than any other method available. The results obtained using this approach will generally be more credible to potential users than will hypothetical figures. This is the preferred method when the sample is of adequate size and appropriately stratified to reflect the major sources of variance in expenditure.

Actual expenditures usually can be used for categories such as instructional supplies, contracted or purchased services, and travel. Although textbooks usually will last more than one year, most educational agencies replace textbooks on a regular basis so that expenditures for textbooks generally do not vary greatly from year to year. Consequently, it is usually acceptable to use actual expenditures for textbooks and similar materials. The exception would be in situations where programmes with high start-up costs are being initiated, in which case such expenditures should be treated as capital investments and depreciated over an appropriate period of time.

Data on certain types of expenditures must be dealt with very carefully. The area of capital investments, for example, is one in which expenditures tend to be 'lumpy' and where the data are likely to reflect unusual patterns. If the facilities are adequate and appropriate for the programme, it is essentially irrelevant for programme purposes whether the facility is old or new. It is not irrelevant, however, in terms of the charge made for depreciation. It is preferable to determine the replacement cost of the existing facility and depreciate the facility over its period of anticipated use. Calculating depreciation based on the replacement cost of facilities and equipment will produce more accurate data for comparative purposes than will depreciating them on the basis of their actual cost.

Expenditures for payment of principal and interest on indebtedness also must be treated carefully because they reflect past decisions, not current decisions. For purposes of comparing programme costs, the use of a standard depreciation schedule and a standard interest factor is appropriate, since an agency's expenditures for debt service are a function of its credit rating and the money market conditions at the time the debt was incurred.

The format which will be used in presenting the data should be determined before the data analysis begins. Consideration should be given to the audience to whom the report is directed, the nature of the decisions to be taken, and the character of the programme under study. Depending on these and other factors, the researcher may wish to highlight cost by programme level (early childhood, childhood, adolescent, adult, and so on), by programme delivery mode (regular classrooms, regular classrooms supplemented by resource rooms, special classrooms, special schools, and so on), or by the agencies providing the programme (existing schools, community agencies, places of employment, and so on). It also may be useful to identify programme costs at various points on a continuum. Depending upon the size of the sample, such distributions might be based on percentiles, deciles or quartiles; or they might indicate only the high, average and low cost per unit of service. Table 13.5 illustrates one format that might be employed in presenting data on programme costs.

Table 13.5
An illustrative format for reporting data on programme costs

	Lowest	10%ile	25%ile	50%ile	75%ile	90%ile	Highest
Direct instructional costs							
Teachers							
Aides							
Instructional supplies							
Textbooks							
Contracted services							
Travel							
Other expenditures							
Indirect instructional costs							
Administration							
Operation and maintenance							
Ancillary personnel (identify major sub-categories if these are a significant component of cost)							
Services (e.g. transportation, feeding, housing)							
Imputed costs							
Facilities							
Equipment							
Debt service							

Interpreting the results

The final task in any study of programme costs is interpreting the results. One of the first decisions to be made is determining the standard against which the cost of a programme for a special population is to be compared. For example, the cost of a programme can be compared with the cost of other programmes serving the same special population, with the cost of programmes serving other special populations, or with the cost of the programme provided for the general population. The results of the comparison are expressed as a ratio of the cost of the special programme to the cost of the programme with which it is being compared. Obviously, any comparisons must be based on comparable units of measure such as cost per full-time equivalent pupil per hour, per day, per month or per year. The choice of the measure to be employed will depend primarily upon the nature of the programmes being compared. It is advantageous to use smaller units of time, particularly in programmes of short duration or in which the participants are engaged for less than full-time. Thus cost per FTE student per hour is generally preferred over cost per FTE student per year.

The standard of comparison used most frequently in studies of this type is the cost of the programme provided for the general population. This has been the conventional standard of comparison in studies of the cost of programmes for exceptional children. The major advantage in using this standard is the fact that most persons are familiar with the nature of educational programmes provided for the general population.

Cost comparisons can be made using the mean cost of each programme being compared, the median cost of each programme, or the cost at a designated quartile or decile. When the cost of special programmes is compared with the cost of the programme provided for the general population, the latter customarily is assigned a value of 1.0. The ratio of the cost of the special programme to the regular programme is referred to as a cost index. A number of studies have been conducted during the past decade to determine cost indices for special programmes for various categories of exceptional children and for various programme delivery systems. When the cost of a special programme exceeds the cost of a programme provided for the general population the difference has often been referred to as an 'excess cost'. This term is not used in an accounting sense where excess cost is equated with unnecessary cost. Rather, it refers to the extent to which the cost of the special programme exceeds the cost of the programme provided for the general population.

Cost indices must be used with appropriate caution. Accurate cost indices can be very useful, for they enable planners and decision makers to make more accurate estimates of the amount of revenue needed to provide programmes for special populations. Cost indices also have potentially serious limitations, however, and those who use them should be aware of their limitations.

One limitation of cost indices arises from the fact that a cost index generally represents a regional or national average. Half of the agencies upon which the index is based will be spending more than the average and the remaining half will be spending less than the average. While the average cost index is useful in projecting the total cost of various programmes, it is obvious that using the average cost index as a basis for allocating funds to individual agencies does not guarantee that adequate provision will be made for the cost of special programmes in these agencies. And using the average cost of a special programme in a region or nation as a basis for allocating funds to operating agencies presents the same problem. Provision must be made in any financing programme to deal with the fiscal needs of individual agencies that deviate from the average for good and sufficient reasons (higher labour costs, diseconomies of scale, and so on).

A second limitation of cost indices lies in the fact that they reflect current practices. That is, they reflect neither the efficacy nor the efficiency of the programme. They reflect only what is currently being done, not what could be done (or what should be done) in the way of programming for the special population. A cost index for a given agency may be high because that agency is not using its resources efficiently. However, a high cost index for a particular programme may be unavoidable in some agencies for reasons such as unusual transportation costs or a limited number of eligible students. Either of these factors, as well as several others, could increase the per student cost of the programme and thus increase the cost index. A programme for financing programmes for special populations must be flexible enough to accommodate necessary differences in expenditures from one agency to another and, at the same time, avoid subsidising inefficiency.

A third limitation of cost indices is closely related to the second. Cost indices show the relative cost of providing programmes for a special population compared with the cost of providing programmes for the general population (or other comparison group). They do not provide information as to how wisely or how efficiently funds are being expended for either regular or special programmes. It is entirely possible that a special programme could be offered to an equal number of students, could provide the same services and could cost the same amount per student in two agencies, but the cost indices in the two agencies could differ because of the differences in the cost of the programme provided for the general population in each agency. Since a cost index provides no information about the efficiency or effectiveness of the programme provided for the general population, a low cost index may mask an inefficient regular programme. The opposite could also be true; if an agency is spending at a low rate per student in its regular programme, the cost index for its special programme will be higher.

A fourth limitation of cost indices can arise if the relative cost of the various delivery systems is not considered when developing the cost index. For example, there is evidence that it costs more to provide special classes for handicapped students than to provide supportive services to these students when they are enrolled in the programme provided for the general population. Care must be taken lest important differences in the cost of various programme delivery systems be obscured by indiscriminate grouping of programme costs.

Finally, it should be noted that for a variety of reasons, costs will vary between agencies for identical programmes. In some agencies, for example, the cost of transporting students will be much greater than in others. Another very important factor in determining the relative cost of programmes is the student/teacher or student/staff ratio. Some agencies will have too few students to operate a programme at optimum efficiency, but students who live in these agencies certainly should not be denied access to a programme. Differences in salaries and in the cost of supplies and materials exist between agencies, and these differences also will be reflected in programme costs and in cost indices.

References

Bernstein, C.D., Kirst, M.W., Hartman, W.T. and Marshall, R.S., *Financing educational services for the handicapped*, Reston, Va., The Council for Exceptional Children, 1976, pp. 7–13.

Churchill, S., Rideout, B., Gill, M. and Lamerand, R., *Costs: French language instructional units*, Toronto, Ontario Institute for Studies in Education, 1978.

Ernst and Ernst, *A model for the determination of the costs of special education as compared with that for general education*, Chicago, Ill., Ernst and Ernst, 1974.

McLure, William P., *The structure of educational costs in the great cities*, Chicago, Ill., Research Council of the Great Cities Program for School Improvement, 1964.

Rossmiller, R.A., 'Coming to grips with costs and expenditures' in *Financing education programs for handicapped children*, report no.50, Denver, Colorado, Education Commission of the States, 1974, pp. 1–18.

Rossmiller, R.A. and Frohreich, L.E., *Expenditures and funding patterns in Idaho's programme for exceptional children*, Boise, Idaho, Idaho Department of Education, 1979.

Rossmiller, R.A., Hale, J.A. and Frohreich, L.F., *Educational programs for exceptional children: Resource configurations and costs*, Madison, Wisconsin, University of Wisconsin, 1970.

Rossmiller, R.A. and Moran, T.H., 'Cost differentials and cost indices: The assessment of variations in educational program costs' in *School finance in transition*, Gainesville, Fla., Institute for Educational Finance, 1973, pp. 63—77.

PART III

Linguistic and cultural minorities

14 Problems and policy instruments in the provision of special education

Stacy Churchill
Ontario Institute for Studies in Education,
Toronto, Canada

The starting point of this review is the fundamental change which has been taking place during the past twenty years in the definition of the content of social equality or even, of equal social opportunity for minorities. At the one end is the definition saying that minority social groups will be accepted into full social participation after their language and culture, at least in the conduct of community life, will have been replaced by that of the majority. At the other end is the definition saying that equality consists in the preservation of minority languages and the cultures whose social status would be equal to that of the majority. In the service of community integration, this latter definition requires that each group, the minority and the majority, would *enter into* the culture of the other, each learning the other's language, for example.

This study shows how the apparent position of various minorities in fifteen industrialised countries along a line between these two definitions, is related to the provision of minority education — generally in terms of its governance, organisation and financing.

The prevailing definitions of the problems and the objectives for the education of cultural and language minorities arises from three general groups of actors: the educators and others who manage and operate the educational system, the majority of the general public and the cultural minority. As a first step in accounting for these definitions it is necessary to review briefly the rich variety of the minority groups appearing in the countries with which we are concerned, to make clear the main factors differentiating them and their situations. Table 14.1 shows at a glance the wide geographical and ethnic range of data available to us for this purpose through the reports and surveys contributed to the CERI programme of inquiry.

Table 14.1
Linguistic and cultural minorities here considered
in the light of information provided in country reports
to the CERI inquiry

Country	Minority group
Australia	Non-English-speaking Aborigines
Canada, Ontario	Francophones, multi-cultural immigrants of their descendants, native peoples
Denmark	Non-Danish-speaking people, including Faroese and residents from Greenland
England and Wales	Immigrants and descendants (Urban Programme), Welsh
France	Non-French-speaking immigrants
Federal Republic of Germany	'Resettlers' of German origin, foreign workers
Netherlands	Cultural minorities (various)
New Zealand	Maori and Pacific Island peoples
Norway	Special language groups (including Lapps/Sami)
Portugal	Portuguese workers abroad
Sweden	Nomadic Lapps/Sami, Estonians, Finnish-speaking and English-speaking minorities, Gypsies, immigrants
Switzerland	Immigrants and foreign language children, Romansch-speakers
Turkey	Turkish workers abroad
United States	Bilingual education students, native Americans

The minority groups: dimensions of diversity

The most important differences between minorities derive from raw demographic facts: absolute numbers, concentration in given areas, relative numbers as part of the total population and recency of settlement in their home area(s). A second set of differences is essentially socio-cultural. It concerns generally the way the members of the minority relate to each other, to their own linguistic and cultural tradition, and to the majority society. Policy-makers must cope with a range of population needs that contrasts with the relatively even distribution of other types of special populations (for example, the deaf, the blind, the retarded) across different countries.

One might note the difference in demands placed upon a country such as Canada, where one minority language group of several million members is concentrated, for the most part, in the single province of Quebec, with those that are generated by a relative handful of political refugees from Southeast Asia in a country such as Sweden. Or, in socio-cultural terms, one can cite the difference between the case of immigrants who arrive in some countries with the firm intention of becoming members of its society and integrating with it, and the case of certain groups who have been known to stick obstinately to their language, religion, and cultural traditions with unremitting persistence over generations (the overseas Chinese of the Pacific perimeter being perhaps the best known, though many parallel examples exist in other countries).

Between these extremes are to be found most of the minorities under study, groups whose members hesitate between identification with their minority role and with the majority society, who practise a form of bilingualism in which two languages alternate in different environments with neither being completely native-like, and whose cultural roots are an eclectic selection of elements of religion, family relationship practices, lifestyle, and folkloric traditions.

As to any specific 'rules' or principles about the relationship between minority population characteristics and public policy responses to their needs, we do not have a great deal of data. Nevertheless, within a given country, one can note the obvious, for example that education provision for minorities usually exists in areas where the minorities are concentrated, as in the United Kingdom where funds are channelled to cities where large immigrant populations are established. Canada provides a somewhat similar example, where the relative degree of control of Francophones over their education appears to vary from province to province as a function of population density and concentration, though not as a function necessarily of absolute size: the New Brunswick Francophones enjoy greater control of their schools than the much larger concentration of Franco-Ontarians, in part because they form a much larger proportion of the population of their province and in part because they are very highly concentrated in some areas.

Such generalisations are much more difficult *across* national situations, simply because so many other factors intervene along with the characteristics of the minority population. Thus one may contrast the almost total exclusion from the political process of millions of resident foreign workers in several European countries with the administrative autonomy of the minute Romansch population in one canton of Switzerland. In dealing with the problem as a whole, the main point to keep in mind is the extreme diversity of situations across countries and, within countries, between regions and even between minorities. With this in mind, we can recall a few of the dimensions of this diversity and the way it interacts with policy.

Length of establishment

The populations fall into three categories. The indigenous peoples are, by and large, the longest established, even if they have often been pushed back from their ancestral territories, the Lapps even further northwards, the American Indians into reservations, and the Australian Aborigines in some of the least hospitable areas of the continent. Most countries have 'established' minorities whose presence predates the period when the modern nation-state took shape — the Welsh in the United Kingdom, the constituent peoples of the Helvetic confederation, the Catalans in Spain or, for the newer countries of America, the Spanish-speakers of the US Southwest and the Francophones of Canada.

The newest group is the result of different waves of European migration, some dating back more than a century but most of it from the period since World War II. By and large, the established minorities are those whose concerns for educational provision are most likely to be dealt with as a matter of 'rights' rather than as a transitory set of measures destined to palliate temporary social disadvantage.

Only the established minorities can lay claim to a right to conserve their identity and back it with political might. Despite their greater antiquity, the indigenous peoples are rarely in a position to assert their claims in ways that affect elections and ballot boxes, though at least in some parts of North America, this situation may be changing.

Geographic isolation

Geographic isolation is a factor in the development of educational policy mainly for indigenous peoples. Such isolation may be viewed as a benefit if the result is to reduce the negative effects of contacts with the mainstream culture of the country involved, or as a disadvantage if it tends to reinforce a socially disadvantaged status. In Norway vigorous financial and other measures have been applied to foster geographical equality of access to education; though not directed to a specific linguistic or cultural minority, the policy helps Lappish Sami populations along with others in the same areas. Sweden and Australia, on the other hand, have adopted specific measures inspired by problems of isolation but have linked them with programmes aimed at specific indigenous populations (Aborigines and Lapps/Sami).

Cultural isolation

Isolation may be a social phenomenon. Ghettoization is primarily linked to groups having inferior social status (in the eyes of the surrounding population). The case studies of the Federal Republic of Germany, France and the United Kingdom all illustrate specific cases of groups having difficulty integrating into, or even establishing contact with, the surrounding society. Such a situation, as for example in the case of resident foreign workers and their children, may so reduce the opportunities for use of the language of the host country that it counteracts the effects of language training classes. However, it also reveals the crucial importance of the school experience, which for many children in such situations, is the *only* place where they have contact with native citizens of the country.

By way of example, immigrant groups in the Federal Republic of Germany may shun contact with immigrants from other countries. The so-called 'Bavarian model' of school, in which non-German students are grouped together for instruction during most of their studies, shows the delicate trade-offs that must be weighed in decision-making: isolation will tend to reinforce the use of the home language of the children but conversely decreases their chances of direct contact with Germans and the German language. Such an effect is consistent with the objective of eventual return of the children to the homeland of their parents but may reduce their freedom of choice with respect to remaining in the new host country.

Geographic 'containedness'

The concentration of a given ethnic or cultural group in a bounded geographic area may encourage the recognition of their needs and the provision of relevant services, quite independently of the total numbers involved. In some countries (for example, Belgium, Canada, Finland, Spain) the areas involved may represent a significant portion of the total national territory and population. The main problem is that of the larger urban areas where very significant immigrant or foreign worker populations may live on a dispersed basis, facing authorities with difficult choices with regard to schooling. Having twenty-five pupils of one nationality in a school at a given age-level makes it possible easily to create special classes; having twice that number split into six nationalities calls for other measures.

As noted in a recent Swedish official circular, the pedagogical advantages of bringing pupils of one nationality together in a central place must be weighed against numerous potential disadvantages: greater distances to travel to school, loss of contact between pupils and other children of same age living in their own area, creation of 'immigrant schools', and difficulty for parents to remain in contact with the school. Geographic containedness has been a very important positive factor in that for stable, established minorities it may be the key to long-term survival (see Danish areas of Schleswig-Holstein, Valle d'Aosta in Italy, Åland Archipelago in Finland).

Political awareness and participation

Provision of special services for a linguistic or cultural minority is seldom a politically neutral act in the eyes of the majority population. The recognition of the need for such services, a first step towards their provision, may depend upon the ability of the minorities concerned to use political power effectively. Access to such power is dependent, in most cases, upon the legal status and history of the group(s) concerned.

Whereas the 'established' minorities have, by and large, political rights, the resident foreign workers of Western Europe usually have little or no right to participation in the political life of their countries of residence; the result has been, in many cases, a very delayed reaction to their needs on the part of the relevant national authorities. The history of arrangements for these groups shows, in a number of cases, the role played by the authorities of their countries of origin, that is, the countries where they do have potentially political rights. The series of bilateral arrangements between authorities in France and Germany with their counterparts in the countries of emigration show how political actions at the international level can supplement the almost non-existent political strength of such groups.

Demography

As mentioned earlier, raw numbers count. The reaction to a given minority depends often upon simple demographic evolution: a group perceived to be numerous and continuing to increase in size is likely to be temporary, whether because the group is declining in absolute numbers through emigration or because assimilation into the majority causes it to lose its separate identity.

Turning from the political level to the one of educational practice, a multitude of decisions regarding services are directly linked to numbers of pupils, their concentration, permanency and so forth. The major difficulties with demographic data are that they are not absolutes: each national situation interprets numbers in widely differing ways. Norwegian educators have been known to point out that a typical secondary school in Norway would be considered too small to be viable in some other countries.

We have, however, one exception that confirms, so to speak, the rule: the decision in Switzerland to create the canton of Graubünden was taken largely because of the perception that, without it, the Romansch language groups would shortly disappear. Where educational (or other social) provision is linked to numbers in some direct fashion, demographic data can be at the centre of controversy, with different groups disagreeing about the basic 'facts' in a situation.

Minority opinion and aspirations

Policy making on education for linguistic and cultural minorities is bedevilled by the general confusion that often reigns among the minorities about the objectives that should be assigned to education. First, multiple minorities may be present in a given jurisdiction, and different groups may have contradictory aims. Secondly, within a given minority group there may be internal differences as between different subgroups. Thirdly, there is often a generation gap between the children attending school and their parents; children of foreign workers, for example, may lose their attachment to the home country of their parents, seeking primarily to make a place for themselves in the new society, whereas their parents may seek to have them educated in a way permitting their eventual return to the home country. Finally, the conditions under which minority groups live may discourage the development of coherent leadership and community organisations, so that authorities do not have a unified, recognised group with which to deal in arriving at decisions about education.

The range of problems posed in dealing with minority group objectives varies rather considerably between the three main groups of minorities: established minorities, recent arrivals (immigrants or foreign workers), and indigenous peoples. The traditional, established minorities appear, by and large, to be the easiest to deal with, simply because they have an established place in the power structure and political life of their respective countries. In different areas of Wales, for example, decisions about the use of the Welsh language are generally resolved at the level of the local school; even though opinions may differ between parents, there are well understood mechanisms for receiving, filtering and deciding on the opinions. By contrast, minorities recently arrived in some countries (for example, England, the Federal

Republic of Germany or France) show a great diversity of national origins, a relatively low level of community organisation (except for Commonwealth immigrants to the United Kingdom) and weak, barely formalised mechanisms for obtaining opinion. The position of the indigenous peoples is somewhat ambiguous. Most have been *in situ* for many generations and have a recognised place in their respective societies with interlocutors recognised by their educational authorities. Available evidence, though somewhat fragmentary, suggests a situation where the established mechanisms are being challenged within the indigenous communities. Furthermore, if one takes the example of aboriginal peoples living in Australian urban areas, they may be present in such small numbers or so submerged by the cultural norms of a different society, that community mechanisms virtually do not exist, rendering dialogue extremely difficult except at the individual level.

The case studies on which this review is based outline the basic dimensions of the internal contradictions within the minority groups. The French study refers to aspirations to 'collective advancement' and 'individual freedom'. The study for England and Wales summarises the issue in one sentence: 'At its simplest we can say that aspirations are either assimilationist or preservationist or combinations of the two'. These same issues of individual choice regarding education appear also in the discussion of Francophones in Canada, as well as in the issues raised regarding indigenous peoples.

The minority group member inevitably is faced with making tradeoffs to determine what is the best way to 'get ahead' educationally — by seeking to merge with the majority group or by retaining a separate identity, by trying to adapt to life in a new country or to return to a distant 'home country'. This dichotomy is often deeply felt by the individuals concerned. Policy-makers are faced with the problems that the dichotomy is not usually clear. Only a relatively few minority group members do succeed in integration with a new society, even over a period of two or three generations. For most minority groups studied the issue is probably not so much whether to be different, but how much difference is necessary and useful and what differences should be, so to speak, cultivated.

For Canada a schema has been worked out for tracing the evolution of policy concerns of linguistic and cultural minorities in terms of their reaction to the different levels of educational opportunities offered them. This appears to be applicable to most countries, even though it must be recognised that the internal inconsistencies of opinion within minority groups mean that the characterisation will not apply to all at any time. In outline, the schema may be presented thus:

(i) *At Level 1, the recognition phase*, the minority group seeks to obtain recognition of its special educational needs and, in many cases, of its own existence as a group having a place in society.

(ii) *At Level 2, the start-up and extension phase*, having obtained a limited response from educational authorities, the minority seeks to obtain the creation and extension of minority language educational services or, where these exist without sanction, the legitimation and improvement of services. The emphasis in this phase is on *quantitative* gains, in amount of instruction offered and in numbers of students served. Two types of objective may be pursued in this phase: 'Transitional' objectives concern use of the minority language and culture as a means of transition to education in the majority language, for example, forms such as initial instruction in elementary school through the minority language, transitional 'bilingual' classes, and so forth; 'group maintenance' objectives attempt to obtain policies that, to the maximum extent possible, involve use of the minority language as a means of instruction to resist assimilation pressures outside the school environment.

(iii) *At Level 3, the consolidation and adaptation phase*, where educational policies have provided access to educational opportunities for most members of the group (fulfilling the immediate quantitative need for provision), the objective becomes to improve the quality and relevance of the education received. Relevance in terms of 'transitional' situations may mean emphasis on goals facilitating social and economic integration (including development of understanding of the minority culture among members of the majority), whereas in 'group maintenance' situations it may mean giving recognition not only to the minority language as a medium of instruction but also to the specific culture as a source of content of instruction.

(iv) *At Level 4, the multilingual co-existence phase*, educational rights for a minority cease to be a major issue. Rights are legally and practically entrenched and different language groups co-exist, not necessarily without friction, but on a basis of quasi-equality. This corresponds mainly to the situation of some of the old established multilingual countries like Belgium and Switzerland.

The classification of different minority situations according to this schema must be qualified to recognise a great many exceptions, particularly when done at a global level: different minorities in the same jurisdiction may have quite different places on the scale, dependent upon their length of residence. Table 14.2 shows a rough classification of minorities for a limited selection of countries. The difficulties of classification are obvious: the great majority of US Hispanics, for example, do not have access to bilingual services, even if certain states and cities have exemplary programmes; thus, the majority might be at Level 1, but a minority at Level 2.

Table 14.2
Impressionistic classification of multilingual situations for a selection of minority groups according to level of development of their aspirations

Level	Transition	Group maintenance
1	Most indigenous peoples UK 'immigrants' Resident foreign workers (France, Germany) Most US Hispanics	
2	US Hispanics, some States Resident foreign workers (Sweden, Denmark) Manitoba (early 1970s)	Lapps/Sami Finns in Sweden Catalans Ontario and Manitoba French Welsh (Level 1)
3		New Brunswick French Romansch
4		Belgium, Finland, Switzerland

Because of the long-standing development of social services in the Scandinavian north, the Lapps/Sami are probably to be classed in Level 2, whereas the bulk of indigenous peoples in other countries are at Level 1. Foreign workers in Western European countries pose similar problems: the breadth of coverage, in terms of proportion of workers reached, places foreign workers in Sweden and Denmark probably at Level 2, but those in France and Germany at Level 1, even if the form of the programmes offered is in some cases the same. Recent constitutional changes in Spain have shifted the Catalans from a Level 1 to a Level 2 status, from which it is expected they would emerge to Level 3 in a short time. Because of their very small numbers, the Romansch speakers of Switzerland would probably best fit situation 3, whereas the remainder of the country's language groups are in a Level 4 situation.

The absence of any candidates for the cell 'Level 3 transition' in the table, together with the tendency of groups, such as the Francophones in Manitoba, to move from 'Level 2 transitional' to 'Level 2 maintenance' suggests that there is little likelihood of development beyond Level 2 if the group goals are transition and integration. After a certain period, if the group goals remain transitional, the success of its members in entering the mainstream of the majority society may cause it to disappear; conversely, if it does not disappear, the longevity of the group's existence inevitably shifts it into a position of seeking group maintenance.

Even if classification of whole jurisdictions within the framework is somewhat loose, the examination of individual minority group situations in the countries under review indicates that most, if not all, can easily be fitted into the schema. Its main utility is to provide a dimensioning of minority aspirations across countries, so that one can see what differences of minority aspirations confront policy-makers.

The educators' view and influence

Before moving on, a brief note is in order on the educator, the second actor in the formulation of public opinion in this field. Studies of Canada, France, Germany and the United Kingdom indicate that by and large initiatives from within the education system are limited to dealing with problems of linguistic and cultural minorities as 'technical issues', that is, the taking of measures to reduce perceived handicaps of minorities in meeting current educational objectives. The range of measures available to the educational establishment appears to be quite limited unless there is strong political backing for change. Beyond a small amount of extra assistance for a foreign group of pupils within a school, a substantial provision of extra hours requiring the mobilisation of large resources is usually beyond the limits available at the school or classroom level.

To introduce new objectives, such as developing language competence in the mother tongue of a minority group, is even more difficult. Teachers are often leaders in providing advice favouring such actions but the studies show that such general changes go beyond the technical decision-making latitude offered to educators who must in fact be backed by political ratification based on a minimum consensus of general public opinion.

Definition of problems and typical policy responses

In the course of studying the many country reports contributed to the CERI inquiry one came to recognise certain definitions that reflected the major public consensus as to the nature of the minority culture and language problem. These have provided a key, as it were, to comprehending the resultant educational provisions, and I shall use them here as a basis for a summary description of these provisions. Seven such 'problem definitions' have been identified and ranked as 'stages' according to the recognition and status given to minority educational needs.

The assumptions behind these definitions and the typical policy responses and expected language outcomes which accompany each of them, are summarised in table 14.3. The regularity of the relationships that appear in this table provide us, as we shall presently show, with a first step in the formulation of a framework for describing the pattern of measures that may be applied to the education of minority groups.

The first of these 'stages of definition', simply ignoring the existence of the problem, is not represented in any of the national education systems under review, and therefore is dropped from further consideration. The remaining six definitions can be viewed as an historical sequence, moving to higher levels of recognition until the problem is defined as the need to give the minority culture and language equal social status. Although these are treated as sequential states they are not meant to represent an inevitable course of history. However, old established minorities, such as in Belgium, Finland and Switzerland, represent something close to the most advanced stage of problem definition while, as the table shows, no new or non-established minority appears to have progressed beyond Stage 4.

Stage 1 — The learning deficit This definition hinges upon the traditional approaches to special education. By various measures, certain groups of students are observed to suffer from scholastic deficiencies. They have poor grades, progress through the system more slowly than others, may have special discipline problems, and drop out of school in greater numbers, and at earlier ages.

Stage 2 — The socially-linked learning deficit In this definition, the student's poor performance at school is seen to be related to unfavourable social economic situations of their parents, and this diminished school performance is expected to lead to social problems later in life connected with this social economic status.

These two stages appear to be universal to OECD countries with the possible exception of two: Finland, where the Swedish-speaking minority was originally perceived by the majority as having a position of higher prestige and social attainment, and Switzerland, where the relationship between the language groups in modern times was coloured by the fact that each of the three major languages (French, German, Italian) was spoken in nearby, culturally prestigious countries, a factor tending to attenuate the superior/inferior status relationships often found in multilingual settings. By contrast, in Canada the same initial (learning deficit) conceptualisation is applied to minority Francophones, whose scholastic achievement was below that of their English-speaking counterparts.

The Stage 1 problem definition, expressed in terms of a deficit model of special education, corresponds to the adoption of pedagogic measures aimed at narrowing the achievement gap. Where minority students are enrolled in the majority-language system (true of most countries except those with long-established minorities) the problem has historically been seen as a language deficit, that is, the students have an inadequate grasp of the majority language. In France and Germany there is a variety of special measures aimed at upgrading knowledge of the second language; educational authorities in England also appear to stress development of English skills for immigrant students. The intent is primarily to bring the students' knowledge of the classroom language up to a level where they can benefit from instruction. This is accompanied by measures of cultural familiarisation in some cases, as indicated in the Danish regulations: 'The purpose of Danish language teaching is for pupils to acquire proficiency in the Danish language, and to familiarise them with conditions prevailing in Denmark'.

The US Title VII legislation for bilingual/bicultural education makes language deficiency the criterion of admission to such programmes. The US programmes also include measures that illustrate the type of action that is characteristic of the Stage 2 model, such as facilitating job training and placement on the labour market for members of minorities. The largest range of such measures, including summer programmes for immigrants and short vocational programmes for all interested youths, is reported from Sweden.

Even though at this stage the primary problem identified is the students' lack of knowledge of the second (majority) language, several countries have introduced instruction in the children's mother tongue for reasons not directly related to the assumptions of the model. The most common case, illustrated by France and Germany, involves the use of language teachers from the home countries of the students (or their parents) to teach the language as a subject and, at least in Bavaria, to use it as a medium of instruction for other school subjects; this reflects the 'external' impetus referred to earlier, the objective being to facilitate eventual return. The case study for England and Wales cites a report from research in the early 1970s, in which 'the authors discovered that although no official policy had been declared, the first limited steps were being taken to provide tuition' in the mother tongue.

Until relatively recently many educators felt that continued use of the mother tongue by students might interfere with the acquisition of

Table 14.3

Major models of problem definition and policy responses

Model	Assumptions about problem causes	Typical policy responses	Language outcomes
Stage 1: Learning deficit	Language deficit in majority language (L2) due to use of mother tongue (L1). Problem similar to retardation or learning handicap common in special education.	Supplementary teaching of L2. Special grouping for initial instruction, rapid transition to instruction in L2.	L1 expected to be replaced by L2, rapid transition to L2 for school.
Stage 2: Socially-linked learning deficit	Language deficit as in Stage 1, instructional problem definition is the same. Causes linked to family status: broad range of problems anticipated, linked to social status, both at school and after leaving.	Teaching programmes similar to Stage 1 model. Special measures to assist adjustment to majority society: 'orientation' for immigrants, vocational counselling, youth programmes etc.	Same as Stage 1.
Stage 3: Learning deficit from cultural/social differences	Language deficit recognised as for Stages 1 and 2. Instructional problem definition the same, but greater weight is given to affective consequences of culture differences (e.g. concern for students' self-concept). Partial responsibility placed on society/schools for not accepting or responding to, the minority culture.	Language component of teaching the same as Stages 1 and 2. 'Multicultural' teaching programmes: teaching about minority culture for all students, sensitisation programmes for teachers, programmes of community contact. Revision of textbooks to eliminate racial, ethnic slurs and stereotyping.	Same as Stages 1, 2 for education and long-term; short-term in-family use of L1 expected, say for one or two generations.
Stage 4: Learning deficit from mother tongue deprivation	Language deficit as for Stages 1, 2, 3 but a major causal factor is assumed to be (premature) loss of L1 inhibiting learning of L2 for cognitive and affective reasons. Social problems recognised as for Stage 2. Cultural differences recognised as for Stage 3 but usually less emphasis placed on need for cultural acceptance by majority school programmes.	Language component the same as for L2 teaching as in Stages 1–3. Support provided for home language by study of L1 as a subject, sometimes also as a medium of instruction. Sometimes may include 'multicultural' component for majority as in Stage 3.	Same as Stage 3, except transition to L2 in school expected to take longer in most cases.

Variant stages 1–4(B): Migratory alienation	Problem definition superimposed on the definition in Stages 1, 2, 3 or 4 regarding problems of contact with, or integration into majority schools and culture. Children are assumed to lose contact with culture of origin as result of foreign residence and require help to prepare for return to culture of origin.	Teaching of majority culture language same as for corresponding stage (1–4 above). Additional instruction in L1 as a subject, often with country's geography and history taught through L1 as medium of instruction. Additional instruction often outside regular school day.	Dependent upon residence: return to home language or, if remaining in new country, same as for appropriate stage of country policy (1–4 above).
Stage 5: Language maintenance for private use	Minority language of group threatened with disappearance if not supported, due to smaller numbers of minority. Minority disadvantaged in education by weaker social position of language and culture, due to smaller numbers. Minority has long-term rights to survival. Minority expected to enter majority society outside school.	Minority language used as medium of instruction, usually exclusively in earlier years. Majority language a required subject of study, at least from late elementary years (10–12) onward. Transition to majority language usually required for higher levels of educational system.	L1 maintained as domestic, private language of group. Outside home, minority uses L2 at work or in business life. Long-term group assimilation if demography unfavourable.
Stage 6: Language equality	Languages of minority and majority assumed to have equal rights in society. Language of smaller group may require special support to ensure broad social use: education viewed as only one field of language policy application.	Minority language granted status of official language. Separate educational institutions by language, usually under administration by relevant language group. Support measures extend beyond educational system to all phases of official business, sometimes private sector as well.	Indefinite, prolonged use of L1 by minority in home and in considerable part of work, business life. Long-term coexistence of minority, majority groups.

247

the second language. Paradoxically, the contradiction between first and second language support measures may not exist, according to mounting research evidence. We shall return to this point. Meanwhile, the common sense belief in the contradiction between the support of the mother tongue and the assumptions of the Stage 1 and 2 models has more influence on public opinion than research findings.

Stage 3 — Learning deficit from failure to appreciate cultural differences
This definition assumes that minorities suffer from learning deficits, at least in part because of the failure of the majority society, particularly in education, to recognise, accept and view in a positive way, the culture of the minority. Thus, a portion of the 'blame' is shifted to the educational system, which may appear to mismatch its programmes and institutions to the minority needs — multi-culturism is the proffered response. The ambiguous aspect of this definition may be illustrated by the fact that the recognition of the culture of children may be endorsed officially without accepting the premise that the language of that culture requires support. Thus, in the United Kingdom, the Community Relations Commission carried out between 1968 and 1976 vigorous programmes to support multiculturalism. However, the Commission showed little or no concern for the maintenance of the mother tongues of ethnic minorities and the West Indian dialects are seen only as causing difficulty in learning, a viewpoint which has been challenged by many social linguistic scholars.

The essence of this definition is the recognition of the right to be different and respected but not necessarily to use a different language. This concept appears to be gaining ground in a number of West European countries, usually with some limited recognition of the utility of instruction in the mother tongue.

Stage 4 — Learning deficit from mother tongue deprivation This problem definition rests upon the idea that failure to develop the mother tongue of children leads to a linguistic deprivation which becomes the major cause of learning deficit among minority children. Research evidence appears to be lending support to this thesis and this idea underlies the educational programmes in a number of countries. The United States' legislation, for example, defines bilingual education as a programme designed for children with limited English language skills in which there is 'instruction . . . in English and, to the extent necessary to allow a child to achieve competence in the English language, the native language of the children of limited English proficiency . . . '.

Countries such as Sweden have adopted far-reaching programmes of home language support, where the goal of transition to the majority tongue is complemented, in terms of the policy statements, by more long-term objectives. A Bill passed by the Riksdag in 1975 set down guidelines for immigrant and minority group policy, with the triple aims of equality, freedom of choice, and partnership. The freedom of choice aim means that the 'members of linguistic minorities must be able to choose the extent to which they will assume a Swedish cultural identity and the extent to which they will retain their cultural and linguistic identity'.

Stage 4 still implies education in the minority language as a transitional measure and therefore this Swedish programme, suggesting the possibility of being able to opt for a long-term maintenance of the language, moves toward Stage 5.

Stage 5 − Maintenance of the minority language for private use This definition of the problem reflects the type of thinking written into the Swedish legislation. It recognises minority groups as being weaker members of society because of their smaller numbers, but recognises their right to maintain and to develop their own languages and cultures in private life. Minority languages are expected to be mainly used in the family, for religion and in private social activities. Educational support for this kind of language development is in terms of using it as a medium of instruction particularly in the earlier years of schooling.

Most minority language students are expected to pursue studies in the majority language if they go on to higher levels of education beyond some point (variable by jurisdiction). The case studies of Manitoba, New Brunswick and Ontario illustrate situations where, over the years, the age of transition to studying through the medium of the majority language has been gradually shifted upwards. The most rudimentary form of this involves initial literacy instruction in the first years of elementary school using the mother tongue, sometimes combined immediately with use of, and instruction in, the majority language. Such programmes are found today in education for indigenous peoples such as the Lapps/Sami and Maoris; it is also the case of certain protected minorities such as the Danish minority in Schleswig-Holstein (albeit in private schools) or the Francophones of the Valley of Aosta, in Italy. Cases such as the latter are almost indistinguishable, in terms of teaching practices, from some identified with Stage 4; the main difference is the assumption made about the long-term role of the minority group in the country involved.

Stage 6 − Minority language equality This definition of the problem involves the granting of full official language status to the minority language for purposes of use in public institutions. Where numbers and social dynamism permit, the minority language may also take its place in the broader economic life of the country, a situation only reached in the very old bilingual or multilingual states (Belgium, Finland, Switzerland). The widely publicised constitutional changes in Spain are obviously intended to move towards a situation like this in areas such as Catalonia. The Canadian case study illustrates some of the potential complications and/or flexibility of moving through these last two stages in a federal system: the policy of official bilingualism adopted by the Federal Government applies only to Federal institutions and services, thereby leaving out entirely the field of education, which is under provincial control. Of the three provinces studied, all have given to the French language the status of language of instruction, but only New Brunswick has also adopted it as an official language of the province for all governmental business.

The students as back-migrants: a special definition A special definition of the problem of educating minority students involves the assumption that the students should be prepared to leave their host country and re-integrate into their mother country. This problem definition does not fit into the stages indicated above, but in practice perhaps involves definitions ranging through Stages 1 to 4. This definition implies that the schools will provide foreign students with instruction in their native language along with some cultural and other information about their parents' country of origin. In practice, such a definition may lead to the kind of school programme which corresponds to the Stage 4 definition.

Policy instruments

The great range and complexity of policy instruments — which can only be selectively treated here — are somewhat clarified and take on a certain order when viewed as a response to whatever is the prevailing definition of the problem of the cultural and linguistic minority concerned. The hierarchy of these definitions, as already outlined, is especially evident in aspects of organisation and governance of education for these minorities.

Instructional provisions

Grouping of students for instruction Two general principles govern the grouping of linguistic and cultural minorities for instruction — either dispersion among the majority students or their concentration apart from them. An examination of practices across countries reveals no consensus with respect to these principles. However, where the problem is defined as one of facilitating transition into the majority culture, the first principle is often evoked, even when minority pupils are grouped for special classes during some part of the day or week. Once the goal is not transition but preservation of the minority language, as in the cases of established minorities, the policy begins to shift to separation.

The place of the home language in the school experience Policy decisions on educational arrangements for the minority language appear less to be oriented around structural relationships to the majority language than to the degree that the minority language can be considered an integral part of the schooling experience. The implications are both pedagogical and symbolic for the students involved. The French case study, for example, quotes a report of discussions held by Yugoslav and Italian teachers regarding the issue of whether the teaching of the home language should be integrated into the regular school programme: 'The very fact that the native language is taught within the normal school curriculum *enhances its value* in everyone's eyes' (emphasis in original). In OECD countries the following range of commitments of the educational system to the importance of the home language of a minority is indicated from the material being reviewed:

(a) no encouragement of the home language in or outside of school;
(b) official encouragement (but not necessarily commitment of resources) to teaching the home language outside school hours;
(c) using the home language as a short-term transitional medium of instruction (e.g. less than two years);
(d) teaching the home language as a subject in school hours (or as part of the programme for which academic credit is received);
(e) using the home language as a transitional medium of instruction for long periods (more than two years);
(f) recognising the home language as an official or quasi-official medium of instruction for major portions of the school experience;
(g) creation of a separate system of education for elementary and/or secondary levels in the home language.

In this list, only the relative positions of items (b) and (c) appear to be debatable in terms of their symbolic value; the case studies provide insufficient information to be sure of their sequence. What is important to note is that official recognition does not efface social distinctions that originate outside the school. Option (e), for example, includes the Bavarian bilingual model. The German case study provides ample evidence, however, that participation in classes for minority groups of any type can have a certain stigmatising effect on pupils and on teachers, both in Bavaria and elsewhere in Germany. If popular opinion considers the minority language to be 'inferior' or a mark of inferior social status (as it often is), then the positive effects of official recognition may be partially offset by this factor. This problem exists to a greater or lesser extent in all countries.

Table 14.4 presents a rough tabulation of different instructional modes selected from across the countries under review. Some of the data on which it is based may not be complete, but the classification provides an initial, intuitive sense of the degree of recognition given to different minority languages and dialects. It does *not* constitute a measure of the degree of social acceptance of the minorities in society at large: the multicultural efforts made in many of the English educational authorities, for instance, are not shown here, but their effect in terms of breaking down out-of-school social barriers may be greater than some higher level of linguistic recognition found in other countries' official policies. The last column in the table distinguishes between three main forms of instruction given in the majority (second) language — L2 — in parallel with whatever is the general form of educational provision: (a) short-term, intensive transitional instruction, (b) long-term remedial type additional instruction, that may be prescribed on an individual basis or given to groups, and (c) study of the second language as a regular school subject on a long-term basis when the dominant medium of instruction is the minority language.

The table illustrates the main types of differences found in the degree of recognition of the minority language as well as the type of variety that may be found in even one country. Two countries are represented by entries both for new and for established minorities, Switzerland and the United Kingdom. In each case, a clear distinction can be seen in the form of educational provision made. To the author's knowledge, a similar distinction is made in most other relevant jurisdictions (Belgium, Canada, Finland), with the higher level of recognition being reserved always for the established minority.

In all but a few cases, the classifications shown reflect an evolution of policy that has occurred within the last ten years: the picture would have been much different had the data been collected in 1970 and would have been unrecognisable if one were to classify the situation in 1965: few jurisdictions would have had a check anywhere except in the first column.

The criteria for establishing separate teaching units Minority language education may be established on the basis of the right of the individual, the right of a group, or the general right of individuals or groups to be educated despite their inability to understand the majority language.

Table 14.4
The role of the home language of minority pupils (L1) in selected jurisdictions

Extent of national commitment	not encouraged	outside teaching encouraged	for instruction short-term	taught as school subject	transition medium for instruction	official medium for instruction	separate system for L1	forms of instruction L2 [1]
United Kingdom: (West Indians)	X							2
Australia: (Aborigine)	X		X[2]					2
Denmark		X						1, 2
Switzerland: (immigrants)		X						1, 2 (?)
United Kingdom: (Non-English speaking immigrants)		X						1, 2
France		X		X elem.				1, 2
Berlin, N.Rhine-Westphalia (prep. classes)		X	X					1, 2
United States (Bilingual Ed. Act)			X	X	X			1 (?), 2
N.Rhine-Westphalia: (long term prep. classes)				X	X			2, 3 (?)
Bavaria: 'bilingual' classes				X	X	?		2, 3
Sweden: options				X	X	X[3]		1, 2
United Kingdom: Wales				X	X	?		3
Manitoba: secondary					X	?		3
Manitoba: elementary					X	X		3
Ontario					X	X		3
Switzerland: Romansch				X sec.		X elem.	X	3
New Brunswick						X	X	3

1 Key to teaching forms for majority language (L2): 1 – short-term, intensive transitional instruction; 2 – long-term remedial type additional instruction; 3 – study as a subject on long-term basis.
2 Experimental.
3 Experimental groups in Finnish leading to secondary school graduation.

The fact that the second concept of group 'rights' is the most common basis for programmes is a source of concern because this right is subject to a criteria of numbers, which means something less than an absolute guarantee for such education.

The training, status and supervision of teachers   The picture that emerges from the partial information available is that unless special measures are taken, the teacher of ethnic and cultural minorities can be assigned a status of second class members of the teaching establishment dealing with second class members of the society.

The examples most contributory to this picture are drawn mainly from the new minorities and indigenous groups, that is, those groups whose status in their host societies is most tenuous. If one turns to the established minorities, the contrast is obvious. The teachers are regular members of their profession with normal opportunities for advancement, at least within their own language system of education.

In the provision of support and ancillary services, although the case studies and country reports do not give full information, the same general division of standards exists between the relatively well-off established minorities and the new minorities and indigenous peoples.

Governance

The response of many jurisdictions to the weaker legal status of linguistic and cultural minorities and, where status is equal, to their numerical weakness, has been to develop mechanisms for associating them with decisions about the education of their children.

Forms of participation   The major forms of participation by minorities in the governance of education for their children include the following.

(a)   *Direct influence through regular governance processes:*   This involves ordinarily participation as electors and/or candidates for boards or nominated offices, acting in a role directly comparable to that of members of the majority. It is only accessible to minorities having the highest level of legal status. The extent of influence effectively exercised depends usually upon absolute numbers and on the local political/administrative traditions. The cases of greatest influence coincide either with areas where the minorities are a majority or near majority (for example, in some Ontario school boards and some localities in Wales) or where the structure of decision-making is itself divided along linguistic and/or cultural lines (for example, in New Brunswick or Graubünden).

(b) *Assigned special status or representation within the regular governance process:* In certain jurisdictions special representation mechanisms are set up so that decisions concerning a minority must be dealt with in consultation with members of the minority, at their initiative or, at least, with their having some right to a voice. In its simplest form, this may involve reserving a limited number of seats or votes for use by minority group members within the regular organs of policy deliberation, for example, one seat on a school board is reserved for parents of Indian children educated in the public school system in some localities of Ontario. The US requirement that applications for funding under the Bilingual Education Act be vetted by an advisory council on which parents of affected children constitute a majority, fits into this same category; the same applies to the French Language Advisory Committees, whose advice must be heard by Ontario school boards that operate French language instructional units at the secondary level.

A somewhat different approach is found in all three Canadian provinces studied, consisting in policies that reserve a certain proportion of administrative posts in the Ministry or Department of Education for members of the minority, including very senior posts (Deputy Minister or Assistant Deputy Minister), and provide specialised sub-units or departments concerned with handling affairs of the minority group.

The US Bureau of Indian Affairs and the Commonwealth Department of Aboriginal Affairs are similar in function as specialised agencies, even if there is no requirement that staff be of the relevant minority group(s). In all these cases, a specialised mechanism is set up, either in representative organs of deliberation or in the administration, to ensure consideration of minority education issues.

(c) *Control or influence over reserved areas outside the regular governance process:* Both in the United States and Canada, a portion of the schools for native American Indians have been turned over to control by Indian tribes or bands, placing them in the orbit of the limited autonomy available on reservation lands. The extent of actual control is difficult to assess from the available data in the studies, but there is obviously a degree of external dependence resulting from the funding of the schools originating from non-Indian sources and, in some cases, from the need for external staffing.

(d) *Control of representation on specialised bodies outside the regular governance process:* New Zealand has set up with partial government funding the Maori Education Foundation and the Pacific Island Polynesian Education Foundation as well as a National Advisory Committee on Maori Education, all with strong representation of the minorities. The Australian Federal Government has helped set up Aboriginal Consultative Groups in all but one of the states; Manitoba has established three advisory councils, though with limited operations; in some jurisdictions (for example, the United Kingdom) voluntary organisations set up independently of government help may play, nevertheless, an important and quasi-official role in providing advice. The common characteristics of these bodies is their role outside the normal governance system with relatively limited competency and control over the main aspects of education affecting the minority. Their existence and function depend in large measure on the good will of associated authorities, which is apparently not lacking in most instances.

(e) *Tutelage by a third party:* The network of bilateral and/or multilateral arrangements growing up in Western Europe, under which national governments assume responsibility for funding and/or staffing portions of the education given to their nationals on foreign soil, effectively transfers responsibility for such matters in large measure to the relevant national government.

(f) *Parental rights:* In the absence of any other mechanisms, most jurisdictions and educational institutions recognise the right of individual parents to be consulted about the education of their children, even if final decisions usually remain with the educational authorities. This is, obviously, an individual rather than a group right.

It is clear that the first two of these forms of participation are associated only with established minorities. Form (b) appears to be quasi-experimental and does not touch the majority of indigenous peoples (though the Sami appear to have a larger proportion of their numbers in situations where their influence is strongly felt). Form (d) is of importance with certain indigenous populations and, to a very limited extent, for some new minorities. However, the bulk of the populations categorised as new minorities and as indigenous peoples in the OECD countries appear to be in situations covered by cases (e) and (f), that is the majority have little or no collective control or consultative role to play in decisions regarding the education of their children.

The obstacles to the current strong tendency to seek better minority group involvement in governance may be cited: small numbers in a given locality, several different minorities with different needs and ideas, lack of experience relevant to governance participation and attitudes of the community or of the professionals concerned. But impetus is derived from broad changes in public opinion and a recognition of the relative ineffectiveness of many programmes that lacked minority involvement.

Locus of control and the strong regulatory stance Analysis of the data available to this study has shown a clear tendency for governments to take a strong regulatory stance towards education of linguistic and cultural minorities. This stance is comprised of a 'bundle' of financial and other regulations which are associated with a preference for categorical funding in all except one country jurisdiction. This raises the general issue of how minority education fits within the patterns of relationship between different levels of governance.

A review of the evidence shows that a variety of factors have contributed to this adoption of stronger regulatory stances:

(i) In countries with relatively strong *traditions of central control* (that is 'central' in terms of the country's individual constitutional structure) the stance is, one might say, a by-product of the normal system of operation. This applies, for example, to France and to the German *Länder* in their dealings with the local school communities.

(ii) *Central authorities have privileged access to certain types of revenue*, therefore providing them with greater financial flexibility in responding to new problems. If a new problem is perceived (for example because of an influx of resident foreign workers), a locality operating within a fixed set of budgetary and staffing constraints may have difficulty in reallocating funds from ongoing programmes to create new ones. This is consistent with the mechanism noted in an earlier CERI study on *Educational Financing and Policy Goals for Primary Schools* where it was shown that erosion of local autonomy resulted in part from ever increasing demands for services whose costs have tended to outrun localities' financial powers.

(iii) *The broad geographic distribution of some populations* appears to dilute their presence in any given locality and to make it easier for central authorities to recognise their problems and to foster a co-ordinated approach. This is particularly notable in the case of the transfer of powers concerning education of Aboriginal populations from the states to the Australian Commonwealth through a 1967 referendum to modify the constitution. On the other hand, the central responsibility for some populations is not necessarily inconsistent with local administration and autonomy. The Australian and Canadian

Federal Governments have both exercised their respective responsibilities for education of indigenous peoples through mechanisms that, for a large part, rely upon the states and the provinces of their jurisdiction.

(iv) *The political influence of minorities*, where it exists, may be more strongly felt at more senior levels of governance, or its influence may be more consistently felt. Within systems with ample autonomy at the local level, the pattern may be very uneven: some localities may prove very responsive to minority needs, whereas others are simply neutral and a few are hostile to them. Attention may focus on local 'trouble spots' that involve resistance to minority rights, thus causing the local level to appear less responsive than it really is. The need to overcome individual cases of resistance may explain in large measure the strong regulatory stances of the Canadian provincial governments.

The majority of jurisdictions have opted for strong regulatory stances combined with varying measures of minority participation in decision-making. However, since this involves strong central authority, reconciliation of local control for the majority with the protection or development of minority educational rights has often proved difficult.

Impact of minority participation in governance Generalisations about the impact of minority participation in decision-making about their own education are difficult to make on the basis of the data available. Only the established minorities have acquired major degrees of group control, and it is difficult to generalise from their experience to the problems of other linguistic and cultural minorities. It is clear that established minorities attempt, wherever possible, to assert control over their educational systems and to expand their degree of autonomy.

The pattern is, nevertheless, clear: the more 'different' and the less 'integrated' a group, the less is the likelihood of control and of educational success. Leaving aside the very particular case of the Sami, the indigenous peoples have all shown various degrees of difficulty resulting from extreme dependency on remote and alien bureaucratic systems. Despite a long tradition of well-intended efforts to promote education of indigenous peoples through decisions by specialised administrators and agencies, all jurisdictions appear to have begun adopting, on at least an experimental basis, some forms of greater indigenous control. The new minorities, by contrast, have been hardly touched in most instances even by experimental schemes to permit their control.

What is clear is that the present tendency to rely upon the home country governments of resident foreign workers for the organisation of some parts of their education, will prove effective only so long as the intention of the workers is to return home. Should the objectives of these groups turn towards remaining as a minority in another country, a means will have to be found to keep in touch with their aspirations and, in particular, the aspirations of their children, socialised into totally new value systems and social conditions.

Financial and regulatory instruments

Modes of finance   In dealing with linguistic and cultural minorities, almost all jurisdictions for which sufficient data are available to classify, have opted for categorical funding. Separate programmes of categorical funding are used even in systems where the main mode of financial transfer is non-categorical. However, it cannot be assumed that this option for categorical funding is automatically linked to a reduction in discretionary powers. Some categorical systems leave very large room for local initiative and decision-making. In the case of linguistic and cultural minorities, nevertheless, the tendency is to use categorical schemes as a means of ensuring special treatment for the populations concerned. The exceptions in Canada and Switzerland are worthy of note precisely because they go against this tendency to focus on a given population, once the population reaches a status approaching equality.

Thus far the discussion has dealt with educational finances in the same context as most other studies, that is, national and sub-national systems of finance. This study has brought to the fore the existence of a new mode of finance: *extra-national subsidies to minority language education.* This takes two forms. In dealing with the needs of resident foreign workers, many Western European countries have opted for a system of allowing the home country of the workers to identify teachers of the same nationality, train them and pay them. The host country typically provides free use of classroom space and, in some cases, educational materials and other support. Most of the home-language education of foreign children in France is paid for in this way, for example.

A second, related form of subsidy has arisen through the action of supranational organisations such as the European Economic Community. Since 1974, for example, the British Government has made applications to the EEC Social Fund in respect of special language teaching and other provision made for immigrant children and has used the money obtained from the fund to make retrospective reimbursements to some local authorities of their portion of expenditure under Section II programmes. The long-term implications of such financial systems are hard to predict, but their rapid development in the field of teaching the home language of resident foreign workers is a major innovation of the last decade and is well worth further study.

Problems of financial subsidies If one seeks to determine why special financial arrangements are made for linguistic and cultural minorities, the problem subdivides into three components: (a) the educational objectives of the policy pursued, (b) the technical basis of subsidy, and (c) the instrumental objectives of subsidisation, that is the way the subsidy relates to the administrative and political environments and results in the mobilisation of resources to serve the policy objective. In a previous section, we have dealt generally with the issue of objectives so, here, our discussion will be limited to the last two points.

As to the technical basis for subsidy, one's primary concern is to know why a special revenue flow should be associated with the education of a linguistic or cultural minority. All the schemes for categorical subsidisation are based on providing a supplement to educational authorities or institutions above the 'normal' amount. In other words, each system is based on some explicit notion of an additional cost, above that which the authority or institution would ordinarily be expected to cover from its regular revenues. In jurisdictions with tightly controlled systems of regulating resource flows (for example, by fixing norms for teacher:pupil ratios and making reimbursements of teacher salaries) the additional subsidy is an automatic by-product of making changes to regulations governing the flows (for example, by setting different pupil:teacher ratios for classes, as in the case of France).

In 'looser' systems the funds may be allocated on bases that are not strictly tied to a defined type of expenditure and may have no control over expenditure. The more obvious case of absence of control is the system of transfers from the Canadian Government to the provinces on the basis of minority language pupil enrolments: the absence of control and therefore of a direct Federal hand in the provincial jurisdiction, is an integral part of the system.

No clear trends are visible in terms of financing ancillary costs such as transportation for scattered populations which can be important. Also, the creation of new services for minorities where none have previously existed or where the minority was not dealt with on a special basis, can give rise to subsidies for *'start-up' costs*. Manitoba operates a so-called 'development grant' that is based on quantitative increases in the amount of instruction given in the minority language for a given group of students; Ontario provides a start-up grant for creation of new instructional units to provide for such expenses as purchase of library and teaching materials, extra recruitment costs and so forth. *Pro-*

gramme and curriculum development is obviously partly included in these grants; it is more specifically provided for in the financing systems of Australia and the United States, where special project funding may be available for experimentation and development of materials. Special programmes for development of curriculum materials and publication of books are also mentioned in some cases (for example, the Ontario French Language Development Fund, or the translation and publication of textbooks in the five dialects of Romansch in Graubünden).

As to the instrumental objectives, even in closely regulated systems, every financial component has a definable 'incentive' value. Explicit incentive schemes are usually reserved to situations where there is a degree of resistance to the policy being proposed; the more the recipients of the subsidy are interested in the scheme's objectives, the less need for incentive. In systems with shared local/central finances, the most simple method is to use the central funds to pay a part, but not all, of the costs of a given programme. This constitutes a way of making it easier to shift local priorities.

Methods of subsidisation often include standard provisions that have a very different effect depending upon the jurisdiction or institutions affected. Thus, if a service for a special group already exists in certain jurisdictions but not in others, a decision at a higher level to subsidise the specific service across all jurisdictions provides additional revenues without additional expenditures in the places where the service exists. The Canadian system of Federal subsidies for minority language education had this effect for Quebec, which had the most developed system in the country for its (English-speaking) minority long before the other provinces began making serious efforts to develop similar provisions for the French speakers in their jurisdictions. Since the largest share of the transfer payments for bilingualism have always gone to Quebec, it must be assumed that this artifact of the system was an integral part of its conception and may have reduced traditional Quebec opposition sufficiently to permit the first major Federal initiative related to the field of elementary and secondary education.

Some systems have rules against supplanting one funding source by another for existing programmes (see bilingual programme provisions in various States of the United States), but funding authorities may be loathe to use them, both because of technical difficulties and because they penalise jurisdictions that have shown initiative in dealing with a given problem while favouring those that have failed to do so.

The effects of regulatory measures

Direct effects on educational treatments   The pattern of financial and regulatory measures of the fifteen countries under study has revealed a tendency toward strong regulatory stances and limited, though improving, minority governance participation. Such measures can directly affect the status of individual minority group members and of the group itself. The instruments can set up conditions for admission to education that may determine individual membership in the group. Australian public policy, including its educational policies, has adopted a definition for an Aborigine as 'anyone of Aboriginal descent who identifies as an Aborigine and is accepted or regarded as such by the community in which he or she resides'. This definition is relatively broad, in that it includes persons of part-Aboriginal descent, and is neutral or non-pejorative.

The US Bilingual Education Act originally limited funding to programmes that served 'children who come from environments where the dominant language is other than English'. The 1974 revisions to the Act changed it to refer to children of 'limited English speaking ability', a term that was revised in 1978 to refer to individuals with 'limited English proficiency'. Up until 1975 there was the further requirement that the children served must come from low income families. This example is typical of definitions that are based upon a deficit model of the members of a linguistic or cultural minority. Moreover the right to remain in a 'bilingual and bicultural' environment is, so to speak, conditional upon not overcoming the deficit. The nuances of wording are, in themselves, quite significant in their effects on individuals and their education. The 1974 revisions broadened the classes of individuals eligible for programmes but introduced a deficit concept for participation. The 1978 changes meant that an individual who had learned to speak English but who lacked other elements of linguistic proficiency (reading, composition and other classroom language skills) would no longer be prematurely removed from the programmes.

The examples are illustrative of the way that regulations related to resource provision can affect individuals by laying down precise conditions for the populations being served and for the personal characteristics of individuals admitted to programmes. In this respect, no definitional scheme is completely neutral. Admission to home language instruction for resident foreign workers in Europe is largely based on nationality, but the definition can have unanticipated effects, for example, if the home language is not the national language of the country (for example, Turkish citizens of Kurdish language, Spanish citizens from Catalonia). The Canadian provinces have opted for definitions based on phrases such as 'French speaking students' but have not applied the definitions rigorously, as this would exclude children of French-speaking parentage who have been heavily Anglicised.

Many educational programmes of a specialised nature are temporarily funded and subject to non-renewal. Disappearance of funding means the end of the programme, a situation that makes the status of the education of affected groups appear to be precarious. If the groups are also weak in a political sense, their continued educational special status can appear to place them in a dependency situation *vis-a-vis* educational authorities. The current US legislation (Bilingual Education Act, as amended 1978), for example, recognises this problem and places strict guidelines on the process of termination of grants to school districts. Non-renewal is, in principle, a possibility for any programme not having automatic funding.

The negative connotations of the analysis given above should not obscure one fact: in many instances, even if the regulations surrounding funding have negative connotations in an absolute sense, the very existence of the programmes is often considered by the minorities concerned as a victory in their attempts to have their status and special needs recognised. Moreover, some of the regulations attempt in a positive sense to provide additional status or political leverage for minority groups. The latest revisions to the US legislation, for example, require that applications for programme funding must be developed in consultation with an advisory council of which a majority are parents of children of limited English proficiency. Systems that tend toward long-term maintenance of minority groups usually have more thoroughgoing provisions that give the group members a formal role to play in the governance process.

Indirect effects of regulatory measures The main effect of regulatory measures on educational treatments, as we have seen, concerned the degree of implementation of policy and, in particular, the *accessibility of educational provisions* to the members of the potentially affected linguistic and cultural minorities. The importance of this effect is, of course, self-evident. The Canadian data indicates clearly the importance placed by the Francophone minorities on ensuring coverage of all their members through the quantitative expansion of the amount of instruction in French both in terms of percentage of instruction given and of numbers of schools and classes. Our previous discussion of minority aspirations has shown this to be a more general phenomenon, common to all the situations under study. However, one *caveat* must be introduced: the implications of incomplete coverage of the members of a minority group by a given type of educational provision depends entirely upon the *appropriateness of the educational experience*. To deal with one extreme: it is known that many indigenous peoples have experienced severe effects of alienation both from their own social ethos and from the dominant values of the 'modern' schools they attend. The extent to which this is traceable to the effects of schooling, by contrast with the general effect of social contact with a European-type society, cannot be determined, but there is no doubt that schooling does play a major role in this process.

Turning to the situation of resident foreign workers in Western Europe, we can note that the models of educational experience pursued in different jurisdictions are sometimes based upon mutually contradictory assumptions. From the point of view of the minorities concerned, the value of universal accessibility to a given educational provision depends ultimately upon whether the assumptions underlying the provision correspond to their interests.

There is extreme variation between jurisdictions in terms of coverage and effects. In France, for example, only one out of five children of foreign workers has a generally 'normal' school career; the German case study expresses severe doubts about the effectiveness of current measures; the results in the United Kingdom refer to unevenness of provision; the US study indicates that only a small portion of the target population is reached by bilingual and bicultural programmes. The most optimistic results are found in the Canadian report. The fact that the latter refers to an established minority and the others to new minorities makes it unlikely that the role of regulatory measures is the main single causal factor; the status of the minority appears, rather, to determine in large measure the regulatory approach adopted. The overall impression derived from the documentation for the CERI inquiry is that the indigenous and new minorities are only poorly covered in most instances, and that the nature of the appropriate provision is not clear.

Conversely, the established minorities are reached in much larger proportions. However, even in this case, there are wide differences as to priorities for content and the feeling of urgency for taking measures. As evidence one need only compare the strong emphasis on use of the minority tongue as the main instructional medium for Canadian Francophones, with the relatively weak role of the Welsh language.

Conclusions

A number of practical conclusions proceed from these findings. The combinations of financial, organisational and regulatory arrangements which are in place still do not provide universal access to minimum standards of service, particularly for indigenous people and new minorities. Even the present knowledge of the way these groups of policy instruments operate allows for distinct improvements in the breadth and quality of coverage. Secondly, while the way must be left open for those minorities who may still voluntarily opt for strategies of integration with the mainstream culture at the expense of the ultimate disappearance of their home culture and language, other options are increasingly evident and their practicality is being demonstrated. However, many difficult problems of effective financing and regulations remain for enquiry and solution. A third consideration is that not only equity values but efficiency and efficacy have been shown to be served by increasing the participation of the minorities in the governance of their educational programmes.

Finally, such interest should give rise to support for research and experimentation toward the development of educational programmes more effective in meeting the needs of the various minority groups concerned. Improvements in the policy instruments will only be meaningful if they provide access to increasingly appropriate educational opportunities.

15 Language and literacy: programmes for linguistic minorities in five countries

Ray C. Rist
Cornell University, Ithaca, New York

A comparison of country settings

Historical and ecological considerations

To define and then examine the range of policy/programme alternatives present in the five countries under review necessitates establishing conceptual boundaries. Indeed, one of the most serious problems that constantly challenges policy-makers is that of containing the definition of the issue at hand. The broader the definition, the larger the net within which to collect extraneous and non-relevant information. Alternatively, defining the issue too narrowly means that one takes the risk of excluding material that ought to be considered. Policy analysis, and cross-national policy analysis in particular, constantly has to deal with the tension between the scope and specificity of the analytic framework.
   For this present effort, a series of criteria will be presented which should be useful in examining the policy/programme variations and alternatives present among the five nations. The goal is to create an analytic framework from which to analyse the variety of means by which countries have confronted their own multiculturalism and its implications for education. The case studies suggest that given different historical contexts, the policy/programme responses are likely to vary. The limits on one's policy options also create limits on one's programmatic responses. Yet these five countries are not so dissimilar in all

ways as to leave no basis for cross-national analysis. The country reports, taken together, suggest that patterns do exist. The task is to formulate a framework from within which to examine them. One should observe here that, on reading the various reports, it became clear that many of the choices were made decades ago. They have become so deeply embedded in each nation's constitutional and institutional structure that they are now extremely difficult to isolate and treat as available levers of change. These historical choices have had many unforeseen effects on the alternatives open to the countries as they have responded to the language and literacy needs of special populations within their respective borders.

A further caveat here is also necessary. No report from any country sought to examine the situation of *all* cultural and language minority groups in that country. The result was selective attention to particular groups. This has meant that generalisations on the national scene are extremely tenuous. To exclude, for example, an examination of the Basque situation in Spain or the Breton situation in France from this present analysis means that the picture is incomplete for those two countries. The same can be said for the remaining three countries as well. In each, the task established by the OECD was to do an in-depth study of a specific group or cluster of groups as opposed to a comprehensive national survey.

To inform the reader of the populations which serve as the basis for this present analysis, the following list indicates the special populations targeted in each of the five nations:

Canada	English-speaking minority in Quebec; and the French-speaking minority in New Brunswick, Ontario and Manitoba.
France	Recently arrived minorities, especially those from Algeria, Tunisia, Morocco, French-speaking Africa, Spain, Portugal, Italy, Yugoslavia, Turkey and Poland.
Federal Republic of Germany	Recently arrived minorities; especially those from Turkey, Greece, Italy, Yugoslavia and Spain.
Spain	The indigenous Catalan-speaking population in Catalonia.
United Kingdom	The Welsh-speaking indigenous population plus recently arrived minorities, especially those from the Commonwealth countries in Africa and Asia.

Geographical boundedness versus dispersal

Perhaps the most readily apparent basis by which to distinguish among the five nations is that of the geographical boundedness versus dispersal of the cultural and language minority groups within their national boundaries. Whereas the United Kingdom, Spain and Canada have clearly defined geographical parameters which delineate the presence of language minorities, that is, the Province of Quebec in Canada, that of the national region or *Communidades Autónomas* of Catalonia in Spain, and that of Wales in the United Kingdom. The same cannot be said of the Federal Republic of Germany or France. Of course with these two countries, there are exceptions. But a characterisation of their 'dispersion' among the language minorities listed earlier is more accurate than it would be to identify the minorities in these countries as geographically isolated or concentrated.

The notion of geographical definitiveness is one that has interested researchers on race relations for some decades. Francis[1] devotes considerable attention to the role that this condition has upon majority–minority relations. Likewise, the recent work of Rex[2] and Allen[3] contribute to our understandings in this area, particularly to that of the origins of the subjective and stereotyped views the dominant group holds about one or more minority groups. The evidence of such separateness on social stratification as well as social perceptions suggests that it is a particularly powerful force in the structuring of inter-group relations. The country reports have explicated a number of ways in which language policy has been central to this organising of the various social systems, not the least of which have been language segregated schools, government prohibition on the use of particular languages, and the refusal of government and business to use any but the dominant language in their activities.

Time the special population has been within the national boundaries

Historical longevity of the language minority within the current national boundaries appears to be a salient distinction among the five countries. Indeed, those with the longest history are also those who are most geographically concentrated. In the Catalonian region in Spain, and the Welsh region of the United Kingdom, the groups of interest in this present analysis have a history dating back several centuries or more.

In contrast, the immigration of language and cultural minorities to France and to the FDR is relatively recent, and their residency in these two countries can be measured literally in terms of months and years.

The major migrations of language immigrants into these host countries has occurred within the past three decades.[4] Though it is not an issue stressed in the country reports, it can be added that the social and demographic characteristics of the latter language minority groups do not approximate those of the former. The migrations into Western Europe in the 1960s and 1970s were migrations of manpower, not of entire populations. These recent immigrants have been overwhelmingly young, actively involved in the labour force, and frequently alone. This is in contrast to the situations in the historical communities of Canada, Wales and Spain where there is an inter-generational continuity and both formal and informal social systems that sustain the mother tongue. While informal social systems are now emerging in France and the Federal Republic of Germany, they are neither so elaborate nor have roots as in the historical communities.

As is evident in the country reports, the discussion of policy/ programme alternatives suggests that the combined factors of dispersal plus recent arrival have influenced governmental efforts in directions quite different from those of the governments addressing issues related to the geographically distinct and long-term populations.

Governmental policy on culture and language

In an earlier draft of this paper, governmental policies on culture and language were treated as distinct entities. Several detailed discussions with colleagues have convinced me that it is important to examine them simultaneously, as they are inextricably interwoven. Thus what follows is an effort to elaborate on the interrelations as well as variations in cultural and language policies for the five nations.

In assessing government policy, what is immediately striking about these five nations is that those three nations with (a) the historical communities and which (b) have been geographically distinct are (c) the same three nations that have most forcefully enunciated a national policy of multi-lingualism, as well as (d) the preservation of the culture of the concerned populations. In contrast, the stance of the Federal Republic of Germany and France appears to be one of stressing monolingualism in the dominant tongue as well as the assimilation of the recent arrivals into the dominant culture. This, of course, may be stating the distinctions a bit too sharply, but the variations *between* these two groups of countries is much greater than the variations *within* the respective groups. Canada, Spain and the United Kingdom do share a common commitment to the preservation of the mother tongue of their respective language minorities and have instituted governmental policies to ensure that this is so. By doing so, they have also given assent to preserving the cultures within which these languages are now used.

A particularly persuasive argument was made in several of the country reports: specifically, the reason that the language minorities in the historical communities have been able to institutionalise and legitimate the use of their own language is that they have successfully used their distinct geographic base for the formation of a political force on the national political scene. A cohesive and politically active population in these areas was successful in efforts to secure governmental sanction for a pluralistic and bilingual policy.

Juxtaposed is the relative powerlessness of the immigrant/minority groups in the Federal Republic of Germany and France. In different variations across these two countries, immigrant groups are restricted in their political participation, their ability to unionise, their ability to seek employment, their ability to gain access to state supported housing, their ability to be granted 'due process' in the judicial system, their ability to protect their current employment from unemployed nationals, and most central to this present analysis, their ability to influence, govern, or direct the educational systems within which their children are educated. With the language minorities being widely dispersed and coming from multiple sending countries (each with a different culture and language), the result is the formation of policy at the national level by the dominant group to encourage a monolingual and assimilationist approach toward these disparate peoples.

An issue raised here deserves further attention. An important distinction to be drawn between the historical communities and those of the recent immigrants is that in each instance, the historical community consists of a single language and cultural group geographically distinct and reinforcing the use of the mother tongue. With the Federal Republic of Germany and France, the minorities in each country come from multiple sending countries, thus creating a cultural and linguistic mosaic. The dispersal of multiple groups across each of the two countries makes within-group cohesion difficult, let alone the consideration of between-group collaboration and co-operation. The preconditions for the development of a national policy affirming multilingualism appear to be nearly, if not completely, absent at present in both the Federal Republic of Germany and France.

*The permanence/impermanence of the
language/cultural minority group*

Public policy and public perceptions within the five countries as to the permanence or impermanence of the language and cultural minorities vary greatly. On the one hand, there are those countries (Spain, Canada, and the United Kingdom) where it is not a question of whether the Catalans, Quebecois, or Welsh shall remain as residents. They have citizenship and a historical claim that makes irrelevant any suggestion of them being transient.

The same cannot be said for the recent immigrants into the United Kingdom from Asia and Africa, or the immigrants into the Federal Republic of Germany and France from the Mediterranean basin. In both countries, there is strong sentiment among a portion of the native population that the new arrivals are not to be thought of as permanent residents. Rather, they are migrants who will eventually (either willingly or not) be going home to their respective sending countries. Indeed, across Western Europe there have been multiple initiatives and proposals for the repatriation of the recent arrivals; for example, the 'Schwartzenbach Initiatives' in Switzerland, the 1975 statement of the Premier of the state of Baden-Württemberg in the Federal Republic of Germany, and the 1978 call from the federation of French employers (Confédèration Nationale du Patronat Français).[5]

Another factor which contributes to the belief that the recent arrivals are not to be thought of as permanent immigrants is that actions have been taken in all three countries to halt further immigration of nationals from the former sending countries. The labour migration halts in 1973 in the Federal Republic of Germany and 1974 in France coupled with the recent proposals of the British government to limit immigration reinforce the beliefs of those nationals who do not consider the new arrivals as potential citizens.

One result of this view is that language and literacy programmes have been developed to both promote and strengthen mother tongue instruction. This is being done, not with the assumption that mother tongue instruction is the necessary precursor to second language instruction, but that mother tongue instruction is necessary for those who will be returning to their countries of origin. One of the clearest examples of this approach is to be found in the *Land* of Bavaria where more than 1000 Turkish teachers have been brought to Bavaria to teach Turkish children the Turkish language and within the context of the Turkish curriculum. German in these classes is taught as a foreign language for no more than eight hours per week.[6]

It must be noted, however, that the issues are not so clearly drawn *vis-à-vis* educational policy in France and the United Kingdom. The situation is somewhat blurred as many of the recent arrivals do speak French or English as their first tongue, but come from a different cultural background. When mother tongue classes are offered, it is more likely that they are given based on the rationale that a basic understanding of mother tongue is essential for learning a second language, that is, French or English. This is the so-called 'transitional approach' to language learning, one of four options for language education discussed in Rosen's study of England and Wales.[7] Yet a third option, as is the case in the United Kingdom, Spain and Canada for the Welsh, Catalan and Quebecois populations respectively, is that mother tongue instruction can be offered as a means to strengthen the commitment and reality of being a multilingual society.

Language and literacy instruction in the mother tongue can be offered for quite different reasons and with quite different social and political goals in mind. Which is only to say that defining the context within which to analyse language and literacy programmes/policies is critical.

Governmental policy-making: centralised versus decentralised

If it were not enough that such wide variations exist in the social and historical context surrounding the presence of language and cultural minorities in the five nations, there is the added variation in the fact that the countries do not share a common framework for governmental policy-making with regard to language and literacy. The country reports provide sufficient data to suggest that the various approaches can be placed on a continuum from highly centralised and nationally administered to highly decentralised and locally administered. When examining the variations and patterns among the five nations, the matrix becomes more and more complex. In matching policy-making approaches against the four historical and ecological factors previously listed in this section, the immediate conclusion to be drawn is that, at best, and only for those populations of direct concern in the present study, one can speak of broad trends. Precise and delimited statements as to the interrelations are outside the domain of presently available data.

The continuum can be conceptualised as one that begins at a centralised and national pivot and moves through regional or state levels of policy-making on to the pivot of local and decentralised decision-making. The reports suggest that France is the most centralised and the United Kingdom the least; Spain might be described as a country where the policy-making is shared between the national and regional or state authorities, while in Canada and the Federal Republic of Germany, the combination is more one of the state governments working with local jurisdictions to formulate overall educational policy. Again, it should be cautioned that this is but an approximation and there are several exceptions that will be discussed later in this chapter.

Having suggested a number of criteria by which an examination of the five nations could provide insights on the study of language and literacy programmes/policies, a central conclusion one can draw is that, indeed, historical and ecological factors are relevant. Important variations are evident: the two countries with recent and dispersed multiple immigrant populations are the same two countries where the diverse immigrant and language minorities are politically weak. These groups have not achieved any governmental legitimation of a pluralistic or preservationist approach to their own cultural and linguistic origins.

Finally, there are the political assumptions and definitions regarding the permanence of the language or cultural minority group within the country. The Federal Republic of Germany, France and the United Kingdom have not defined themselves as countries of immigration, thus implying a tenuousness to the residency of recent arrivals.[8] While Spain has been primarily a country of emigration, Canada has served as a country of immigration for both English and French speaking people. In these varying circumstances, the responsiveness of the five governments and the willingness of the educational authorities to stress either the integration or separation of the linguistic and cultural minority groups is evident. The policy formulation and programmatic responses are influenced by the assumptions regarding the political legitimacy and permanence of these same groups, not the least of which is how the language groups themselves define their presence.

The major policy instruments

It is within the context of these distinctions among the five nations that the following analysis of the policy instruments of *organisation, financing* and *governance* of language and literacy programmes for young people of diverse linguistic or cultural backgrounds is to be undertaken. The data supplied by the national studies suggest not only policy and programmatic commonalities and/or differences among these western, industrialised nations, but also re-emphasise yet again the substantive and symbolic importance of language within multicultural societies.

Organisation

From the writings of Archer,[9] Persell,[10] and Summerfield[11] among others, the evidence continues to build and support the notion that the social organisation of education rests upon fundamental political and ideological considerations. Thus the definitions of problems, the manner in which resources are marshalled to address these same problems, and the programmatic form such responses take are integrally related. How the issue is defined significantly influences and limits the alternatives.[12]

An examination of the organisational framework for literacy and language programmes created to assist young people of diverse linguistic and cultural backgrounds firmly supports this line of analysis.

First and perhaps most revealing is the finding that language and literacy programmes throughout the five nations tend to be decentralised in their administration at the national level. Indeed, not one of the five nations has established a separate ministry, or even more plausible, a single department responsible for the co-ordination and implementation of language and literacy programmes for immigrant and cultural minority youth. What is evident is that the various national administrative hierarchies for education have not seen this issue as so distinctive and separate from other aspects of educational policy and programmes that they need organise sizeable aspects of their bureaucracies to respond.

What are in evidence are multiple sub-ministry departments each with partial responsibility for language and literacy programmes. This organisational form, in particular, characterises Canada, France and Spain. Spain and France are both centralised in their decision-making and reflect this in their administrative hierarchy. The national governments within these two nations play a decisive role in the formulation and implementation of educational policy. Canada, alternatively, has a more decentralised administrative system with each of the provinces assuming many of the key administrative responsibilities granted national officials in Spain and France. That Canada is decentralised is evident in the country study when one examines how each of the three predominantly English-speaking provinces have organised their language services for the French-speaking minority. No two of these three provinces have created the same organisational form. That Canada has such an administrative hierarchy suggests an approach of national goals being implemented through provincial policy.

Data on the Federal Republic of Germany and the United Kingdom indicate that both have an extremely diffuse organisational structure for the administration of language and literacy programmes. There is no visible responsibility in this area within the Federal Republic of Germany, and it is spread across a number of sectors of the central administration. The German situation is understandable in light of the post-war diffusion of educational authority to the eleven *Länder*. The federal role within the Federal Republic of Germany is weak in all areas of education. Within the United Kingdom, the diffusion of responsibility to local educational authorities thus limits the authority the central administration is able to exercise.

What is of some import in the British and German situations is the fact that these are the two countries that have been most ambivalent about the presence of recently arrived language and cultural minorities within their national boundaries. Second generation persons born in the

United Kingdom of non-Anglo backgrounds are yet commonly referred to as immigrants, denoting their 'newness', their assumed lack of permanence, their lack of historical ties, and their fundamental lack of an 'English identity'. Recent articles by Kirp[13] and Killian[14] and the book by Freeman[15] have all explored this phenomena in some detail. Killian writes:

> Many white Britishers are aware of the use of the term 'immigrant' as a euphemism and many minority members violently protest it, but it is nevertheless widely used to mean 'nonwhite' or 'colored'. The British race problem, unlike that in the United States, is dealt with as an immigrant problem, although the flow of newcomers from the West Indies, Asia and Africa (particularly Uganda) was heaviest from 1948 until 1961 and despite the fact that a whole second generation now entering adulthood was born in England.... For a number of years, the Department of Education and Science officially defined an 'immigrant child' as one who was born abroad or whose parents had lived in the United Kingdom for not more than ten years.[16]

The ambivalence in the Federal Republic of Germany and the United Kingdom towards immigrant and cultural minorities is reflected in a myriad number of programmes on the regional and local levels. In the Federal Republic of Germany, the various *Länder* have developed quite different programmes, several in fundamental opposition to each other, for example, Berlin and Bavaria. While Berlin treats the *Gastarbeiter* as new immigrants into the country and as persons to be assisted in their integration into the mainstream of German society, the Bavarian approach is one predicated upon the eventual return of the *Gastarbeiter* to their home countries. Bavaria presumes the rotation of the foreign workers out of the Federal Republic of Germany while Berlin presumes their performance within it.[17]

In those countries where the future status of the language and cultural minorities is least clearly defined at the national level, one also finds that educational policy is inconsistent and not uniformly adopted *vis-à-vis* language and literacy programmes. The educational programmes, furthermore, do not necessarily assist in clarifying the situation. They may, in fact, actively contribute to the confusion. Indeed, here is but another instance of political realities superseding and defining educational realities. Choosing not to define one's national culture as multicultural influences educational policy and practice as much as a choice to do so.

A second finding from this survey is that there exists, almost without exception, a confusing array of overlapping jurisdictions involving the national government, the provincial governments (especially Canada, Spain and the Federal Republic of Germany), and the local educational authorities. These overlaps influence not only the administration and organisation of language and literacy programmes for immigrant and cultural minorities, but the financing of these programmes as well. The maze of administrative regulations, the variations in inter-governmental policies and the location of programme decision-making in countless agencies, boards, committees, sub-committees, ministries, departments, and co-ordination councils thwarts any coherent comparative analysis along this dimension.

Of special interest is that this overlapping and confusing set of jurisdictions appears just as readily in those countries with indigenous language minorities (Spain and Canada) as it does the countries where linguistically and culturally different groups are recent arrivals. (The United Kingdom fits both sides of this proposition, depending upon the group in question.) The longevity of a language or cultural minority within a country does not necessarily imply that the relations between that group and the remaining portions of the society are either stable or well articulated. The opposite appears to be more nearly the case at present in both Canada and Spain.

Confusion in administration and organisation perhaps reflects confusion over goals. Each of the five nations are in a state of flux regarding their language and literacy policies. Whether the various nations be characterised as opting for centralised decision-making or decentralised decision-making; whether they have concentrated or dispersed language and cultural minority groups; and whether these same groups are of recent or long term presence, variation and uncertainty characterise current policies in the respective countries.

Central to this confusion is the major political issue of the degree to which minority language education can be considered a 'right' as opposed to a 'privilege' and the extent to which the exercise of such a right should be the responsibility of the varying jurisdictional levels of education, that is, national, provincial, or local.

In Canada, Wales and Spain, the language minorities appear closest to having instruction in their own language considered a right; for the remaining groups of concern in this analysis, it is considered a privilege. Neither the Federal Republic of Germany, France, nor the United Kingdom considers it a formal constitutional responsibility to offer mother tongue instruction to recent arrivals. They choose to do it for pedagogical reasons, for reasons of bi-national agreements, or to comply with the European Economic Community agreement of 1977. (This agreement binds the participatory nations, 'within the context of their national situation', to provide mother tongue instruction to children of immigrant workers.) Only in those countries which have adopted policies legitimating the creation of a multicultural national identity has instruction in mother tongue been considered a protected right.

Financing

The financing of language and literacy programmes for special populations of youth involves two interrelated and reciprocal processes: taxation and distribution. While taxation has, for the western democracies, been an activity that has cut across all levels of government, distribution has always been under more heavy national influence. This is because the growth of the welfare state was initially a national enterprise. Transfers which could be easily standardised, for example, old-age pensions, unemployment benefits, and health care payments, have been almost universally handled at the national level. They quite easily can be made without the assistance of the local governments. These are personal transfers and make up a large percentage of the total transfer payments in all the modern democracies.[18]

This is not to say that as the welfare state expands, there is not more activity at the local level; there is. But the situation is one of the national governments making the decisions on how resources are to be allocated and how benefits are to be delivered. The increased size of the welfare state has, almost without exception, resulted in greater national restrictions on local decisions. As the western societies increasingly expand their definitions on the role and responsibility of the state towards its citizens, the responsibility for the financial burden is almost always carried by the national government. The corollary to this is that the role of the national government in taxation has also been commensurately increased.

But when one turns to an area like education, where the direct transfer approach is less appropriate, the alternative is reliance on indirect transfers. Funds are supplied to institutions to supply goods and services to specific groups of clients.

The country reports suggest that the national governments move resources to lower levels within the educational system through a host of programmes, agencies, and types of formula funding. The reports also suggest that local governmental agencies vary widely in their access to these channels of funding. Each country appears to have developed a different pattern of access. For example, interactions between the national and state/local levels of government in France are clearly concentrated around patterns of transfer between the national government and the local educational agency; in England and Wales, as well as Spain, it is much the same; in the Federal Republic of Germany the relation is one between the individual states and the local authorities. Only in Canada are all three levels of government — national, provincial, and local — involved in both the taxation and subsequent distribution of resources.

As might be expected, the result is that the politics of educational finance differ greatly from the economics of educational finance. Relatively small sums of money come to take on immense political importance and large blocks of funds may well elude political influence. (The paper on England and Wales in particular lends considerable weight to this last contention.)

An oft-cited truism suggests 'He who pays the piper calls the tune'. Stated alternatively, financial resources can be used as a means of power and control. Data from this present study suggest that while such may be true in particular instances, it is by no means a universal set of relations. An examination of the financial resources and the control of their allocation for language and literacy programmes provides an interesting window from which to study such provisions as do exist for language and cultural minority youth.

Integral to the examination of power and control are the matters of form and source of funding for language and literacy programmes. Table 15.1 suggests the form and source of funding across the five nations.

Table 15.1
The form and source of funding for language and literacy programmes

	Form		Source		
	Categorical grant for language instruction	General formula assistance	Federal	Provincial	Local
Canada					
Quebec	X		X	X	X
Manitoba	X		X	X	X
New Brunswick		X	X	X	
Ontario	X		X	X	X
Spain		X	X		
France	X		X		
United Kingdom		X	X		X
Federal Republic of Germany					
Berlin	X			X	
Bavaria	X			X	
Nordrhine-Westfalen	X			X	

While at first glance this table suggests no discernible patterns, closer examination provides several insights. First, Spain and the United Kingdom have a quite comparable set of arrangements whereby the source of support for language and literacy programmes comes from the national government and comes in the form of block grants or formula assistance to local educational authorities. But what makes this situation of particular interest is that the two countries which have centralised funding vary considerably in the level of central planning and policy co-ordination that occurs *vis-à-vis* language and literacy programmes. The United Kingdom is quite decentralised. As Rosen's country report has noted:

> Frankly, in the British system, control is usually too strong a word: influence and persuasion are more apposite. However, if there is any control regarding language and literacy provision, then, in practice, it is vested in the local authorities . . . and in their existing educational infrastructure.[19]

Spain is clearly centralised in its planning (though a proposed set of revisions in regard to decentralising educational decision-making has been made).

A second implication of the table is that inter-governmental collaboration is selective. Of concern is how this pattern of selectivity bodes for future funding through established budget channels. One can observe only in Canada, for example, the instance of all three levels of government — national, provincial, and local — involved in the funding of language and literacy programmes. Of the remaining four countries, the United Kingdom alone involves local support for language and literacy programmes. In France and Spain, the funding is exclusively national while in the Federal Republic of Germany, the funds come from the individual *Länder*. What lends a particular urgency to this issue is that, however imperfectly or reluctantly, all levels of government must learn to live with reduced growth, if not an outright steady state. The fact that many of the basic functions of education must continue, regardless of local choice, means that those functions which are financed by discretionary resources are more vulnerable. As the number of instances multiply when educational authorities will have to choose between the continuation of basic programmes and those designed for special populations, the likely direction of those decisions is already clear. To maintain special programmes may depend upon the readiness of individual localities to tax themselves at increased rates.

The United Kingdom is between these two poles, drawing upon financial support from both the national and local levels. The author of the paper on England and Wales also notes that such collaboration should suggest optimism regarding future expenditure programmes for language and literacy efforts. The United Kingdom is also something of an anomaly in this context, as it is the one country of the five where language minorities are few in absolute numbers. Recent (and not so recent) arrivals are, more likely than not, English-speaking. Thus there has occurred a slight and often subtle shift in the goal of the programmes — away from that of language and literacy to the broader matter of cultural awareness. Local, community-based efforts provide the framework within which varying ethnic and cultural groups are recognised and responded to by British policy-makers.

The third implication, and a corollary to the second, is that the fate of language and literacy programmes is integrally linked to decisions made at the national level. Only the Federal Republic of Germany does not involve the national level in the support of these programmes. On the one hand, proponents of language and literacy programmes for immigrant and cultural minorities can applaud this situation as it suggests that the discriminations of hostilities often found in local communities cannot, of themselves, eliminate the programmes. Parallel to the argument made in the United States during the time of the civil rights movement that 'locals could not be trusted' to uphold and support civil rights programmes, the argument can be made that what educational services do exist for the minorities are there because they are supported at the national level.

Alternatively, one can argue that the central role played by the national government in all but one of the countries also makes the long-term existence of these programmes somewhat precarious. The political decisions on how resources are allocated at the national level are often influenced by the various vested interest groups involved and the support they direct towards propositions favouring their own objectives. The fact that the language and cultural minorities are frequently unorganised politically (indeed, they have little or no political voice in the Federal Republic of Germany or France) suggests that the resources now allocated for language and literacy programmes are vulnerable to being allocated elsewhere. This is particularly so if the funds are categorical. When the category is eliminated, so are the programmes.

It is important in an analysis of the allocation of resources to separate out the *source* of funds from the matter of *control* over the funds. Previously, it has been noted that in the United Kingdom context, overt control and power by the national government was not evident and perhaps even shunned. Authority had been granted to the local educational administrators. It was they who defined the programmatic response to the language and literacy needs of special populations.

In the Federal Republic of Germany, the situation is different. Federal control is extremely weak, as is local control. The decision-making power rests at the provincial level. Thus the policies and programmes that are in place in the various *Länder* reflect more accurately regional as opposed to federal or local views. It is within this regional context that one can assess the political and ideological views of those in power regarding the place of the *Gasterbeiter* and their families in German (read regional) society. The discussion in the German country report on the approach of the three *Länder* towards both mother tongue instruction and bilingual instruction is particularly informative in this regard.

The Spanish situation is one in flux. While, heretofore, the funding and control has been quite centralised, there are at present efforts underway to decentralise the authority over language and literacy programmes to various regional governments. Funding, however, would remain within the federal domain. There appears to be no pressure to modify the current general formula assistance that local school districts receive from the national treasury.

The Canadian situation is unlike that of the other four nations. Canada has involved all three levels of government in the funding of language and literacy programmes. All three also appear to have some if not equal input into the policy process as to the form and content of the funded efforts. If there is a weak member in this triad, it appears to be the national government.

In France, the source of funding for language and literacy programmes is the national level. It is in this same arena where the control of the policy process resides. But as the CERI analysis of the French situation suggests, it is this centralisation of the decision-making process that stands in constant tension with the pluralism and growing tendency towards diversity evident within French society. The government favours a hierarchical and unified policy approach to all matters affecting education. Yet this implies that there are necessarily situations where national policies are not particularly appropriate nor well received at the local level. The result is that these initiatives are not always well or enthusiastically implemented. Yet few public resources or institutional channels exist at the local level to provide alternatives. This disparity, in part, accounts for the large private sector involvement throughout France in matters related to language and cultural minorities.

In sum, the distribution and allocation of public resources in each of the five countries tends to rather closely reflect the political realities of how language and cultural minorities are perceived. When efforts are made to institutionalise a national commitment to bilingualism, the financial resources and programmes they support tend also to reflect this commitment. Likewise, when the host societies are ambivalent over bilingualism, there is evidence of a lack of institutionalisation of the funding. *Indeed, in none of the five countries does one find a mismatch between the political or ideological views towards immigrant groups and/or cultural minorities and the financing of language and literacy programmes.* If the policy process is one of 'rationalising' the allocation of goods and services, then the present instances suggest the effort has been successful.

Governance

To describe the current situation with regard to the governance of language and literacy programmes within the five nations is to say that the issue is one that has stirred passions and generated no small amount of controversy. The substance of the debate appears to have two tightly interwoven aspects: *who* shall govern and *how* shall responsibility be divided. With respect to the question of who shall exercise governance over language and literacy policy, the data suggest that it is not merely a matter of pin-pointing which administrators within which bureaucracies. It is also necessary to be cognisant of the current political forces at work changing the very form of governance.

Both in Quebec, Canada, and in the Catalan region of Spain, governance is at the root of the current efforts to realign the relations of these regions to the remaining parts of their respective countries. What one confronts directly in both instances are the political choices between national affiliation and regional 'self-determination'. In both situations, the language minorities have clearly defined geographical boundaries, have a history which pre-dates the emergence of the modern nation-state, and have amassed sufficient political power to be able to translate many of their aspirations into policy.

The Canadian situation is slightly more evolved than in Spain. In Canada, the emergence of a national policy of bilingualism has been in response to the recognition of the sizeable French-speaking population in the country as well as the political force they represent. Not to have opted for bilingualism would have been an open invitation to the irrevocable division of the country. (That this is yet the goal of many within Quebec suggests that concerns for political and economic autonomy weigh heavier in the final analysis than do matters of language.)

In Spain, the acknowledgement of Catalan as the official language of discourse within the province of Catalonia is yet to occur. Nevertheless, the report from Spain suggests that it is but a short time before this acknowledgement is a reality. Within Spain one finds the development of a two-tier policy: at the national level, Castilian will remain the official language, but regional languages will be recognised not only as the form of daily discourse, but as the official means for the transaction of regional governmental and economic affairs.

Within both of these nations, the governance issue appears to be one of ensuring, from the point of view of the language minorities, that they govern language and literacy programmes within their respective regions. (In Canada the country report suggests that the issue is not merely one restricted to the French-speaking region of Quebec, but that the concern is now national in scope, that is, that French-speaking people wish for an autonomy and responsibility over French language instruction in all parts of Canada.) Thus the recent language laws enacted within Quebec as well as the declarations by Catalan officials give evidence of their concern to *institutionalise* within all major social and economic sectors their respective languages.

In those remaining parts of Spain where the Catalan speaking people are in a minority, the situation is much more closely akin to what one finds in the nations of the United Kingdom, France and the Federal Republic of Germany. In these latter three countries, the recent immigrant groups speaking other than the dominant language are in a distinct minority and there appears to be little enthusiasm for allowing the language minorities to obtain separate control of the educational process for their children. (The exception to this is in the area of religious and cultural instruction. In the Federal Republic of Germany, for example, the 'national classes' that meet after school and on weekends are organised and supported by private religious and cultural groups.)

Arguments in favour of this local control by minority language groups appear to be largely dismissed for two reasons in the United Kingdom, France and the Federal Republic of Germany. The first is that the creation of a separate school system would be expensive, and in a time of retrenchment within education, such an expansion would be unacceptable to the language majority group. The second reason for the rejection of separately controlled local educational agencies is that the diffusion of the various and multiple language minority groups throughout the respective countries means that in a large number of instances, there would not be the 'critical mass' of either students or teachers necessary to sustain an educational programme. Thus the services would be sporadically available to some minority group youth and not to others. This lack of 'distributive justice' would also make the policy extremely untenable.

As an option to the separate systems based on language or nationality, there is that of a fully multilingual and integrated school system which would protect the rights of the minority students, but ensure that they were mainstreamed within a unitary organisation. This appears to be a realistic possibility only in the English language provinces of

Canada. Matching a national commitment to bilingualism with considerable financial support for language programmes appears absolutely essential for the minority language youth within majority systems to be afforded some degree of protection and legitimacy.

This latter option also does not appear feasible for recent immigrant minorities in the United Kingdom, the Federal Republic of Germany, or France. In none of these three countries is there evidence of a commitment to supporting full multilingualism as a goal for the educational system. Rather, all three appear committed to an assimilationist position (with only regional variations, for example, Bavaria). This, in turn, necessitates the use of the dominant language as the single medium of communication within the schools. What evidence is available from the three country reports on instruction in mother tongue suggests that this is most often done in conjunction with effecting an eventual transition into the dominant language.

One response documented in the country reports is that private and religious groups have undertaken on a broad scale to provide cultural awareness and mother tongue instruction to the minority children. Much as was the situation in the United States when the language minority groups established parochial schools to protect their language and religion, so the same responses now appear in Western Europe and in the English speaking regions of Canada. Indeed, the data are quite persuasive in documenting the efforts of the various language and cultural minority groups to undertake such projects on their own behalf. Establishing these organisations in the private sector becomes one means by which to compensate for the lack of policy-making authority in the public sector.

Juxtaposed to the question of who governs is the matter of the scale at which decisions are to be made. In Spain and Canada, the move is towards decentralisation, shifting the policy process with respect to language and literacy from the national to the provincial level. No evidence of this appears in the description of France, while the United Kingdom and the Federal Republic of Germany already exist with decentralised policy-making authority. The United Kingdom system is the most decentralised with the local educational authorities exercising more responsibility than in any of the four remaining countries. The German system has institutionalised the authority at the provincial level and there is no indication that this is changing.

In sum, an examination of the governance issue suggests the following:

(a) Political and ideological considerations are uppermost in many of the decisions regarding language and literacy policy. The fact that when new Italian or Turkish immigrants arrive in

Quebec, they have no choice but to send their children to French-speaking schools, or to 'transition classes' were they in Berlin or London, suggests something of the manner in which control is exercised and to what ends.

(b) There is an interesting hiatus between the concerns with controlling language and literacy policy and the monitoring of how effective or efficient are the subsequent policies. Here may be but another instance of the symbolic overtaking the substantive. None of the five countries appear particularly well informed on whether their linguistic and literacy policies either match the pedagogical needs of the youth or impact in the desired manner upon the target groups.

(c) The matter of governance creates a continuing dilemma for language minority groups in terms of self-determination and autonomy versus their institutional mainstreaming. Countless arguments can be offered on both sides of this issue. Yet 'real life' decisions have to be made. The choice of moving in one direction tends to preclude the options available within the other.

(d) Governance is predicted upon power and influence, commodities which are never static. Consequently, one can anticipate that the actors, the goals, and the means used to achieve them are all constantly changing. Language and literacy policies are not likely to escape — nor should they — the transitions under way amidst these five countries.

Postscript

There is one commonality across the five nations that deserves special mention. All share a cultural and linguistic diversity that is really quite extraordinary. There is an enormous complexity to the linguistic 'infrastructure' of these nations, a complexity that has been understood in only the most superficial of ways. It still awaits a full description and this complexity appears not to have influenced language and literacy policy in any demonstrable fashion. The nuances in the linguistic groups, the multiplicity of dialects within each group, and the effects of interaction with the dominant language in the society all appear to be bypassed within the policy process. Less critically, one might suggest that the policy process has worked precisely by avoiding such distinctions. Allowing the groups themselves to sort out and decide on whether and how to allow private and religious classes to support mother tongue and cultural awareness classes provides both autonomy and diminished government influence. Such a mechanism may be the best means by which to allow each linguistic or cultural group to internally differentiate itself into various clusters and thus achieve greater attention to its specific language needs.

There is yet another issue which cuts across all five nations and cannot go unmentioned. Throughout this paper, words such as 'racism', 'prejudice', and 'discrimination' have been studiously avoided. What has been presented has been an analysis of language and literacy policy in each of the countries as if those countries were 'colour blind'. To suggest in general terms that the policy process is one which emanates from and functions within the political workings of any particular society obscures as much as it illuminates. It is something quite different to suggest that policy is not necessarily rational nor linear, but that deep-seated prejudices and racial antagonisms also must be accounted for. That such conditions exist in each of the five countries is beyond doubt. What remains to be done is to trace out the impact of these belief systems upon the opportunities/constraints experienced by the language and cultural minorities.

Last, and in light of the comments made in the discussion on governance, it should be reiterated that language and literacy policies accurately reflect social and political conditions in each of the societies. As the status, permanence, and political influence of the various language and cultural groups change, so also will the policies affecting these groups. But the linguistic and cultural minorities are not merely passive recipients of decisions made elsewhere. They, too, are involved in creating the future for themselves and their children. As such, the interactions between these groups and others will determine the shape of future policies — policies which will not only influence the cultural identities of millions of people, but impact upon fundamental characteristics of the societies themselves.

On future study

Heretofore, the focus of this paper has been primarily descriptive and analytic; it has not been proscriptive. This present section seeks to redress this omission by means of outlining in some detail what the 'next steps' might be in further development and elaboration of the issues raised by this OECD five-nation study. In specifying areas for further investigation, an effort is made in each instance to build upon what has been learned through the present endeavour. It should also be noted that the focus of concern is with policy issues. The task now is one of translating into policy concerns the findings generated by the work done to date.

A first area that bears scrutiny is that of the form and content of policy with respect to those groups that are the sole possessors of a cultural/linguistic tradition. This is in contrast to policy responses to those groups that are but one of many possessors of such a tradition. The case study from the United Kingdom prompts this analytic distinction. The situation of the Welsh, who are the sole possessors of the Welsh language and culture, is not equal to that of those who have come to the United Kingdom, for example, from the Indian subcontinent. Succinctly, if the Welsh lose in any degree their mastery of the Welsh language and understanding of Welsh culture, that represents an absolute loss of the amount of Welsh culture/language now present. It is, as it were, a diminution of the 'critical mass' of those who possess Welsh attributes. This is in contrast to those who would come to the United Kingdom from India or Pakistan. If these groups lose aspects of their original culture, the loss or demise of that culture is less threatened, if at all.

The policy questions to be investigated in this area are complex. When, for example, can a group make a claim to be the sole possessor of a cultural/linguistic tradition? Furthermore, if such can be determined, where ought the decision-making responsibility lie for ensuring the preservation of that tradition? Ought it to be centrally administered or decentralised among those so defined as possessing the tradition? Related to the management questions are those of financing. From where ought support come to sustain the various cultural traditions? And perhaps more fundamental, through what process is agreement reached on which cultural traditions are to be supported and which are not? In short, how are political decisions made about what constitutes a viable 'culture' worthy of preservation and nurture?

Related to this area is that of the role for the state in supporting cultural pluralism. Is it appropriate for the state as a political entity to support diversity, or is it more appropriate for the state to support efforts at unanimity of cultural expression? Such questions lead in turn to a concern with stability and cohesion of the modern nation-to-state. Does such come from 'unity through diversity' or from 'unity through sameness'? The manner in which such a question is answered can have a profound impact upon the policy decisions made regarding support for language and cultural minorities.

In many OECD nations, this latter question appears to have been answered in the affirmative through the support of diversity, for example, language policy in both Canada and the United Kingdom. With the initial assessment of these policies now available through the present study, further effort is needed to learn more of the specifics of these provisions, of their means of financing, of strategies for administration, and of their impact upon programme development and implementation. The pivots of 'government directed' versus 'group directed' are critical to our understanding of the means and mechanisms by which public resources are allocated.

A second key policy area, and one that has come to the forefront throughout the industrial nations of the Western world, is that of the response towards those groups defined as impermanent. This issue is particularly relevant to the nearly fifteen million guestworkers and dependents in Western Europe and the approximately six to fourteen million undocumented workers now in the United States. The fundamental question is one of whether policy with respect to these large groups be predicated upon the presumption of the 'rotation' of these same groups in and then out of the respective host countries, or upon the presumption that these same groups will remain and essentially take on the characteristics of immigrants.

In policy terms, the matter appears to hinge on the decision as to whether to attempt to organise educational provisions for the young so as to maintain their options to return to the sending country with the necessary literacy and cultural skills to compete in that country, or to press for the integration of these same youth into the host society, thus defining them as new immigrants. The organisation, governance, and financing of either of these approaches suggests complexities that are only now beginning to be addressed. Further, the response is not merely one of hypothetical alternatives. The reality of literally hundreds of thousands of 'second generation youth' in the host countries is not to be denied.

What is unknown at present is whether it is possible for the host society to *simultaneously* maintain a two-track educational system for these youth — the one track allowing for and fostering appreciation of the mother country language and culture while the other track equipping the youth to enter the economic and cultural activities of the host society. That this issue has not been resolved and that no models for accomplishing such dual socialisation on a large-scale level now exist suggests important areas for investigation in the coming years.

A third area of policy study concerns when it is that the size influence of a culturally different group is sufficient to warrant public intervention and support. The present five-nation study suggests that quite different criteria are applied across the countries. In several instances, the numerical considerations appear paramount. If a group reaches a particular figure, it is recognised and the government then makes resources available for the preservation of that same group. In other instances, size appears secondary at best as it is the political influence of a group that largely determines the policy response. The interesting generic policy question that arises from such variation is one of ascertaining when and under what conditions do governments recognise and then support educational programmes for various ethnic and cultural groups.

This is a particularly salient question with respect to the future of bilingual education. When is it that educational systems choose to respond? What are the mechanisms that instigate support? Is that 'critical mass' essentially numerical or political? Do the policy decisions take into account concerns of effectiveness and efficiency? (It is qualitatively as well as quantitatively different to instigate a bilingual programme for 12 as opposed to 2,400 students.) Stated somewhat differently, upon what premises do the various member countries respond (or choose not to) to the support of hyphenated identities among those from culturally different groups?

The tension between scope and specificity in targeting programmes for different populations represents a fourth important area for further policy analysis. The choices in providing services to youth from special populations range on a continuum from those efforts that are highly targeted towards specific groups to those where there is little or no means testing and programmes seek to encompass large numbers of participants. This tension, and one that is especially acute with regard to the needs of special populations, is fundamentally non-resolvable. At best, what each educational system appears to have done is to make decisions on strategies of inclusion/exclusion based on economic, political, and cultural concerns salient to that society.

What has been unexplicated to date, however, are the relative influences of various economic, political and cultural concerns and how these are juxtaposed in the decision-making process. If all do not carry equal weight, which are of more importance and how is this relative importance translated into policy? Of additional concern is the matter of how it is that these broad forces influence the pedagogical responses of the various educational systems. It is the educational system, after all, that has responsibility for creating programmes that in some form reflect the broader contours of the society, including the factors of race, social class and ethnicity. So long as politics remain the art of deciding who gets what when and at whose expense, the creation of educational programmes for special populations will be a critical arena in which the various forces at work in the member countries will be evident.

The four policy areas detailed above suggest fundamental tensions in the organisation, governance and financing of educational programmes for special populations. Yet this ought not to deter further study and analysis, especially as these four are not exhaustive. Rather, it is that in an area of considerable complexity and political sensitivity, cogent and considered attention is of the utmost necessity. To avoid the issues outlined above because of the highly charged reactions to them is to take flight from the realities all five of the nations participating in this present study have begun to face.

What appears particularly important at present is to build upon the contributions of the studies completed to date. Having mapped and charted the broad outlines of how services are organised, financed and governed for special populations of young people, it is now possible to move towards a more detailed policy assessment of alternative responses and how it is that present policies have come to be what they are. For it is in this manner that not only may the present be better understood, but also illuminate something of the options for the future.

Notes and references

1   Francis, E.K., *Interethnic Relations*, New York, Elsevier, 1974.
2   Rex, J., *Race Relations in Sociological Theory*, New York, Schocken, 1970.
3   Allen, S., *New Minorities, Old Conflicts: Asian and West Indian Migrants in Britain*, New York, Random House, 1971.
4   Rist, R.C., *Guestworkers in Germany: Prospects for Pluralism*, New York, Praeger, 1978.
5   Rist, R.C., 'Migration and Marginality: Guestworkers in Germany and France', *Daedalus*, American Academy of Arts and Sciences, Boston, Mass., vol.108, no.2, 1979, pp. 95—108.
6   Rist, R.C., 'On the Education of Guestworker Children in Germany: A Comparative Study of Policies and Programs in Bavaria and Berlin', *School Review*, Chicago, vol.87, no.3, 1979, pp. 242—68.
7   Rosen, H., *Case studies of linguistic minorities: England and Wales*, Mimeo. See Appendix, p.364.
8   Rist, R.C., 'Migration and Marginality: Guestworkers in Germany and France', op.cit.
9   Archer, M.S., *Social Origins of Educational Systems*, London, Sage, 1979.
10 Persell, C.H., *Education and Inequality*, New York Free Press, 1977.
11 Summerfield, H.L., *Power and Process: The Formulation and Limits of Federal Educational Policy*, Berkeley, McCutchan, 1974.
12 Pressman, J. and Wildavsky, A., *Implementation*, Los Angeles: University of California Press, 1973.
13 Kirp, D., 'The Vagaries of Discrimination: Busing, Policy, and Law in Britain', *School Review*, vol.87, no.3, 1979, pp. 269—94.
14 Killian, L., 'School Busing in Britain', *Harvard Educational Review*, vol.49, no.2, 1979, pp. 185—206.

15   Freeman, G., *Immigrant Labor and Racial Conflict in Industrial Societies: The French and British Experience, 1945–1975*, Princeton, Princeton University Press, 1979.
16   Killian, L., 'School Busing in Britain', op.cit.
17   Rist, R.C., 'On the Education of Guestworker Children in Germany: A Comparative Study of Policies and Programs in Bavaria and Berlin', op.cit.
18   Ashford, D., 'Political Choice and Center–Local Finance', *European Studies Newsletter*, vol.9, no.2, November 1979, pp. 12–19.
19   Rosen, H., *Case studies of linguistic minorities: England and Wales*, op.cit.

16 Indigenous cultural minorities — concepts pertaining to their education

Frank Darnell
Centre for Cross-Cultural Studies,
University of Alaska

Economic conditions and legal systems and the way they are related to education vary considerably among OECD Member countries. Many efforts have been made by all to understand and describe the numerous factors that are involved in governing, organising and financing education, both in the context of their own national conditions and in studies of an international comparative nature. This paper adds to that large volume of material by specifically addressing but one small segment of the broad topic: the education of indigenous minorities in those Member countries where this is now a concern. Given the space and resources allocated to it, especially when the extensive geographic, economic and political dimensions of OECD membership are considered, even this segment is far too broad a topic for a comprehensive review and analysis. Thus, this paper is not a detailed account of provisions for indigenous minority education found in member countries, nor is it a comparison of provisions: what has been attempted here is an 'introduction' to certain governance and financial notions or concepts that may universally pertain to education among indigenous minorities wherever they are found.

This paper, then, is one among many on school finance, organisation, and governance; and has as its primary purpose the introduction of one phase of what is an otherwise extensive, detailed and complex subject. As such, it is offered for consideration by policy-makers anywhere, be they in governmental agencies, indigenous minority groups, or educational establishments.

The limited scope of this paper should not lead to the conclusion that the topic itself is either limited or unmanageable. By initiating discussions on a complex subject, it is intended that the paper also serve as a point of departure from which more detailed papers will emerge. Fundamental ideas that pertain to education among indigenous minorities, properly coupled with detailed fiscal, legal and organisational information from concerned member nations, open up potentially promising means for improvements in schools attended by indigenous minorities.

Theme

Indigenous minority peoples in many parts of the world have had their relatively stable way of life interrupted by the demands of Western technology and social thought. Traditional ways of subsistence, art forms and indigenous material objects, while still found and valued (although in varying amounts and degrees of authenticity), seldom fulfil current everyday needs. At the same time, many individuals lack the skills and cultural orientation necessary to succeed economically or to 'feel comfortable' in Western technological society, evidence of which is found everywhere about them. Because of an uncertain future and inadequate means to acquire or understand the things and ways of Western society, frustrations abound, especially among the young in indigenous populations. At times there may be seen proud and successful efforts to cope with the situation by clinging to indigenous life styles of earlier times, but even these efforts are sometimes distorted because they are unrealistically idealised and romanticised, further adding to the confusion and frustration.

Growing out of this situation, that is, where uncertainties prevail more often than do either old or new ways, is a lack of a sense of direction and purpose which leaves individual youth vulnerable to negative influences. Public education, its curricula, faculty, and the ways schools are organised and supported, is frequently at the centre of the conflict. Subsequent issues that have grown out of this dilemma are often clouded because they are inadequately understood or because they have sometimes been distorted for political gain.

Many of the changes that have resulted in a deleterious effect on the values and life styles of indigenous minorities have been categorised as the people's loss of control over the circumstances of their daily lives. Frequently given as a reason for this situation is the formal system of education that was developed and has been controlled for many years by non-indigenous, centralised governmental agencies. Many indigenous minority peoples believe that school systems so constituted are biased against indigenous cultures. It is also contended that schools fail to adequately prepare indigenous people to participate in modern economic and social development when such participation is elected. In short, it is believed that cultural and ethnic considerations in the schools, coupled with more realistic and sensitively constituted educational programmes, may eventually enable indigenous peoples to deal more effectively with the contemporary world.

School finance, governance and organisation, when combined with cultural topics and education for indigenous minorities, can become a cumbersome subject. Even when treated separately, these complex topics have seemingly endless factors to be analysed, each with specialised vocabularies. However, it is essential to link contemporary thought growing out of a variety of ways schools may be financed, organised and governed to minority—majority situations and relationships. Also, it is necessary that the ideas introduced have more or less international applicability; that is, no specific element under discussion should be so narrow that it pertains to the interests of only one or two member nations.

A central theme that cuts across the topic and across national frontiers is reflected in a view expressed by Carnoy: 'For an institution to play an important role in society, it must be "legitimate": people who use it must believe that it serves their interests and needs'.[1] A cardinal requirement in financing, governing and organising schools among indigenous populations, wherever they may be, is that schools be perceived by the people they serve as acceptable or 'legitimate'. How education systems can meet this requirement in face of a multitude of conflicting elements and issues is the problem and, thus, the theme of this paper.

Definitions

There is little uniform use of educational terminology within nations and even less internationally. Consequently, terms used herein, or those that may be used in discussions on the subject of the paper, require delineation.

Reform and change are among the most frequently encountered terms in current literature on education. School reform, as it applies here, refers to improvements in student learning. Educational change refers to any planned alteration or intended innovation in the educational enterprise. Obviously, changes take place that are unplanned or evolutionary and thus are not to be disregarded when reform is a concern. But change more often than not has come to be considered a planned circumstance and will be used in that sense.

Organisation and governance of education are fairly straightforward terms. Organisation, the environment of an enterprise, is the setting in which decisions are made, leadership exercised, and routine tasks carried out. Governance is synonymous with control and is considered to be the legal authority and the means (usually money and political influence) to exercise that authority to decide one's own affairs and determine one's own circumstances.

Finance reform refers to improvement in the way schools are financed. However, there are two major dimensions in school finance where improvements may be made: the allocation (or distribution of funds) dimension and the revenue (or sources of funds) dimension. Included in the allocation dimension are the populations to be served and the programmes, services and facilities necessary to serve the populations. Also considered in the allocation dimension is the means by which unit costs for programmes are computed and whether local ability and/or effort will be considered in the allocation of funds from more general sources. Included in the revenue dimension are considerations such as percentage of revenues to be provided from the whole range of education fund sources; the type of taxes to levy; the amount of revenue to allocate for school support from specific tax types; and the characteristics of the tax itself, such as the extent of progressivity or regressivity.[2] It is necessary to keep each dimension separate when issues in school finance reform are discussed since often individuals or groups, depending on their basic orientation, are more interested in one than the other. Such is the case in this paper; the allocation dimension is often of greater critical importance to indigenous minorities than is the revenue dimension.

Those peoples originally found in a given location, but because of the effect of immigration are now in the minority, are the subject of this paper. They are the indigenous minorities who until quite recently were ignored or rejected by the majority. They are the peoples who have felt the pressure of mass permanent immigration, especially to the Americas, Australia, New Zealand and Arctic Europe.

The terms native, aboriginal, indigenous and autochthon have more or less similar dictionary definitions. Each is in use in one part of the world or another depending on local preference rather than difference in precise meaning. To avoid negative connotations ascribed to one or more of the terms, the term indigenous, considered the least stigmatised by many, will be used throughout this paper to designate those people who exist 'naturally' in a region. As such, indigenous peoples are those who 'belong' to a region and who are considered to be the first people as opposed to those who are settlers, immigrants, or intruders.

Minority, in addition to its obvious meaning of lesser or smaller, that is, less than half of a total, is not necessarily limited to numerical strength. Where groups have numerical superiority, but lack adequate influence or authority, they are considered to be in the minority.

The word culture, with a multitude of definitions, illustrates the need for terms with more than one meaning to be kept in their proper context. Culture is generally viewed from one of three perspectives:

(a) From the standpoint of civilisation as a whole, culture is seen as the cumulative store of expressive works preserved in the form of literature, art and music;

(b) From an individual's point of view, culture is seen as the training and refinement of mind, taste and manners;

(c) From an ethnic point of view, and thus the most important definition from this paper's perspective, culture is seen as the way of life of a particular people which includes a catalogue of diverse traits from traditional or ancient cultures and beliefs, and covers such things as food, shelter, material, equipment and the various ways these are respected and treated.

Terminology directly applicable to indigenous minorities often lacks consistency and is sometimes confusing to the casual observer. For example, terms such as multicultural education, multi-ethnic education, ethnic studies, and cross-cultural education are freely used about the world today, but not always with consistency.

Multicultural education is an educational approach intended to reduce discrimination against stigmatised cultural groups and to provide them with equal educational opportunities. It focuses on the study of cultural groups which experience prejudice and discrimination.

Likewise, multi-ethnic education is intended to reduce discrimination against ethnic groups and to provide all students with equal educational opportunities. Nothing in the way of majority–minority relationships is to be implied by use of the term ethnic. Ethnic groups anywhere are the intended beneficiaries by modifying the school environment to reflect the diversity of multi-ethnic populations.

Ethnic studies deploy teaching strategies that modify courses so that they include information about ethnic groups and thereby help students to develop valid concepts about groups other than their own. By so doing it is expected that negative attitudes to ethnic and racial situations will be reduced.[3]

The terms cross-cultural education or intercultural education are among the most frequently used by those dealing with education among indigenous minorities. The terms, which may be interchanged, refer to ways of accomplishing goals of multicultural education. Intercultural education is a means to realise the goals of multicultural or multi-ethnic education. According to Walsh:[4] 'Intercultural education is the process by which one looks beyond his own culture and attempts to understand and appreciate how persons of other cultures interpret the life of man and the things of nature, and why they view them as they do'. Use of this definition requires that no one in an intercultural situation be exempt from conditions required by the concept. The very use of the prefixes cross and inter requires that programmes developed under their meaning must apply equally to the teacher and the learner. It is every bit as damaging to the learning situation for the teacher to fail to 'look beyond his own culture' as it is for the pupil.

Most of the terms used to deal with indigenous minority education are based on the philosophical concept of cultural pluralism:

> One of the most difficult words for people to understand when they look at various cultures or sub-cultures is different. *Different* means *different*; it does not mean *better than* or *worse than*. This wholehearted acceptance of one's own culture and other people's culture is basic to the development of a sense of cultural pluralism....[5]

Cultural pluralism, a society of diverse ethnic cultures, is seen by many as the ultimate goal of society and thus is considered an ideological position. On the other hand, ethnic pluralism and biculturalism, unlike cultural pluralism,

> are empirical concepts used to describe relationships between groups in society. Ethnic pluralism describes a society composed of various ethnic groups fully participating in ethnic sub-societies but having allegiances to the nation state and accepting its idealized values. Biculturalism is a process in which ethnic group members are socialized to participate both within their ethnic cultures and within the universalistic culture.[6]

School reform efforts for indigenous minorities, both in the way of providing improved control mechanisms and financial resources, need to be developed and implemented in forms consistent with these concepts. Biculturalism, multicultural education, multi-ethnic education, ethnic studies and intercultural education are assumed to be the processes and means by which the ideology of cultural pluralism can be realised.

In any consideration of the subject of financing, organising and governing education to the advantage of indigenous minorities, regardless of the nation in which the effort is being made, concepts at the base of such effort are of great importance. They influence the programmes, the research and attitudes of policy-makers, and the amount of funds available. But because terms associated with education for indigenous minorities are often used interchangeably, and have different and at times ambiguous meanings, there is often confusion over educational goals and strategies. This condition speaks to the need for a sustained effort to clarify, specify and consolidate the vocabulary of education for indigenous minorities within and across international boundaries.

Issues

Issues in financing, organising and governing education for indigenous minorities are complex and numerous. Those included in this paper are considered to be the most vexing issues presently confronting indigenous minority peoples and policy-makers in several member nations. Issues listed contain elements of controversy and differences of opinion regarding each. Posed as questions, the issues vital to indigenous minorities include:

1. Does educational equality refer to equality of opportunity or equality of results?
2. Should there be different educational goals and different levels of expenditure for different pupil populations?
3. For whom are the concepts of fiscal equity to be applied: the student population as a whole? Taxpayers? Or special populations for whom compensation for previous shortcomings may be given priority?
4. Is it inevitable that when funds are increased at one level of government or from specific agencies that control over the education process inextricably accrues to the level of government or agency providing the funds?
5. How can sources of funds from multiple levels of government be co-ordinated? What organisational schemes are necessary to guarantee optimal co-ordination?
6. How can equal access to education be assured in light of the extraordinary physical and/or social environment of many indigenous minority peoples?
7. Can extraordinary provisions for indigenous minorities be justified and funded in a manner that exceeds programmes for the majority? If so, how can such programmes be endorsed and supported by the majority?

8   Should schools be concerned primarily with future incomes of its indigenous minority pupils? Cultivating an awareness of the student's ethnicity and appreciation of cultural diversity? And/or fostering a common national heritage?

9   How much of society's need to foster and guarantee equality should be met by the school *vis-à-vis* other elements of society?

10 Can the education system create the means for acquisition of improved economic opportunities by indigenous minorities without their rights to being culturally/ethnically distinct being destroyed?

11 Is local control a necessary provision to assure educational reforms for indigenous minorities? Is local control a sufficient condition?

12 What are the limits to which education systems should go, both in expenditures and programme aims?

13 How can changes and reform in education for indigenous minority peoples, especially equity- and equality-related changes, be measured and evaluated?

14 Who should have responsibility for formulating policies that may be necessary if answers to the above questions require changes in financing, organising and governing schools?

Delineating the above questions that identify the issues associated with indigenous minority education is not to suggest that the list is exhaustive nor that each question is of equal concern among member nations. Other questions may well be added and some deleted depending on local circumstances. But the list is a convenient way to distinguish what appear to be the most vexing and contentious problems in financing, organising and governing education in member nations with indigenous minority populations.

Discussion

Many issues in financing, organising and governing education for indigenous minorities are indifferent to international boundaries. The need for schools to be constituted in such a way as to be positively perceived by indigenous minorities is a universal problem. Thus, the considerable extent of transferability of ideas that address the means to resolve such issues is one of the most compelling reasons for examining them.

Not all issues introduced in this paper are necessarily concerned with indigenous minorities. Some apply to general educational reforms irrespective of the population under consideration. But whether the issues are general or relate directly to indigenous minorities, they should be considered from the perspective of equity and equality concepts that favour the financial, organisational and governance needs of indigenous minorities.

Also, issues and the way they will ultimately be resolved are directly subject to constitutional and statutory limitations placed on education systems. These vary in such a way among member nations that solutions in one nation may not be feasible in another, thus the need to identify these limitations prior to considering the issues. In addition to constitutional and statutory considerations when considering issues, there are a number of factors in each country that bear on the way issues may be resolved. Some are of a general nature that affect all education regardless of target populations, while others pertain in particular to indigenous minorities. These factors include such things as:

— public shifts in attitude toward education as a whole;
— public resistance to spending levels;
— gross demographic changes, especially those that alter population composition proportions;
— laws enacted with one population as a general target, but which have unplanned consequences for others;
— clashes between two or more major educational movements;
— periods of rapidly changing social values, especially when changes necessary for accepting a new set of values requires that another set be rejected;
— fragmented power resources, such as legal authority, funds and political influence;
— higher costs to deliver educational services in sparsely populated or economically depressed areas where there are many indigenous minority peoples;
— extraordinary expenses of extraordinary education, such as alternative or compensatory educational programmes;
— influence of special interest groups (whose position is often adverse to indigenous minorities) which prevent needed changes in education and are sometimes protected by laws and policies unfair to indigenous minorities.

These, and other factors depending upon local circumstances, bear on the nature and severity of issues in just about all locations where there are indigenous minorities.

Equity, as used in this paper, is derived from the doctrine of fairness and impartiality. Answers to the questions generated by the issues obviously must be answered in terms of fairness; but they must also be answered in terms of applying educational equality. This is a more difficult doctrine to apply because of the variety of concepts that have variously been ascribed to the term, educational equality.

Our discussion of educational equality must start by delineating the various types of equality; and the question, 'What is the purpose of educational equality for indigenous minorities?' must be asked. Until recent times, inequality was accepted as the norm. Now, however:

> The one universally accepted criterion of a public activity is that it affords equal treatment to all. With respect to schooling, this implies that any two children of the same abilities shall receive equivalent forms of assistance in developing those abilities . . . .[7]

How to develop the means and find the resources to guarantee that this notion is reflected in educational policy is the essence of a problem in need of consideration in many, if not all, member nations. But as fundamental and necessary as the principle of equal treatment to all is considered to be, it may not be enough where indigenous minorities are concerned.

Although each of several forms of educational equality is based on the doctrine of equity, some may actually work to the disadvantage of indigenous minorities. It is necessary, therefore, to sort out the various forms of equality and agree on the forms most appropriate to the needs of indigenous minorities. An educational equality concept that is indigenous-minority-specific needs to be formulated; each concept to become the basis for policy development in each member nation. Once this is done, the issues listed above are more apt to be resolved in favour of indigenous minorities.

Listed below are seven concepts of educational equality generally found in the literature on the subject. In particular, I am indebted to Arthur Wise for his treatment of this subject in *Rich Schools, Poor Schools*.[8] The list includes:

- the foundation system concept;
- the equal-dollars-per-pupil concept;
- the competition concept;
- the fiscal neutrality or negative concept;
- the levelling concept;
- the minimum attainment concept;
- the concept of full opportunity.

All of these concepts have their complex features and all have been variously described by several authors. In a brief and general way they may be summarised as follows.

The foundation system concept requires a satisfactory minimum offering, expressed in money to be spent, which shall be guaranteed to each pupil. Many complex formulas have been derived to satisfy the guarantee feature of this system, but they are based on the fundamental idea that certain minimums are essential for all, regardless of local resources. If local resources are inadequate they are increased by resources from elsewhere.

The idea of 'equal-dollars-per-pupil' approach to educational equality assumes there is no reason for one individual, minority or majority, rural or urban, bright or dull, to be granted more resources than another. Ability is not considered a reason for differential allocation of funds. Each individual is entitled to an equal portion; how that portion is to be spent depends on the circumstances of the individual.

The idea of 'competition' as an approach to educational equality suggests distribution of educational resources to students according to their talent. In this definition, equality is an individual focus rather than a social focus. It simply means the more able students deserve more education, regardless of wealth of parents, ethnicity, or location.

The nature of a student's education should not depend upon where he/she lives and what his/her parental circumstances are. Because of its 'should not' feature this concept has been named the 'negative definition' of educational equality. It applies without regard to the place where one lives and favours no individual or class. As such, it may be considered to be fiscally neutral. The difficulty with this particular definition is that it does not specify conditions necessary to assure equality. It fails to acknowledge the possibility of legitimate reasons for group differences in average share sizes, but it does suggest each child should be able to reach the limits of his/her abilities even though levels of expenditure will be different for various students.

The 'levelling' concept requires that resources should be allocated in inverse proportion to the ability of each student. In effect, this approach compensates for shortcomings of some pupils and is typically provided in categorical, compensatory programmes.

The 'minimum-attainment' concept of educational equality requires that each student shall receive educational resources until he/she reaches a specified level of achievement. This approach requires greater expenditure for some students than for others.

The concept of 'full opportunity' assumes that students may differ in their ability to learn, and that each person should be given an opportunity to develop his/her abilities to the fullest. In this concept the cost of every individual's education would vary. There would be no cut-off of educational services until there is nothing more to be gained.

Each of the above concepts has utility as the basis for financing, organising and governing education. But not all favour indigenous minorities, and therein lies the danger of accepting any concept arbitrarily. Based on the first two, the foundation system and the equal-dollars-per-pupil system, policies can be formulated that would be detrimental to the needs of indigenous minorities although they could meet tests for equity and equality in the minds of many.

The final three concepts — levelling, minimum attainment, and full opportunity — can be said to favour indigenous minorities, but none is sufficient in itself to guarantee all of the necessary reforms. To derive an indigenous-minority-specific concept it is desirable to relate equality to equity in such a way that 'fairness' does not limit special resources and considerations necessary for indigenous minority education reform. Educational equality is the means to assure equity for indigenous minorities, but only if the definition of equality is indigenous-minority-specific. This notion is best explained by reducing the seven concepts above to two equity principles:

(a) the equal treatment of equals or horizontal equity principle;
(b) the unequal treatment of unequals or vertical equity principle.

Berne and Stiefel[9] explain the two principles this way:

> Horizontal equity is concerned with the equality of revenues for all children.... The equal treatment of equals is a specification of the horizontal equity principle. Children are assumed to be equally deserving, and horizontal equity measures the difference between the actual distribution and a perfectly equal distribution. The smaller the difference from equality, the greater the horizontal equity....
>
> If members of the group are not equal and some are judged to be deserving of more or less of the object of concern, then the application of the vertical rather than the horizontal equity principle may be appropriate.... If learning handicaps are recognized as a characteristic that identifies children who should receive more revenues than children without learning handicaps, then the principle of vertical equity is applicable.... Vertical equity can be expressed as the unequal treatment of unequals....

Each of these ideas is based on concepts of equity. Only the latter principle, vertical equity, truly favours indigenous minorities. And, before it is used as the guiding principle, it needs to be coupled with the idea that there should be no systematic relationship between wealth per child and revenues for education per child, that is, there is an absence of discrimination based on availability of money.

Because there is no single group or type of indigenous minority in the OECD member countries, and legal and economic conditions vary appreciably between them, no single statement of educational equality can be made to fit perfectly in all countries simultaneously. However, the principle of vertical equity, favouring the needs of indigenous minorities, has universal application to formulating a concept of equality. Thus, the following concept of educational equality, derived from the principle of vertical equity, may serve the need for an indigenous-minority-specific concept or serve as a point of departure for a more locally tailored statement: *School systems should provide the opportunity for every student to develop his/her abilities and interests to the fullest, regardless of where he/she lives, regardless of his/her parental circumstances, and regardless of the ultimate level to be attained.* With this definition we can posit that the purpose of educational equality for indigenous minority children is to ensure that each student may develop his/her abilities regardless of the accident of birth or geography.

Answers to the questions posed in the section on issues are not easy to arrive at nor will they always be the same from nation to nation. But if the above statement, or one similar to it, is used as the basis for arriving at answers, the position of indigenous minorities should be enhanced. Basic policy needs to be formulated on the premise that students can be afforded, without rancour, substantially different educational programmes for reasons of differences in where they live, differences in economic status, and differences in ethnic and cultural backgrounds, even though they will be expensive and demanding on patience and energies.

> There can be no blinking the enormous and unique set of handicaps which our whole history, right to the present, has imposed on those who are not white. . . . You must spend time and money beyond your normal standards in helping them [minorities] survive and succeed. Precisely because it is not yet 'racially neutral' to be [a minority], a racially neutral standard will not lead to equal opportunity. . . .[10]

It is axiomatic to this assumption that 'to offer students of different [backgrounds, circumstances, and] ability similar amounts of resources may, in fact, be to treat them unequally'.[11]

Regardless of the importance of ample financial resources to improve education for indigenous minorities, or the formulas devised to allocate these resources derived from an indigenous-minority-specific concept of equality, the way schools are organised and governed may have even greater long-range implications for reform in education for indigenous minorities. A historic root of discontent is that from the very beginning the dominant Western society has developed education programmes under the premise that they knew what was best for indigenous minority people without affording them a major share in decision-making. Among all the issues posed in the preceding section, those that deal with local control are the most fundamental. Conflict is perennial between centralisation and decentralisation and between local values and values reflective of wider realms. The pervasiveness and durability of the value of local self-determination consistently reappears in arguments addressed to this subject.

For years the problem has been failure to understand the fundamental difference between perceptions of control or autonomy by central governmental agencies (the Western view) and the way control of schools is perceived by many groups of indigenous minorities. Central, Western style agencies have agreed in the recent past that authority might be allocated to indigenous minorities in certain instances to certain degrees, but decentralisation as an ultimate granting of authority is often seen by central agencies as a *tendency*, while indigenous minorities perceive it as an *event*. The two different interpretations lead to qualitatively different activities desired over long periods of time. Decentralisation as a tendency connotes an 'allowance' of greater control bestowed upon the consumer at the pleasure of the parent agency. Decentralisation as an event connotes arrival at a specific state. The event has a defined end and a planned beginning, but the tendency has a defined beginning with no specific end other than to find that point where consumer pressure to decentralise is reduced.

The granting of autonomy outright results in a different relationship between central authorities and local indigenous minorities than the award of it in increments of indefinite size and duration. The value attributed to the ability of local people to make intelligent choices reflects directly in the school programmes. Programmes developed under one perception of intellectual ability are apt to be substantially different from programmes developed under the other. What would have been the levels of educational achievement of many indigenous minorities today if earlier programmes of education had been developed *with* rather than *for* them?

At present, there is too little relationship between what happens at home and in the community and what is experienced at school. The need to fuse the culture of the community and the school is a critical requirement before schools will be perceived as legitimate establishments. Substantial attempts to introduce multicultural or multi-ethnic education in the classroom began in earnest in many countries in the

1960s and continue today, probably more intensely and more effectively now than ever. Minority languages in the classroom, minority music and dance, minority arts and crafts, minority subsistence techniques, and minority legends have found their way into the school, with varying degrees of success. Other innovations, such as flexible school calendars to accommodate traditional, social and subsistence activities, and visits by indigenous minority leaders and artists serving in classrooms as supplementary teachers, have contributed to an indigenous minority presence in the schools. But there are problems in sustaining these efforts, especially when sources of funds for extraordinary categories of the curriculum become exhausted or are withdrawn.

The multitude of cultures further compounds the problem, there being no single indigenous minority culture in any of the OECD member countries. Incidence of high teacher turnover further aggravates the situation, especially when particularly culture-sensitive, creative teachers move on or become disillusioned because of intense multicultural situations. When one adds to this the meagre population in some locations and the efforts required of the relatively few individuals, the number of indigenous-minority-oriented programmes that do exist is more surprising than the number that do not. But even those most committed to programmes stressing cultural enrichment are coming to recognise limits to such programmes and are looking for more profound answers to the problems of previous educational shortcomings.

Also, much attention is being paid to cultural relevance because it has become an emotional issue. But the emotional nature of the issue has also caused confusion and polarisation of positions among those debating the topic. As pointed out previously, the definition of 'culture' depends on the perspective of the user, and its use and misuse contribute to the uncertain nature of the problems. Until the word culture has a common realistic meaning and is used in both the school room and the community, the problems associated with it are likely to go unresolved. Educators often miss the basic problem by oversimplifying notions of culture. They expect every educational issue to be simply explained by culture difference, and to be resolved by adapting the educational programme to a minority culture in a perfunctory way. Coping with the situation, however, cannot be handled so simply.

> Cognitive sophistication makes it possible to know both one's own cognitive system and that of the different group with which one works so that one may be able to translate both talk and actions from one such system into the other while recognizing the conventional and arbitrary nature of both . . . [however] cognitive

sophistication is so rare and so difficult to acquire that interaction of cultural barriers is a frequent cause of conflict. This applies to all relationships across cultural barriers — not only to those of other nations and major cultures, but also to those within a culture, such as relationships between suburbanites and slum dwellers or between races or social classes.[12]

Where there is centralised authority, staffs employed to administer school systems seldom have the cognitive sophistication necessary to relate in a realistic manner to the indigenous minority population.

Furthermore, in most instances where local control or school governance is an issue, indigenous minorities are unable to secure their legitimate rights to influence policy decisions because there are so many levels of individuals in educational policy-making that it is unclear who makes decisions and how decisions are made. The primary purpose, therefore, in moving toward local control is to bring about shifts in authority and a redistribution of power so that decisions can be made that will more quickly and realistically improve learning conditions. Decisions at the local level must: (a) enable local authorities to vary the total amount of money available for school purposes; (b) adopt regulations governing organisational policies; (c) establish procedures for the operation of schools; and (d) adopt programmes congruent with local community needs. The need for local control in this sense is based on the premise that the level of decisions required at the local level must be commensurate with the level of authority to make those decisions.

> If a group is discriminated against in a negative sense, the basic requirement is to build up the strength of that group. It becomes a tactical problem whether this can best be done through maximizing the access of the particular group to the educational system as it is through increasing its bargaining power in relationship to that system . . . or through the establishment of separate and sheltered parts of the educational system governed by the group's own values.[13]

Either of these two ways, increased bargaining power or establishment of separate parts, require legal authority and fiscal resources favouring local control.

A popular premise among many indigenous minority leaders is that school systems can more effectively meet the education of indigenous minorities when authority to control education is moved from central administrative agencies to local, predominantly indigenous minority groups. Whether this is done by maximising access to the educational system or by establishing separate systems is a decision that depends on several factors and must be made locally. Each way holds potential for improved education and will tend toward realising the purposes of developing educational equality.

These observations should not be interpreted in such a way that they suggest the qualities of Western life style or value of Western education be disregarded or dismissed when programmes of education for indigenous minorities are developed. Nor does it suggest that responsibilities for education be abandoned at the central level. In many instances, there remain among indigenous minorities technical inadequacy, personnel underdevelopment, and functional isolation of social services that can only be improved in partnership with professional workers. Also, an indigenous minority emphasis or point of view does not necessarily mean that Western education has little value. There are common norms toward which all school systems should strive. Professional educators must be able to determine the cognitive, affective and motor needs of each student to such an extent that programmes of education, professional staffs, and other resources are sufficient to meet such needs — an awesome task it should be added, and a capability among educationists yet to be achieved.

Thus, a need exists for a partnership between indigenous minorities, with their particular and specialised perspective, and professionals (so much the better should they happen to be indigenous minorities), who are trained to recognise the means by which objectives of education may be met. Concerns increasingly being expressed by indigenous minorities may be looked upon as essential elements necessary for substantive reform. The growing bank of academic and research skills emerging in the profession must be brought to bear on the perspective and intuition of indigenous minority peoples. To realise this condition, ways will have to be found to bring the perceptions and intuition of indigenous minorities together with the knowledge and skills of trained educationists. Such a merger has the potential to eliminate the frustrations of both groups.

Conclusions

Throughout much of the world, substantial interest is now being shown in improved education for and among indigenous minority peoples. The favourable extent to which the concept of educational equality has become a fixture of contemporary social thought reveals a major shift in attitude among large segments of the populations. It was not many years ago that 'education was a privilege of the privileged, inequality was expected and accepted . . .'.[14] Today, minority—majority relationships are not inevitably negative situations. Greater knowledge among and between cultural groups has brought about more friendly and co-operative perceptions of each other. Commingling of cultural groups provides a constant source for new thoughts and ideas.

Positive developments in recent years notwithstanding, consequences of the supposed demise of the idea of inequality have, in many instances, yet to be translated into policies and programmes. Because many indigenous minority children remain between two cultures, firm psychological and intellectual foundations will be required to enable these children to cope with a life divided between majority and minority worlds. Inadequacies in providing these foundations persist at both the policy-making and programme-execution levels.

To address the problems of inadequacies it is necessary to better understand the relationships between current programmes of education and the needs of indigenous minorities. A detailed study of the special educational needs of indigenous minority children, nation by nation, is essential in order to clarify what is expected of schools and other agencies concerned with the children's welfare.

Data need to be accumulated which suggest the means for evaluating and predicting the impact of changes in school finance and governance schemes. Because there are many ways to evaluate school finance systems, the standard of equity to be applied in any evaluation must first be satisfactorily defined. A standard based on the principle of vertical equity will lead to judgements quite different from judgements based on the horizontal equity principle.

> Apart from choosing the equity concept to be measured, efforts to evaluate major reforms in school finance involve three tasks. The first is to measure the amount of prereform inequality; the second is to measure the changes in inequality after the reform has been adopted; and the third is to anticipate the effects of policy changes before they occur — a task that is critical for the design and evaluation of alternative policies.[15]

It is also necessary to identify the object being measured. Is the object (a) expenditure per child (either actual or cost adjusted); (b) real resources such as teachers or supplies per pupil; (c) output, such as achievement test scores or years of schooling completed, or (d) the outcome of education, such as income, satisfaction, or status? Each of these must be measured in different ways and some are more problematic than others. All are subject to value judgements.

Regardless of local circumstances and choices of equity principles and objects of evaluation, certain preconditions to change must exist if reforms are to take place. Anderson[16] has identified four conditions of change appropriate to the theme of this paper:

(a) the existence of incentives to change;

(b) the existence of power to change in the sense of freedom from external constraints that prevent or severely restrict any alteration in the *status quo*;

(c) the existence of leaders capable of carrying out the various functions necessary to bring about change;

(d) the existence of a plan for change that grows out of a systematic self-examination of past practices and current problems, and which anticipates and provides for the technical assistance and material resources necessary to support the change.

No matter how positive governmental agencies may be toward indigenous minorities, no matter how adequate the funds or complete the legal authority to act at the local level, little in the way of sustained, substantial reform is likely without all four preconditions to reform being present. This assertion is made on the premise that genuine reform is only possible when it is derived from a grass roots movement. If this premise is valid it may explain why the process of education reform among indigenous minorities has been so slow to arrive. To be inspired, to acquire power, to exhibit leadership, and to have a plan require information — information seldom sufficiently available to indigenous minority peoples in their present status. This is so simply because existing educational and governmental agencies usually do not provide information to indigenous minorities in a form or an amount sufficient to engender change even though these agencies ostensibly subscribe to a principle of educational equality. As Kjell Eide has said in chpater 9, 'equality is rarely given to a group, it is achieved through the stirrings of the group itself. And in so doing, it is essential that a group is capable of defining what equality means in its own terms. Its ability to do this, in fact, is probably the best measure of the degree of equality it has achieved'.

For all of the necessary conditions to come together among indigenous minorities, several things must happen simultaneously. Especially necessary is knowledge of organisational and programmatic options. To assert the fundamental right of self-determination, or to redistribute power without alternatives, results simply in political conflict, not school reform. Unless indigenous minority peoples have the technical resources, the organisational capabilities, and competent personnel requisite to meeting their demands, the demands cannot be satisfied irrespective of their legitimacy or intensity.[17]

Public educational investments represent the principal method by which society attempts to equalise opportunity among children born into different circumstances.[18] This condition speaks to the need for long-range, ongoing comparative studies that will provide indigenous minority peoples with the background materials and knowledge of options required to meet their educational goals. Also, policy-makers in governmental and educational agencies require information that will better enable them to relate the various principles of equity to plans now in effect and to better judge the validity of the demands and claims of indigenous minorities.

Differences in education expenditures are caused by differences in the costs of providing services and in the quality or level of services provided. Thus, comparison of costs can be meaningless unless several variables are accounted for. Indices that accurately measure differences in education costs require complex statistical methods and a firm economic model. Controllable and uncontrollable variables must be separated so that accurate indices can be based on the uncontrollable variables. Analysis of any member nation's system of financing schools may be done by one of several different procedures. Evaluation of finance systems within a single nation is complex; comparisons between nations even more so.

Because of the complexity of school finance plans it is difficult, but not impossible, to interrelate all of the elements bearing on the process. A need to monitor trends, in both the distribution and revenue dimensions, exists in all OECD countries. Also, because so little is known about the effects of reforms in both equity and educational equality issues, it is suspected that long-range consequences of any reform may be significantly different from their short-term effects. Because of this, continuous study of the subject and development of techniques for forecasting long-range trends is warranted. The impact of school finance reform on a wide range of education systems may be more adequately predicted where an analytical framework for understanding the consequences of finance reform and shifts in authority has been developed.

Quality and scope of educational programmes, irrespective of the populations served, are often determined more by the philosophy of those in control than by available financial resources, especially in multi-cultural situations. Control has always been a vexed school problem, especially when multiple standards conflict. As a problem it can be minimised, if not eliminated, however, when people are willing and conscious participants in shared enterprises.[19] It is to this end, shared enterprise and the subsequent minimising of the vexing nature of educational control, that studies of specific situations and conditions in OECD countries should be undertaken.

> Cultural differences are facts of life in much the same way that air, water, and fire are. It is what men think about these differences, their attitudes and feelings toward them, and what they finally decide to do about them which determines whether there will be harmony or discord.[20]

So that issues and concepts that bear on educational programmes for indigenous minorities are considered from several points of view and discord reduced, it is recommended that a series of studies and reports that would explore, describe and analyse parallels and contrasts in financing, organising and governing education for and among indigenous minority peoples in member nations be initiated.

The theme of this paper was developed with the idea that indigenous minority peoples in many parts of the world have had a relatively stable way of life interrupted by the demands of Western technology and social thought. Indigenous minorities, undergoing changes as profound as those in many OECD countries, are bound to experience unrest.

> When technological innovations or new behavior patterns impinge on society living in relative equilibrium, their values become disturbed. This is so because such innovations create new strains and demands and effective ability to meet them.[21]

The education systems of many of these countries are caught up in the struggle of the people to regain a new form of stability; a struggle compounded by a paradox that exacerbates the problem. Education, as an element of Western society, is a source of strain on the traditional indigenous society while simultaneously offering a means to cope with change and ultimately a new form of stability.

The purposes of education, its programmes and personnel, will remain the centre of controversy until pressures causing stress are reduced — in other words, until schools are perceived more as the means to enable indigenous minority peoples to cope with their present situation than as sources of irritation.[22] The necessary criterion for eventual success of educational programmes among indigenous minority peoples is the provision that the education they receive corresponds to their interests, norms and values: when this criterion is met, the schools become 'legitimate'.

Notes and references

1   Carnoy, Martin, *Education as Cultural Imperialism*, New York, David McKay, 1974, p.1.
2   Johns, Roe and Morphet, Edgar, *The Economics and Financing of Education* (3rd ed.), Englewood Cliffs, New Jersey, Prentice-Hall, 1975, p.252.
3   Banks, James A., 'Issues and Trends in American Education — Pluralism and Educational Concepts: A Clarification' in Borg (ed.), *Readings in Education 1979/80, Peabody Journal of Education,*

January 1977, pp. 26–9, Guiford, Connecticut, Duskin Publishing Group.
4   Walsh, John, *Intercultural Education in the Community of Man*, Honolulu, East–West Center, University Press of Hawaii, 1973, p.13.
5   Rivlin, Harry, 'Preface' in *Cultural Pluralism in Education: A Mandate for Change*, p.vii, Madelon Stent, William Hazzard and Harry Rivlin (eds), New York, Appleton-Century-Crofts, 1973.
6   Banks, James A., 'Issues and Trends in American Education – Pluralism and Educational Concepts: A Clarification' op.cit., p.29.
7   Benson, Charles S., *The Cheerful Prospect: A Statement on the Future of Public Education*, Boston, Houghton Mifflin Co., 1961, p.62.
8   Wise, Arthur E., *Rich Schools, Poor Schools*, Chicago and London, The University of Chicago Press, 1972.
9   Berne, Robert and Stiefel, Leanna, 'The Equity of School Finance Systems Over Time: The Value Judgments Inherent in Evaluation', *Educational Administration Quarterly*, 15, Spring 1979, pp. 18–19.
10 Bundy, McGeorge, 'The Issue Before the Courts: Who Gets Ahead in America', *Atlantic*, November 1977, pp. 42, 45.
11 Wise, Arthur E., *Rich Schools, Poor Schools*, op.cit., p.156.
12 Quigley, Carroll, 'Needed: A Revolution in Thinking', *NEA Journal*, May 1968, in *Contemporary American Education*, p.23, Stan Dropkin, Harold Full and Ernest Schwarcz (eds), New York, Macmillan, 1975.
13 Eide, Kjell, in chapter 9, 'A researcher's assessment of the autonomy problem', p.161.
14 Wise, Arthur E., *Rich Schools, Poor Schools*, op.cit., p.6.
15 Friedman, Lee S. and Wiseman, Michael, 'Understanding the Equity Consequences of School-Finance Reform', *Harvard Educational Review*, 48, May 1978, p.205.
16 Anderson, Lee, 'School Reform, Educational Change, and Public Policy', Report of the Summer Institute on the Improvement and Reform of American Education, DHEW, Office of Education, no.74-12008, 1974, p.263.
17 Anderson, Lee, op.cit., p.267.
18 Levin, Henry, 'Equal Educational Opportunity and the Distribution of Education Expenditures' in *Rethinking Educational Equality*, edited by Andrew Kopen and Herbert Walberg, Berkeley, McCutchan, 1974, p.27.
19 Dewey, John, *Experience and Education*, Macmillan (Collier Books), 1938.
20 Walsh, John, *Intercultural Education in the Community of Man*, op.cit., p.2.

21 Goulet, Denis, 'An Ethical Model for the Study of Values', *Harvard Educational Review*, 41, May 1971, p.206.
22 Darnell, Frank, 'Education Among the Native Peoples of Alaska', *Polar Record* 19, May 1979, p.445, University of Cambridge, Scott Polar Research Institute.

17 Reactions to these concepts from Aboriginal Australia

Colin J. Bourke
Centre for Research into Aboriginal Affiars,
Melbourne, Australia

Professor Darnell has covered the major issues relating to the education of Aboriginal people with an international perspective and his general conclusions are relevant to the education of Australian Aborigines.

It needs to be stressed, however, that his paper's parameters are somewhat limiting. While the finance, organisation and governance of education are important, they do not have exclusive impact on the education provided to the client population. Throughout the paper the author equates education with schooling. Unfortunately, Professor Darnell does not differentiate between the two concepts.

Education cannot be isolated from other costs associated with living in society. The cost of freeways, water supply, sewage disposal, local government services and other costs associated with urban areas cannot be ignored whilst those associated with education of more isolated communities are highlighted. The financing of education should be viewed as only one cost factor in the total community expenditure by governments, Federal, State and local.

The Aboriginal pattern of population distribution differs to that of non-Aboriginal Australians. According to the 1971 Census, some 56.4 per cent of Aborigines lived in rural areas compared to 14.3 per cent of the total Australian population. This Census also showed that only 14.7 per cent of Aborigines lived in major urban centres compared to 64.5 per cent of the total Australian population. These differences have important implications. Higher education institutions and specialist education facilities are located in urban areas. The majority of Aborigines, therefore, experience difficulty in gaining access to these facilities. Cultural and family considerations and the time demands, aggregate with geographic, economic and social factors to deny most Aborigines access to higher education. As a result they lack opportunities to gain expertise and the educational experience which will meet their individual and community needs.

In discussing the education of Aborigines it is essential to define who is an Aborigine and relate this to the system of education.

Soon after the arrival of Europeans in Australia, Aboriginal societies and cultures were placed under enormous pressure and changed drastically. One of the results of white colonisation was the appearance of a group of people of mixed ancestry. These people were not accepted by European society and they identified with their mothers and the Aboriginal people. The number of these Aborigines has steadily increased until today they constitute the greater proportion of the Australian Aboriginal race.

To be classified as an Aborigine under official government definition a person has to be *of Aboriginal descent, identify as such* and *be recognised as an Aborigine by the community* in which he/she lives.

Unlike most other people in the world the Aborigine is dependent upon the community to give him/her a legal identity as a member of his/her own race. This enables him/her to vote in National Aboriginal Conference elections and obtain some special assistance in housing, employment and education. For the purposes of this paper the term Aborigine encompasses all who are descended from the indigenous peoples of Australia, including Tasmania and the Torres Strait Islands, identify as such and are so recognised by their community.

The 1976 Australian Census indicated that 160,000 Aborigines lived in Australia. Although constituting only one per cent of the total population, they are found in most parts of Australia:

Table 17.1
Distribution of Aborigines by State

Victoria	New South Wales	Queensland	South Australia	Western Australia	Tasmania	Northern Territories	Total
14,739	40,450	41,345	827	26,126	2,942	23,751	160,913

Source: 1976 Australian Census

Aborigines are found in most Australian communities but in many cases there is no sense of belonging to the community. Aboriginal people are aware that they are different from the rest of the population. A common language and a common situation are not enough. Aborigines have communal social relationships which rest on various affectual, emotional and traditional bases. They may live within the geographic confines of a community but the difficulties and discrimination they encounter in housing, employment, education, health and legal services reinforces their feeling of difference.

Aboriginal people have been subjected to numerous research studies regarding their group identification and solidarity. R.C. Hausfield stated:

> No study has established that Aborigines anywhere in Australia exist other than as members of distinctive Aboriginal groups. It is realised of course that some isolated Aborigines are living as members of the general community but no studies have been carried out which establish that these individuals are socially similar to other members of the general community.

When writing of her experiences among Aborigines in Melbourne, Diane Barwick concluded that kinship still regulated most activity in this population. 'Few as yet desire the breakdown of extended family and kinship bonds . . . group ties are reinforced by strongly developed sentiments of loyalty and kinship.'

Barwick's stance is supported by Inglis who, when discussing urban Aborigines in Adelaide, stated: 'The majority of dark people place a high value on their sense of community'. Beckett also affirmed:

> It is possible for an Aboriginal to escape from the community and become a citizen of a white neighbourhood . . . but to do this he must . . . dissassociate himself from his more 'backward fellows'. Deprived of the support of the community, he must face alone a new world, which has customs and mores he knows imperfectly.

The latter is a somewhat negative view because the Aborigine could well argue that he has rejected the non-Aboriginal world because of its values, customs and beliefs.

Aborigines are distinct from the remainder of the Australian population. While some may be regarded by non-Aborigines as being of similar ancestry to their own, few people of Aboriginal descent choose to pass as white. They identify with their relations whose skin colour and physical characteristics make them a visible and identifiable minority. Discrimination and racial prejudice from non-Aborigines reinforces the group perception Aborigines have that they are different.

Aborigines are bound by a strong sense of identity, even though internally, within their society, there can be extremely disruptive conflict. Barwick noted that Aborigines in the Victorian capital city, Melbourne, had basic cultural values concerning locality and family as well as reciprocal obligations in regard to help and hospitality.

Today, Aborigines are developing greater pride in their own identity, a deeper interest in their history and a greater understanding of their uniqueness. These developments are assisting Aborigines in strengthening their feelings of belonging to a recognisable and viable community.

Australian Aborigines are a distinct racial group and see themselves as a separate community. They desire an independent and equal place in Australia even though they can be distinguished from the remainder of the Australian population because of their unique cultures and sub-cultures. Socio-economic indicators also show that they are different from other Australians in regard to education, health, housing, employment, demography, economic development and social welfare needs.

In the area of education the difference in academic attainment between Aborigines and non-Aborigines helps perpetuate the dependency syndrome which has afflicted the Aboriginal population since colonisation. Few Aborigines are gaining the academic qualifications necessary for equality in Australian society or the expertise to mount education or other programmes for their own people.

The Aboriginal unemployment rate is also an indication of the vast differences that exist between Aborigines and non-Aborigines. Department of Employment and Youth Affairs figures for May 1980 indicated that 36 per cent of the Aboriginal workforce was unemployed compared to 6 per cent of non-Aborigines. The effects of such a high unemployment rate on the Aboriginal community is a matter of grave concern and has serious implications for Aboriginal education.

During their 50,000 years-plus occupation of this country, the Aboriginal people developed unique cultures and a viable form of education. It was an education system in which schools were not needed. Learning occurred through interaction with other people.

According to Penny the education of the tribal Aborigine was deliberate, systematic, comprehensive, very lengthy and most searchingly examined. The curriculum was not set out in books: it was the living culture of the people. Learning did not happen in a separate place, but directly in the environment.

Tribal Aborigines were educated people. Education was universal. Learning was a co-operative exercise, education belonged to the family. All people were teachers because they learned from each other. The motivation to learn came from the satisfaction gained in being a competent person. Aboriginal education was soundly based on a hierarchical learning model. It was an education for living, everyone was educated so that all could contribute to the group to the best of their ability.

Today, Aboriginal communities need to develop their own educational institutions or schools if the students are to achieve their potential. Such institutions would recognise the reality of being Aboriginal in the twentieth century. The philosophy, curriculum and teaching techniques would reflect those of the contemporary Aboriginal community. The resources of the community could be used and developed by such institutions and this would strengthen the feeling of common kinship among Aboriginal people. Aboriginal educational institutions would ensure the perpetuation of Aboriginal cultures including Aboriginal norms and values. Aborigines would once again be custodians of their own cultures. These institutions should also develop in their students a critical awareness of the local community and the broader Australian society.

Most non-Aboriginal people seem to view schools as having an integrative role. They appear to believe that they should contribute to the unity of the wider society by providing similar educative processes for all citizens. Any move by Aborigines to establish schools on racial grounds is usually labelled as separatist and is deplored as being divisive. Apartheid is a term frequently used. In many cases moves to establish Aboriginal schools are even interpreted as an attack on democracy itself. Yet a large number of private schools in Australia have been established on educational, religious, racial and economic grounds without protest from wider society.

While seeking cultural continuity and their own communal life Aborigines must remain full citizens of Australia integrated, both politically and economically, into Australian society. They need to seek cultural pluralism. Cultural pluralism is not a new concept for Aborigines because even before the arrival of the 'First Fleet' from England in 1788, the Australian population had many different cultures which co-existed as entities of their own.

Some Aboriginal people live in areas where they form a statistically insignificant proportion of the total population. Despite their lack of demographic significance these people are Aborigines and have educational needs similar to their relations who live in areas with significant Aboriginal populations. In many respects their needs are even more urgent because they lack the support and reassurance that is given by an Aboriginal community and may be struggling to retain their Aboriginal identity.

To ensure that Aboriginal education programmes meet the needs of Aborigines, a process of consultation must be developed. Such a process would involve the relevant state Aboriginal education consultative group, meetings with Aboriginal parents and probably the establishment of local Aboriginal education committees.

For structural and cultural pluralism to develop in Australia so that Aborigines can have equal societal status with non-Aborigines a decision to that effect will have to be made by the majority society. Aborigines are an impoverished, relatively powerless minority in an affluent Anglo-Saxon society whose goals and values are decisive. Non-Aboriginal society is so powerful that even whilst it acknowledges the rights of Aborigines to self-determination, it can so structure the situation that it is *its* hopes, not Aboriginal hopes, that are realised.

When discussing consideration in financing, organisation and governing education of indigenous minority populations, it is important to recognise that if education programmes for them are to be successful they must be supported by education programmes for the majority non-indigenous population so that the indigenes will be able to achieve their educational and community goals and not be subjected to prejudice and racism.

The maintenance and development of viable Aboriginal cultures would enrich the lives of all Australians through popular traditions, arts, literature and the development of an enriched perspective of the Australian environment. Until all Australians develop a greater understanding of Aboriginal cultures, and have a more realistic appreciation of the effects that colonisation has had on Aboriginal society, it is doubtful if a truly national Australian identity can emerge. A national identity must take cognisance of the culturally pluralistic nature of the Australian population.

To be effective, education for non-Aborigines must take place both inside and outside the present school system. Lippman undertook a survey of race relations in New South Wales and Victorian country towns. Part of the survey involved interview situations; 52 per cent of all respondents freely mentioned attributes of an unfavourable nature which they considered to be characteristic of Aborigines in general. Their comments were completely unsolicited and yet all of them were unfavourable.

A large-scale education programme will be necessary to overcome the racism and prejudice exhibited by so many Australians. Such a programme will, of necessity, involve the media (radio, television, newspapers and magazines). In addition, schools, public education programmes, teacher training and the training of other professional and para-professional groups need to involve a sensitisation process. A total approach using all avenues will be required. It is not possible to legislate racism and prejudice out of any community. They can only be lessened through education programmes.

Conclusion

Aboriginal people have particular educational needs that can only be met by specific education programmes developed by Aborigines. This can be interpreted as a demand for separatism, but Aboriginal educational programmes and institutions are essential if the indigenous people of Australia are to maintain and develop their cultural identity.

Australia is the only country in the world where Aboriginal cultures can survive. They offer a unique view of life. Aboriginal organisation and cultural values have much to offer a world which is having great difficulty in coming to grips with its own development.

A strong, healthy, well-educated Aboriginal community should reduce racial tensions rather than develop them. Lippman stated that the stronger a minority group was in relation to its own ethnicity, the easier was its integration into the general community. Education programmes can also generate the necessary enthusiasm for a minority group to improve its situation. Greater involvement by individuals in their own ethnic community can develop greater tolerance towards others who are different.

Aboriginal education programmes which involve the development of Aboriginal educational institutions can only increase the strength of the Aboriginal people. This would also promote a concept of equality based on a recognition that Aborigines are the indigenous people of Australia. Education programmes developed by Aborigines for Aborigines will allow Aboriginal people to develop themselves and enable them to achieve their natural potential and not destroy their birthright.

It is time that Aborigines took the initiative so that once again assured, self-reliant individuals will be developed who are proud of themselves and their people. This will require a total approach to education involving all members of the community, both Aboriginal and non-Aboriginal. Success will see future Aboriginal Australians as confident and capable citizens contributing to their own community and to mainstream society.

All Australians will benefit because successful Aboriginal education programmes will develop a deeper appreciation of cross-cultural situations for all Australians. This will enable them to communicate with people of different backgrounds from their own, think multi-culturally, empathise deeply and have an increased sense of identity and worth as members of the human family.

18 The situation of the Sami people in Norway

Anton Hoem
Institute of Educational Research,
University of Oslo, Norway

Ethnic minorities and formal education: theoretical considerations

The past

There has never been a society in which socialisation has not taken place. Transmission of knowledge, upbringing of individuals with a view to responsible citizenship, institutions for cultural inheritance have existed for a long time. However, the socialisation processes, their institutionalisation and other types of institutions have shown a wide variety of pattern when viewed historically.

As a rule, one can say that the simpler a society is the fewer are its institutions. At the start, the complexity and manifold character of the single institution were inversely proportional to the number of institutions in a society. The simple hunting society, for instance, had few institutions and none of which was specialised for a single function. Thus, the development from a simple to a complex society can well be described as a development from multifunctional and general to unifunctional and specialised institutions.[1]

An obvious example of a single specialised institution is the school, the development of which into a specialised educational institution has occurred relatively late in history. In all small-scale societies that have existed in different degrees up to modern time, the school is a new and foreign innovation. These societies existed without schools until the missionaries and others from abroad came and established them for their children. This has led to problems at both individual and society level.

On the one hand at the individual level, the teachers and schoolmasters were met with practically no understanding of the great importance they attached to formal education. On the other hand, the local parents received little understanding from the school authorities for their own particular priorities of knowledge and skills. To close this gap (often called the cultural barrier), various pedagogical methods have been tried, the main difference between them being the degree the minority culture has been used as an educational tool. In this, the main element of the minority culture that has been employed is its language. Alternatives have been tried between teachers from outside and teachers recruited locally, between big and small schools, between different ways of organising the school year. The financing of the school has mainly been from outside — an especially interesting feature because it shows how foreign the school really was to the societies in which it was implanted.

The school, as introduced to the minority populations we have in mind, was based upon urban areas with dense populations. Scattered populations, however, demanded small schools with few divisions or larger boarding schools. New ways of arranging the school were also created to meet the needs of different population patterns. At the same time, the school was developed in a society where learning and work were separate. As long as this was not the case in small-scale societies, different systems within the school were adopted to give the older children an opportunity to take part in family life and thus get traditional knowledge of work at home. Thus far, the development can be summed up in the statement that the school is a sub-system of a total system where the degree of integration in the total system defines the way and degree of function.[2]

As long as the school was a foreign innovation in a small-scale society and not an integral part of it, the minority group tried not to be affected by it. At individual level, this showed itself in minimal school attendance, passivity during classes and poor recruitment locally to the teacher profession. At society level, the result was lack of investment — both economically and culturally. It is reasonable to draw the conclusion, then, that in this period the school was a poor agent for the transmission of culture and knowledge. It is surprising in these circumstances that the establishment of urban institutions in rural districts has been so little questioned. Why was a system of formal education established in a society where informal learning was sufficient and natural? The lack of adequate evaluation of the consequences of these schools, and the gross overestimation of their effect on the traditional minority culture, can be explained, I think, by looking no further than the experience of the single individual. All children were involved with school for shorter or longer periods of time and they all either liked or disliked it. It was in the majority society that the school was largely 'liked', and this because of the importance traditionally attached to it in their particular culture. Still at the individual level, let us remember too that those with their professional careers linked to education had special reason to advocate the importance of school, both at home and abroad.

The present position

The school, however, never functions alone. It has always entered the small-scale society along with other institutions from nearby more complex and larger societies. At a certain point, therefore, the ethnic minority can no longer regard it in a mainly negative way; sooner or later it emerges clearly as a positive resource. This happens most often when the technical and economic integration of the ethnic minority has developed so far that this minority's present and its future lies in an urban and industrialised society. For the single family the school becomes a necessity when, as we have seen, work and learning are divided and traditional ways of acquiring knowledge are no longer enough to give understanding of the total society into which the minority has been absorbed. The school then acquires a second function of great importance for the minority, namely the maintenance and transmission of its own culture. It also becomes a resource for an individual career for the minority man or woman in the new, complex and urbanised society.

These end-terms may sound somewhat in conflict. The reason for this is that, while the school has now become an organised and integrated part of the incipient urbanisation and industrialisation of the minority society, culturally it still remains foreign. Changes do not take place at the same rate in the various sections of a society. This is true for ethnic minorities as well as for all groups of people. Changes are most rapidly brought about in technical and economical spheres and more slowly in social and cultural values. This is true in spite of the fact that participation in technical and economic innovation is often dependent on mastery of the language of the majority. At individual level this sometimes leads to a rejection of native language and culture and an overestimation of the language and culture of the majority. In this situation a revitalisation of the traditional culture of the minority, especially its language, often occurs. The problem then is that economic and social life represent an urban, industrialised society based on human conditions more than on the natural conditions traditional to a small-scale society. The fundamental basis for the minority culture no longer exists, nor do the central institutions that maintained it. The traditional culture then has to be nurtured and further developed in accordance with the (probably quite different) characteristics of a new and alien society.

For the educational and cultural sector at macro-level, this situation will raise questions like this: is the minority to be fully responsible for the development of the educational system, based on their own traditional culture, and should the majority at the same time provide the economic, administrative, and general resources needed for this task? Put in a different way: in this situation, cultural and educational questions at the macro-level are bound to concern the cultural and political autonomy of the minority. At individual level, pedagogical questions will be raised as to how and in what degree the individual pupil can be helped by his own and the foreign culture to become resourceful and active in the new society.

Regardless of the political solutions to these questions, the minority school will demand considerable resources to assure its equality with the majority school. Such equality means either a school based upon and developed out of the traditional society (although the notion of school is foreign to this society) or a school based upon and developed in accordance with the existing society with the prevailing mixed-, bi-, or multi-lingual environment. In addition to this demand, there is another claiming a pedagogically superior school that will rapidly and effectively promote an assimilation of the minority into the majority. Regardless of which alternative is chosen, the development must correspond closely with the general social development of the minority society. This means that a school based upon the traditional society and the minority culture is doomed to failure if the general development of the minority is in the direction of assimilation.

All three of these alternatives for the development of a school are relatively expensive. If the policy aim is to maintain and develop the culture and lifestyle of the minority, it follows that the minority should get its own educational and cultural institutions equal and additional to those that already exist. This must be attained by the minority, but with economic and technical help from the majority society. Less comprehensive is the assimilation alternatives which are, therefore, less demanding in all respects — for instance, the educational system will be worked out mainly by the majority society.

If an educational and cultural policy aimed at revitalising the minority culture and lifestyle is to have a fair chance of success, the general social development must, as we have seen, go along with this same policy. The size of the minority is also a factor of importance. For instance, it is scarcely likely that a minority of less than 50,000 people will be able to run all the institutions and attend to all the different interests that arise in modern society without assistance from outside — that is, from members of the majority culture.

The Sami people and the school

The year when the first order calling for formal education for Sami people arrived from outside is usually taken as 1889.[3] Since then a Norwegian educational system has been developed in the Sami districts which in many ways has been remarkable.[4] Particular ways of financing the schools have been developed that assure building standards equal to the rest of the country. To motivate Sami students to become teachers, scholarships have been offered and possibilities for educational specialisation have been opened up. A written Sami language and literature have been evolved, while in the schools, the role of the language has changed in accordance with the views taken from time to time as to the proper pedagogic role of minority languages in teaching. The schools in the Sami districts are, therefore, part of the national educational system, both in organisational and economic terms. An important exception are the boarding schools which were established in 1905 with special sources of financial support.

Today, the educational policy takes as its starting point the social and cultural situation of the Sami population. Their total number in Norway is difficult to estimate, but the current assumption is that there are about 30,000 of them, half of whom live in Finnmark, the most northern county. Northern Norway as a whole has 90 per cent of the Sami people, most of them in districts with scattered populations. The development of the inner part of Finnmark, however, has resulted in a more dense urbanised society. Simultaneously, there has been a steady circulation of Sami people between traditional Sami districts and the bigger Norwegian cities. Of the total population only about 10 per cent are concerned with reindeer herding; the rest are employed in the ordinary industries of the country. Taking into consideration that reindeer herding, both technically and economically, is highly integrated into the national system, it is reasonable to say that the present occupational and economic situation of the Sami people is no longer rooted in their old traditional way of life.

Of the total population it has been estimated that between 15,000 and 20,000 have Sami as their first language.[5] Most of these people (about 75 per cent) belong to the North Sami language group; the remaining 25 per cent speak Lule Sami. The South Sami people are more or less completely Norwegianised so far as language is concerned. In these districts, the distinctive features of ethnical affinity are reindeer herding and where one lives.

Although it is possible today to identify the Sami people geographically and by language, they do not constitute a specific entity in terms of international law and are fully integrated into the political and administrative system of the country. In recent years, however, Sami organisations have grown up on both national and Nordic basis. These organisations have been especially active in questions of cultural policy and law. In the central Sami districts in the northern part of Norway where the Sami people are in majority, they also have the majority in political decisions by the local authority — the relative size of different groups throughout the country deciding where political power is placed at the local level. In Norway as a whole, however, the Sami people have always been a miniscule minority and have consequently never obtained any direct influence.

Nevertheless, the Sami people are exerting increasing influence on national policy through their organisations and by representation on important boards and committees. In the local councils where they are in majority, they also have a decisive influence on the management of their schools. This extends, in accordance with the national system, to educational planning, educational materials, teacher education, financial planning and the organisation of individual schools. Since 1967 Sami for beginners has been taught in the schools of the central Sami districts. The pupils who choose Sami for beginners get lessons in Norwegian as a foreign language. Later on, they can choose which one of the two they want to have as first or second language. This is also valid for the secondary school. Children with Norwegian as their mother tongue can also choose Sami as their second language.

The National Standard Plan of Primary Education which regulates all teaching in Norwegian Primary schools does not take education in the Sami districts into consideration. This means that work has to be done at local level to adjust it to the needs of the Sami schools. In addition to the pedagogical challenge represented by this task, the situation has led to economic problems as well.

The number of pupils in each class in the Norwegian school is standardised in relation to the amount of work the teaching of Norwegian-speaking pupils in a homogeneous class represents. On this basis, the school is financed by national and local budgets. A normal-sized Norwegian class numbers thirty pupils. In the Sami districts a functional class will consist of ten to twenty pupils. This is paid for after special applications each year. To find out about the most appropriate number of a class a combined experiment with increased lessons and reduced number of pupils in each class has been tried out. Together with new rules of financing and new ways of organising within the school, new educational materials in Sami language have been attempted. This again has led to an increased need for adequate teaching plans and for an adequate teacher education. The development of teaching plans, educational material, educational methods, and education of teachers is a national responsibility.

Since 1974 the practical work of development and specialisation of teachers' training for the Sami school has been done in Alta. Among the matters that have been of interest for the teachers' training course is whether the school should have different teachers for Sami and Norwegian. Another important matter for discussion relates to schools of multi-cultural teaching: should they employ the system of form masters or of subject teachers? There has also been an attempt to achieve a common pedagogy for teachers in pre-primary and those in primary schools. Possibilities have also been developed for secondary education. Since the primary schools for the Sami people are directed towards the present society in the Sami districts, the question has been raised as to how teachers' training is to be developed in relation to the Norwegian society and the Sami culture. For the staff in the department of Sami teachers' training, knowledge of Sami language and culture has been the most important qualification. For the students one has seen general teacher education as the most important educational aim. Education in the Sami districts is now classed as a subject for specialisation.

In 1975, the Sami Council of Education was established. Before then, the responsibility of pedagogical development in the Sami school was in the hands of the Advisory Board for primary schools in general — namely, the National Council for Primary Schools. Today, responsibility for the professional development of the school system in the Sami districts has passed into the hands of the Sami Council of Education, and among its important tasks is educational planning. Since the schools in the Sami districts aim at the Norwegian society and the Sami culture, an important task is to decide on the relative distribution of educational topics and educational time. For both Norwegian and Sami subjects, it is necessary to create new plans involving new subject combinations. Likewise new learning materials must be developed in both Sami and Norwegian and for this a combination of experts and practising teachers has been engaged. In fact, a hindrance so far has been a lack of teachers and experts, and whether or not to take Sami people out of teaching to do developmental work presents quite a dilemma. If they are, the teaching of Sami children must be taken over by Norwegian-speaking people who have not had the advantage of a teachers' training course. All this mainly concerns the North Sami districts.

Parallel to the development of educational plans and materials has been a search for new organisational patterns. Reduction in the number of pupils to match an increase in the number of lessons has already been mentioned. Another innovation is a regrouping of pupils to correspond with their level of achievement in different subjects.

Closely connected to this is expansion of the financing system. In Norway each local council is responsible for the daily running of its primary school, but the expenses are covered by the state in accordance with the economic situation of the local society. For the Sami districts, this means that the state meets all the expenses of the primary schools. An urgent task today is to find a norm for expenses of the Sami school and to get it accepted nationally. Another new task for the Sami Council of Education is an analysis of requirements for the various parts of the school system. For this to be worthwhile, however, adequate finance and qualified personnel must be assured.

The establishment of South Sami schools will be an altogether different matter because this will involve cultural revival in a district where even the language is more or less dead and the Sami population amounts to no more than 3,000 people, if that. What is more, they are spread over a large area and it would be impossible to establish a school in every neighbourhood.

Discussion

Both the Norwegian authorities and the Sami organisations are working for the principal of equality in the schools in the Sami and Norwegian districts. This means equality of possibilities and equality of results for each pupil whether his or her mother tongue is Sami or Norwegian.

At the macro-level, the situation is different. The Norwegian primary school relates to the Norwegian society, and only this. The primary schools in the Sami districts, however, have both the Norwegian and Sami societies as their frame of reference. This means that while the Norwegian society has its own school, in the cultural sense the Sami society does not, so for them there is neither equality of possibilities nor equality of results.

This survey of the situation in Northern Norway shows, we believe, that the approach to the financing, organisation and governance of education for indigenous minorities adopted by Professor Frank Darnell in his contribution to this volume needs further elaboration if it is to cover the case of the Sami people. Equality of possibilities and results at micro-level need, by no means, be the same at macro-level. Darnell distinguishes between the two levels when he is considering questions of finance, organisation and governance, but he looks at pedagogical and cultural questions in no more than a micro-perspective. Here we have shown that problems involved in education need to be examined at both levels — macro and micro.

In the Norwegian Sami districts proper development of the school has been resolved pragmatically. In reply to the demand for equality at micro- and macro-level, the response of the Sami school may seem modest; but in the light of what is physically possible, it is all too easy to become over-ambitious.

In defining the Sami school at the beginning of this paper, we stressed that the degree of integration of the minority into the larger society will determine its function. On the other hand, it follows also that the establishment of a school will lead to the development of other Sami institutions. The teaching of the Sami at school presupposes some form of Sami language institutes. The teaching of Sami literature presupposes specialised publishing and printing houses. Living Sami literature presupposes Sami theatres, radio and television. All this presupposes Sami organisations and bureaucracy to take care of the various cultural activities; and this in its turn presupposes Sami people with various educational backgrounds. The education of Norwegians in Sami language and culture to help such cultural revival and development is, in principle and in practice, a non-starter. If there is to be revitalisation of Sami culture, this must be brought about by the Sami people themselves. Otherwise it will end up as an advanced form of museum activity.

Here we come to the heart of the matter: how large must the Sami population be if the traditional culture of a nomadic people engaged in hunting and fishing is to have a reasonable chance of growing in an urbanised and industrialised society? To start with, the lack of human resources is a visible obstacle to such a cultural development. The same individuals are seen in the various institutions, in the educational system and in cultural life in general.

Another knotty matter is control and management. Darnell touches on this in his Question 4 under 'Issues' on page 299. As far as one can see, increased state grants are not leading to increased state control over the Sami school — on the contrary; but as the Sami school develops closer integration results with that part of the Norwegian economic and cultural life associated particularly with the Norwegian school. The consequences of this seem inescapable: since the school is an urban phenomenon, the establishment of a Sami school will promote urbanisation of the Sami society. Over this process, the Sami people will have little control, solely because of their relatively small number. Partial governance over the cultural life of the Sami people through normal operation of the national economic system is not necessarily a negative factor; but it will make a revival of Sami culture on Sami premises a much more difficult process.

In a search for common elements in the problem of education for ethnic minorities, it seems that pedagogical thinking offers the best approach for comparisons at the individual level. It is here, for instance, that attempts have been made to achieve some degree of equality. It is, however, far more difficult to find common elements at the macro-level. These difficulties do not lie so much in differences between ethnic minorities as in differences between majority societies. If one compares, for instance, the educational systems of the ethnic minorities in Alaska with the schools in the Sami districts, the extent to which the financial arrangements for the latter are more stable and less flexible than in Alaska is most striking. The question of control, governance and organisation is not so acute in the Sami school, on the other hand; the concentration of resources around pedagogical and cultural qualities, which might be called the inner life of the school, is the big difficulty.

Suggestions for future work

At the present juncture, more attention must be given to educational questions at the societal level. As a start, we suggest:

(a) In relation to cultural revival and development, one of the first tasks is to find variables that indicate the minimum size a minority must have if the desired development of school and society shall have any chance of success.

(b) Parallel with (a) must be a recognition of such cultural institutions as must be established in a small-scale society if a minority cultural school is to be started.

(c) Following this, the optimal accordance between the developmental level of the school and of the minority must be determined.

(d) A fourth task might well be the development of parameters indicating the time needed for a real improvement of pedagogical standards.

The results from such work should then be regarded from an economic, organisational and administrative point of view to find optimal solutions.

At the individual level, it should be of value:

(a) to find ways of teaching that had the local culture of the pupils as its starting point, and yet was seen in relation to the national culture;

(b) to find a way of calculating the costs per pupil, when the starting point is teaching for equality for the pupil of the ethnic minority — in other words for equal possibilities and equal results;

(c) to find indicators for grouping of pupils when they represent differing degrees of ethnocultural adherence;

(d) to find a form of teacher education that in the best possible way combines the social advantages of the form master with the professional advantages of the subject teacher.

All these studies should throw light on the various aspects of pedagogical method, teaching plans, teaching materials and school building. They also have bearing on the economic dimension.

These few points are suggestions for starting points for future work. Yet, though suggestions, they are not occasional for they are deduced from a theoretical framework and consequently show a systematical pattern and indicate priorities. The theoretical basis can be concentrated thus: the possibilities of the school are determined by the society of which it is a part. The possibilities open to the pupils are determined by their own achievement and the pedagogical qualities of the school.

Notes and references

1   Hoem, A., *Sosialisering. En teoretisk og empirisk modellutvikling* (Socialisation. A theoretical and empirical model for development), Oslo, Universitetsforlaget, 1978.
2   Hoem, A., *Skolen og fornorskninsprosessen* (School and the process of Norwegianisation), 1; Heimen nr.4, Oslo, Universitetsforlaget, 1980, p.512.
3   Dahl, N., *Språkpolitikk og skolestell i Finnmark 1814 til 1905* (The politics of language and schooling in Finnmark 1814 to 1905), Oslo, Universitetsforlaget, 1957.
4   Hoem, A., *Skolen og fornorskninsprosessen*, op.cit.
5   NOU 1980:55, pp. 12–13.

19 An American Indian view on education for indigenous minorities

William G. Demmert
University of Washington, Seattle, USA

Response to Dr Darnell's concepts

Opinions on financing, organising and governing educational programmes or systems serving or specifically designed for indigenous minority populations depend on a variety of circumstances. For me, these opinions are a result of being a member of an indigenous minority in a national and a regional setting, but being of the majority, locally. They are also a result of having a family of educators, my experiences as a student in public schools, private schools, and special schools for Indians or Native Alaskans, and my professional life at the local and national levels as an educator/administrator. These experiences include working in schools where American Indians are a minority, schools where they are the majority, schools exclusively for Indians, and in programmes designed to meet Indians' 'special educational needs'.

With this in mind, you are now ready to read my position in the following response to Dr Frank Darnell's paper.

I will start by saying that this paper reflects the informed state of the art. It accurately represents points of view common to knowledgeable leaders in the field who are inside, as well as outside, indigenous minority populations I have worked with. I will, therefore, attempt no further analysis of the paper; nor will I attempt to challenge or support those parts I agree or disagree with. Rather, I will present some additional considerations or rationale representing a different way of perceiving the issue of improving educational opportunities for indigenous minorities.

337

Many aboriginal peoples developed a highly skilled technological society that may have been as complicated or demanding as the one we find ourselves in today. There is no doubt that it was different. There might have been a better understanding of the environment, that is, the Inuit's ability to live in the cold North; the Australian Aborigines' life in the 'back country'; the use of natural medicines and psychology by many Aborigines to treat physical and mental disorders. The development of complicated social orders or structures and art forms among the Tlingits of Southeastern Alaska and among other groups, leads one to question the validity of 'uncomplicated societies'. The advanced technology of the Aztec, Mayan and Inca peoples, and the loss that occurred as a result of intruders not being able to understand or comprehend the existence of a different level of thought and development should cause us to wonder if Western cultures are still short-sighted on occasion (for example, resistance to the art/skill of acupuncture).

If societies are different, not more complicated or less complicated (viz. better or worse), if traditional life styles of indigenous minorities were or are as complicated and demanding, and if technology has moved in different paths, should we be talking about developing an educational system for indigenous minorities or should we be asking ourselves how two systems can be merged or operate concomitantly, mutually benefiting from each others' knowledge and understanding? Are we talking about a different kind of 'legitimatising'? I propose we are talking about a 'sense of ownership', maybe even 'partnerships'. Going one step further, maybe we are talking about regaining a 'meaningful role' in the education of our children — a role in conceiving, planning, implementing and evaluating a system and continuously adjusting to individual, local, national and international needs.

Finally, it might be more appropriate to view differences which hinder learning in the tradition of the dominant culture, not as learning handicaps, but as differences in conditioning. These learning differences should not require remedial approaches but, rather, curriculum alternatives.

Discussion of issues

The following issues, put as questions, are different from those presented in Dr Darnell's paper and represent a different priority and way of viewing the problems we have encountered in educating American Indians and Alaskan Natives. They are those I, personally, believe to be important, being taken from my own experience, from suggestions made by various professionals and from other sources available to me as part of my participation in special projects.

Does the local community view the school and the educational system as belonging to them, and their responsibility, or is there a general feeling that the school and system are external?
Generally speaking, Indian communities in the United States have felt that the schools belong to the Government (Bureau of Indian Affairs), or to the non-Indian community (public schools), and have developed very negative attitudes towards them. These attitudes influence their children, and have an effect on the students' success or failure in school.

My impression is that in Indian controlled schools (schools run and operated by tribes or members of the Indian community), student attitudes are more positive, and problems like attendance and drop-out rates improve significantly.

I believe that a sense of ownership (that is, having a meaningful role in the development, operation and governance) is critical to the success of any school and/or system.

An important part of this issue is, of course, whether the school reflects the cultures of the students and the communities they come from, or whether this aspect of 'legitimacy' is ignored. Schools generally pass on and support the cultures of those in control. If the retention of an indigenous minority culture is important, then the question of ownership is critical.

What are the appropriate circumstances, if any, for tribal administrative control and priorities for education to supersede parental or local control and responsibility?
Traditionally, the educational responsibilities for Native youth rested with parents or members of a clan or family. Among the Tlingit of Southeastern Alaska, the responsibility for a male child fell to the maternal uncle. With the advent of the white man, this fell to the church, the federal government, and/or to the State. Where this abdication of responsibility and active involvement in the education of their youth occurred, a deterioration of skill level and academic achievement became evident.

Some tribes and Indian professionals are advocating that tribes have the ultimate responsibility for the education of their youth, and that everyone (parents, community, state and federal government) ought to be under that jurisdiction.

Is this a concept that has surfaced as a result of the majority system; and will it experience similar problems?
Most tribes have not considered education as important as self-

determination, protection of land and resources, or economic development in contemporary times. The movement, therefore, toward local control has come from Indian professionals and Indian organisations.

The dollars available for education from the US Government have reached a substantial level, and with other kinds of money becoming harder to obtain, competition for control of education has become important to tribes and communites alike.

What is the federal government's intent, and how committed is it to following through with anything it starts?
Acculturation, termination, assumption of land and resource rights, and the right to govern have been the agenda of the US Government during different phases of its history and have caused tribes to question virtually every effort the government has made on their behalf.

In addition, many project proposals or actual legislation have been implemented with little or very short-term fiscal support. Programmes like the Indian Education Act of 1972, Part B, will fund a project for one or two years and drop the funding. This has caused confusion and negative attitudes to develop.

Another good example of a lack of commitment or responsibility on the part of the federal government and public schools where the needs exceed $1 billion, and Congress appropriates less than $100 million per year.

Will outside pressures (political and financial) have more influence on what is planned and done, or will indigenous minority needs and priorities receive adequate consideration?

Should the educational systems or programmes for indigenous minorities be integrated or segregated?
The Bureau of Indian Affairs has a segregated educational system for Indians living on or near reservations and where a public school is not available (with some exceptions).

The US Education Department and the Bureau of Indian Affairs fund special programmes for Indians attending public schools through the Indian Education Act of 1972, and the Johnson O'Malley Act of 1934.

Do these special programmes, in public education systems, for one minority group (indigenous minorities) create barriers with other minority groups not having special programmes?

These questions have not been answered in the United States, but there are advocates for both sides within the Indian community.

Have the impacts of a technological society and technology itself been analysed, and adjusted for?
There are a number of important questions under this issue that need answering at the outset. Who should exercise control for technological impact? How has the indigenous minority/government been prepared for impacts on their economies, politics, social structures, and cultures in general?

What is the proper role of a culture outside its traditionally defined settings in areas like religion, language and customs?

Has the lack of one's ability to play a meaningful role in today's world caused problems like psychological depression, drinking, suicide, deterioration in cultural development, or some other kind of defensive reaction?

The impact of oil among the Eskimo of the north and Indians of Oklahoma, and timber sales in the Olympic Peninsula of Washington and southeastern Alaska, are good examples of extensive technological/economic change. In some cases, the Natives are still attempting to adjust, in other cases, the impact of sudden change is just beginning to be fully felt.

To what extent is current knowledge on the 'state of the art' available to, and understood by, the policy-makers, practitioners and community members alike?
Of greatest concern here is the question of how well informed is the community concerning: (i) its legal authority; (ii) government policies; (iii) scientific/theoretical research; (iv) cultural research (that is, perceptions, cognitive styles, traditional decision-making processes (authority/power)); (v) ultimate age-levels for learning new skills and adjusting to different systems of education.

Adequate information is as important to making sound decisions as are experience and understanding. A good mix of people representing professionals (educators/researchers), community members (parents/leaders), and technicians are important to developing programmes that are as complex as are those involved in education.

The practitioner seldom utilises the researchers' findings. The community's potential contributions are often overlooked by educator and researcher alike.

Information flow and an atmosphere of mutual trust and respect are important when working on complex problems involved in developing an education programme for indigenous minorities.

Should responsibility for financial support be national, regional, local, or some combination of each?
In the United States there are two predominant points of view. One is

that the federal government is responsible for the education of Indians because of treaty obligations, legislation and a moral obligation to righting some of its past injustices. Another is that education is a responsibility reserved for the respective states by the Constitution of the United States.

Land held in trust by the United States and certain income from trust property is not taxed by either state or federal governments. Therefore, when the question of who should pay for the education of Indians becomes real, each government is inclined to say: 'It's your responsibility', totally, or in part, depending on which system and in what State the student is attending.

The issue has become important enough for the federal government to finance a study of tribal, State and federal responsibilities.

Is there a source of stable and reliable funding?
Tribal schools spend too much time looking for monies to operate their schools, and have to depend on too many sources for basic programme operations. Federal schools have had to depend on the 'whims' of Congress and the Administration, with no real method for determining need and acceptable levels of funding. Public schools are continuously looking to the federal government for supplementary or basic support for Indians (JOM, Title IV, IEA, or P.L.874).

More time is spent looking for monies by administrators than for planning good educational programmes. In addition, one never knows whether money will be available for a programme's continuation.

A parent-based early childhood education programme was funded by the Indian Education Act of 1972 for two consecutive years, then was dropped and picked up by Johnson O'Malley funds on an emergency basis, then later refunded by the Indian Education Act. The anguish and uncertainty of the professionals, local community participants, and concerned people at the national level, was very evident.

Has the importance of supplementary/discretionary programme support above 'basic programmes' been recognised as critical to success?
Financial support for the core of basic curriculum tends to foster conservatism, or an inability to try new or innovative ideas. Supplementary support like the Indian Education Act of 1972, the Elementary and Secondary Education Act of 1965, and others allow the federal government and local schools to try a variety of approaches to educating children. As a result, members of the Indian community have had opportunities to try out many of their ideas.

The United States Office of Education has published several editions of a text on educational programmes that work. They represent local programmes operating for a number of years that have evidence of effectiveness.

Is the government running programmes or are indigenous minorities allowed to run programmes themselves?
Legitimacy, a sense of ownership and policy-setting all fall under this concern. The Bureau of Indian Affairs has run schools for American Indians for many years. Public schools have allowed Indians to attend with little or no opportunity for them to participate in the design or implementation of programmes. In both cases, these schools have produced large numbers of drop-outs. Church schools have been more successful, but they attract a different kind of student. More recently, tribal schools have been started and appear to have reduced drop-out rates.

Has the need for a good staff with proper training been recognised as important to a programme's success? Has the need to train and acquaint lay persons to new responsibilities been taken into consideration? What is the availability of good top and middle-level people from the indigenous population? Will natives be trained to take over positions at all levels, now occupied by the dominant society?

All of these questions must be addressed as one deals with the issue of who runs the schools.

Additional concerns

The following concerns should be considered by the local professionals and community leaders alike. They are worth mentioning now and discussing at some later date when these issues are ready to be addressed.

- Does a major focus on culturally relevant curriculum ultimately inhibit or stimulate success in academic subjects?
- What are the differences between the programmes indigenous minorities need in areas of concentrated population versus areas of scattered population patterns?
- Should equalisation formulas be allowed to take into account special funding for minorities in their calculations?
- How aware is the national government about traditions of indigenous minorities?
- Are local leaders politically astute to deal with national, local and regional politics?

- Has the need for planning and evaluation responsibilities been given enough consideration?
- Is there a 'key group' of supporters prepared to support the new movement, programme, or administration?
- Is the academic programme separate from a residential programme in the boarding school setting?
- Is there a key person ('linchpin') with the commitment to see that the project succeeds?
- Are accreditation alternatives available to the schools?
- Is there an economic base in the community that allows for some fiscal independence?
- Is the state of cultural development important to the kind of education programme/system developed?
- Is the social standing of the developers in both the external and internal community important to its acceptance among the community members?
- Is cognitive style different from cognitive level of development and, if so, what does this mean to programme development?
- Is the question of educating indigenous minorities and special programmes one of equal versus unequal treatment of students, or one of proper treatment for students of different cultures (requiring different approaches to learning)?

Having raised some of the issues and concerns identified as important to me, I must ask myself if there is a prior question: 'Are there some goals in life common to us as indigenous minorities, as groups, or individuals?' If there are, 'what must we do to reach them?'

My response to the first question is, we are probably interested in retaining a sense of identity to our basic culture, including the retention of those things important to its uniqueness. We are also probably interested in preserving whatever rights and resources we still have as indigenous peoples. Finally, we are probably interested in having a decent livelihood with opportunities to play a meaningful role in today's world. For the sake of moving to the next step, let us assume that I am not too far off. Generally speaking, these goals are common to a large enough group so that the question of, 'how can these goals be accomplished', is now appropriate. My response to this question is 'education'.

The next logical level of thought introduces the question of, 'how can this best be accomplished quickly and economically?' The educational systems developed to date have not been able to do this effectively. There are still large numbers of poorly educated people, a large number of school drop-outs, and many untrained and unskilled adults. What are our educational alternatives? What educational system(s) has worked? Can we develop a system that accommodates the variables important to success? What are these variables?

What would I do if I were given a free hand in the development of a programme for educating all of the members of my community?

My first step would be to develop a list of programme priorities; identify a process for planning, implementing and evaluating them; and gather the resources necessary to accomplish these tasks.

Programme priorities

1 A parent-based early childhood education programme A programme designed to bring members of the local and professional community together that would allow for maximum preparation and stimulation of things important to success in both communities. Key actors from the local community would represent qualities and attitudes important to the culture, well-trained, informed and sensitive educators committed to excellence in process and product would be important to that mix.

Such a programme would include components for working with expectant mothers and prospective fathers (including school-based programmes for students); a home-based activity that would allow individual co-operation between mothers of infants, with appropriate professional or semi-professional personnel; and group activities that would provide children with opportunities to learn and play together in a well-thought out, planned setting.

2 A comprehensive education programme for children and young adults A programme that continues and expands upon the concepts developed in the early childhood programme would be important. Group and individual education plans would be an integral part of the operations.

The programme would need to focus on academic skills and training, and other skills important to the community. Its setting would have to take the local culture into account in its organisation, physical setting and curriculum.

Considerations about local life styles, the physical environment, customs, and recognition and acceptance of a new educational system, would all be important to a more formal system.

3   *A post secondary system for students who are ready to move out of the elementary and secondary school programmes*   This system would include programmes for graduate, undergraduate, and technical training, and basic educational programmes for adults that still need basic reading, writing and computation skills.

Special programmes as well as preparation for entry into an educational system need to be available for students.

A process for planning, implementing and evaluating programmes

Identification and selection of local political, community (parents) and education leaders.

Three small groups, each with an interest in one of the three programme priorities, would discuss the gathering of support for their respective areas. Once discussions have taken place in detail, a proposal or plan would be developed for consideration.

Once a plan has gathered sufficient local support for implementation, and conditions of a predetermined funding source have been met, staffing and in-service training activities will become critical to success. Physical location and type or condition of facilities for each of the programmes are also considerations that must be met.

Concomitant to planning and implementation, evaluation considerations for process and programmes must be made and included. Local and outside entities are important for appropriate feedback, adjustments as the groups move forward, and future considerations.

Each of the priority groups will work independently of each other, but must co-ordinate their planning, implementation and evaluation to ensure continuity and co-operation.

Resources necessary to carry out the priorities

Basic support for programme stability and supplementary support for exploration and meeting unforeseen immediate needs are two resources which must be available.

Basic support could be tied to some kind of formula or foundation programme that would set standards for: staff/student ratios, physical plant and daily operations. Supplementary support could be provided either as part of an entitlement for each school or through some kind of competition that allows developing new or different programmes which are not part of the regular system.

The importance of adequate and predictable resources cannot be over-emphasised. They are critical.

Conclusions

I believe traditions and culture are important to the stability of an individual as well as his/her indigenous group and schools should reflect the cultures of the people they are serving. Most of the educational systems with which I have come into contact do not accept this nor do they adjust their educational programmes to take that factor into account. The absence of that ingredient appears to cause many minority groups to reject the school, what it stands for, and see the school as the enemy.

The most important issue concerning the education of indigenous minorities, it seems to me, is 'what do we want out of life?' Once we decide that as individuals and as a people, we can identify specific goals and objectives, outline a plan of action and begin carrying out that plan. A proper role for indigenous minorities, as a whole, is probably not possible to define. Individual goals and/or roles are much easier to work with, and ought to be the focus of the eductional system's activities.

We should concentrate on an educational system for indigenous minorities that is flexible, allows a sense of community ownership, is well supported financially and politically, has a good mix of competent, sensitive and dedicated professional and community people, and a system that represents a partnership or joint venture between the people served and the responsible government.

The issues and concerns I have listed in this paper as they relate to financing, organising and governing education as a consequence of the needs of indigenous minority populations, do not represent a comprehensive research effort. Rather, they are a report of what my impressions are concerning the subject mentioned. They are an accumulation of ideas from personal experiences that have resulted from running local and national programmes, keeping up with some of the literature, and discussing issues, priorities and local problems with my peers.

Acknowledgements

I wish to thank Mr Myron Jones, Indian Education Training, Inc., Albuquerque, New Mexico; Mr Dillon Platero, Headmaster, Navajo Academy, and Instructor, Centre for American Indian Community Education, University of New Mexico, Albuquerque, New Mexico; Mr Joseph Abeyta, Superintendent, Albuquerque/Santa Fe Indian

School, All Indian Pueblo Council, Inc.; and Dr Dave Warren, Director, Research and Cultural Studies Development Section, Institute of American Indian Arts, Bureau of Indian Affairs, Santa Fe, New Mexico; for their contributions to this paper.

20 A response for the Maori population of New Zealand

Allan F. Smith
*Department of Education,
Wellington, New Zealand*

Professor Darnell's paper looks at and discusses the issues in terms of notions and concepts that he considers have general application for education among indigenous minorities wherever they are found. The subject is a complex one and is fraught with difficulties when attempts are made to apply generalisations in particular cases. As he says, 'because there is no single group or type of indigenous minority in member nations and legal and economic conditions vary appreciably between member nations no single statement of educational equality can be made to fit perfectly in all countries simultaneously'.

Background to the problems and developments in New Zealand

In New Zealand the indigenous Maori population makes up about 9 per cent of New Zealand's total population (270,035 out of 3,129,383 in the 1976 census). This population is youthful with about 45 per cent under the minimum school leaving age of 15 years. Whereas some 30 years ago Maoris were largely rural in location now more than 76 per cent of them live in towns of 1,000 or more. They now find themselves in a minority situation in most urban areas and in State primary and secondary schools. This is different from the situation in many other countries. It would be very difficult to apply the principle of local control except in a few rural and sometimes urban areas where Maoris make up the majority of the population.

Provision for education in New Zealand is part of a centralised system of organisation and finance and, while room has been found for considerable and increased devolution of responsibility and governance, the source of finance remains the responsibility of central Government. Questions of self-reliance, funding, motivation and support at local level in New Zealand must, therefore, be seen in this perspective where centralism and decentralisation in governance are more important issues than that of financing.

Professor Darnell has provided an institutionalised and sectional approach to the question of the education of the indigenous minority. In the New Zealand situation one must note the great importance of the 'grassroots' movement among Maori people and their morale and commitment to improving education. It is they, and the Maori community — not the educators or teachers — who are the true focus of effort in education. This self-reliance and the strong moves to self-determination are in marked contrast with any paternalistic provision in which the parameters are set by others.

In the historical development of New Zealand society the Maori has been seen in terms of equality and any assimilationist stance has been abandoned in favour of integration and bicultural development. However, the successful development of Maori people in education as in other things has never been seen as possible in isolation from the majority culture. Their view is summed up in the *poroporoaki* (farewell) of Sir Apirana Ngata to his grandchild.

> E tipu e rea mo nga ra o to ao
> Ko to ringa ki nga rakau a te Pakeha
> Hei ara mo to tinana
> Ho to ngakau ki nga taonga a o tipuna
> Hei tiki tiki mo to mahuna
> A, ko to wairu ki to Atua
> Nana nei nga mea katea

> Grow up oh tender plant in this world
> Your hand to the Western tradition
>   for your physical wellbeing
> Your heart to the treasures of your ancestors
> As a plume for your head
> Your spirit given to God
> The source of all things

Ngata showed how a Maori child should handle the two categories of information — the first concerned with Pakeha traditions (those of people not of Maori ancestry), the second with Maori. He believed at that time that the passing on of the Maori side could be done by the

Maori community itself. But the forces of our changing society, including urbanisation, have rapidly destroyed their means to do so. As the recent report of the National Advisory Committee on Maori Education asserts, 'It is now the urgent task of the schools, for which the Maori people pay taxes like anyone else, to assist in this role'.

Maori tribal life before the arrival of white settlers (Pakeha) in the early nineteenth century was socially sophisticated and culturally advanced. The Maori showed great adaptability in face of the growth of settlement accepting Christianity without any major conflict with their own religious beliefs and values. They did not cling to any indigenous life style. At the same time there has been a persistence of language and cultural values to the present time, although these are now under threat.

The Marae has remained as the important cultural institution and adapted to provide for groups in urban situations, thus helping the process of integration to urban living and providing the means for the continuity of values and traditions. There are now moves in a growing number of schools for the building of Maraes within them as a focus for Maori language and studies programmes and bringing the values and cultural activities of the Maori community to the school in a visible and tangible way.

Schools have been seen by Maoris, in a way similar to other minorities, as carrying one code of knowledge, one set of values — those stemming from the majority Pakeha tradition. Maoris have seen the schools as Pakeha institutions with a bias against the indigenous culture. However, the benefits that education has brought with wide opportunities for academic and material advancement, have been eagerly sought by Maoris, even to the extent of supporting the exclusion of their own language. The Maori private secondary schools established by the Churches — St Stephens, Te Aute, Queen Victoria — sought to provide courses and educational programmes predominantly in the English mould — extremely formal and examination oriented. Maoris now see that their children have not done as well as majority group children. Schools have failed to prepare them adequately to enter the modern mainstream of economic and social development. Some 67 per cent of Maori secondary pupils do not have any success in the external School Certificate examinations, so they are doing about half as well as other pupils who sit the examination.

I shall now look at the issues Professor Darnell indicates as vital to the financing, organising and governing of education for indigenous minorities.

What kind of educational equality?

The question of whether educational equality refers to equality of opportunity or equality of results has been of considerable significance in New Zealand. Here, the major concern for education up to the sixties was to ensure that all pupils had a right to equality of educational opportunity. Some special attention has been given to the special needs of Maoris since the late eighteenth century by the provision of merit scholarships to allow able Maori pupils to receive secondary education. The establishment of the Maori Education Foundation in 1961 was a further attempt to provide additional assistance to people of Maori ancestry assisting them to pursue educational goals within secondary schools and at tertiary level. The policies of the Foundation allow for continuing support of this kind as well as support for early childhood education in Maori communities, research and post-graduate study.

A move towards the development of compensatory programmes in education — especially in language, increased staffing and teacher training — was given greater point by the report of the National Advisory Committee on Maori Education in 1970 which advocated that unequal measures had to be taken to bring about quality of educational opportunity. The most recent report of that committee, *He Huarahi*, also makes the point that there is nothing more unequal than providing equality of treatment to pupils who suffer educational disadvantage. The recent review of Maori education which led to the report was prompted by an awareness that, in spite of considerable improvement, there was still an unacceptable disparity in educational outcomes between Maoris and non-Maoris.

This issue, along with the others which follow, needs to be seen in the context of the historical development of Maori education in New Zealand. Following the development of Mission Schools for Maoris, from 1816 they eagerly sought education. In those schools Maori was the medium of instruction. From 1867 the Government accepted direct responsibility for the education of Maoris. In the Native Schools Act 1867 the Native Schools Service was established to provide educational opportunities for Maori children, virtually all of whom lived in rural districts remote from the European settlements of the mid-19th century. Two of the leading features of the Act were, in the words of one of its proponents, firstly, 'the promotion of local interest and the securing of as much local management as is at present desirable', and secondly, 'making knowledge of the English language an indispensable requisite in all native schools in receipt of Government aid'.

The land wars of the 1860s and 1870s led to a retreat of the Maori people to their remaining rural lands, a disenchantment with Pakeha government and institutions (including education) and a rapid decline in numbers. But segregation did break down and from 1900 onwards there were more Maori children enrolled in 'Board' schools than in native schools. The Maori schools were nevertheless regarded as a Maori institution. The task of teachers in Maori schools was to introduce Maoris to what was best in modern civilisation whilst safeguarding the Maori traditions and skills and virtues upon which depended his pride of race and ultimately his self-respect.

In the three decades following World War II came the rapid urban migration of Maori people in search of job opportunities, economic betterment and improved education. In 1969 the Maori schools were transferred to Education Board control following the advice of the National Advisory Committee on Maori Education which maintained that the long-term policy of the Government should be the development of a single system of administrative control of primary schools. The Committee affirmed that although the basic educational needs of Maori and European children were identical, Maori children, especially where associated with European children, had a special need for security and a sense of identity and personal worth.

Few of the outstanding Maori leaders or educationalists up to World War II like Buck, Ngata, Pomare or Carroll saw the impending effects of education and the majority language and culture on what was then a comparatively stable rural Maori population. The ending of historical separation meant also an end to idealistic views of the Maori by Pakeha members of society and tensions became inevitable when Maoris found themselves in urban situations clearly suffering from social, educational and economic disadvantages in comparison with the majority. So, the basis for acceptance of equality of educational opportunity and the provision of measures to bring about greater equality of educational outcomes was laid.

Different goals for different populations?

Should there be different educational goals and different levels of expenditure for different pupil populations? The provision of different levels of expenditure for Maori education is accepted as a necessary consequence of policies which recognise special needs to bring about equality of educational achievement. These policies include additional staffing, grants, scholarships, advisory services and special programmes and the successful programmes of work exploration and trade training promoted by the Departments of Maori Affairs and Education.

In many countries problems related to the indigenous population are linked to problems of rural education. In New Zealand the attention given to educational equality and the acceptance of additional costs for provision of education in rural areas has been helped by the importance of the political representation of rural areas. Approximately one-third of the seats in the New Zealand House of Representatives are for rural areas. Measures such as improved staffing, housing and bursaries given to rural schooling were likewise similarly applied to Maori schools where until 30 years ago most Maori pupils attended.

Until recently educational goals were not seen to be basically different for the Maori child. While this assumption is now questioned, the only survey of Maori views on education (Royal) confirms that view. In the 1930s, however, educational goals for Maoris were sometimes seen by those in the system as rather different but all aimed at bringing them into the mainstream of Pakeha society. There was an emphasis on the learning of English, some practical skills, housekeeping and health. Now many Maoris are questioning the usually accepted outcomes of the Western education system. For instance, besides strongly advocating the vigorous promotion of Maori language teaching, the National Advisory Committee suggests that forms of success other than academic may be important to Maori children. These include success in cultural activities, success in becoming bicultural and as co-operative members of a group. It comments that the demand to be bicultural is a demand which society at present makes only on children of minority groups.

To whom are the concepts of fiscal equity to be applied? As I have indicated, Professor Darnell has tended to look particularly at the institutionalised forms and provision of education and in particular the place of school education. As Eide has pointed out in his paper, 'in purely cognitive terms education presents youngsters with a tiny fraction of potentially available knowledge' (p.155).

In the same way institutionalised education provides a very small part of educational opportunities and provisions. In New Zealand there is a considerable focus by Maoris on educational opportunities provided within the community outside the formal institutions. And it is likely to be these factors — self-relevance and self-determination — rather than institutional provision within the boundaries set by others which will provide the inputs seen by Maori people as important. New Zealand has a nationally funded system of education able to respond on a national or local regional level to meet specific cases of educational needs. The provision is not circumscribed by the ability or inability of any group to recoup any outgoings by taxation; the critical issue seems to be provision of an effective consultative machinery to bring the issues to attention and action. The National Advisory Committee on Maori Education, the Maori Women's Welfare League, the New Zealand Maori Council, the Maori Affairs Department, the four Maori representatives in Parliament and other active groups ensure that the issues are brought forward.

New Zealand recognises that to some extent individual children may need different treatment in educational situations because of differences in ability and background experience. We have only recently, however, begun to recognise that children and their parents may have a wide variety of interests, values and expectations, with corresponding differences in what they want from education. In the past we tended to study the differences in terms of access to education, the distribution of resources, educational attainment and various measures of 'success' in society with an assumption that the education offered served all groups equally well. Any ideas of assimilation, integration or the melting pot as an institutional goal for New Zealand society are out of favour. The recognition of Maori cultural and tribal identity, while still controversial, is accepted as a basis for policy. In the same way some geographical districts by virtue of their isolation or some other special nature are being regarded as having a special identity.

The issues of control and co-ordination over education by funding through multiple levels of Government do not really apply in New Zealand's centrally funded system. There is no confusion because of differing local, state, or federal funding. Recent attention in New Zealand has been focused on the Maori Affairs Department's *Tu Tangata* programme. The title means 'the stance of the people', and is an assertion of the importance of identity and pride. In the programme there is an emphasis on improving the education of the Maori and economic development through self-determination. It has provided an interesting exercise, not without some tensions, for the Maori Affairs and Education Departments, at both national and local levels in providing co-ordination. Local *Tu Tangata Whanau* committees are being established and funded to support local initiatives, to develop homework and education centres, run local programmes and seminars and to assist Maori language and pre-school education developments.

It is too early to evaluate this interesting development. Certainly the dispersement of funds to local groups has evoked considerable response and interest from the Maori community.

Additional funds for educational awards based on the dual criteria of merit and need are provided by the Maori Education Foundation. Established by Act in 1961 the Foundation had some initial capital provided by the Government and any donations and income attract subsidy. Substantially, however, the Foundation uses Maori monies and disperses these to support Maori secondary pupils at secondary school level, **tertiary** and post-graduate studies, research and early childhood education. As with the Ngarimu VC Fund Board, which makes prestigious awards to Maoris for university study, the Foundation has close links with the Department of Education which provides its staffing and administrative support and is represented on the Board of Trustees.

Access to education by Maoris is not a major problem in geographical terms. Rural isolation, once the lot of most Maoris, is no longer so. Many of the more isolated rural communities in the Bay of Plenty, East Coast and Northland are dominantly Maori. But they are provided as indicated before with excellent school facilities, good transport, better than usual staffing and special assistance is given through scholarships, boarding allowances, assistance through the Maori Education Foundation and Maori Trust Boards. With 76 per cent of the Maori population now living in urban areas, the problems of disadvantage are more often those related to economic disadvantage, larger families or lack of parental supervision. Both the Housing Department and the Maori Affairs Department housing policies have resulted in large groupings of Maoris and Pacific Islanders in certain urban areas. Very often they have relatively poor transport, poorer access to health services and are demanding additional welfare and educational services. They are often the seedbed for social discontent, ethnic gang formation, unemployment, vandalism and delinquency. In such areas teacher turnover and inexperience was considered to be high although a recent study relating to Wellington has shown that this is no longer true in one such area, Porirua. Change is probably related to a new community coming of age, the development of community facilities and provision for cultural activities, urban Marae, Pacific Island Churches, Polynesian Community centres, and local body representation.

Some implications of biculturalism

There is some backlash in New Zealand about unequal provision made for the indigenous Maori minority generally in the additional individual assistance provided through scholarships and awards. There are some also from labour groups against the trade training programmes for Maoris and there is much contention about the place of Maori language in schools and efforts made for its maintenance and retention. The inclusion of language and culture is seen by many Pakehas as a challenge to their institutions. However, almost half of the secondary pupils now learning Maori are Pakeha and when programmes of Maori language are introduced with full consultation with parents few problems are encountered. The reaction about the provision of a reserve quota in which priority is given to the recruitment and training of Maoris as teachers has been minimal and this policy is now fully supported by the New

Zealand Educational Institute. In 1980, 7.9 per cent of the intake to primary teacher training was Maori or Polynesian.

The major difficulty in providing a social and educational environment which promotes Maori achievement is related to changing the understanding of Maori culture by the majority group, in particular among other teachers. Teacher training programmes in Maori language and studies, cross-cultural programmes and English language teaching are now important courses in all teacher colleges. To help counter the same problem in the schools, in-service training and Marae-based courses for principals and senior teachers have been established. The Marae courses give the community a major educative role in widening teacher knowledge about Maoritanga and the educational aspirations of the Maori people.

The promotion of identity, recognition of ethnicity, appreciation of cultural pluralism and biculturalism are the basis of *He Huarahi*, the 1980 Report of the National Advisory Committee on Maori Education. While seeking immediate solutions for the non-realisation of Maori potential, it examines the roles of the educational institutions, provides ideas on the differing views that constitute success in Maori and Pakeha society, examines the importance of a sense of identity in creating a harmonious multi-cultural society and the implication for Pakeha society in changing attitudes and improving Pakeha knowledge. It goes on to make some fundamental assertions:

— that every child in New Zealand should have the opportunity to learn Maori;

— that bilingual instruction in schools where the local population is willing should be considered;

— that the values of the Marae are as significant for all our schools as the values of Western technological society: both are important to the identity of the New Zealander;

— that we urgently need to use community expertise including that of Maori parents, many of whom are richly skilled in cultural terms;

— that urgent steps need to be taken to recruit more Maori teachers so that the teaching force becomes more representative of the whole community;

— that we need to give whatever practical support we can to have the Marae recognised as a place of learning, a unique New Zealand institution for culture transmission.

In particular, the Committee feels that advice about the education of Maoris and decisions about their education should come from Maoris.

In all areas of education there is a need to be open, innovative and flexible, and to look for alternative ways or providing educational services.

Along with the Maori re-assertion of tribal and cultural identity as exemplified by the *Te Rua Mano Whakatupuranga* of Raukawa and the political movement of *Mana Motuhake* many also argue for greater attention to a common national heritage. These days Maori and Pakeha culture have tended to become more closely entwined and increasing intermarriage will continue this trend. Many of the elite Maori private church schools, Te Aute, St Stephens, Queen Victoria, Wesley, have integrated into the State system and others are planning to do so.

In these moves for greater equality in the fullest educational and cultural sense, the schools and education are likely to be in the vanguard of change but reacting in response to the pressures and moves which have come from the Maori community and with the growing measure of support from majority groups. Whether improved economic opportunities for indigenous minorities can be created within the education system without such rights to being culturally and ethnically distinct being destroyed is still not clear. On the one hand Maoris desire the rights and advantages within the education system, opportunities for employment, professional and trade training. Some Maori leaders see this as being achieved through the emphasis in identity, Maori language and tribal self-determination with state support.

In a study of Maori graduates, Fitzgerald (NZCER) examines how Maori graduates were forced to give up their Maori values to achieve Pakeha educational goals, but returning often to their Maoriness later. Changing the 'mainstream' Pakeha culture to include the norms and values of Maori culture may be a laudable but impossible dream. If it could be achieved it would avoid the negative effects of segregation while maintaining the cultural integrity of the individuals and groups concerned. Perhaps the best that can be done is to develop and provide for greater tolerance — avoiding the possibility of allowing either group to exploit the other. However, equality has more than simply economic dimensions and the different value structures of Maori and Pakeha make this difficult. In the educational context where education is concerned with the transfer of values we 'socialise' groups into what is assumed to be a common cultural heritage. It seems almost inevitable that in this situation the stronger majority cultural values predominate. Maoris are at present resisting this attack and their leaders see that if they accept indiscriminately all values as equally valid, all behaviour equally acceptable, then Maori culture like the language will rapidly weaken.

New Zealand initiatives in Maori education have been the result of a partnership with national policy being developed in response to local as well as national consultation. In general the local controlling authorities, education boards and secondary school boards have been slower to respond to Maori wishes. In the New Zealand situation where Maoris generally make up a minority in most schools local control would not ensure any control in the interests of the indigenous minority group. The reverse often seems to be the case. Central direction and support is used to ensure that the interests and the educational needs of Maoris are kept in mind. The *Tu Tangata* programmes, the activities of the Maori Women's Welfare League groups, District Maori Councils and Marae Committees provide important local inputs supportive to the education system rather than providing any alternative. Present developments are those of homework centres, assistance with school cultural activities, language programmes, Marae-based programmes for teachers and pupils, counselling and assisting communication between home and school.

The limits within education for expenditure to meet programme aims are constrained by the total availability of resources for education in New Zealand at a time of falling school rolls, increasing difficulties of employment, especially as it affects Maoris. Both expenditure and programme aims need to ensure the improvement of educational outcomes for Maoris.

The evaluation of change

The measurement and evaluation of changes and reform were issues discussed this year by a conference of Maori community members, researchers, administrators and teachers brought together to look at priorities for research with multi-cultural education. Participants at the conference brought to the discussions the knowledge and feelings gained from their involvement in the revival of Maoritanga. Their desire for changes in the education system were inseparable from their aspirations for Maori society generally. Education must be related to its social and political context.

Criticism of previous research (and evaluation) for being Pakeha initiated, directed and judgemental led to a call for action research which would evaluate specific projects concerning, for example, the teaching of Maori in schools. Such research should be initiated by Maori people, and conducted by a multi-cultural and multi-disciplinary team using appropriate (often ethnographic) methods. If such research were mounted as part of a community development project results could be fed directly back to the instigators. The role of educational administration would be supportive (providing funding, training researchers) rather than directive. More quantitative approaches and the attempt to measure equity and equality related changes have not been very satisfactory in New Zealand because of the complexities of factors which need to be considered. These include socio-economic and cultural complexities including the very difficult question of deciding who is to be considered Maori.

The responsibility for formulating policies in the New Zealand setting is clearly seen as that of the Central Government, but carried out in close consultation with consultative groups and agencies allowing the greatest degree of flexibility for responses and initiatives at local level which can be supported within a broad framework of national goals and objectives for Maori education.

Conclusion

New Zealand uses a variety of forms of funding to support Maori education. They include that provided by the Maori Education Foundation and scholarships, compensatory programmes such as teaching English as a second language, additional staffing for schools with special needs, the provision of additional teachers' aides and ancillary staffing. The goal of 'full opportunity' with each to be given the opportunity to develop his/her abilities to the fullest has, since 1940, been at the heart of New Zealand education. The education of Maoris and other cultural minorities in New Zealand is now given greater priority by the stated aim of the Director-General to provide an education that produces a greater equality of outcomes.

The report of the National Advisory Committee affirms this direction when it re-emphasises the need to take measures that are themselves unequal in order to meet special needs. Nothing could result in greater inequality than providing the same treatment for all in education. It goes on to give as a major school objective, the significant reduction of numbers of children leaving school who have not reached the highest level of attainment they are capable of speaking, listening, writing, reading and calculating and to create a 'climate of success' for Maori pupils within the schools.

Professor Darnell's statement that 'School systems should provide the opportunity for every student to develop his/her abilities and interests to the fullest, regardless of where he/she lives, regardless of his/her parental circumstances, and regardless of the ultimate level to be attained' is thus much in accord with New Zealand objectives. But it contains a majority cultural assumption of what constitutes the 'fullest' abilities and interests of pupils.

Measured by the Pakeha School Certificate examination in New Zealand, Maoris do badly. Where within the system is the opportunity to evaluate ability and interest in other cultural terms? Even with the acceptance of policy and programmes formulated on the basis of differences in economic status, and differences in ethnic and cultural background, there remains the difficulty of providing for the parallel wish to succeed in the mainstream majority culture with its overriding values and those which stem from Maori cultural roots.

Professor Darnell is correct in saying that at present there is too little relationship between what happens at home and in the community and what is experienced at school and that the need to fuse the culture of the community and the school is a critical requirement before schools will be perceived as legitimate establishments. There has been an attempt to do this in New Zealand with the teaching of Maori language and culture measures for the recruitment and training of Maoris as teachers, the inclusion of Maori cultural activities — songs, dances, arts and crafts and bilingual programmes. All such measures are made easier by national centralised financing of education in New Zealand. Nevertheless there are still some hard questions to be faced.

(a) Is it possible to teach a culture in a formal educational setting?

(b) Which cultures should be incorporated in education programmes where there are other significant minority groups?

(c) Is a policy of multi-cultural education compatible with the maintenance of quality in education as defined by any of the groups involved? Although the knowledge codes of the education system have a clear relationship to Western cultural and social contexts this is difficult to do and there is a danger of 'integrated' type knowledge as being seen as peripheral or alternative. While it is true that cultural minorities have to earn their living in a modern industrialised labour market (implying a 'common core') there must be a significant place given to elements of other cultural knowledge.

(d) Can a multi-cultural or bi-cultural educational system succeed in a society that generally rejects socially, politically and economically the reality of bi-culturalism in its public institutions?

(e) How do we recognise and provide for cultural differences in educational programmes and policies without increasing divisions both in the classroom and society?

There are many other such questions so far unanswered as, for instance, the implications for the selection, training and administration of teachers, or ensuring an adequate supply of resource material prepared by people who know what they are talking about for both teachers and students.

The New Zealand problem is at least in a major part a political one and concerns the development of a clearer awareness of the needs and priorities for multi-cultural education. As the Maori people, now better educated, with an increasing awareness of how to work the system, with leaders at all levels in society, bring greater pressure through their representatives for change, their aspirations in education should get greater realisation. There are at present strong incentives and a greater willingness to change amongst the majority and a growing community and an organised grass roots development which will demand an increased share in the educational partnership.

There is already a base for consultation and growing political pressure to bring about change within education and New Zealand institutions. The community provides a major focus for change and possesses the capacity to bring it about.

The response of the Government in terms of finance, organisation and direction needs to continue to be the acceptance of the right of Maori people to maintain their identity and justifying placing a positive bias in policy to bring more Maoris into the schools and education system. There are accepted implications for affirmative action, positive acceptance and support of differences in language and cultural background. Until these are used to positive ends in the classroom and supported in community programmes no improved financing for intervention programme is likely to bring about the changes in educational motivation advancement, achievement and learning among the indigenous Maori minority group.

Appendix

The CERI project enquiring into the financing, organisation and governance of education for special populations

Country Surveys of Current Practice
to which reference is made in the text

(copies are held at OECD Headquarters, Paris, for consultation by those who are professionally interested)

Australia	Ken McKinnon and Karen Bisset *Schools Commission, Canberra*
Canada (Ontario)	Ralph Benson and Wayne Burtnyk *Ontario Ministry of Education*
Denmark	Knud Hjorth *County School Psychologist*
England and Wales	K.H.L. Burgin *Department of Education and Science*
France	A. Labregère *National Ministry of Education*
Federal Republic of Germany	Peter Siewert *Max-Planck Institute, Berlin*
Ireland	T. O'Cuellenain *Department of Education*
Netherlands	M. Molenaar *Netherlands Ministry of Education*
New Zealand	Murray Burns *Department of Education*
Norway	Kjell Eide *Royal Ministry of Church and Education*
Portugal	Amilcar C. Branco *Ministry of Education and Scientific Research*

Appendix (cont.)

Sweden	O. Wennas *School Inspector*
Switzerland	André Chappot *Swiss Office of Special Education*
Turkey	Saban Dede *Ministry of National Education*
United States of America	Allan Odden and Robert M. Palaich *Education Commission of the United States*

Case Studies of Linguistic Minorities

Canada	Stacy Churchill *Ontario Institute for Studies in Education*
England and Wales	Harold Rosen *Institute of Education, London University*
France	Leslie J. Limage *CERI Secretariat*
Federal Republic of Germany	Ursula Boos-Nünning *University of Dusseldorf*

Secretariat for the project

Beresford Hayward, *Counsellor*, and G.A. Hancock, *Senior Fellow*, *CERI, Project Officers*; Wyn Courtney, *Consultant*

The research was supported by a grant from the United States National Institute of Education

Index

Alternative educational experiences, 20: clinics, 21, 23; tutoring by parents at home, 23
Australia:
Aborigines: cultural education system, 320–1; cultural identity, 319–20; education, 39; educational requirements, 321–2, 323; factors limiting access to education, 317–18; identification and definition, 318; not fully integrated, 319; population pattern, 317;
aim of special education programmes, 125; change in attitudes to girls' education, 44; dealing with geographical isolation, 237;
Disadvantaged Schools Program, 19, 131–3, 137; funding, 30;
political aspects of policy-making, 54–5

Behavioural disorders: Danish investigation, 111; screening criteria, 85; therapy in Sweden, 66
Bergen project, 68
Blind, see Visual handicap

Canada: control over funding, 282; grants related to economic and social disadvantage, 130–1; Heritage Languages Program, 148–52; levels of funding, 280; minority language policies, 41; Ontario's funding of special education, 19, 31; organisation of language programme, 275; policy on Fancophone education, 235; policy towards indigenous population, 283; special cultural populations, 268; special provision in Ontario, 139–53; teaching English as second language, 146–8

365

Capital investment costs, 225
Central governments: allocating general revenue to local authorities, 32–3; finance for special education, 28–30; funding by variety of government departments, 33–4; funding specific services to local authorities, 31; funding specific services to schools, 31–2
Changes in education, definition of, 295
Charities, see Voluntary organisations
Clinics for severe reading retardation, 21, 23
Conflict, advantages and disadvantages, 172
Control of special educational provision, 52, 53, 165–76, 293, 295, 312: administrative costs, 171; advantages of higher level, 169; agents, 166; area for future study, 58; by experts, 170–2, 175; by parents, 166, 168–70, 174–5 by political agents, 172–3, 175; definition, 296; different perceptions of, 306;
  evaluation of systems, 310: criteria, 174–6;
  government policies on culture and language, 270–1, 273–4; impact of minority participation, 258–9; in Denmark, 105–6; input control, 173–4; levels of, 166–73; of language and literacy programmes, 283–6; of Sami schools, 333; output control, 174; overlapping jurisdictions, 276–7; process control, 174;

Control of special education provision (cont.)
  regulatory measures, 259–60 direct effects, 262–3; indirect effects, 263–4;
  role of students and parents, 53
Costs and costing: as actual expenditure, 224–5; bearers, 204–5; comparison techniques, 227; control programme, 201; distinguishing *ex ante* and *ex post* factors, 200–1; dynamic, 200; economic concepts, 192–3; estimation, 197–8; importance to decision making, 191, 211; indices, 227–9, 312; inflation effects, 201–2; interpreting data, 227–9; of alternative programmes, 214; of education in relation to other living costs, 317; of personnel, 223–4; of public and private services compared, 194; opportunity, real and historical compared, 192–3; public and private sector compared, 202–3; reasons for variation between programmes, 229; related to circumstances, 194–5; scale factors, 195, 207; split between agencies, 220–1; standard, 224; time aspect, 195; to achieve correct service specification, 197; types, 203–4
  see also Finance
Cross-cultural education, definition of, 297
Cultural handicap, 86
  see also Ethnic minorities

Cultural pluralism, 298, 307–8; government attitudes, 288–9; in Australia, 321, 322; in New Zealand, 361; relationships across barriers, 308
Cultural relevance, 307
Culture, definition of, 297
Curriculum: at primary and secondary levels, comparison of, 123; grants for development, 261; supplementation, 20, 21; to encourage disadvantaged students, 115–16

Data analysis, 223–6: format for presentation, 226; interpreting results, 227–9; using standard costs or actual expenditure, 224–5
Data collection:
for cost analysis, 220–3: strategy, 217–20;
for cost control, 201; for evaluation of services, 188–9
Decision making: analysis of processes, 172–3; at individual school level, 106; importance of cost information, 191, 211; levels of, 6
Denmark: central government provision for special education, 32; funding special categories, 32; per capita expenditure, comparisons, 102–4
Depreciation costs, 225
Disadvantaged students, 6: inner-city programmes in Toronto, 145–6
see also Economically disadvantaged students; Geographically disadvantaged students; Social disadvantage

Division of labour, related to per capita cost of education, 104
Dyslexia, Bergen project on, 68–9

Economic aspects, influence on educational policies, 44
see also Costs and costing; Finance
Economically disadvantaged students, 11: additional resources to compensate, 129–30; costing alternative programmes, 205
Education: difficulties of research, 155–6; factors encouraging change, 5; formal, superimposition on simple societies, 325–6; institutional development, 325–6; measuring success of outcome, 17
see also Schools; Special educational provision
Emotional disturbance, 11
see also Behavioural disorders
Equality of education, 302: concepts, 302–3: definition, 305
equity principles, 304–5;
in New Zealand, 358: position of Maoris, 352–3
Equality of opportunity: analysis, 127; and resource allocation, 15
Ethnic minorities, 6, 11, 37–8, 133–4: areas for future study, 60; cultural emphasis in schools, 133–4; culture threatened by urbanisation, 327–8; duration of special provision, 134; encouraging grass roots movements, 59;

Ethnic minorities (cont.)
  English language teaching in Toronto, 146–8; Heritage Languages Program in Canada, 148–52; immigrant students in Sweden, 69–72; language and literacy programmes, 40–2; learning deficit from cultural misunderstandings, 248; learning dominant language, 133, 134; mother tongue deprivation, 248–9; need for legislation, 54; permanence/impermanence factor, 272–3; returning to mother country, 250, 272, 289; screening criteria, 86; special provision, 24; Swedish 'household language' teaching, 64, 69–70; view of advantages of education, 327
  see also Indigenous minorities
Ethnic studies, definition of, 297
European Economic Community, Social Fund grants for language teaching, 259
Expenditure, see Costs and costing

Finance, 45–9, 293, 295: advantages of special funding, 137; allocation, 28; as basis of educational equality, 304;
  at central government level, 28–30: methods, 182–4; varying level of provision, 121;
  co-ordination with general policies, 135–6; changes in cost over time, 48–9; control, 37, 201; cost estimating, 46–7; costs involved in raising funds, 197; equity and funding policies, 46;

Finance (cont.)
  evaluation of systems, 310; for indigenous minority education in USA, 341–2; for minority language programmes, 41; in total community expenditure, 317; links between central and local government and schools, 30–4; modes, for ethnic minorities, 259–60; multiple sources, and equitable allocation, 16–17; national variations, 278–83; non-renewable funding, 263; of Maori education, 353, 355–6, 360; of Norwegian schools, 330; problems of identifying costs and funding, 35; scope for improvement, 296;
  sources, 28: and control, distinguished, 281–2;
  strategies, 34–7; student weighting factors, 47–8; subsidies for language teaching, 260–1; targeted to special populations, 136–7
  see also Costs and costing; Resource allocation
France: control over finance, 282; funding boarding schools for itinerant workers' children, 32; minority language policies, 41; organisation of language programme, 275; sources of finance, 279, 280; special cultural populations, 268
Funding, see Finance

Geographically disadvantaged students, 11–12
Germany, West: control over finance, 282;

Germany, West (cont.)
 financing of Hanover Children's Centre, 35, 37; minority language policies, 41; organisation of language programme, 275; sources of finance, 279, 280; special cultural populations, 268
Gifted students, 6, 11: allocation of extra resources, 15; screening criteria, 85
Girls, education of, see Sex discrimination; Women, education of
Governance, see Control of special education provision; Legislation

Handicapped students, 6, 10–11: co-ordination of services, 51; disallowing integration, 96; effects of post-school life, 79–80;
 integration into main classes, 21: in Sweden, 74
 long history of provision, 12; medical model for identification, 65; recognition of needs, 157; specialisation of institutions, 88–9; specialisation of staff, 89–90
 see also Hearing disabilities; Intellectual disability; Mental handicap; Physical handicap; Visual handicap
Hearing disabilities, 10, 84: integration, 77–8; placing strategy in Sweden, 66; Toronto programmes, 143–4
Historical costs, 192–3
Home tuition, 23: methods, 24
Hospitals, students in, 12

Indigenous minorities, 11, 38–40, 133: alignment with remainder of country, 283; common goals in education, 344; cross-national analysis, 267–8; cultural isolation, 237; cultural merging and differentiation, 160–1; cultural sophistication, 338; definition, 296–7; demographic and cultural factors, 234–5, 238–9, 289–90; desire to improve services, 309; development of education programmes, 345–6; distinguished from recent immigrants, 271; education conflicting with culture, 38–9; educational equality, 302, 305; effect of technological change, 294, 313; financial aspects, 259–60; fusing home and school cultures, 306–7; future development possibilities, 334–5; future educational concerns, 343–4; geographic isolation, 236–7; geographical spread, 257; government policies on language and culture, 270–1; grouping for instruction, 250–1; increasing recognition of culture, 156–7;
issues for education policy, 299–300: considerations affecting, 301–2;
length of time in country, 236, 269–70; nature of special problems, 243–50; need for legislation, 54; need for series of studies, 287–9, 310, 313; opposition to separate education, 284;

369

Indigenous minorities (cont.)
own objectives in education, 239–43; participation in governance of programmes, 254–6; partnership with professionals, 309; permanence/impermanence factor, 271–3; phases of special programmes, 240–1; range in OECD countries, 233–4; requirements for successful programmes; 311–12; restricted access to minimum service standards, 264; retaining cultural identity, 347; role of educator in special programme policy, 243; share in decision making, 306; sole possessors of a cultural tradition, 288; special provision for, 24; strong regulatory stance, 257–8; use of community mechanisms, 240;

well-defined boundaries of settlement, 237–8: *versus* dispersal, 269;

see also Australia: Aborigines; New Zealand: Maoris; Norway: Sami people; USA: American Indians

Inflation: effect on costing, 201–2

Information: for evaluation of services, 188–9; for indigenous minority programmes, 311–12

Inner-city provision, *see* Disadvantaged students

Integration into main groups, 50, 125: cost analysis, 216–17; different forms, 76–7; functional, 76; in Sweden, 74; limits and conditions, 96–7;

Integration into main groups (cont.)
of ethnic minorities, degrees of, 240, 242–3; of Maoris, 350; of school premises, 76; of students with hearing difficulties, 77–8; partial, 97; progression towards, 181; releasing resources for other purposes, 95; requirements for success, 157; serving coherent education policy, 158

social, 76–7: outside school environment, 75–6;

to overcome cultural isolation, 237; *versus* educational segregation of American Indians, 340

Intellectual disability, 10: screening, 84, 91

see also Mental handicap

Intercultural education, 298

see also Cultural pluralism

Interest payments, 225

Ireland, education of itinerant workers' children in, 23–4

Itinerant families, children of, 12: special provisions, 23–4

Language: diversity, 286; education of ethnic minorities in official language, 70–1; English as second language in Canada, 146–8; full multilingualism not envisaged, 284–5; Heritage Languages Program in Canada, 148–52; linguistic handicap, 86; major policy instruments, 274–86; minority: criteria for separate teaching units, 252, 254: for private use, 249; official status, 249–50;

370

Language (cont.)
  minority:
    range of commitment to preservation, 251–2, 253; status of teachers, 254; teaching in schools, 251–2
  mother tongue: deprivation, 248–9; instruction, 272; national attitudes to teaching, 277;
  organisation of programmes, 274–8; political and ideological aspects, 42; problems of minorities, 40–1; programmes to eradicate deficits, 24, 245, 248; uncertainty in national policies, 277
  see also Ethnic minorities; Indigenous minorities
Learning ability, assessment, 66
Legislation: control function, 172; covering special programmes in Ontario, 140–1; in favour of ethnic minorities, 54; role, 52, 53
Local authorities: financial arrangements with central government and schools, 30–4; fiscal autonomy, 33

Media, influence of, 6
Mental handicap: early screening, 91; identification in Sweden, 64; integration in Sweden, 75–6; screening criteria, 84–7; variety of causes, 92; too severe for integration, 96
  see also Intellectual disability
Migrant workers, 270: German view of, 276; policy options in education, 289
Multicultural education, 297
Multiethnic education, 297
  see also Cultural pluralism

Netherlands, distribution of financial resources, 32
New Zealand: consultative machinery, 354–5; education system, 350; funding special education programmes, 33; Maoris, 349–63: areas of disadvantage, 356; biculturalism, 354; degree of educational equality, 352–3; demographic factors, 349; development of Maori self-determination programme, 355; education outside formal institutions, 354; educational development, 39, 352–3; educational objectives, 353–6, 360–1, 362; finance for education, 360; language teaching, 356; need for educational research, 359; pre-colonialism, 351; promotion of cultural identity, 357–8, 361; strong self-reliance, 350; view of schools, 351;
  rural resources, 19
Norway: central government funding of special education, 31; geographical equality of access, 236–7; inequalities in education, 332–3; local funding of special education, 33; Sami people, 39–40: Council of Education, 331; degree of power, 330; development of education services, 329; development of teaching materials, 331; geographical distribution, 329; identity problems, 333; language, 329; school finance, 330; territorial equalisation of provision, 18–19

371

Opportunity cost, 192, 193: symmetry, 196
Organisation of special education, 49–52, 293, 295: cooperative aspects, 50–1; definition, 296; of cultural minorities, 274–8

Parents: attitudes to special services, 185–6; control of special education programmes, 166, 168–70; problems of lack of information, 168; rights to consultation, 256: in Toronto programme, 143; in USA, 174
Pareto improvements, 185
Physical handicap, 11: early screening, 91; enforcing periods of absence from school, 84; identification in Sweden, 64; screening criteria, 83–4
Political aspects and conditions: ability of special populations to gain power, 161–2; and the identification of special populations, 9–10; control of special populations, 172–3; equality concept, 163; influence on educational policies, 44; of education finance, 105, 279; of ethnic minorities, 258, 271;
power of indigenous populations, 236: not available to foreign workers, 238; special provisions in Ontario influenced by, 139
Pre-school education in Sweden, 67–8
Psychometric tests: limitations, 91–2; Swedish, 65

Racial prejudice, 287: in Australia, 322–3
Real costs, 192
Reforms in education, definition of, 295
Religious groups, segregated education of, 158
Remedial teaching programmes, 21;
see also Special educational provision
Resource allocation, 15–17, 26–7: according to number of teachers, 49; areas for future study, 60; areas of study on equality, 156; as form of input control, 174; cost of ignoring less able, 123; determinants of access in Sweden, 63; differential, 119;
equality: concepts of, 16: difficulty in assessing, 120; research inputs, 162–3
equity and funding policies, 46; for research projects 128–9;
per capita expenditure, 120, 121: at primary, secondary and tertiary level, 122–3
rationales, 104–8, 114; reasons for additional allocations, 101–17; reasons for inequalities, 15, 101, 102–8; related to period in education, 120; specifications for equality, 16; styles of provision, 17–27; teachers' span of control, 170; to economically disadvantaged areas, 129–30; to ensure equality with mainstream, 328
Rural areas: resources for, 19–20;
see also Home tuition

School readiness, assessment, 67–9
Schools: variations in organisation, 7
see also Education
Screening special populations: criteria, 83–7; early, 90–3
Sex discrimination: against female subculture, 157; change in Australian policies, 44; creating special populations, 12; single sex schools, 23
see also Women, education of
Slow learners, 11: curriculum supplementation, 21
Social class: and judgemental ability of parents, 169; and level of education of girls, 135; as distinct subcultures, 157; compensatory resource allocation, 114; conferring early differences in attainment, 109–10; effects of concentration on performance, 130; effects of differences, 126–9; influencing perception of need for remedial help, 128; 'problem children', relationship to, 111; related to resource allocation, 129
Social disadvantage, 34: allocating additional resources, 114–15; English resource allocation, 19; in indigenous populations, 244; reinforced by school, 127–8; Sweden, 65–6
Social equality, 105
Social factors: community attitudes to special populations, 185; favouring special programmes, 10; in determining school readiness, 67

Social mobility, as measure of equality, 162
Socialisation process, 160, 325
Socially disturbed students, 11
see also Behavioural disorders
Spain: control over finance, 282; developing policy on indigenous populations, 283–4; organisation of language programmes, 275; sources of finance, 279, 280; special cultural populations, 268
Special educational provision: and segregation, 94–6; areas of research, 59, 125–6; arrangements for delivery, 187–8; as parallel stream, 93–4; Australia's Disadvantaged Schools Program, 19, 30, 131–3, 137; consequences of different control systems, 175–6; continuum of objectives, 212–13; cost benefit approach, 198–9; costs, 203, 204; country studies, 56; decision making process, 43–4, 58; defining programme delivery system, 216–17, 219; English system, 18–19; evaluation, 188–9: as form of output control, 174;
factors affecting delivery, 180–7; full-time equivalent (FTE) student computation, 221–3; future directions, 57–60; general availability in all countries, 124; identifying programme structure, 213–16; implications for OECD Members, 54–5; importance of school atmosphere, 184–5; main characteristics, 90–3; measuring yield, 41–2; Ontario's programmes, 19

373

Special educational provision (cont.)
 outcomes, areas for future study, 59; parents' attitudes, 185–6; principles and issues, 57; problems of segregated education, 95;
 programmes in Toronto, 140: parents' prerogative, 143; Work Group, 141–3
 reasons for, 178; research design, 55–7; services required, 179–80; styles, 17–27; success in promoting equality, 159;
 Sweden: changes in emphasis, 72–3; effects, 78–81; growth in services, 74; staffing policy, 73; working method, 74
 variations, 6–7; working relationships with other agencies, 186–7;
 see also Alternative educational experience; Control of special educational provision; Curriculum: supplementation; Finance; Legislation; Organisation of special education provision; Special populations

Special populations: ability to influence provision, 141, 143, 144; adverse self-concepts 80–1; aims of education, 177; annual and total expenditure per capita, 105; areas for future study, 58–9; as separate subcultures, 156; assessment of individual needs, 178–9; attitudes of regular school system to, 180; bearers of costs of, 204–5; case studies, 56–7; community attitudes, 185;

Special populations (cont.)
 composition, 211; defining categories, 109–14; diagnostic teams, 90; early diagnosis, 203, 204; effects on community, 206;
 estimating costs, 198: additional, 209
 identification, 9–13, 49–50, 83, 178, 212–13; as form of input control, 174; costs, 203, 204, 209–10; criteria, 213; in Sweden, 63–82
 see also Screening process
 inclusion of 'difficult' students, 94; inputs from variety of agencies, 186–7; integration into ordinary groups, 50; internal and external causes, 12, 13, 64; methods of allocating additional resources, 114–16; need for interdisciplinary programme, 205–6; non-exploitation of or by other groups, 159; Norwegian system, 18; policy variations, 13; preconceptions of potential, 10; provision in Ontario, 139–53; rationales for additional resources, 108–16; rejecting education offered, 157; scope or specificity of programmes, 290; segregated schools, 158; socialisation procedures, 160; specialisation of institutions, 88–9;
 subdivision into categories, 87–8; variation between countries, 49
 Sweden, measures to deal with in, 64–5; transfer payments to, 203, 204, 206–7; utilisation of information on, 188–9; with multiple handicap, 88

Specific learning difficulties, 11: Bergen project, 68–9; curriculum supplementation, 21; in Sweden, 65; screening criteria, 85
Standard setting, 47
Student numbers, computing full-time equivalents (FTE), 221–3
Sweden: aim of special education programmes, 125; dealing with geographic isolation, 237; identification of need, 63–82; language deficit programmes, 245; minority language for private use, 249

Teachers: attitudes causing disadvantage in some groups, 127–8; control of special programmes, 170–2; inappropriateness of attitudes, 184; qualification as form of input control, 174; ratio to pupils, in resource distribution, 121; relative wage levels, 106; special responsibility allowances, 184; training courses in special education, 180, 184–5; 331
see also Costs and costing: of personnel
Technological environment: and investment in education, 104; causing employment problems for early school-leavers, 123–4; effect on costs of special programmes, 208; effect on indigenous minorities, 294, 313
Transfer payments: indirect, to education, 278; to special populations, 203, 204, 206–7

Unemployment: affecting school-leavers, 12, 123–4; among Australian Aborigines, 320; creating special populations, 49–50; link with inflation, 202; recruitment of school-leavers with basic qualifications, 64; Swedish training scheme, 72
United Kingdom: emphasis on cultural groups, 281;
finance: control over, 281; sources, 279, 280–1;
funding special populations, 18–19; long-term view of immigrants, 276;
minorities: cultural, 268; language policies, 41; public policies, 235
organisation of language programme, 275; teachers' pay supplements in disadvantaged areas, 131
United States of America: aim of special education programmes, 125;
American Indians, 40, 337–48: development of education programmes, 342–3, 345–6; educational integration *versus* segregation, 340; government's ambiguous attitude, 340; impact of technology, 341; sources of finance for education, 341–2; tribal administrative control, 339–40; view of educational system, 339
Californian School Improvement Program, 137; decentralised control of education, 170;

United States of America (cont.)
federal aid earmarked for special areas, 32; funding for compensatory education schemes, 31; language deficit programmes, 245; legislation on language programmes, 262; local funding of special education, 33; number of special programmes, 124; parents' rights over education of handicapped child, 174; special grants to disadvantaged areas, 131–3

Visual handicap, 10, 84
Vocational training: category missing out, 111–12; discrimination in selection for, 116
Voluntary organisations: contributions to funding, 33; mother-tongue teaching, 285; role in special education, 52: and diversity, 181–2;
Voucher system in education, 168

Warnock Committee, 179
Women, education of, 5, 134–5; *see also* Sex discrimination